IN
SEARCH
OF
AMERICA

IN
SEARCH
OF
AMERICA

Transatlantic Essays, 1951–1990

MARCUS CUNLIFFE

Contributions in American Studies, Number 98
Robert H. Walker, Series Editor

GREENWOOD PRESS
New York • Westport, Connecticut • London

Library of Congress Cataloging-in-Publication Data

Cunliffe, Marcus.
    In search of America : transatlantic essays, 1951-1990 / Marcus
Cunliffe.
      p. cm.—(Contributions in American studies, ISSN 0084-9227 ;
no. 98)
   Includes bibliographical references (p.) and index.
   ISBN 0-313-27712-5 (alk. paper)
   1. Washington, George, 1732-1799. 2. United States—Politics and
government—1789-1797. 3. United States—Civilization—1865-1918.
4. United States—Foreign public opinion, European. 5. Public
opinion—Europe—History. 6. Presidents—United States—History.
I. Title. II. Series.
E312.29.C85 1991   90-47538

British Library Cataloguing in Publication Data is available.

Library of Congress Catalog Card Number: 90-47538
ISBN: 0-313-27712-5
ISSN: 0084-9227

First published in 1991

Greenwood Press, 88 Post Road West, Westport, CT 06881
An imprint of Greenwood Publishing Group, Inc.

Printed in the United States of America

The paper used in this book complies with the
Permanent Paper Standard issued by the National
Information Standards Organization (Z39.48-1984).

10 9 8 7 6 5 4 3 2 1

for
Phyllis

true, sage, delightful, partner

Contents

List of Photographs

Preface and Acknowledgments

These essays comprise about half the ones I would like to have seen reprinted. However, they are a generous selection. What they may not fully reveal is the extent of my interest in the uniform-wearing Americans, professional and amateur, of the nineteenth century; in the evolution of the presidency; in certain cultural-literary-intellectual issues (touched upon most accessibly in the 4th, 1986 edition of my Penguin *Literature of the United States*, which Einaudi has brought out in a felicitous new translation [1990] by Massimo Bacigalupo and others); and in a quantity of material, still awaiting final form, on the history of the idea of private property in America. Otherwise I feel well represented, and am beholden to Greenwood Press for not grumbling at the largeness of the manuscript, as well as to the Greenwood series editor, Robert H. Walker, having first met him in Laramie, Wyoming, in 1958, when the United States and ourselves all seemed much younger.

Over such a span of time I have incurred hundred of debts, personal and institutional. I ask my innumerable benefactors will take the gratitude as read. Apart from Phyllis Palmer, to whom the book is dedicated, I must also pay special tribute to Nan Thompson Ernst. Without her editorial talents and sustaining good sense, *In Search of America* would have remained a jumble of papers, lacking order, bibliography or index.

Introduction

A selection of essays — even a rather large one — only suggests the range of serious interests reflected in the career of Marcus Cunliffe. Here is a man who has studied, spoken, written, and published on Crèvecoeur and Stephen Crane, F. O. Matthiessen and James Madison, Mark Twain, and Frances Trollope. His most widely read works deal with literary history, military history in both its narrow and broad dimensions, George Washington, and the American presidency. He has published two ambitious period histories: 1789-1837 and 1848-1917. In addition, Cunliffe has produced substantial works on education, historiography, property, and republicanism.

The key to appreciating this personal intellectual history, however, only begins with an admiration for its breadth. There are a small number of large topics that have provided substantive focus within the canon. Furthermore, there is a remarkable consistency of tone. Over four decades, while literary theories and fashions in historical interpretation have brushed all colors of the spectrum, Cunliffe's irenic voice has maintained its own tenor, avoiding fads and controversy, beguiling auditors of every persuasion.

This Englishman's direct discovery of America started in 1947 with a two-year fellowship at Yale University. Thereafter his presence here, frequently as a visiting professor and since 1980 as a permanent resident, has made him the most American of Englishmen.

Moreover, as a student at Yale, Cunliffe was caught up very early in an excitingly controversial and thoroughly American intellectual movement. Introduced by David Potter to the sociological study of the American national character and by Ralph Gabriel to an original style of intellectual history, Cunliffe absorbed the new scholarship that was bringing out the unities in American culture, while playing down the sharp social conflicts that an older generation of

progressive historians and critics had emphasized. It has somehow been easy not
to notice, or perhaps not to remember, that Cunliffe's career as an Americanist
began in the thick of a battle of interpretations. His position was unmistakably
on the "consensus" side.

Cunliffe's first important book, *The Literature of the United States* (1954, since
grown to a much larger fourth edition, 1986), was written during the armed
warfare between the New Critics and the social critics including some
distinguished and stubborn rearguard Marxists. Prophetically, Cunliffe's book
took neither side. Grouping authors perforce by region and epoch, the historian
of letters refused the temptation of trendy categories and misleading
classifications. As much as possible he preserved the distinctiveness of the major
writers, presenting them unencumbered to readers who preferred literature to
literary criticism.

Cunliffe's first major venture outside literary history offered exemplary and
unanswerable testimony in favor of the triumph of national unity. The historian
stepped forward with a succinct, persuasively designed biography, *George
Washington: Man and Monument* (1958). Without a trace of theorizing, we are
shown the beginnings of national cohesion in the interaction between a leader
and a culture. Cunliffe depicted Washington as the greatest unifier this country
has produced and did so with deeply sympathetic insight into the remarkable
resemblance of the man to the myth his fellow countrymen built around him.

A year later, in *The Nation Takes Shape*, a short history of the period from 1789
to 1837, Cunliffe did not avoid an explicit interpretation. The significance of the
period, he declared, lay in the emergence of a national character and in
widespread social fluidity, which blurred the sharper class struggles visible in
Europe. Thus Cunliffe embraced the essential tenets of "consensus" history. He
did so, however, in a way that removed the ideological coloration and political
bias that argument usually carried. Instead of disparaging the great social and
political conflicts of the past as shadow-boxing, he found them real and
important. Cunliffe looked, as always, for the partial truths in rival claims. In
sketching an outline of the national character, he offered a diagram of basic
antinomies. Americans were "a people at once erratic and straightforward, self-
conscious and demonstrative, friendly and suspicious, tolerant and bigoted,
radical and conservative, confident and nostalgic." Quoting Samuel Johnson in
conclusion, Cunliffe intimated that the contradictions in American life arose
ultimately from divisions in human nature. "Inconsistencies cannot both be right,"
Johnson's spokesman had remarked in *Rasselas*, "but, imputed to man, they may
both be true."

Cunliffe's principal historical work to date displays most amply his genius for creating a tapestry of inconsistencies. *Soldier & Civilians: The Martial Spirit in America, 1775-1865* (1968) capped a long-term interest in military history, going back to his own service in the Royal Armoured Corps in World War II. Cunliffe took as his subject the puzzling contradictions between three American ways of responding to war: the special strength of a pacifist tradition in America; the respect, on the other hand, for professional warriors, incarnated in the pride and honor of West Point; and, in counterpoint to professionalism and pacifism alike, an irrepressibly belligerent enthusiasm for amateur recruits and guerrilla fighters — for the civilian soldier. As the tapestry unfolds, we see the three strands intersecting with one another, overlapping but never dissolving. In Cunliffe's empathy for a complex American heritage, a reader may sense the author's own vivifying involvement in the tensions of his story: his gentle love of harmony seemingly at odds with the fascination of war; his respect for unflinching professionalism tugging against the broader, egalitarian appeal of an amateur spirit.

In brief, having no taste for academic disputes, Cunliffe extracted from "consensus" history its ideological sting and placed its vision of America in a wider context, both human and humane. His is a style of thought that relies on clear, logical distinctions but refuses to impose them categorically on the tangles of history. Again and again we find him exploring an argument rather than building one, always acknowledging its tentativeness and its dependence on the corrections pressed by the other side.

Consequently, the virtual collapse of the consensus approach to American history in the 1960s did not leave Cunliffe stranded. America no longer seemed as distinctive or cohesive as it had in the 1940s. But the general repudiation of consensual integration as the mainspring of American history merely freed this Anglo-American to look outward to linkages across the Atlantic. As some of the essays in the present volume demonstrate, Cunliffe's gradual shift from internal to external unities — his widening exploration of connections and continuities between the Old World and the New — has kept him on the cutting edge of historical inquiry.

As much as any single factor, it is Marcus Cunliffe's engagement with individual lives and careers that has kept him out of the dead-end streets of passing fashions. Not only did he preserve the distinctiveness of literary personalities but, when he turned to the study of the presidency, he furnished his insights with individual cases in point, often involving crucial decisions. One rebounds upon another, as in Cunliffe's haunting comparison of the use of foreign policy by Theodore Roosevelt and Richard Nixon. Both inherited a war in Asia —

Roosevelt in the Philippines, Nixon in Viet Nam. Both sought a place in history as peacemakers, one by mediating a settlement between Russia and Japan, the other by detente with the USSR and an opening of relations with China. But the Nobel Peace Prize went to Roosevelt — and to Henry Kissinger.

One notices also the strongly individual coloration of Cunliffe's principal contribution to historiography, *Pastmasters: Some Essays on American Historians* (1969), edited jointly with Robin W. Winks. Here the editors inveigh against assigning individual scholars to predetermined categories. It is hardly surprising that more than half of the essays in the present collection are about individuals.

To find the wellsprings of Cunliffe's encompassing flexibility, we must obviously look beyond the scheme of thought he encountered at Yale in the 1940s. An important source may have been a model of intellectual life that a young Englishman could have acquired from an undergraduate education at Oxford. Cunliffe has always maintained — without the usual pomposity — the breadth and style of a nineteenth-century English Man of Letters: a type of cultural critic we would in this country simply call an intellectual, but which in Britain, though now largely extinct, has carried a special cachet as the last amateur in a world of professionals. Although Cunliffe gladly mastered the professional skills of academic scholarship, he never sought a Ph.D. (Altogether, he spent only five years as a university student.) Nor did he yield to the pedantic fault-finding, the over-developed rigor, or the intensely competitive drive of professional life. He kept his uncontentious independence and ranged across the widest expanses of American life with allusive good sense rather than possessive appropriation.

Instead of partisanship and pedantry we have been given polish and originality of expression. Marcus Cunliffe has worked from the reader's susceptibilities and expectations. He has given them a bouquet of pleasant surprises: juxtapositions and contrasts that entertain while making a set of deliberate points. As a case in point, consider the aptness of this passage from the epilogue to *The Age of Expansion, 1848-1917*. Then consider whether this is not the work of a literary historian turned to writing history of literary quality.

> *The world scene at the end of 1916 appeared to invert and caricature all the values that the dynamic societies had trusted in. Technology turned vile. Inventiveness produced high-explosive and poison gas. The lofty pretensions of the nation-state were invoked to encourage masses of men in one kind of uniform to slaughter men clad in a slightly different uniform. Dreams of rebirth of old, chivalric, pre-commercial gallantries stirred some. Others were bored with bourgeois urban sameness. Instead they died in droves, butchered like cattle; and the incessant pounding of artillery created*

a terrain infinitely more monotonous than the streets of peacetime — a featureless lunar landscape, a waste packed with shell-craters. Hopes that all mankind could be brought together in peaceable assemblies, as in the ceremonies of the revived Olympic Games, were travestied on the main fronts of the war. There was a gathering of the tribes: contingents from Britain and France and Germany and Portugal and Belgium and Italy and Russia and Austria-Hungary, from Canada and Australia and South Africa and the United States, from Serbia and Greece and Turkey and India, came together into the terrible fraternity of the killing-grounds of the world conflict.

In one of his earliest books Cunliffe needed to explain the complex ingredients that made up the new nation. Rather than retreat to anecdote or advance to abstraction, the author developed a triad of archetypes: the Quaker (Franklin, Whitman), the Rifleman (Washington, Jackson), and the Chevalier (J.E.B. Stuart, Robert E. Lee). Each explains aspects of American goals as well as qualities identified with leadership. At times they blur and merge; none is categorically absolute. Yet how ingeniously these types facilitate sectional contrasts, simply by pointing out how replete was the South with Riflemen and the occasional Chevalier, and yet how lacking in the attributes — abundantly present in the North — symbolized by the Quaker. (*Soldiers and Civilians*, 412-23.)

This exercise appeared in a book about attitudes toward the military: a book which palpably transcends its topic. How readily it leads to a compact sectional portrait propaedeutic to literary considerations:

In the old North-South diagram the South had symbolized a set of good things: lordly grace, courage, courtesy, leisure, family and local ties, stability, love of the past. The reverse side was a set of antithetical vices: snobbery, brutality, affectation, laziness, parochialism, standpattism, mythologizing. Twentieth-century literature gained immeasurably, while keeping the idea of the South, by admitting its multifarious ambiguity. Perhaps the idea would ultimately lose all magic out of its very diversity, and its openness to parody.

The liveliness of Cunliffe's prose arises in part from his stress on history as a dynamic, continuous process — as opposed to a set of separate stages. When, for example, he takes his reader back to the colonial origins of the Washington family, he anticipates the device chosen by Kurt Vonnegut to undo the bombing of Dresden:

As in a film projected in reverse, we demolish the monument. The plinths and statues disappear; the wings of the mansion at Mount Vernon are whirled away, and the portico, the dove-shaped weathervane, the furnishings, and then the very core of the house and its foundations, leaving no trace. The roads are peeled from the surface of the land; the farms and inns and churches and courthouses are scraped off. Old tree stumps shoot up again into branches, trunk and leaves, then dwindle backward to sapling, to seed. The Indians and the buffalo they hunted are once more found along the seaboard. Like iron filings answering a magnet, the ships are drawn in, stern first, eastward across the Atlantic; their cargoes are magicked from the holds, their living freight of settlers, servants, convicts and slaves disgorged. The sun climbs in the west from darkness to sunset, rises to high noon, and falls toward the eastern dawn.

Appropriately, after depicting Washington's death, Cunliffe turns the pages of the calendar as they might have passed before the eyes of the Father of the Country had he been spared, allowing him to see the capital moved and named in his honor, projecting his disapproval of Jefferson's victory and his mixed reactions to the Louisiana Purchase and the death of Alexander Hamilton. (143) The *moving picture: rewind and fast forward.*

Dynamism is not just a sequence of life, death, and the march of public events. In his uniquely valuable portrait of Parson Weems, Cunliffe ends by speculating that the dynamics of history may conspire to confuse the wheat of truth with the chaff of invention. W. C. Fields, he reminds us, does eventually portray Mr. Micawber, and the writings of Weems, the shameless allegorist, have ended by thickening the useful package of the past.

If Cunliffe is quotable — and he surely is — it is in part because he has learned so well to find and focus the best of what others have written. To put Abraham Lincoln in a capsule, he uses James Russell Lowell's ode, describing the late president as rising from the "sweet clay" of the "unexhausted" West: "Sagacious, patient, dreading praise not blame . . . the first American." And for Washington, there is Emerson:

The head of Washington hangs in my dining-room for a few days past, and I cannot keep my eyes off it. It has a certain Appalachian strength, as if it were truly the first-fruits of America and expressed the Country. The heavy, leaden eyes turn on you, as the eyes of an ox in a pasture. And the mouth has gravity and depth of quiet, as if this MAN had absorbed all the serenity of America, and left none for his restless, rickety, hysterical countrymen.

                              Ralph Waldo Emerson, *Journals*, July 6, 1849

We are accustomed to taking Emerson with such gravity that we often fail to grasp his sense of the droll — even in the foregoing passage. We are in no such danger in the presence of Marc Cunliffe who informs as much with riddles, jokes, and transpositions as he does with sequence and analysis. In what is probably his best known platform performance, he opens by describing one George as though he were a prototype for all that was to become American and another George as though he were a member of a royal British family. Just as the audience is wondering how historical figures could have been so well placed, symbolically, the sly deceiver pulls his scarf away from the pedestals and . . . here are George Washington and King George III each perched where one had been led to expect the other!

A volume of selected essays does not begin to indicate the number of occasions, great and small, on which Marcus Cunliffe graced a public rostrum, a television panel, or the pages of a popular newspaper or journal. These experiences provided their own discipline, emphasizing fluency and brevity. They also showed a figure endowed with wit and insight but also with grace and charity.

The author has subtitled his collection "transAtlantic essays." Born, reared, and educated in England before he made his first American trip, Cunliffe has become one of a sequence of British observers of the American scene dating from Captain John Smith, including George Alsop, Frances Trollope, Charles Dickens, Lord Bryce and many others. As an expositor of American topics in Europe, Marcus Cunliffe had to learn how to present figures and events from an American context his audience did not share. His subtly persuasive explanations and his ingeniously uncondescending supply of background information have made his views of America readily comprehensible in Europe while giving Americans new angles on familiar horizons.

The American reader also acquires, once he has alerted himself to the subtext, a cumulative portrait of the European intellectual. However long he has resided in the United States, Marcus Cunliffe never gave up his English birthright. Attached to two continents he is also, in different ways, detached from both. Marcus Cunliffe is, most assuredly, not an exile. He is a comparativist incarnate. From this combination of mind and circumstance has come a set of enduring perceptions expressed with uncommon style.

John Higham
Robert H. Walker
July 1990

Postscript

Allusion has been made above to the way Marcus Cunliffe allowed a calendar to turn its pages before the eyes of George Washington as though he had outlived himself and could see the future he had wrought. Now Marcus has himself died, after a long struggle with leukemia, on September 2, 1990. Thus, instead of a tribute, this introduction and this collection become a memorial.

Although published posthumously this volume reflects the choices, logic, and words of the author — at times overruling the preferences of others. It includes the characteristically reflective headnotes, each adding to the coherence of the collection.

Fortunately, Marcus lived to see this work in its nearly complete form. His conscientious assistant, Nan Thompson Ernst whose help he acknowledges, faithfully and meticulously finished the work. Happily for John Higham and myself, Marcus read this introduction and let us know how he appreciated our perception of his intellectual life.

As the pages of the calendar continue to turn, they will reveal a lengthening list of debts to Marcus Cunliffe along with a growing inventory of ways in which he is missed. They will also show what he so longed to see, this book in print: an artfully arranged suite of chambers in the edifice by which he will be judged.

Robert H. Walker
September 1990

IN
SEARCH
OF
AMERICA

1

Backward Glances

My links with the British Association for American Studies, of which I had once been chairman, went back to the early 1950s. So I was happy to contribute "Backward Glances" to the BAAS *Journal of American Studies* jubilee issue (April 1980). The assignment was to reminisce informally and candidly about one's own involvement with American Studies. In common with other contributors I wrote autobiographically. The essay moved on to discuss some problems and some ways ahead. In this reprinted version I have omitted the last few pages, which deal with possible comparative approaches. These are alluded to here and there in several other essays, particularly "New World, Old World: The Historical Antithesis," first published in *Lessons from America: An Exploration*, edited by Richard Rose (London: Macmillan, 1974).

My first steady job, if one leaves out four years of wartime soldiering, began at Manchester University in 1949. It was a lectureship in American Studies and followed a two-year Commonwealth (Harkness) fellowship at Yale, also in American Studies, under the benevolent guidance of Ralph Gabriel. I have been in the same line ever since.

In my own evolution four roughly successive stages can be discerned. They constitute four ways in which one might regard America. At the outset it was a place to visit. Second, America also figured as a great discovery. This was however countered thirdly, by the notion of America as a great mistake. The fourth stage takes us into the consideration of the United States merely or mainly as a nation among other nations. I shall generalize from personal experience within that sequence.

"How did you get interested in this country?" Travelers in the United States grow used to the query. My own replies have varied according to time and circumstance. Sometimes I have inflicted upon the questioner extensive pieces of autobiography, beginning with scenes from adolescence: how teachers at school put me on to James Thurber (bliss), Crane's *The Red Badge of Courage* (more bliss), *The Faber Book of Modern Verse* (bits of bliss, and occasional bafflement, from Pound, Cummings, Marianne Moore, Wallace Stevens, Allen Tate, John Crowe Ransom), Henry James's *The Golden Bowl* (which did not initially bowl me over); FDR's voice on the "wireless" (not yet radio to us); movie-going (films? flicks?) in the same era (infatuation, soulful or erotic, with Garbo, Jean Harlow, Joan Crawford; different emotions aroused by the rhetoric of Pare Lorentz's *The River* and the richly ominous sepia in the film version of Steinbeck's *Mice and Men*); or how at the end of the 1930s cinema coalesced with assembly-line technology to envelop and rescue Europe from the Axis (Clark Gable overhead in his real B-17, Hemingway in his jeep braving the London blackout or the snipers around the Paris Ritz. We ourselves, khaki-clad, blasted at tin silhouettes with tommy-guns, like trainee G-men. When Telly Savalas won the Battle of the Bulge in his Sherman tank, I could reflect that I too had been there in mine). So naturally I would seize the earliest opportunity to cross the Atlantic to that fabled shore.

Or I have concocted briefer explanations. For instance: secretly ashamed of big feet and gangling arms, I found that in the United States, where the skinny-gorilla physique was common enough, I was not misshapen but Lincolnesque. Shoes and shirts in my size were everywhere: no problem of special measurement or plain brown wrappers. Therefore a need to come back regularly to replenish my wardrobe. The truth? No European who lived through the 1930s and 1940s could avoid being affected by the American ambience. Most of us warmed to Franklin Roosevelt, as we later liked Ike (while he still wore battledress). Yet I am obliged to recognize that in the prewar and immediate postwar years America was far from being our sole concern. Most of the films still lodged in my memory from before 1939 are French: Jean Gabin appeared more compelling than Jimmy Cagney — though Bogart was another matter. I recall the impact of an English amateur performance of Odets's *Waiting for Lefty*. I can remember reading through Sinclair Lewis, Upton Sinclair and Hemingway in about 1937, also the effect of *Typee* and *Walden* published in Penguin illustrated editions in 1938. But such works did not hold primary place in the imagination. They coexisted, perhaps subordinately, with contemporary productions of Auden and Isherwood (e.g. *The Ascent of F6*), the novels of Graham Greene and Kafka, or the European avant-garde represented in John Lehmann's volumes of *New Writing*.

In a way this was also the case in 1946-47, when I was back at Oxford as a history student. The United States was inconspicuous in the curriculum, though one could have gone looking for it. Seeking a broad view of the nineteenth century in Bertrand Russell's *Freedom and Organization*, I lost my bearings in his account of the American Civil War. Between Federals and Confederates, which was North and which South? The plays and fiction of Camus and Sartre engrossed my leisure. A Rhodes Scholar in my college tried to convey his admiration for sundry American novels. His recommendations left me unmoved. I felt ashamed of my complacent ignorance only when I went to America in 1947 and hit upon two of the books he had praised: *The Great Gatsby* and *Look Homeward, Angel*. A retrospective excuse is that they were probably not even in print in the skimpy England of the Attlee era. And when I applied for my American fellowship and had to express a preference, I listed the three institutions Englishmen like me had heard of: Harvard, Yale, Princeton. We knew there were others but supposed they did not count. Sharing a cabin en route with Mark Bonham-Carter, I was surprised to hear he was bound for the University of Chicago. Was this eccentricity, a blunder, or proof of a sophistication beyond mine?

In other words, I became an Americanist without forethought. Several ex-service friends were entering the Civil or Foreign Services. If I had not been given a fellowship, I might have joined them. In 1947 the nicest alternative to regular employment was further study in some foreign country. It was especially pleasurable to go to the United States under the auspices of the Commonwealth Fund, which looked after us as if we were princes traveling incognito. Indeed the Fund stipulated that we should explore the land in vacation. Most of us criss-crossed the continent, paying little heed to the Fund's wise warning not to go too far too fast and unconsciously aping the proverbial behaviour of American tourists in Europe ("I would have done the Louvre in ten minutes but my shoelace broke"). For us the slogan might have been: "If it's Tuesday this must be South Dakota."

I could claim that my study at Yale was eclectic. Haphazard is possibly more accurate. When Manchester's recently appointed Professor of American Studies, Isaac Kandel, told me of a job there, this — in the absence of other immediate prospects — was an offer I could not refuse. Chance appeared to take me to Manchester. I did not know what to expect — only that my salary would be £500 per annum, payable quarterly in arrear, and that I was to offer three concurrent year-long survey courses, American History, American Foreign Policy, and American Literature. My blithe tourism was at an end.

Many careers start from apparent accident. However, while one's first visit
might be a casual business, serious concern with American Studies was usually
confined to those with whom America had "taken." This applies with double
force to Americanists of my exact generation. We assumed that Britain, the
Commonwealth and Russia could not have won the war without the United
States. We knew how vast and omnipresent the American involvement had been.
We had driven in American vehicles and fired American guns. I had seen Flying
Fortresses spiral into formation at dawn over East Anglia and come back in mid-
afternoon from their daylight raids, singly, sometimes in dire trouble, barely able
to clear the hedgerows. I had seen the American dead in Normandy, Holland
and the Ardennes. Our bias, if that is what it was, made most of us momentarily
grateful for the bombs on Hiroshima and Nagasaki which — we believed — had
saved us from the carnage of invading Japan. Cheered by the Marshall Plan and
"Give-'em Hell" Harry Truman, we did not then agonize over the apportionment
of blame for the onset of the Cold War. We were further cheered by the easy
abundance of postwar America. We were, for the most part, half-ready to accept
the tenets of "consensus" scholarship in the 1950s, according to which the wartime
arsenal of democracy had, under Truman if less emphatically under Eisenhower,
continued its transition from "innocence" to mature "responsibility." Communism
was "the god that failed"; American democracy had demonstrated the superiority
of pragmatism to ideology. We were predisposed to agree that the United States
was different from and in important respects better than Europe: exceptional
and exceptionally good.

In the Attlee-Truman years, however, one could appreciate the United States
without abandoning Britain. An English accent helped. Ivy-League anglophilia
was manifest; and Britain, its war-reputation still vivid, its great Cunarders
punctually docking at Pier 90, still passed for a first-rate power. The gold-and-
scarlet crest of my college blazer conferred unearned advantages at Yale, which
I was tempted to exploit. On being asked whether I was related to various
prominent Cunliffes, such as the Sir Robert Cunliffe mentioned in *The Education
of Henry Adams*, I might respond with ambiguous formulae such as "Distantly,
perhaps," or "Ours is the slum branch of the family," half-hoping these would be
glossed as British understatement. My interrupted spell as a wartime
undergraduate made me hardly more of an authentic "Oggsford man" than Jay
Gatsby. The comforting American presumption seemed to be that everyone from
Oxbridge was ipso facto a scholar and a gentleman.

It was thus possible to love America without losing England. Nevertheless
people of my kind were eager to meet the United States on its own ground. My
Oxfordish vowels flattened. After a few months, visiting Englishmen began to

strike me as affected and absurd. Their voices, their mannerisms and what I now took for tedious gamesmanship offended me. When Wallace Stevens let fall an inaudible lecture I readily forgave him. I was severer on Osbert Sitwell, who descended on Yale with his sister Edith, for a performance that was patently slipshod. Stevens in this new phase was to me a genius, Sitwell a fraud. I was inclined to suppose that America was as brimming with talent as England was bereft of it. Or rather, I assumed the decadence of London, Oxford and Cambridge, being by birth and upbringing a Northerner. By the close of my stay at Yale, about to depart for Manchester, I was ready to draw a map, historical and current, of contrasting regions. There was Little England, the region of the Home Counties, parochial and snobbish and retrograde. There was the larger, livelier hinterland, in which the back country — progressively speaking — held the foreground. This stretched in a big arc: northern England and Scotland, Ireland, Wales and possibly Devon and Cornwall, together with their natural extension, North America.

Such a division grew not only from Northern nurture but from observation of how people from Britain reacted to the United States. The gentry, I decided, were ill at ease, as they always had been in that bantering, undeferential land. An Etonian acquaintance at Yale, afterwards a Tory M.P., confided that he found it an uncouth community. One reason was that the college porters — affable, large-bellied men, some of them ex-cops — never called him sir. On the other hand, the scholarship boys, the Scots and Celts, *novi homines* such as myself, felt liberated from the intricate discrimination of the mother country — the queer hesitancy, for example, over whether to shake hands when introduced to a stranger and whether to divulge one's name to him. I knew at the back of my mind that this was not quite just to England, whose system at Oxford and elsewhere had operated generously for me. Nor was Yale exactly a cross-section of America, even with its contingent of young veterans admitted under the G.I. Bill.

Nevertheless on my return to England I started out as a sort of New-World missionary — at least in my own estimation. The sense of having "gone native" was heightened by having married an American. Commitment to another country was not of itself unusual. Manchester's French department was headed by a Frenchman. Russian Studies were presided over by a Russian. The Professor of German, though English, had a German wife. Many scholars begin and continue a species of love-affair with their field. Affection for one's subject is a better basis than antipathy. In general, *-philiacs* teach and write with more insight than *-phobes*. My particular case was, though, a little special. Not only was I a spokesman for the American "minority" inside Anglo-American culture:

my wife was Jewish and an artist, which gave me a proxy attachment to two other minorities. I would like to have linked these outsider intimations with the fact of living in the North. But this was not always easy, though I used to pass a Lincolnesque statue of Abraham Lincoln on my way to work. "NO DOGS, JEWS, OR CHILDREN" was the sign that greeted me on a flat when I was house-hunting in 1949. Hopes for a rapid triumphal growth of American Studies at the University were to prove naïve, even if American history lay within the frame of reference of such colleagues as Lewis Namier, his protégé Eric Robson, and the Ulsterman Rodney Green.

Yet much in the first years was exhilarating without being impossibly difficult. I was a missionary in no danger of martyrdom. American Studies was tolerated, if not cosseted: other Americanists were appointed in the next decade or so — Maldwyn Jones, Geoffrey Moore, Howard Temperley, Dennis Welland, etc. The University's library holdings in American history and literature were patchy, except for Namier's beloved eighteenth century. But here and there Manchester's archives yielded pleasant surprises. The John Rylands Library (now part of the University collection) turned out to have a good many antislavery publications of the 1830s and 1840s. In the University library I came across a scrapbook on Buffalo Bill's Wild West Show. It had been compiled by a young Lancashirewoman who had cherished her souvenirs of Colonel Cody's tours in England. I surmised that she had developed a crush on one of the Indians in the show; for the scrapbook included a reply to a letter she had sent to Cody's manager, wanting to know why her Indian had failed to appear on the last European visit. The sad explanation: he had died somewhere on tour in America — falling from a train. In a Manchester second-hand bookshop I found maps of Colorado goldmines, with pencilled notations. Some Lancashireman, I supposed, had gone to Pike's Peak and busted. The same bookshop had several editions of the sermons of DeWitt Talmage of the Brooklyn Tabernacle. In the 1870s the breezily homiletic Talmage had edified a congregation of thousands by preaching on topics such as "The Sins of Watering Places." The bookseller said Talmage's discourses still found customers, principally (he thought) among lay preachers wishing to warn their flock against the snares of Blackpool, Morecambe or Colwyn Bay.

Again, I became friendly with a Manchester bank manager who had a remarkable grasp of American history. His curiosity had been stirred as a small boy in Liverpool by a meeting with an ancient mariner. The old man claimed to have been a deckhand during the Civil War aboard the *Alabama* — the Confederate raider built at Birkenhead by Cammell Laird and crewed in part by local sailors. The old man had told my friend:

The Alabama was a long time at sea. We put into Cherbourg, not before time, to scrape the bottom and make repairs. We were all paid off, in gold coin. But before we got a chance to spend any, the Kearsarge [a Union warship] was there waiting for us outside the harbour. They challenged us to come out and fight. In our state we were no match for them, and we knew it. But our captain had to take the challenge; so out we sailed. The Kearsarge opened fire before we did. The very first shot struck our helmsman — hit him right in the body and cut him in half. His blood spurted on to the deck. So did his money. Gold coins! Twelve months' pay! But somehow none of us picked them up. And in a few minutes the Alabama was sinking.

Everything about the United States, old or current, interested me in the early 1950s. All seemed part of inexplicitly vast terms of reference, elementary yet arcane knowledge that was a duty as well as a pleasure to thrust upon audiences. I was obsessed by the need to develop our library, which had, for instance, only a handful of twentieth-century texts in American fiction and poetry. By degrees the effort showed results. Manchester put in its own money. Various cultural attachés and Maggie Haferd at the London Embassy assisted us substantially. So eventually did the Rockefeller Foundation. My very rawness made teaching the more enjoyable. With American literature I could feel that Manchester University and I were breaking new ground. The pioneering image is apropos, in that often I had arrived at a particular book only a few days before the class. Or if it were a treasured (though belated) discovery such as *The Great Gatsby*, I regarded it as fresh, delicious terrain to be revealed to and shared with students. Perhaps that is why I have been intrigued by a remark of Santayana's, to the effect that the activity of pioneers is paradoxical: in settling the wilderness they destroy it. At any rate I have occasionally regretted the celebrity achieved by *Gatsby*, and wished for dictatorial powers to impose a five-year ban on any allusion to its final page — or to the American Dream, for whose clichéification I am in small part responsible.

Such thoughts never troubled me in the 1950s, although as I shall explain I did have reservations about the propensity of American Studies to take as axiomatic the unlikeness of the United States to all other nations. At Yale I had been greatly impressed by F. O. Matthiessen's *American Renaissance*. Soon it was joined by other writings — those for example of Henry Nash Smith, Leo Marx, Daniel Aaron, David Potter, John William Ward, Richard Hofstadter, C. Vann Woodward, Marvin Meyers, R.W.B. Lewis, Perry Miller, David Riesman — in what struck me as an extraordinarily imaginative and persuasive canon. They appeared to range with assurance from politics to fiction, from art to sociology. If this was interdisciplinarity, let us have more of it. I still cherish the memory of hearing them lecture at Manchester and elsewhere in Europe.

There was an even greater tonic provided by big subsidized seminars which enabled Britain's scattered Americanists to hobnob together. The first of these ambitious rallies, at Cambridge in 1952, featured Henry Steele Commager, Allan Nevins, Alfred Kazin and others, together with Cambridge's own encyclopaedic Denis Brogan and Oxford's Herbert Nicholas. The BAAS grew out of these jamborees. At early BAAS conferences we pooled our problems and stimulated each other to think about our prospects. Among the problems was a doctrinal issue that also engaged colleagues across the Atlantic. Like them we debated whether American Studies could be both a discipline and an inter-discipline. Like them we never reached a satisfactory conclusion. Gradually, as jobs and departments were established, the answer defined itself. American Studies, in common with other fields, existed when enough people believed it to do so (cf. Eneas Sweetland Dallas, *The Gay Science*, 1866, on "a splendid definition of art which I once heard. When the infinite I AM beheld his work of creation, he said THOU ART, and ART was").

Alfred Kazin's memoir, *New York Jew* (1978), describes the other side of the 1952 Cambridge meeting. I do recall that some of the British participants were less enthralled than I; and people can be astonishingly resistant to performances offered free. Alan Pryce-Jones, then editor of the *Times Literary Supplement*, gave a debonair, faintly patronising introductory address — as if in his eyes the conference was much ado about not very much. Kazin speaks of Pryce-Jones's "silky insults," and remembers being urged by a group of redbrick lecturers to hurl back a refutation on their behalf and that of the United States. (Could I have been among them?) In Kazin's recollection the "young dons" at various sessions "looked on America with fascinated dislike." Everyone, even the teachers from the outer provinces, "talked about a monster called America, but, icily looking each other over, thought mostly of getting a hoist up England's greasy pole."

I don't think we were quite so bad. But I had become sensitive to the kind of reaction Kazin depicts. It took some while to grasp that my miscellaneous courses at Manchester might be suspect to pure practitioners of History or English. Or that the creation of an American Studies programme might be a leftover from wartime rather than a clear, principled intention. Or that my Americanized, missionary zeal might amuse or irritate senior colleagues.

At any rate the early 1950s were sometimes frustrating. Isaac Kandel soon departed from Manchester. American Studies was of only marginal concern to other large, strong groups. The librarian, while personally amicable, was a paleographer who I suppose graded centuries in descending order, so that the twentieth was nearly beneath contempt, culturally speaking, and America was not even in his cosmos. At first he held back on my request lists for the work of living American authors. "We don't want Book-of-the-Month-Club stuff," he patiently explained. The Professor of English Literature, H. B. Charlton, expressed blunt disapproval of the bulk of American literature. Should one of his junior lecturers, he inquired, be encouraged to research on "that dismal fellow Hawthorne"? And ought he not to dissuade a graduate student from a projected thesis on Henry James, who was merely "inferior Meredith"? The Manchester historians were more polite. But they too declined to sanction American Studies courses within their required curriculum. It was easy to become neurotic: to imagine hostility among preoccupied mediaevalists and wait for the sort of comment I never heard at the University, but frequently outside: "You teach American . . . *history*? *Is* there any?"

American friends in those years would sometimes confess to a puzzled annoyance at British stinginess, incompetence, hauteur, frivolity, etc. On the whole I agreed, for as a semi-American I was vicariously touchy and hesitant about giving my nation the benefit of the doubt. I brooded over a thirty-second meeting with the Oxford historian A.J.P. Taylor which I am sure he at once forgot — stung by his remark and my inability to say anything in reply. Taylor, on being told that I was "in" American Studies, said: "Oh, so that's your racket." (Since then I have heard comparatively dismissive verdicts on American Studies from academics in the United States.) I was in sympathy with Richard Hofstadter when he recounted his moments of discomfort as a visiting professor at Cambridge, despite or possibly because of the well-meant round of hospitality. He had come to loathe the ritual of sipping sherry — "sticky and warm, like someone else's blood." I forbore to tell him of the comment made to me by a Cambridge don, according to whom Hofstadter (in my experience, a delightful companion) had not been a social success — poor at high-table talk, and a sartorial sinner (brown shoes and woollen pullovers with dark suits).

I convinced myself that the British *did* condescend to the United States as J. R. Lowell had maintained, and that the habit was centuries old, predating the American Revolution though heightened by it. I came across examples in a copy of Robert Walsh's *Appeal from the Judgement of Great Britain* (2d ed., 1820). Thus, at the close of the War of 1812, the annual Latin play at Westminster School concluded with an epilogue on the theme of emigration. "Davus," a patriotic Englishman, warned "Geta" of the folly of settling in America:

> *No man is a slave there, for negroes are not considered as of the human
> species. . . . The young men spurn the restraint of laws and manners: his
> own inclination is there every man's sufficient diploma. Bridewell and the
> stews [prisons and brothels] supply them with senators, and their . . . chief
> justice [John Marshall] is a worthless scoundrel.*

Merchants were liars; violence was rife. The expenses of removing would cripple
Geta: "your destiny at last would be to feed the rats of a prison." Davus urged
him to "think better of this scheme. . . . Let the ruined man, the impious wretch,
the outlaw, praise America; if you are yet in your senses, Geta, stay at home."
Almost no-one, it appeared, was free from the taint of prejudice — not even
William Hazlitt, the Orwell of his day:

> *America is just setting out in the path of history, on the model of England,
> without a language of its own, and with a continent instead of an island to
> run its career in — like a novice in the art, who gets a larger canvas than
> his master ever had to cover with his second-hand designs.*

The disdain of Davus emerged again in the travel accounts of Dickens or
Frances Trollope; in the scorn with which *Punch* and *The Times* first greeted the
American contributions to the Great Exhibition of 1851; and in the hostility to
the Union displayed by the privileged classes during the Civil War. Or so I
thought. I was horrified by Matthew Arnold's inability to appreciate the style of
General Grant's memoirs, and delighted by Mark Twain's counter-attack. How
could Arnold be so dismissive of Grant's plain easy prose? How could he decide
that America was not "interesting"? The real deficiency surely lay with the
British. They had failed to grasp what America signified, politically or
technologically; they had been guessing wrong ever since the reign of George III.
They (we?) had not expected the Union to survive, just as they had been startled
by the Colt revolvers, Yale locks and McCormick reapers at the Great Exhibition.
In this vein, I was not surprised to learn of Anthony Wedgwood Benn's findings
on the history of the telephone while he was Postmaster General. Benn
discovered that in 1875 a post-office official named Priest reported to a
parliamentary committee on this American innovation. He informed them that
the telephone was unnecessary in Britain: we had a plentiful supply of messenger
boys. Years later, when telephone lines had nevertheless been installed in
Britain, the same man assured another parliamentary committee that the
American automatic exchange was also unnecessary: we were amply and

economically provided with female telephonists. The last mention of Mr Priest recorded by Benn was an obituary of 1912. It dubbed Priest "the father of the British telephone system."

No doubt these attitudes reflected metropolitan contempt for Anglo-America's outlying provinces. It was the barbarians who needed missionaries, not the other way round. Whatever the explanation, I found the old snobberies depressingly tenacious. The Southern poet Allen Tate told me of being escorted to a London performance of John Drinkwater's successful play *Abraham Lincoln* in the 1920s. Tate was startled to see Lincoln's generals clad in the enemy's Confederate grey instead of Union blue (by then I understood the difference.) When Tate pointed out the error to his English host, the reply was: "Oh, I'm sure Mr Drinkwater would know about that sort of thing." Innocent prejudice was still alive in the 1950s. I heard the elderly chairman of the Manchester branch of the English-Speaking Union announce: "Most of us here are of course English. However, the secretary informs me that this evening we have guests from New Zealand, Canada and the United States. Our regular members will I am sure wish me to extend a warm welcome to these friends from the colonies."

In the early 1950s gentry-disdain found common cause with left-wing criticism of cold-war America. "Americanization" was an evil to both parties. Correspondents in *The Times* and *Listener* blamed the United States for London's new rash of multi-storey building. One aspect of the threat, for a writer in the *New Statesman*, was the sheer presence of Americans, "with their big cars and expensive teeth." The McCarran-McCarthy witch-hunt was, of course, a prominent theme.

I was not aware of much leftist sentiment at Manchester University. McCarthyism was an embarrassment mainly because it supplied ammunition for anti-Americanism ("Bridewell and the stews supply them with senators"). My friends in the United States loathed McCarthy and what he represented, perhaps even more comprehensively than did friends in Europe. Nor did I have qualms about writing for *Encounter*, whose CIA funding was later to be disclosed. I thought it a very good publication. Its pro-American, anti-Russian emphasis was rationally maintained, and the "consensus" position it on the whole embodied was obviously congenial to a numerous and varied company of American contributors, from Lionel Trilling to Leslie Fiedler. C. Wright Mills once reproached me for a flippant autobiographical note in *Encounter*. I had referred to my army service as four years of free board and lodging and said that a sequence of Anglo-American scholarships had made me a contented "traveller on gravy-trains." Perhaps the facetiousness was injudicious. Mills cited it as evidence of cold-war myopia and complacency. But, as I was able to argue with him when we found ourselves teaching together at the Schloss Leopoldskron in Salzburg, I felt my time in uniform entitled me to a joke. Mills himself had not served in the war, though he dressed like a paratrooper and bragged of his gun-toting Texas grandfather — shot up as I recall by an irate Mexican, whose wife was being pursued by the ancestral Mills. My Mills, the Mills-bomb of *The Power Elite*, was himself a beneficiary of American largesse. I doubted whether he handed his lecture fees to the poor. Did not the vehicles he brought from Copenhagen to Salzburg — a huge motor-bike, a command-caravan of a minibus — constitute a kind of gravy-train, with Mills pretending to double as driver and conductor?

Nevertheless I was intermittently uneasy in those years. I did not believe American Studies was a racket. But I could see why others might think so. In early days some of our activities were seeded with American funds. There was a small worry that British academics might regard us as corruptible. At the other extreme was the feeling that American Studies was as yet a frail plant, artificial to the degree that it required irrigation. What if the assistance dried up: if the United States Information Service or the American Council of Learned Societies ceased to fund the initial cost of new posts? Though we would not disappear, development would be stunted and retarded.

Few colleagues did take the trouble to investigate what we were up to. By and large their scepticism was ill-informed. Their own *raisons d'être* were not beyond question. It was sometimes suggested that American Studies, lacking an agreed method and corpus, was a concoction rather than a properly rigorous field of study such as History, English, Sociology or Geography. This was dubious a quarter-century ago and has become more so. I have never heard a satisfactorily precise definition of any of these recognized disciplines. "Historical method," for example, is basically an injunction to weigh evidence scrupulously and sensibly. In fact, History like other established subjects is a coalition of different interests and approaches. Only a fraction of the material in *History* or the *English Historical Review* has immediate relevance for the average specialist. At least that is true in my case; whereas I find myself engaged by most or all of the material in *American Quarterly* or *Journal of American Studies*. This is, of course, one-country scholarship, and limited to a span of about four centuries. But of necessity most historians limit themselves similarly. And the great historians are often those who transcend the common boundaries and orthodoxies.

Yet institutionally there were vulnerabilities in the theory and practice of American Studies. Thus, one might be impatient with the notion of demarcated disciplines. But there were practical problems. Which department should an American Studies lecturer go into? How should he or she be recruited? What of promotion chances? More fundamentally, might interdisciplinarity prove as much of a fiction as disciplinarity? Or of an additional burden upon teacher and student? What really happened in an interdisciplinary seminar in American history and literature? The use of two teachers, one on each "side," might imply that there were still two supposedly distinct disciplines, aiming not at a merger but merely a treaty of trade. If that were the intention, fair enough — but hardly a bold demonstration of interdisciplinarity. The student might fancy he was being expected to be more flexible than his tutors. And between their two approaches, one was apt to prevail — the other supplying the "background." If pride of place went to literature, was there then a danger of assuming that a batch of novels sufficed to explain an era? Imaginative writers may neglect or evade uncongenial yet essential themes. As Daniel Aaron has shown, American novelists were strangely hesitant to tackle their nation's Civil War: *The Red Badge of Courage* appeared thirty years after Appomattox (though it is also true that Zola waited twenty years after the Franco-Prussian War to write *La Débâcle*). As for the treatment of class and ethnicity in American fiction before the 1890s, and even beyond, the most significant point may be how far authors fudged or ignored such matters.

Another question was whether the body of American literature was substantial enough to sustain the attention increasingly lavished upon it. For a time I reviewed American material for *The Year's Work in English Studies*. Some was excellent. The remainder tended to be laboriously chic. What, *another* scrutiny of "My Kinsman, Major Molineux," *another* monograph on *The Scarlet Letter*? Publish or perish? Quite a high proportion of what was published seemed pedantic or perverse — in short, perishable. So far as American literature before 1850 was concerned, could Sydney Smith and his fellow-disparagers have been right, if for the wrong reasons? Perhaps it *was* provincial — even, as Martin Green has subsequently maintained, a failure, in the light of so much confident prophecy that American genius was about to dazzle mankind? There were signs of nervous provincialism — the supposed fear, in Malcolm Cowley's phrase, that "the game was in the bag for Oxford and the Sorbonne" — lingering well into the twentieth century.

At the opposite pole of American Studies, I was also now and then perturbed by the aggrandizing mode: the assumption, tacit or explicit, that the United States constituted a unique civilization. There were two corollaries. The first was that America formed a *Gestalt*: everything fitted, everything served to illuminate and vindicate everything else. The development of the United States was therefore organic, basically harmonious, and foreordained — almost providentially. Such an interpretation minimized conflict and error and absorbed them within the sphere of Americanity. There was a resultant prompting to generalize about American character — to engage even in a quest for some central, unifying key. This impulsion was a stimulus but could be an overstimulus, with tinges of chauvinism.

The second corollary implicit in some American Studies generalizations was that the United States was to be defined as not-Europe and more particularly not-Britain. The New World-Old World antithesis stressed the innovative energy of America in contrast to the reactionary torpor of Europe. As a proposition it had the advantage of boldness and clarity. In teaching, for example, I found British undergraduates almost unduly responsive to Frederick Jackson Turner's frontier thesis. They seemed grateful for a generality that was appealingly simple. Perhaps I only confused them by suggesting that the theory was *too* simple: that it underestimated influences from Europe and lumped Old-World nations together as uniformly "feudal" and inert. I had similar reservations about Oscar Handlin's study of immigration, *The Uprooted* (1951), though his argument was more subtle. As a European I was piqued by the tone of a book like Bernard DeVoto's *Westward the Course of Empire* (1952), an account of exploration in North America in which DeVoto's countrymen figure as brave, hustling pragmatists and Europeans as in some degree effetely theoretical ("Maurepas sat in Versailles, polishing epigrams and moving dividers across fantastic maps"). According to DeVoto, "The American teleology is geographical" — and about chaps rather than maps. Had Britons never been adventurous nor concerned for humanity? Was it all Home Counties? I sensed a divided allegiance. In the act of propagating the American viewpoint one was liable to distort one's own heritage.

Disquiet was not altogether allayed, in the early days, by university circumstance. American Studies was a separate department. But this status could also be a liability. In fortunately rare moments of paranoia I felt segregated rather than separate — shut out from the curricula of neighbouring departments, and yet for other purposes subsumed, as if we were "different" but somehow nonexistently so. The only remedy appeared to be to insist upon independence — empire building, if that is not too grandiose a description. This recourse in turn impelled us to emphasize the exceptionalist doctrines of American Studies.

These perturbations reawakened reflection on the problem of national allegiance. Henry Adams, writing to Henry James about the inward or actual expatriation of people like themselves, called them "improvized Europeans." Were people like myself "improvized Americans"? Did we unwittingly reveal the desire to please, characteristic of converts and immigrants? An American sociologist once spoke of "Alistair-Cookeism," with reference to Cooke's pieces in *The Guardian*. I asked what he meant. "Well, Cooke is a talented journalist. He gets his facts and opinions from *The New York Times*. Then he rewrites them in better prose. I'm sure he's genuinely fond of the United States. But he's a first-generation immigrant. So inside himself he doesn't feel at liberty to offer any searching criticism. He's inhibited as a native American wouldn't be."

Whether or not this is true of Cooke, I remember thinking about the possible application to myself. Publication exposed the difficulty. A remark by me in print that could be construed as "anti-American" was so construed, now and then, by American reviewers, whose umbrage-sensors would not have registered an identical remark from a fellow-American. Coming from me, it was condescending: back to James Russell Lowell! Again, books about the United States written by our Americanist fraternity did not as a rule attract much attention from reviewers or purchasers in Britain. The audience and market were primarily transatlantic — a factor that reinforced the Americanizing of one's outlook.

Ironically, Americans flattered us, with allusions to Tocqueville and Bryce, by declaring that "foreigners understand us best." I was often told that I must as an Englishman be endowed with additional insight/detachment/perspective. I felt it *ought* to be true. Able Americanists were multiplying in Britain. Reputable books and articles were beginning to flow from them. By a Stakhanovite standard of quantity, however, our output was a tiny fraction of academic production in the United States. We must be measured by quality. To make an impact we must be original as well as meticulous. Yet could we be "original" by speaking in non-American accents? Were we likely to hit upon hypotheses that had eluded the intense surveillance of American academe? When the best of American scholarship in our field was so ingenious, so aided, so masterful, one might conclude the game was in the bag not for Oxford and the Sorbonne, but for Harvard, Yale, Princeton, Chicago, Hopkins, Amherst, Minnesota, Ann Arbor, Berkeley, Stanford, and so on and so on.

What I have said so far relates mainly to the olden days of the 1950s and to an interdisciplinary conception of American Studies. Colleagues who worked in other "straight" departments probably had rather dissimilar experiences. For all of us much has changed and on the whole for the better. Anglo-American ripostes can no longer rely upon the ancient clichés. The self-confidence of both nations has been shaken. In the 1960s the "homogenizing" consensual mode of American thought (as analysed by John Higham) shifted toward a new interest in conflict and ideology. This development appeared radical in more than one sense. American foreign policy, for instance, was viewed with far more scepticism than in the diplomatic histories of Samuel Flagg Bemis (though he was affectionately nicknamed "American Flag Bemis" even when I was at Yale). The received wisdom on America's relative classlessness was challenged more sharply than in the previous sociology of Lloyd Warner or Talcott Parsons. Black militance, together with that of American women, Indians and "ethnics," seemed to deny the very existence of a unified national character. The heritage of Africa, we now learned, had remained stubbornly alive in America's black communities. Women had been excluded in large part from the American polity; and their perceptions were perhaps unlike those of men. The Indians had never become assimilated to white ways. The melting pot had failed to melt. According to such arguments, male WASPS were not only in decline; they had at no stage been properly representative of so diverse a scene.

I was intrigued by the further implication that the United States was not as "exceptional" as had been assumed. In the familiar American-Europe antitheses, common or comparable phenomena — urbanization, industrialization, democratization — had been somewhat overlooked, or posed as contrasts, as in the anecdote of the mayor of Dublin who attended a St. Patrick's Day parade in New York. One New Yorker to another:

> *"You know he's Jewish?"*
> *"No, I didn't. Ah, it could only happen in America."*

The notion of a Third World effaced the New World-Old World distinction. In that context the United States was aligned with the affluent societies of the northern hemisphere, as against the have-nots who were concentrated chiefly below the equator. So it might now be necessary to reinterpret American history and culture *vis-à-vis* Europe on a comparative instead of a contrasting basis. In this light, Anglo-American relations might be evaluated afresh, not as a story of American repudiation and supersession but as a more richly complex set of attempted divergences and convergences.

This idea was of course not my invention. It was finely demonstrated in J. R. Pole's *Political Representation in England and the Origins of the American Republic* (1966); and some of the possibilities had already been discerned in H. C. Allen's *Great Britain and the United States* (1954). Courses of a comparative nature were proliferating across the Atlantic. The trend was fortified by the spread of interest in intellectual, cultural and social history, for it was clear that ideas — whether in philosophy and economics or in architecture, music and dress-design — moved across frontiers almost as irresistibly as migrating birds or contagious diseases.

Jefferson's trinity of great minds (Bacon, Locke, Newton) were Europeans. A twentieth-century Jefferson, required to name three later geniuses who had powerfully influenced his country, might specify Marx, Freud and Einstein — again, Europeans. One could list a number of important counterinfluences upon Europe. The point, however, would not be to proclaim the superiority of one continent over the other, but to stress their mutual involvements.

This essay appeared in the *Journal of American Studies* 14 (April 1980): 83-102.

BIRTH PANGS

As I explained in the previous essay, "Backward Glances," my first teaching about the United States in an English University called for an expertise in history, literature and international affairs of the most startling dimensions. Fortunately the specification was reduced before long. Even so, job expectations remained large. Fortunately, so were my tastes. It was most enjoyable for a while to offer historical *and* literary courses.

To some extent, however, I did concentrate upon the Revolutionary and early national era. In addition to biographical and other studies of George Washington, which are represented in the next section, I became absorbed in the cultural as well as military aspects of the break with Great Britain and in the efforts of the newly independent United States to define its own identity and its appropriate political styles. Some of these themes were outlined in *The Nation Takes Shape, 1789-1837* (1959), a book of mine commissioned by Daniel J. Boorstin for the Chicago History of American Civilization series. Subsequently in another book, *Soldiers and Civilians: The Martial Spirit in America, 1775-1865* (1968), I carried forward for a few more American decades an interest in military history that had grown out of service in the British army during World War II.

In this Part I of the present book, a couple of essays on George Washington and on James Madison deal with military leadership in the Revolutionary encounters of 1775-83 and then in those of 1812-15: two conflicts often linked as America's formative pair of wars of independence. Although Washington and Madison can both be described as commanders-in-chief during those episodes, Madison was, of course, not a field general but acting as commander-in-chief by virtue of his position as president of the United States. By the time General Washington became president in 1789, his years of field command were behind him. Nevertheless the political-military overlap is an instructive feature of the crucial formative period of American nationalism.

That this period was crucial and even critical for the nation's survival is suggested in the term "Birth Pangs" used to group the topics of Part I. The early history of the presidency is a central concern of the essay on the elections of 1789 and 1792, when Washington and his countrymen cautiously introduced a novel experiment in republican executive office. Madison's attempts to define the powers and responsibilities of the White House in the War of 1812 supply another chapter, so to speak, in the evolution of the presidency. A broad account of this process, *American Presidents and the Presidency*, first appeared in 1968. In its latest revised edition (*The Presidency*, Boston: Houghton Mifflin, 1987) I have carried the story from the tribulations and triumphs of George Washington to the triumphs and tribulations of Ronald Reagan.

The other two essays in "Birth Pangs" address cultural problems of early nationalism in the young United States. The one on Crèvecoeur focuses not on his initial delight in what was being achieved in the New World, but rather upon the dislocations of independence. The other essay, "They Will *All* Speak English," also examines the sometimes frustrating literary and linguistic consequences of repudiating the political ties that had hitherto been acknowledged by the mainland colonists of British North America. Such questions crop up now and then throughout the material assembled in the present volume.

2

Crèvecoeur Revisited

A version of this essay on Crèvecoeur was first presented in Washington D.C. in 1968 at a symposium to celebrate the opening of the National Portrait Gallery. It appeared in its present form in 1975, for the British *Journal of American Studies*. Three years later I abridged the two Crèvecoeur collections, *Letters* and *Sketches*, in one volume for the Folio Society, as *The Divided Loyalist: Crèvecoeur's America* (London, 1978), with an introduction. European and American scholars, literary and historical, devoted considerable attention to Crèvecoeur in the 1980s, though not always with a full awareness of one another's work. "St. John de Crèvecoeur in the Looking Glass: *Letters from an American Farmer* and the Making of a Man of Letters," (*Early American Literature* 19 (1984): 173-90), by Bernard Chevignard, is a good example. Other essays by him, in French, are listed in his helpful bibliography, which also draws attention to the article on Crèvecoeur by A. W. Plumstead in *American Literature, 1764-1789*, ed. Everett Emerson (Madison: Univeristy of Wisconsin Press, 1977), 213-31. Everett Emerson is the author of "Hector St. John de Crèvecoeur and the Promise of America," in *Forms and Functions of History in American Literature: Essays in Honor of Ursula Brumm*, ed. Winfried Fluck (Berlin: Erich Schmidt Verlag, 1981), 44-55; and he has been engaged in work on Crèvecoeur manuscripts acquired in the 1980s by the Library of Congress. There are interesting ethnic speculations in Moses Rischin, "Creating Crèvecoeur's 'New Man': He Had a Dream," *Journal of American Ethnic History* 1 (1981): 26-42. On Crèvecoeur within the context of perceptual geography see Robert Lawson-Peebles, *Landscape and Written Expression in Revolutionary America* (Cambridge and New York: Cambridge University Press, 1988), 100-109. A few fresh biographical details are offered in Gay Wilson Allen and Roger Asselineau, *St. John de Crèvecoeur: The Life of an*

American Farmer (New York: Viking, 1987), a Franco-American collaborative
work.

———————————

Almost every twentieth-century discussion of American history, literature, culture
or character makes reference to J. Hector St. John de Crèvecoeur's *Letters from
an American Farmer*, a book first published in 1782. Anthologies usually find
space for an excerpt from Crèvecoeur.[1] A particular favorite is the third chapter,
"What Is An American?" Here is the best-known, the most-quoted, the almost
tediously familiar paragraph from that chapter:

> *What, then, is the American, this new man? He is neither an European
> nor the descendant of an European.... He is an American, who, leaving
> behind him all his ancient prejudices and manners, receives new ones from
> the new mode of life he has embraced, the new government he obeys, and
> the new rank he holds. He becomes an American by being received in the
> broad lap of our great Alma Mater. Here individuals of all nations are
> melted into a new race of men, whose labours and posterity will one day
> cause great changes in the world. Americans are the western pilgrims who
> are carrying along with them that great mass of arts, sciences, vigour, and
> industry which began long since in the East; they will finish the great circle.
> ... The American is a new man, who acts upon new principles; he must
> therefore entertain new ideas and form new opinions. From involuntary
> idleness, servile dependence, penury, and useless labour, he has passed to
> toils of a very different nature, rewarded by ample subsistence. This is an
> American.*

Earlier in the same chapter Crèvecoeur says:

---

[1] Three mentions out of many: Henry S. Commager, ed., *America in Perspective: The United States
Through Foreign Eyes* (New York: Mentor, 1948), 25. Commager reproduces the third chapter of
Letters, and says: "Crèvecoeur, who lived half his mature life in America, can scarcely be classified
as a foreigner, and indeed ... he knew his adopted country better than most native-born Americans
did — knew it, understood it, and loved it."; William J. Chute, ed., *The American Scene, 1600-1860*
(New York: Bantam Matrix, 1964), 73:   "No book of readings in American history could be
considered complete without Crèvecoeur's essay, 'What is an American?'."; Richard B. Morris, *The
American Revolution: A Short History* (New York: Van Nostrand, 1955), 139: "Embraced in the new
spirit of nationalism which pervaded the Revolutionary movement was an idyllic concept of America
as a land of opportunity.... No one expressed these ideas with greater fervor nor gave a more lucid
account of the effects of the melting pot on the molding of the American character than did ...
Crèvecoeur."

We are the most perfect society now existing in the world. Here man is free
as he ought to be, nor is this pleasing equality so transitory as many others
are.[2]

Crèvecoeur is then a standard exhibit: the man who analyzed the essence of
Americanness, including the famous melting-pot, at the very period two centuries
ago when the United States was in the act of achieving independence. And there
are other almost equally familiar passages in Crèvecoeur's *Letters* that serve to
establish him as a prime early generalizer about the United States. Again and
again he conveys the liberation, the enlargement, the wonder felt by men when
they arrive in the New World and enter into "that great field of action everywhere
visible." They undergo, says Crèvecoeur, a "resurrection". The new land
transforms them. It is amazingly fertile. "Men are like plants, the goodness and
flavour of the fruit proceeds from the peculiar soil . . . in which they grow." If
they will take off their coats and set to work, they are bound to succeed.

Again, the new country is so *big*. When the European gets to America, he
therefore "suddenly alters his scale: . . . he no sooner breathes our air than he
forms schemes and embarks in designs he would never have thought of in his own
country." Environment, it would seem, is almost everything. In Crèvecoeur's
view such a settler does not lose his identity in exchanging for the tight social
order of Europe, the shifting, amorphous American situation. On the contrary,
the settler now assumes for the first time a genuine personal identity. He is no
longer a vagrant or a "nobody," left outside the respectable enclosure of Europe;
for in America he swiftly acquires a home, land, neighbours, a district, a country.
Acquires is the proper word — an active verb. The settler gains his identity in the
act of acquiring property and improving it. This is his stake in society: *his* stake,
not one that he has been "staked *to*" by somebody else. Nor does Crèvecoeur fail
to distinguish between the various regions of America. He provides an affecting
and gruesome account of a Negro slave, locked up in a cage in South Carolina,
to die of starvation and be tormented by voracious birds and insects. Crèvecoeur
has an eloquent section on the hardy, self-reliant whalers of Nantucket. He

---

[2] Hector St. John de Crèvecoeur, *Letters from an American Farmer and Sketches of Eighteenth-
Century America*, ed. Albert E. Stone, Jr. (New York: Signet, 1963; New York: Penguin, 1981), 60-
64. All subsequent quotations from *Letters* or *Sketches* are drawn from this, the only one that prints
both books in one volume. There is another paperback edition of *Letters* (New York: Dutton,
Everyman, 1957) with some interesting editorial comment by Warren B. Blake. The most detailed
biographies of Crèvecoeur are by Julia Post Mitchell (New York: Columbia University Press, 1916);
and Howard C. Rice, *Le Cultivateur Américain: étude sur l'oeuvre de Saint John de Crèvecoeur* (Paris:
Champion, 1933) — a most useful work. A good brief study is Thomas Philbrick, *St. John de
Crèvecoeur* (New York: Twayne, 1970).

writes circumstantially and charmingly on farming in the middle states. He praises the Quakers for one kind of simplicity, and the Indians for another.

This is everybody's Crèvecoeur: farmer, optimist, expounder of the preordained American success story. Here, it would appear, is an eighteenth-century chronicle whose elements have been absorbed into the United States' cosier beliefs about itself. We might feel that George Washington summed up the virtues and limitations of Crèvecoeur in a letter of 1788, replying to someone who sought advice on whether to leave Europe and come to the United States. Among published guides to the new nation he recommended a treatise by Benjamin Franklin and Thomas Jefferson's *Notes on Virginia*. Washington ended by adding that the book by Crèvecoeur, a person who had "actually resided twenty years as a farmer . . ., will afford a great deal of profitable and amusive information, respecting the private life of the Americans, as well as the progress of agriculture, manufactures, and arts, in their country. Perhaps the picture he gives, though founded on fact, is in some instances embellished with rather too flattering circumstances."[3]

Crèvecoeur is however a more equivocal witness than General Washington could have realized. True, some of the artifices in his book were perfectly acceptable to Americans of his day. Many of them knew, as Washington no doubt did, that the man Washington referred to as "Mr. Crèvecoeur (commonly called Mr. St. John)" was by birth and upbringing a Frenchman. They may not have been precisely aware that he was a gentleman of Normandy, born in 1735, who had fought as an army officer in Canada under Montcalm; who had been wounded in the battle for Quebec in 1759; and who, entering the American colonies in that year, had eventually bought a farm a few miles west of the Hudson River in Orange County, New York. Contemporaries would not have been amazed to learn that Crèvecoeur had spent some time in England before going to Canada and had come near to marrying an English girl. These details — or his naturalization under the name of John Hector St. John, or his actual marriage to a lady in Orange County named Mehetable Tippet — were arguably of no great consequence. Perhaps it was not important that in the *Letters* he posed as a native-born Anglo-American, self-taught, ignorant of Europe, who was farming in Pennsylvania — even if these supposed "facts" have misled some

---

[3] Washington to Richard Henderson, June 19, 1788, in *The Washington Papers*, ed. Saul K. Padover (New York: Harper, 1955), 358.

twentieth-century scholars.[4] Such expedients, including the pretence that he was writing to an acquaintance in England, did not make him a liar. He was merely adopting the common authorial devices of his era. Pennsylvania, the home of the Quakers and of the renowned Benjamin Franklin, had a greater symbolic attractiveness than New York. Exaggerating his own lack of education enabled him to heighten the literary contrast between the virtuous innocence of the American country-dweller and the somehow less virtuous sophistication of his imaginary English correspondent. Eighteenth-century readers would not have been alarmed to discover that certain passages in the book (for example on the deep South, which Crèvecoeur may never have visited) had been borrowed from other writers. In that epoch, plagiarism was only a minor offence and had not yet become a moral crime. For this reason they may not have thought it odd that the central themes in Crèvecoeur — such as the dislike of cities, the praise of rural life, and the sentiments on slavery — probably derived from a European work, the *Histoire philosophique et politique* by the Abbé Raynal, to whom Crèvecoeur dedicated the first edition of his own book.[5]

Again, it was not exactly Crèvecoeur's fault that the book soon ceased to be popular. Tastes change, after all. The first London edition of 1782 brought him some fame. So did the revised French editions of 1784 and 1787 (*Lettres d'un Cultivateur Américain*). But an American edition of 1793 fell flat; and for the next hundred years Crèvecoeur dropped out of sight. In 1851 the French literary historian Philarète Chasles made only brief mention of *Lettres d'un Cultivateur*, "un livre . . . peu connu aujourd'hui," and seemed to assume the author was an Englishman, "Sir John Crèvecoeur."[6] The *Letters* did not come back into print again until editions (in English) of 1904 and 1912. The explanation for this revival appears to relate to the famous chapter already quoted. He had, in other words, stumbled upon the melting-pot metaphor long before it came into vogue. In the opening years of the twentieth century, at a time of polyglot mass immigration, Crèvecoeur's vision of "individuals of all nations . . . melted into a

---

[4] Max Savelle, in *Problems in American History*, ed. Richard W. Leopold and Arthur S. Link (Englewood Cliffs, N.J.: Prentice-Hall, 2d ed., 1957), 32-33, describes Crèvecoeur as "a Frenchman who lived for a time in Pennsylvania." J. C. Furnas, *The Americans: A Social History of the United States, 1587-1914* (New York: G. P. Putnam's Sons, 1969), 239-40, refers to Crèvecoeur as "a middle-aged Norman . . . who had spent much of his life in the Middle Colonies."

[5] "Behold, sir, an humble American planter, a simple cultivator of the earth, addressing you from the farther side of the Atlantic and presuming to fix your name at the head of his trifling lucubrations." *Letters*, ed. Stone, 29-30.

[6] Philarète Chasles, *Etudes sur la littérature et les moeurs des Anglo-Américains au XIXe siècle* (Paris, 1851), 11.

new race of men" was suddenly apposite and reassuring to Americans of the liberal persuasion. It had thus an accidental and rhetorical value: hence its place in the conventional anthologies of the twentieth century, as a striking early statement of American heterogeneity.

Yet the more explanations we offer, the more we involve ourselves in puzzle and paradox. Here is a supposedly classic text that described and predicted the shaping of the American character. Yet it was practically forgotten, on both sides of the Atlantic, throughout the nineteenth century. Crèvecoeur's book is, for example, not mentioned at all in Charles Sumner's *Prophetic Voices Concerning America* (Boston, 1874), though there are several pages on the Abbé Raynal, and accounts of various other "prophets" whose names are less familiar than Crèvecoeur's to the present-day reader. Here is a man whom some commentators have taken for an American and some for an Englishman, but who was not really either. Here is a man often cited as a Founding Father of American cultural patriotism, but who also figures in specialist histories of the American Revolution as a Loyalist: that is, a person who sided not with the colonists but with the British.[7]

These mysteries are worth unravelling for their own sake and for things they may tell us about the whole realm of transatlantic generalizations. There is an intriguing speculation by an unfriendly English reviewer of the 1782 edition, who found *Letters from an American Farmer* so peculiarly uneven in tone that he maintained it must have been composed by two different men. His guess was perceptive. Crèvecoeur *was* two different men inside one physiognomy — at least two, if not more. As far as citizenship went, he was never an American. Crèvecoeur was naturalized in 1765 as an Englishman. He left the colonies in 1780, half way through the War of Independence, in a British ship, and made his way from London to his native France. When he returned to New York in 1783, he came as French consul, having resumed French citizenship. In 1790 he left New York again for France and in the remaining twenty-three years of his life never revisited the United States. Brissot de Warville, a compatriot who knew him well in the 1780s, described Crèvecoeur as a gloomy person, sometimes apparently "appalled" rather than pleased by the success of his book.

---

[7] See, for example, William H. Nelson, *The American Tory* (repr., Boston: Beacon Press, 1964); and Wallace Brown, *The Good Americans: The Loyalists in the American Revolution* (New York: Morrow, 1969).

Crèvecoeur, said Brissot, behaved like a man with "a secret which weighed down upon his soul and whose disclosure he dreaded."[8]

Other evidence, including Crèvecoeur's own testimony, confirms that he was miserable in those consular years from 1783 to 1790. This is understandable. When he set foot in America at the end of the war, after a three-year absence, he had had no news for even longer than that of the family he had left behind. What he learned seemed to fit only too justly the French surname, Crèvecoeur, that he had taken up again. He learned, heartbreakingly, that his wife was dead; his children had barely survived, thanks to the kindness of a stranger; and his beloved farmhouse, Pine Hill in Orange County, had been burned down in an Indian raid. The "American Farmer" had no more appetite for agriculture in the New World: he sold his property in 1785.

But the full force of his misery, a semisecret misery, was not revealed until 1925, when some further literary endeavors of his, dating back to his first American sojourn, were at last released from the obscurity of a French attic and printed as *Sketches of Eighteenth-Century America*. The *Sketches* make strange reading when set beside the *Letters*. Only at the end of the 1782 book did Crèvecoeur touch upon the strife of the Revolutionary War. He declared then that he would seek refuge by abandoning his farm, in fact by renouncing civilization altogether, to go and live among the Indians. It was so fanciful a project that no casual reader could take it seriously. In fact, as D. H. Lawrence derisively noted in his *Studies in Classic American Literature* (1922), Crèvecoeur had done the exact opposite. He had retreated *into* civilization by going to Paris, where he mingled with *salon* intellectuals.

To underline the contradiction, Lawrence stressed the discrepancy between the Frenchman's real passion for nature in America, which Lawrence called "blood knowledge," and his artificial enthusiasm for Nature in the abstract. Lawrence wrote before the publication of *Sketches*. And in any case, being magnificently egocentric, Lawrence was more interested in his own idea of Crèvecoeur than in Crèvecoeur's actual predicaments. Lawrence therefore missed the truly

---

[8] "Crèvecoeur portait partout un front sombre, un air inquiet. . . . Jamais il ne se livrait aux épanchements, il paraissait même quelquefois effrayé du succès de son ouvrage, il semblait enfin qu'il eût un secret qui lui pesât sur l'âme et dont il craignait la révélation." Brissot, quoted in Rice, 43n.

remarkable discrepancy between what Crèvecoeur proclaimed in print and what he inwardly felt.[9]

In the *Letters*, remember, Crèvecoeur announces: "We are the most perfect society now existing in the world. Here man is free as he ought to be, nor is this pleasing equality so transitory as many others are." But in the *Sketches* he speaks in another voice altogether:

> *Could I ever have thought that a people of cultivators, who knew nothing but their ploughs and management of their rural economies, should be found to possess, like the more ancient nations of Europe, the embryos of these propensities which now stain our society? . . . The range of civil discord hath advanced among us with an astonishing rapidity. Every opinion is changed; every prejudice is subverted; every ancient principle is annihilated; every mode of organization, which linked us before as men and as citizens, is now altered. New ones are introduced, and who can tell whether we shall be the gainers by the exchange? . . . But why should I wonder at this political phenomenon? Men are the same in all ages and in all countries. A few prejudices and customs excepted, the same passions lurk in our hearts at all times.*[10]

The difference, of course, is that in the meantime the American Revolution had begun. Worse than that, the mild, Quakerish Crèvecoeur could not bring himself to rejoice at the rebellion. His "secret," to use Brissot's term, may have been that patriots had regarded him as pro-British during the conflict. Here and there surprise was expressed that the French should have appointed such a dubious person to represent them as consul, so soon after the war. Back in New York, where the courts were full of cases involving the property of former Loyalists,[11] Crèvecoeur may have lain awake worrying that some malicious enemy would denounce him as a collaborator.

---

[9] Lawrence's essay on Crèvecoeur first appeared in the *English Review* (January 1919). It is longer than the version printed in *Studies in Classic American Literature* but equally off-hand about the actual circumstances of Crèvecoeur. See Armin Arnold, *D. H. Lawrence in America* (London: Linden Press, 1958), 50-53. The two sides of Crèvecoeur are well brought out in Vernon L. Parrington, *Main Currents in American Thought* (New York, Harcourt, Brace, 1927-30), 1: 140-47.

[10]*Sketches*, ed. Stone, 342-43.

[11] See Oscar Zeichner, "The Loyalist Problem in New York after the Revolution," *New York History* 21 (July 1940): 284-302.

Loyalist is probably too strong a word to define Crèvecoeur's position; and so is *collaborator*. His agony was that he had no defined position. He was, rather, a *neutralist* or a *quietist* in a situation that did not permit quiet or neutrality. He therefore got the worst of both worlds during the Revolution. Neighbors expected active proof of his support for the American cause. His oddities as a part-time man of letters aroused suspicion. Why did he shut himself up and scribble? What was he writing about, and to whom? His half-fictional, half-autobiographical essays became, one guesses, an essential release. He could not stop committing them to paper. But they now contained dangerous sentiments. He could envisage no satisfactory outcome for the Revolution. For him, living in an area of exceptionally confused allegiances, the immediate reality was violence, bloodshed, hypocrisy; the suppression of free speech; intimidation and robbery in the name of high-sounding ideals. So Crèvecoeur composed frantic sketches with titles such as "The Man of Sorrows" and "The American Belisarius" (an allusion to the Roman general who, having been disgraced, blinded, and deprived of all his property, was reduced to begging by the roadside). Crèvecoeur, portraying himself or his friends or his wife's Loyalist kinfolk under various disguises, poured out his soul in bitter anecdotes of persecution and confiscation. His emotion found vent too in a number of remarkable dialogues or playlets that he calls "Landscapes." In these the patriots are shown as sanctimonious thugs. Their victims, on the other hand, are harmless Quakers, decent farmers, upright gentlemen. One of the victims, a woman whose husband has been hunted like a wild beast, wearily observes that "the world was created round to convince us that nothing therein is stable and permanent." She says of a patriot colonel, who is also a deacon: "As a county canting, religious hypocrite I had always known thee; now as Congress delegate, and in that service dost thou use thy former qualifications."[12]

These heartbroken essays, together with some more cheerful earlier ones, accompanied Crèvecoeur to New York City at the beginning of 1779, when he at length set out to quit the colonies. Leaving was easier said than done. The town was in the hands of the British. A local official in Orange County reported: "the people of our country are much alarmed at their apprehensions of St John's being permitted to go to New York." The British did not quite trust him either. They opened up the little trunk in which he guarded his papers. A British officer testified that it contained "a great Number of Manuscripts, the general purport of which appear to be a sort of irregular Journal of America, & a State of the

---

[12]*Sketches*, ed. Stone, 450-58.

Times of some years back, interspersed with occasional Remarks, Philosophical
& Political; the tendency of the latter is to favor the side of Government and
throw Odium on the Proceedings of the Opposite Party, and upon the Tyranny
of their Popular Government."[13]   In other words, two types of essay: the
optimistic ones that made up the volume of *Letters from an American Farmer*, and
the pessimistic ones that were to remain unprinted until the *Sketches* volume of
1925.

An anonymous informer denounced Crèvecoeur to the British authorities in
New York as a patriot spy.   They put him in jail — from which he was released
after three months only on the pleading of an impeccably Loyalist friend.   Some
of his papers went astray.   On arrival in London he sold a portion of the
remainder to a pair of booksellers.   Hence the publication of the *Letters* in
London in 1782 — by which time Crèvecoeur was in France.

He did not think the British completely blameless for the Revolution.   Perhaps,
he conjectured, their appetite for conquest had disturbed the balance in North
America.   Crèvecoeur was much more positive that, whatever the long distance
workings of history, the Revolution was without rational justification.   The
colonists had no real complaint.   "It is to England," says Crèvecoeur in one of his
pre-Revolutionary essays, "we owe this elevated rank we possess, these noble
appellations of freemen, freeholders, citizens; yes, it is to that wise people we owe
our freedom."   In a later essay he gropes for an understanding of what has gone
wrong.   "Ambition," he suggests, is

> an exorbitant love of power and thirst of riches, a certain impatience of
> government, by some people called liberty — all these motives, clad under
> the garb of patriotism and even of constitutional reason, have been the
> . . . foundations of this, as well as of many other revolutions. But what art,
> what insidious measures, what . . . masses of intricate, captious delusions
> were not necessary to persuade a people happy beyond any other on earth,
> . . . receiving from Nature every benefit she could confer, enjoying from
> government every advantage it could confer, that they were miserable,
> oppressed and aggrieved, that slavery and tyranny would rush upon them
> from the very sources which before had conveyed them so many blessings.[14]

---

[13] Major-General James Pattison, quoted in Rice, 57-58.

[14] *Sketches*, ed. Stone, 399.

Consider the ironies of Crèvecoeur's situation. When he speaks in his lyrical, pre-Revolutionary writings of "government," he means the benevolent, far-off yet powerful British government, the guarantor of the colonists' contentment. The American, "this new man," is actually an Anglo-American; "the new government he obeys" is actually an Anglo-American government. And when Crèvecoeur talks of government in his subsequent essays, he refers to the truculence of patriot Congressmen or the spleen of the New York board of commissioners established in 1777 to smell out un-American activities in Orange County and elsewhere.

Before the troubles came, Crèvecoeur's dual allegiance — to old England and the New World — involved no strain. He was doing well in British America. He was writing essays, no doubt with a view to publication, that ought to gratify English citizens on both sides of the Atlantic. Then his world split apart. He still contrived to salvage the book, or some of it, and to appeal to a now-divided double audience.   But when his book reached the public it was already anachronistic, and he was a changed man.   *Letters from an American Farmer* glows with a ruddy optimism. The narrator is the architect of his own fortune; his latchstring is always out for visits from neighbors and strangers alike. But by 1782, as the author must have been more painfully aware than anyone, the optimism of the *Letters* was absurd. The latchstring had proved to be out for visits from commissioners and raiders. Literally and metaphorically, the structure of Crèvecoeur's farmhouse lay in ruins.

He tried, we can see, in the later work (published eventually as the *Sketches*) to reorder his mind, to arrive at philosophical detachment, to admit irony into his mental scheme: to turn, so to speak, from Rousseau into Voltaire. The task was too difficult. He could manage only an occasional gleam of humor or a half-hearted effort at philosophical detachment. Never a systematic thinker, he wrote incoherently about the incoherence of human history.

Crèvecoeur also tried to reshape his Anglo-American into a Franco-American identity. Soon after reaching France, in August 1781, he contacted Benjamin Franklin, expressing himself "glad ... as a good Frenchman and a good American to contribute my Mite towards the Success of this grand, this useful revolution." After the Franco-American victory at Yorktown, he wrote again to congratulate Franklin as the representative of the United States on an event that must "convulse with joy the hearts of every loyal American as well as those of every good Frenchman." In the next couple of years things improved for Crèvecoeur. By the end of 1783 the War of Independence was over; his English edition was being discussed and on the whole applauded; he was respected among some of the *philosophes* of Paris; and he had prepared a French version of his book. But

these consolations were offset. His own part in the Revolution may now have
struck him as inglorious and even cowardly. He had been proved too pessimistic;
and ought he to have left his family behind in America? He experienced more
subtle anxieties. The London edition of the *Letters* contained no hostile comment
on the mother country. The French edition, however, introduced many partisan
interpolations, so as to present the English as the villains of the story and the
Americans as heroes. The old dedication to the Abbé Raynal was gone: the
Abbé's advanced opinions had put him out of favour with the French court.
Instead, the Paris edition of 1784 was dedicated to the fashionable new Franco-
American idol, the Marquis de Lafayette. Crèvecoeur, though, can hardly have
forgotten the manuscripts still in his possession — unpublished and now
unpublishable. In one of them, "an American gentleman" observes:

> When the accounts of this mighty revolution arrive in Europe, nothing will
> appear there but the splendid effects. The insignificant cause will be
> overlooked; the low arts, this progressive succession of infatuations which
> have pervaded the whole continent will be unknown.[15]

When Crèvecoeur was installed as French consul in New York, in 1783, nearly
all his former friends and connexions had departed into Loyalist exile. Silence
about those old ties was his only recourse. Then and for the rest of his days,
Crèvecoeur busied himself as conscientiously as he could with Franco-American
exchanges. Most of them had to do with plants, which he perhaps found safer
than people to deal with. He produced pamphlets recommending the cultivation
in France of the potato and the false acacia. Scientific societies elected him to
membership. He refurbished old notes to make a book of his bygone travels,
Voyage dans la Haute Pennsylvanie et dans l'Etat de New-York (1801) — dedicated
to Napoleon.[16] On the title page he described himself as an adopted member of
the Oneida Indian tribe: a detail that would have amused D. H. Lawrence.
Silence and discreetly timed absences from France enabled him to survive a
second revolution there, followed by the marchings and countermarchings of the
Napoleonic wars.

---

[15] Rice, 166-70; *Sketches*, ed. Stone, 422. This particular dialogue anticipates the complex responses
to the Revolution and to American democracy of James Fenimore Cooper — for instance, in his
Littlepage Manuscripts trilogy.   See Marcus Cunliffe, *The Literature of the United States*
(Harmondsworth: Penguin, 4th ed., 1986), 95-96.

[16] Available in an English edition as *Journey into Northern Pennsylvania and the State of New York*,
trans. Clarissa Bostelmann, (Ann Arbor: University of Michigan Press, 1964).

What then is this Crèvecoeur? Is he an American, or a European, or an unhappy hybrid? I described him earlier as a would-be neutralist or quietist. Does the additional evidence make him seem more like a Vicar of Bray, one of those "trimmers" of chameleon-like adaptability who modified their attitudes according to circumstance? It is clear that he was a romantic rather than a political ideologue. He never showed much interest in constitutions or manifestos. *Quietist* is a fairer description than *trimmer*. More bewildered than agile, he reveals anguish rather than relish when he has to change his line, and he is clumsy at covering his tracks. But perhaps in most cases a trimmer is merely a quietist who has been forced out into the open. Such sudden and cruel exposure is a feature of revolutions, civil wars and military occupation. It is not my concern to indict Crèvecoeur for inconsistency or insincerity. The charge against him is that Crèvecoeur adopted fashionable notions of life in the New World and convinced himself they were as powerful as a creed, when in fact they were only a conception. If so, he paid quite a heavy psychological price.

Fate was fairly kind to him after the shock of the war years in America. A good many Loyalists came back to New York when peace was restored, and most of them were able to come to terms with the new régime. They were not harassed unduly; Crèvecoeur seems to have gone unscathed. He was treated as a respectable, well-informed foreign diplomat. He corresponded now and then with such American dignitaries as Thomas Jefferson. There was no disposition in Britain to attack his record. His few English critics, agreeing with George Washington, merely complained that the *Letters* painted too rosy a picture of American life and hinted that his motive was to encourage emigration.[17] Otherwise, the British gradually forgot him. So, as we have seen, did the French. If they wanted to read about America, Chateaubriand and later Michel Chevalier, Tocqueville and Beaumont were more to their taste. Crèvecoeur may have been frightened that someone would take the trouble to compare the British and the French edition of the *Letters*. It appears that nobody did. People had other things to worry about in the tumult of the time. His death in France, in 1813, went almost unnoticed.

But that is not to say he is unimportant to us. Looking behind the twentieth-century Crèvecoeur of the textbooks and anthologies, we can use him to shed light on various reactions of people who leave their own country for some other

---

[17] Rice, 63-6. Complaints as to the unreliability of Crèvecoeur's accounts of America were also voiced by French consular colleagues, one of whom dismissed his book as a "novel": see Peter P. Hill, *French Perceptions of the Early American Republic, 1783-1793* (Philadelphia: American Philosophical Society, 1988), 6, 18, 161.

one. Such departures are either voluntary or involuntary. The voluntary leavers
are usually called *settlers* or *emigrants*. The involuntary leavers are often labeled
as *exiles* or — in the English usage of the French word — *émigrés*. Which of
these was Crèvecoeur? A mixture. The mood of the *Letters* is, in general, that
of the voluntary voyager. The mood of the *Sketches* is that of the involuntary one.
But the story goes further back. For some reason his brother officers were eager
to push him out of the French regiment in which he was serving in Canada in
1759. In this respect his arrival in the British colonies makes him appear an exile
or émigré from France. When he came back to his native land in 1781 he had
almost forgotten how to speak French.

As to the voluntary leavers, the rather indistinct association between the two
categories, settler and immigrant, helps to explain why the *Letters*, though
popular for a while, lapsed into obscurity and were then resurrected. It is mainly
as a spokesman for emigration (to put the emphasis on *arrival*) that we read
Crèvecoeur today. An immigrant — in my sense of the word — is a man who
severs his connexion with the past. He transfers to another sovereignty, another
flag, another loyalty, and in so doing must repudiate his previous existence. For
Crèvecoeur to come to British America probably involved a quite complete
repudiation of France: of French citizenship and possibly of the whole
atmosphere of exclusion and oppression of Continental Europe. It may be
significant that he named his daughter America-Francès.[18] Recalling that as a
young man he lived in England and nearly married an English girl, we may regard
him as an example of the Anglomania professed by various French *philosophes*.

The important element is that if his French origins and his repudiation of them
made him an immigrant to America, his Anglophile instincts made him a settler.
Defining that term in a restricted sense, a settler is a person who despite his
territorial movement remains under the same flag, the same dispensation. He
does not swap allegiances, he amplifies them. He takes pride in the mother
country *and* in its new, extended universe. So Crèvecoeur, in his celebrated
chapter "What Is an American?", pictures an "enlightened Englishman" landing
in America and delighted to find what his countrymen, even the disadvantaged
and lowly, have been able to accomplish. "They brought along with them," he
says, "their national genius. Here [the enlightened Englishman] sees the industry
of his native country, displayed in a new manner. . . . What a train of pleasing
ideas this fair spectacle must suggest!" Crèvecoeur to some extent visualized

---

[18] Thomas Jefferson attended the wedding of America-Francès. See *Dictionary of American
Biography* (New York: Charles Scribner's, 1943), 4: 543.

himself as an English settler-citizen: an Englishman *and* an Anglo-American. His literary *persona*, significantly, was that of an Englishman, and the son of an Englishman, though also American by birth. He pretends in the *Letters* that it was his grandfather who came from England to British America. Crèvecoeur, in short, intended to write as a settler, for a largely European audience. The twentieth century, somewhat misreading him, has interpreted him as an immigrant, writing for an American or would-be American audience.

His personal trauma was double. During the War of Independence he was required to affirm that he was not an Anglo-American but an American: not a settler but an immigrant. New York State demanded a loyalty oath from what it called "persons of neutral and equivocal character." They were to acknowledge that New York was "of right, a free and independent state." Crèvecoeur could not at that stage bind himself to agree. His second tragedy was to be thrust back into the dispossessed plight of the exile or émigré and to feel that none of the possible roles was satisfactory.

Among the elements that the settler and the immigrant have in common is a disposition to be optimistic, and to think in the future tense of what *is* to be. If, says Crèvecoeur, the new American "is a good man, he forms schemes of future prosperity. . . . He thinks of future modes of conduct." Such men have gambled on tomorrow. Being newcomers, they are also extremely reluctant to criticize their new environment. Their enthusiasm may thus be both sincere and oddly circumspect, even artificial. In Crèvecoeur's case, he was compelled for a while to renounce this optimistic mode. As exile or émigré, he faced the irony of having lost England as well as America and of having to strive to renew an allegiance to France that he had almost abandoned. Far from gaining a habitation and an identity, the exile or émigré is deprived of his. Not the future but the past is their tense: not *I shall be* but *I was* is their avowal. It is terrible for a man to be shifted from one extreme to the other, as was Crèvecoeur's lot. "I am no longer the old me" (l'ancien moi) "that you knew in the days of my happiness and my liberty," he lamented to a friend. "Before this fatal era," he wrote (c. 1778), "no man was happier than I was, I . . . was full of hopes and confidence." But the previous three years had brought "nothing but . . . acrimonious reflections which have made me a very different man from what I was."[19] *What I was* — hence the almost schizophrenic difference of outlook between the genial *Letters* and the gloomy *Sketches*.

[19] Quoted in Rice, 162.

Obviously Crèvecoeur's problems were peculiar. His difficulties of national identity were compounded during the Revolution because his farm happened to be in a chaotic debatable zone between the British and American forces. His wife's family seems to have been chiefly Loyalist. But fascinating though his story is in its own right, it carries broader lessons. In some respects Crèvecoeur reveals himself as a typical man of the pre-Revolutionary Enlightenment. Like a good many European contemporaries, he was not sure whether America was fundamentally different from Europe or fundamentally similar: whether the effects of environment outweighed the effects of heredity. His answers are not always consistent: a comment that can also be made about Alexis de Tocqueville's *Democracy in America*, written sixty years later. In places, Crèvecoeur seems to think that, for good and for ill, America's characteristics are entirely environmental. Elsewhere, especially in the *Sketches*, the argument tends to be that human nature is everywhere the same. Elsewhere again, Crèvecoeur appears to be saying that America is a melting-pot of all nations (the assumption of his mentor Raynal) and yet that its character has been formed on the basis of the colonies' British origins.[20]

This range of possibilities has continued to underlie nearly all subsequent discussions of the America-Europe relationship. As a man of the Enlightenment, Crèvecoeur probably did not feel the need for any greater analytical rigor. He does not wave the flag for any one nation, including the United States. He attempted to look upon the world with a transnational benevolence. On the whole he did not see America and Europe as distinct, rival civilizations but as societies bound by a principle of complementarity. In praising America so highly he was imparting a message of hope for mankind everywhere. The intended moral of the *Letters* was that simple prosperity was the best guarantee of human happiness and that such a goal could be universally attainable.

Up to the time of the American Revolution, most of the big generalizations about America had come from Europe or were identical with American formulations. In this respect, Crèvecoeur summed up in the *Letters* two or three

---

[20] Winthrop D. Jordan, *White Over Black: American Attitudes Toward the Negro, 1550-1812* (Chapel Hill: University of North Carolina Press, 1968), 334-41, argues that Crèvecoeur's melting-pot vision was not representative of American thinking in Crèvecoeur's own day, nor of the state of affairs in subsequent decades. His, says Jordan, was the hopeful attitude of a non-British, though distinctly Anglophile, settler. Most other works of the period, more accurately predictive than Crèvecoeur's, stressed the dominant influence of the English (or at any rate Anglo-American) culture in subjugating other cultural strains — a dominance that persisted through the nineteenth century. Jordan also detects another limitation: that Crèvecoeur's melting-pot allowed no place for the Negro American. Apart from his one chapter on the fate of the slaves in the South, Crèvecoeur refers without embarrassment to the supposedly happy and submissive blacks whom he himself owns.

centuries of the more favorable kinds of comment on America: the *Sketches*, consciously or unconsciously, recapitulate some of the unfavorable views, according to which America was a disorderly, degenerate place. For a century and more after the Revolution, the America-Europe relationship tended to become polarized into a principle of stark contrast. The gentle and rather ambiguous messages of *Letters from an American Farmer*, in an era of nationalistic scholarship, failed to excite the imagination of readers on either side of the Atlantic.

The *Letters*, as we know, were given a new lease of life at the beginning of the twentieth century. Not only did they appear to describe the conditions of melting-pot America: in general the book provided a welcome additional item to augment the none too abundant shelf of early American literary sources. Crèvecoeur ministered to the cultural and academic nationalism of the twentieth-century United States, as typified by the American Studies movement. Portions of the *Letters* — the bits to be found in the anthologies — are so fitting for the purpose that one almost thinks they would have had to be invented if they did not already exist.

Such an interpretation, of course, depends upon a highly selective reading of Crèvecoeur. With the exception of his biographers, scholars have been content for the most part to reproduce a few paragraphs from the *Letters*, to ignore the *Sketches*, and to accept the *persona* of the *Letters* as an essentially accurate portrait of the author.

The result is a grossly oversimplified rendering. It prevents us from recognizing that the European-American relationship contains all sorts of nuances, with a considerable element of mythologizing. Crèvecoeur's writings, the *Sketches* no less than the *Letters*, are even more relevant for the twentieth century than conventional interpretations claim. They help us to grasp the ambivalences of departure from one society and arrival in another, and therefore the whole drama of New World settlement. Crèvecoeur also has become relevant because our time is more aware of the similarities between New and Old Worlds than was the nineteenth century. We are once again inclined to think transnationally. In the perspective of the 1970s, the United States and Western Europe, in spite of their many dissimilarities, are seen to be running on more or less parallel lines. In the context of world history, both communities are relatively rich, relatively sophisticated, relatively urbanized and industrialized. They share common heritages, though admittedly eclectic ones. The New World is in some ways now old, the Old World in some ways new. One advantage to be gained from a close reading of Crèvecoeur is the realization that this interplay between Europe and

America has been going on for a very long time, and that it has never been straightforward.[21]

This essay appeared in the *Journal of American Studies* 9 (August 1975): 129-44.

---

[21] In addition to the works cited in note 2, there are signs of a more knowledgeably sophisticated approach to Crèvecoeur in a number of recent books and articles. See, for example, Elayne Antler Rapping, "Theory and Experience in Crèvecoeur's America," *American Quarterly* 19 (1967): 707-18; and James C. Mohr, "Calculated Disillusionment: Crèvecoeur's Letters Reconsidered," *South Atlantic Quarterly* 69 (1970): 354-63.

3

George Washington's Generalship

I produced this for a book of essays on Washington and his commanders, published in 1964, and have made only small changes, including the addition of a few more titles of subsequent work on the wartime phase of George Washington's career.

At first sight there is little new to be said about George Washington's generalship. With hardly an exception, contemporaries and biographers alike have agreed that he was an exemplary leader. Not even his few detractors have denied that he possessed certain essential attributes. Thus, he was personally brave. In the fighting on Manhattan in September 1776, at Princeton in the following January, and at Germantown in September 1777, he displayed conspicuous courage. Tall, handsome, composed, an expert horseman, he *looked* the part of a commander. He had great physical stamina; unlike some of his generals he survived years of arduous campaigning without a serious illness. While less well educated than a number of his associates, he managed to express himself in conversation and correspondence, with clarity and vigor. He was a methodical and energetic administrator. However despondent he might appear in private correspondence he never wavered in his public insistence that the American cause was righteous and would triumph. Nor did he waver in his loyalty; the British admiral, Rodney, hopelessly misread his character in assuring Lord George Germain, as late as December 1780, that "Washington is certainly to be bought — honours will do it."[1] Then, early in the struggle he realized that crisis could be defined as peril

---

[1] Quoted in Henry S. Commager and Richard B. Morris, eds., *The Spirit of 'Seventy-Six: The Story of the American Revolution as told by Participants*, 2 vols. (Indianapolis, 1958), 2: 70.

plus opportunity. The limitations of his command — miscellaneous and inexperienced troops, inadequate equipment and supplies, lack of naval vessels — must determine military policy. "[W]e should on all occasions," he told the President of Congress in September 1776, "avoid a general Action, or put anything to the Risque, unless compelled by a necessity, into which we ought never to be drawn."[2] But these words were written at a time of grave danger, when his troops were raw, hard-pressed and considerably outnumbered. He never ceased to seek out the possibility of what he called a "brilliant stroke": a sudden assault, that is, like the one across the Delaware in December 1776. When he felt more confidence in the quality of his men, he did not shun large-scale encounters. Finally, though he had a high sense of his own reputation, he resisted the temptation to abuse his authority. No scandal, financial or moral, attached to his name. Though he kept a punctilious record of the expenses owed him by the United States, he took no pay for his services. British propaganda alleged that he had a mistress: the *canard* gained no credence. He made it plain beyond doubt that he cherished no overweening dream of military dictatorship. In emergency, Congress twice entrusted him with exceptional powers. Some of his officers were prepared to hint in 1783 that he might become king of the new nation. In such situations he responded with the utmost rectitude. No wonder that the contrast was so often drawn between his own career and that of Napoleon Bonaparte.

On this there is virtually no argument. But to probe deeper, to offer any reassessment of Washington's relative military talent, or of his standing vis-à-vis his brother generals or the Continental Congress, is difficult. Some of the evidence we need — for example, on the true nature of the so-called Conway Cabal — is lacking. The story has become fixed in its main outlines. Between us and what might be a fresher truth lie the famous tableaux, apocryphal or authentic. Through portraiture we see Washington as elegant, severe, unruffled. We recall a whole sequence of static scenes: Washington placed in nomination for the chief command by John Adams at Philadelphia in June 1775; Washington reviewing his army on Cambridge Common a couple of weeks later; Washington sharing the miseries of the Valley Forge winter of 1777-78 with his men, yet (in our minds' eye) less affected by the cold than they; Washington rebuking Charles Lee at Monmouth Court House in June 1778, his soldiers broiled and parched, yet himself neither thirsty nor perspiring though angry enough with Lee; Washington superb in triumph at Yorktown, when Cornwallis surrenders to him

[2] Letter of September 8, 1776, in John C. Fitzpatrick, ed., *The Writings of George Washington*, 39 vols. (Washington, D.C., 1931-44), 6: 28.

in October 1781; Washington equally superb in his fatherly wisdom, when he puts on his spectacles to reply to the Newburgh Address of his discontented officers in March 1783; Washington bidding farewell to his officers, who now weep, at Fraunces Tavern in December of the same year. With such scenes are associated smaller vignettes: of nice young Lafayette, gruff old Steuben, jealous Gates and Conway, robust John Stark, comical Artemas Ward, villainous Arnold, loyal Greene, fat Knox; of Major André the British spy, so polite as to be almost masochistic; and of the Continental Congress, peevish, erratic, self-important. The total effect is that of an old-fashioned engraving in which a central subject or person is surrounded by a decorative border of tiny subordinate figures. The achievements of others are dwarfed and made to seem dependent upon Washington's direction.

Awareness of this disparity accounts for much of the carping or malicious comment about him that circulated among such prominent soldiers and civilians as Joseph Reed, Charles Lee, Benjamin Rush, James Lovell, and John Adams. Admired, deferred to, secure in seniority, Washington as they saw it could easily afford the luxury of *noblesse oblige*, just as the wealthy, well-born Lafayette could easily rise to a nobility of conduct that endeared him to Washington but made him an exasperating example for a hard-up comrade like "Baron" de Kalb.

The nature of the war itself creates further difficulties of interpretation. Though we call it the Revolutionary War or the War of Independence, it was also a civil war.   It was an improvised, embittered struggle. We do well to remember, for instance, that John Stark, the hero of Bennington, had a loyalist brother William who fought on the opposite side and was killed in the Battle of Long Island in August 1776.[3] The British were not sure how to define the conflict. The simplest answer was to call it a rebellion. Indeed, the British might have noted that such disturbances were apparently subject to a thirty-year cycle: 1775 was preceded by the Jacobite risings of 1745 and 1715 and by Monmouth's rebellion of 1685. The difference was that the American rebels were more remote, and the extent of their threat to British power less starkly obvious. So George III's advisers and generals fell into confusions over strategy and policy comparable to those that were later to perplex Abraham Lincoln. Both sides complained that they did not know where they stood or where they ought to stand in a war that was much easier to lose than to win.

In the circumstances, British generalship was often so hesitant and mediocre that Washington's own prowess is not easy to determine. When he tried to write

[3] Maldwyn A. Jones, *American Immigration* (Chicago, 1960), 53-54.

this portion of his biography of the American commander-in-chief, Washington Irving confessed his bewilderment. The military campaigns, he said, reminded him of two drunk men trying to hit one another yet failing to connect. An English observer (in *The Gentleman's Magazine* of August 1778), while seeking to denigrate Washington, admitted to a similar inability to make sense of events:

> *Nature has certainly given him some military talents, yet it is more than probable that he will never be a great soldier. . . . He is but of slow parts, and these are totally unassisted by any kind of education. Now, though such a character may acquit itself with some sort of éclat, in the poor, pitiful, unsoldierlike war in which he has hitherto been employed, it is romantic to suppose he must not fail, if ever it should be his lot to be opposed by real military skill.*

The anonymous commentator continues:

> *He never saw any actual service, but in the unfortunate action of Braddock. He never read a book in the art of war of higher value than Bland's Exercises; and it has already been noted, that he is by no means of bright or shining parts. If, then, military knowledge be not unlike all other; or it be not totally useless as to all the purposes of actual war, it is impossible that ever Mr. Washington should be a great soldier. In fact, by the mere dint and bravery of our army alone, he has been beaten whenever he has engaged; and that this is left to befall him again, is a problem which, I believe, most military men are utterly at a loss to solve.*

The author is ungenerous. Washington had had several years of soldiering in the French and Indian War. He had "heard the bullets whistle" more than once, before and after Braddock's disaster at the Monongahela. And it would strain the imagination to see the actions at Trenton and Princeton as proofs of British military superiority. Still, the commentator's puzzlement is understandable. For whatever reasons, and with the doubtful exception of Monmouth Court House, Washington *did* get the worst of the principal engagements he had a hand in during the first half of the war. The English writer goes on:

> *It should not be denied . . . that all things considered, [Washington] really has performed wonders. That he is alive to command an army, or that any army is left him to command, might be sufficient to insure him the reputation of a great General, if British Generals any longer were what*

British Generals used to be. In short, I am of the opinion . . . that any
other General in the world than General Howe would have beaten General
Washington; and any other General in the world than General Washington
would have beaten General Howe.[4]

Without taking the last observation too seriously, we can agree that Washington came near to catastrophe in the latter part of 1776. With a little more persistence and audacity from Howe, the army led by Washington might have been destroyed. If so, and if he himself had fallen into British hands, the struggle might have continued and Washington would have been dismissed by posterity as a well-intentioned but outmatched amateur.

As this *Gentleman's Magazine* assessment indicates, the war defied measurement according to European standards. It was a civil war, or a rebellion, or a popular patriotic rising, or a mixture of all three. Washington was a novice, with a reputedly limited intelligence; and yet he had "performed wonders."

Two of the most decisive factors were perhaps not personal but geographical: the huge extent of America and the width of the Atlantic. We have said that Washington's own eminence has made the activities of his officers seem minuscule. Geography, as Washington Irving came to feel, had a similar diminishing effect upon the commanders of both sides. A third factor, the French alliance, was almost equally decisive. Its inception might be counted as a diplomatic rather than a military success, while the all-important victory at Yorktown may be seen primarily as a Franco-British affair — a blow struck in a century-long contest.

When we attach the proper weight to such elements, what is entailed in the estimate of George Washington's generalship? Some scaling-down of the wilder claims: claims, it must be said, that he did not advance on his own behalf and that have not been asserted by reputable historians in the past half-century. We must discard the legend, disproved but still lingering on in folklore, that Frederick the Great ever sent Washington a sword with the engraved inscription, "From the oldest soldier in Europe to the greatest soldier in the world."[5] Instead, let us

---

[4] "Particulars of the Life and Character of General Washington, Extracted from a Letter in Lloyd's Evening Post of Aug. 17, Signed An Old Soldier," *The Gentleman's Magazine*, vol. 47 (August 1778). This is conveniently reprinted in Martin Kallich and Andrew MacLeish, eds., *The American Revolution Through British Eyes* (Evanston, 1962), 111-13.

[5] The results of various scrutinies of the legend are summarized in Francis V. Greene, *The Revolutionary War and the Military Policy of the United States* (New York, 1911).

consider his stature as a fighting general or field commander and secondly, as an organizing general or commander-in-chief.

Washington's talents as a field commander were not tested often enough or upon a big enough scale to rank him automatically with the prodigies of military history. Like the other American generals at the beginning of the war, he was, after all, deficient in experience. At the outset this recognition weighed upon them. None had had much formal training on the European pattern. They were, at best, veterans of colonial warfare, unaccustomed to the handling of large bodies of troops or to the employment of special arms such as cavalry. Washington never had the responsibility for campaigns on the Napoleonic scale, not to mention those of the American Civil War. He might have risen to the occasion, but the giant occasion did not present itself. We can only guess what his "ceiling" of achievement might have been in the tactical disposition of one big army confronting another.[6]

On the debit side, Washington made some mistakes. Possibly he was too ready to shift the blame for a reverse on to a subordinate. This has been said of his treatment of Nathanael Greene after the loss of Fort Washington and of his more peremptory reaction to Charles Lee at Monmouth Court House. Still, few senior soldiers in history could be held entirely innocent of such a charge. Washington's record is, for example, no worse and probably better than that of Stonewall Jackson in this respect. As for actual mistakes, he is most commonly accused of the following:

Long Island (August 1776): *Splitting his army between New York and Brooklyn; failure to appreciate the value of cavalry for reconnaissance purposes, and so being taken by surprise through a flank attack; failure to*

---

[6] "His courage is calm and brilliant, but to appreciate in a satisfactory manner the real extent of his . . . ability as a great . . . captain, I think one should have seen him at the head of a greater army, with greater means than he has had, and opposed to an enemy less his superior. At least one cannot fail to give him the title of an excellent patriot, of a wise and virtuous man, and one is . . . tempted to ascribe to him all good qualities, even those that circumstances have not yet permitted him to develop." This is the rather feline opinion of Colonel de Broglie, a young French nobleman who joined his regiment in 1782. W. S. Baker, *Character Portraits of Washington* (Philadelphia, 1887), 18-21. Perhaps its coolness, unusual for this late stage of the war, has something to do with family history. Four years earlier, another de Broglie was being hinted at as a candidate for what would in effect have been the chief command in America. See Douglas S. Freeman, *George Washington*, 6 vols. (New York, 1948-54), 4: 99.

give close supervision to General Israel Putnam's dispositions, which led to raw troops fighting without benefit of entrenchments.[7]

Fort Washington (November 1776): *The loss of 3,000 men when the Fort was captured through his own indecision.*[8]

Brandywine (September 1777): *Failure to use his Light Horse to gather information of enemy moves, or in other ways to anticipate Howe's flank attack; general lack of firm direction.*[9]

Germantown (October 1777): *Reliance upon too intricate a plan of battle.*[10]

Campaigns of 1777: *A strategic error in deciding to march south against Howe's invasion of Pennsylvania, instead of joining Gates and Schuyler so as to crush Burgoyne in the north and then swing south, with reinforcements from the Northern army, against Howe.*[11]

In extenuation, it should be said that most soldiers, even celebrated ones, make mistakes. Stonewall Jackson, brilliant in the Shenandoah Valley in 1862, was sluggish in the Peninsula fighting a few weeks later. Washington's errors were concentrated in the first half of the war, when he was a learner in command of learners, face to face with professionals. Probably Howe could have destroyed him at the end of 1776. But Howe hesitated; Washington's response was the

---

[7] Greene, *The Revolutionary War*, 41; Christopher Ward, *The War of the Revolution*, 2 vols. (New York, 1952), 1:229; George F. Scheer and Hugh F. Rankin, *Rebels and Redcoats* (Cleveland, 1957), 174.

[8] This criticism has been most bluntly formulated by Bernhard Knollenberg, in *Washington and the Revolution: A Reappraisal* (New York, 1940), 129-39.

[9] For some representative comments, see Willard M. Wallace, *Appeal to Arms: A Military History of the American Revolution* (New York, 1951), 139; John R. Alden, *The American Revolution 1775-1783* (New York, 1954), 123; Freeman, *George Washington*, 4:488; and Scheer and Rankin, *Rebels and Redcoats*, 240, 293-94.

[10] Ward, *The War of the Revolution*, 1:364-71; Alden, *The American Revolution*, 125; Scheer and Rankin, *Rebels and Redcoats*, 244.

[11] One of the first books in Washington historiography to express serious reservations as to the commander-in-chief's military prowess (including his failure to understand the value of cavalry) was Charles Francis Adams, Jr., *Studies Military and Diplomatic, 1775-1865* (New York, 1911). For the campaigns of 1777, see pp. 132-49.

splendidly impudent *coup* at Trenton. It was a raid rather than a battle; part of the plan miscarried, but the effect upon American morale was tremendous. It was a needed victory at the time, as was the more ripely comprehensive and more thoroughly professional victory at Yorktown five years later. The difference in the scope and context of the two engagements defined the distance that Washington and his army had traveled in skill, in offensive capacity, and in assurance. Valley Forge and the French alliance represent the turning point. After the winter of 1777-78, the troops close to Washington began to correspond to the notion he had always stressed: namely, that America must have a disciplined national force, as trained and tried as the best European ranks that could be brought against them.

Here we come to a point that is worth stressing. Ever since the Revolution, Americans have been debating the respective merits of professional and of amateur soldiery. It has been a heated debate, for it embodies quite fundamental divisions of opinion as to the true nature of American nationalism and democracy. The contenders have both managed to find ammunition in their interpretation of the Revolutionary War. The professionals cite Washington's highly critical references to the militia and to all short-term enlistments; the conflict was won, they believe, by the Continental regiments. The amateurs dwell upon the battles in which the militia fought stoutly and upon the superior qualities of initiative, patriotism, and ingenuity which derive from an amateur tradition. George Washington, the Virginia planter, could be seen as the highest product of an essentially civilian approach to warfare.[12]

That he retained some "civilian" characteristics is undeniable. His deference to Congress and to civilian authority generally may be interpreted in this light. It is arguable that the tactics to which he sometimes resorted show a refreshing freedom from military orthodoxy, and that the British generals were hopelessly hidebound. No doubt the achievements of Washington's lieutenants — Greene, Knox and Morgan especially — are striking illustrations of amateur proficiency. But the professional-amateur debate is misleading in various ways. On the British side, many of the officers prided themselves on a dilettante approach to warfare. Nor do we give proper credit to the Americans if we caricature the British conduct of operations as a series of brutally stupid frontal attacks on the Bunker Hill pattern. On occasion the British showed considerable enterprise.

---

[12] One stout upholder of this view is John A. Logan, *The Volunteer Soldier of America* (Chicago, 1887), 484: "No amount of preliminary technical education could have made a greater general of the hero of Trenton, Princeton, and Yorktown. His genius was natural, and bloomed into the perfection attained under the developing influence of actual warfare."

One example of this would be Grey's night assault on Anthony Wayne at Paoli in September 1777, when the British killed, wounded, or captured nearly 400 Americans for the loss of only 8 of their own men. On the American side, amateurishness may have been evident — perhaps all too evident — in the war's initial stages. But after two or three years of campaigning, Washington, his officers, and his Continental rank-and-file had become professionals in all important respects.[13]

This was what Washington himself ardently desired. He did not visualize himself as a guerrilla leader, a will-of-the-wisp harassing the stolid British like some brigand chief. From the start he strove to build an army able to meet the British in open battle and beat them at their own game.[14] He knew that this was only a dream in the early stages, and he acted accordingly. But his was no idle dream; it was an ambition that he labored to fulfill. As his correspondence shows, he hammered away at the task of creating an army officered (as far as possible) by gentlemen observing strict discipline, properly armed, accoutered, paid, rewarded, punished. His was no doubt a sensible conservatism: even the most revolutionary armies discover the advantages of well-established procedures and hierarchical distinctions. "Let us have a respectable Army," was his plea from 1776 onward, "and such as will be competent to every exigency." In other words, an army much like that of Howe or Rochambeau.[15]

But George Washington was not merely a field commander, though he maintained his headquarters in the field with whatever troops seemed to be best placed for his manifold purposes. He was commander-in-chief. The limits of his

---

[13] There are intelligent comments on these matters in Walter Millis, *Arms and Men* (New York, 1956), 32-33; Daniel Boorstin, *The Americans: The Colonial Experience* (New York, 1958), 364-71; Theodore Ropp, *War in the Modern World* (Durham, 1959), 71-80; and Alfred Vagts, *A History of Militarism*, rev. ed. (New York, 1959), 92-101.

[14] An excellent recent study is Russell F. Weigley, *Toward an American Army: Military Thought from Washington to Marshall* (New York, 1962). See especially pp. 1-7.

[15] By the closing stages of the war he had gone far enough in this direction to astonish discriminating Frenchmen, although previously Mifflin and other generals had enjoyed a reputation for being somewhat more effective disciplinarians. "I had expected to see," wrote the Comte de Ségur, "unkempt soldiers and officers without training. . . . I saw a well-disciplined army presenting in every detail the very image of order, reason, training and experience." Chastellux was equally impressed. "When one sees . . . the General's guards encamped within the precincts of his house; nine waggons, destined to carry his baggage, ranged in his court; . . . grooms taking care of very fine horses belonging to the General Officers and their Aides de Camp; when one observes the perfect order . . . within these precincts, . . . one is tempted to apply to the Americans what Pyrrhus said of the Romans: *Truly these people have nothing barbarous in their discipline!*" Gilbert Chinard, ed., *George Washington as the French Knew Him* (Princeton, 1940), 37, 57. If these officers had visited Washington's headquarters in 1776 or 1777, instead of 1781 or 1782, they would, of course, have found a more rough-and-ready atmosphere.

authority could not be exactly defined, in a situation without precedent. Even if a precise definition could have been formulated, much else would have remained hazy. He had a large but vague jurisdiction. His commission came from the Continental Congress, a body speaking for a then-nonexistent nation. Congress entrusted him with considerable powers. But Congress itself was only a comity, or perhaps more accurately a committee, of thirteen semi-sovereign states. Washington was clearly senior in rank to all the other generals. But what control was he to exercise, theoretically or actually, over armies that might be several hundred miles away from his own headquarters? To what extent could he give orders to the French military and naval leaders when their expeditions began to arrive in 1778? Who was to formulate strategy? With whom was he to communicate, and on what terms — governors of states, other commanders, the President of Congress, the Board of War? If he lost favor, was he removable?

Like the rest of his countrymen, Washington had to proceed by trial and error. That he did err now and then seems both undeniable and forgivable. His appointment was meant to symbolize the spirit of union. In 1775 such spirit was more an aspiration than a reality. Through indiscreet early letters he let it be known that he, the Virginian, was not much impressed by New England's military prowess. Some harm was done. He had one or two awkward passages with the French, again through indiscreet and possibly disingenuous correspondence which fell into the wrong hands. For a prudent man he sometimes expressed himself with dangerous candor in letters to his family and to friends in and out of Congress. Yet he learned by his mistakes. He shed all trace of Virginia localism until he, more than any other person or any institution or symbol, became synonymous with America's cause. And compared with most of his prominent fellow countrymen — soldiers and civilians — he was a model of discretion. His letters are sometimes angry and self-righteous; they are never whining, silly or malicious.

It was both a strength and a weakness of his position that he seemed, in more than one sense, irreplaceable. In retrospect the critical mutterings of 1776-77, in Congress and among certain army officers, strike us as petty and perhaps even treasonable. We find it absurd that Washington's military policy should be subject to the scrutiny of the five men whom Congress constituted as the Board of War and Ordnance in June 1776. What assistance could be rendered by such a member of the Board as the utterly unmilitary John Adams? It was replaced in 1777 by a new Board not composed of congressmen. But was this not even worse, when intrigue might place disgruntled army officers upon it? Or what of the six special committees sent by the Continental Congress to inquire into the army's affairs? Knowing what befell Gates at Camden — or thinking we know

— we wonder how anyone could have entertained the notion of substituting him for Washington in the supreme command.

But this is hindsight, and a hindsight which may be cruelly unfair. On the whole Congress and Washington worked together well — fantastically well if we compare their relations with those between Congress and Lincoln's wretched generals in the Civil War. The boards and special committees of Washington's day had next to nothing in common with the inquisitorial Committee on the Conduct of the War. They were anxious to help, and rendered all the aid within their power. It is doubtful whether there was any serious and concerted scheme to supplant Washington. There was something of a crisis of confidence in 1777-78. His more demonstratively enthusiastic supporters may have persuaded him that an organized plot existed. In the subsequent jockeying for position certain officers — Conway, Gates, Mifflin — may have been identified as a coalition hostile to Washington. Whether they were is dubious. Washington and posterity have treated them with marked disdain.

Whatever the inner history of a situation that may have had *no* inner history, Washington emerged as the undisputed commander at the head of a group of competent and devoted officers. If there was a plot, it hardly deserves the name. If there was a counterstroke by Washington, it was far from being a Putsch.[16] In the long run, the effects of the entire episode were probably beneficial. The army could rely on Washington to put its case before the country; Congress could feel reasonably sure that with Washington in command there was no risk of subversion by a military junto. It would have been amazing if there had been no friction, no dissension, no backbiting. Once his position was secure, Washington was able to display a remarkable magnanimity. True, he complained unceasingly of the difficulties in his path. The war dragged on and on. The French had their own views of fruitful strategy. There were ominous mutinies in the Continental line. Yet there was a good deal more acrimony in the British camps and council chambers and far more in that later American conflict of 1861-65.

Washington's ultimate success may owe as much to British limpness as to his own firmness. It has been plausibly maintained that the British situation was impossible from the start and that no amount of brilliance in leadership could have offset the formidable disadvantages of having to fight an unpopular war, with resources strained by other global commitments, in a terrain in which merely

---

[16] The undercurrents of hostility and rivalry are closely analyzed in Knollenberg, *Washington and the Revolution*, 30-77; and in Kenneth R. Rossman, *Thomas Mifflin and the Politics of the American Revolution* (Chapel Hill, 1952), 91-139; as well as in Freeman, *George Washington*, 4: 581-611. An older account, which assumes that opposition to Washington was organized, is Louis C. Hatch, *The Administration of the American Revolutionary Army* (New York, 1904), 23-34.

to feed or move an army — let alone fight major battles — was an administrative problem of daunting dimensions.[17] The surrender of Cornwallis could not have been encompassed without the French fleet and army. Washington's own growing military capacity would have counted for little if his generals, junior officers, and enlisted men had not grown commensurately in competence and assurance. The heroic efforts of Greene, Knox, Lafayette, and others ought not to be underrated in the apportionment of credit. Greene was accurate as well as warmhearted in writing to Knox after Yorktown:

> *Colonel Lee who has lately returned from the Northern Army says you are the genius of it, and that everything is said of you that you can wish. . . . Your success in Virginia is brilliant, glorious, great and important. The commander-in-chief's head is all covered with laurels, and yours so shaded with them that one can hardly get sight of it.*[18]

As Washington himself was quick to acknowledge, there was room for more than one set of laurels.

Nevertheless, his devoted subordinates and his admiring French allies gladly yielded to him a major share of the glory. We may discount some of their compliments as flattery or as formal rhetoric. Yet they knew him, closely and testingly, from day to day and month to month. If he had been indecisive, or unduly arrogant, nervous, or reckless, he could not have won and held their respect. The British army no doubt labored under handicaps; yet those of Washington's army were sometimes very similar. Long after the war, John Adams is said to have growled that Washington was "a block of wood!"[19] If he really made the remark, which is likely enough, it can be understood as an oblique commendation, a grudging testimony to the vital elements of character. He won, that is, by taking to the field and staying there; by tenacity rather than by Napoleonic *brio*. Though he could be dashing in action, his overriding service to America lay in his steadfastness. He was a fixed point in a shifting universe.

Washington's role in the War of Independence was extraordinary. There are no close historical parallels. Yet two comparisons can be made, each of which

---

[17] See Eric Robson, *The American Revolution in its Political and Military Aspects* (London, 1955), 93-152.

[18] Greene to Knox, December 10, 1781, quoted in North Callahan, *Henry Knox: General Washington's General* (New York, 1958), 93-94.

[19] An anecdote relating to *circa* 1816, recorded by John G. Palfrey; see *William & Mary Quarterly* 15 (January 1958): 190.

helps to remind us that the commander-in-chief was only in part a military leader. The two comparisons are with Charles de Gaulle and Dwight D. Eisenhower. Like de Gaulle, though with less conscious purpose on his part, George Washington symbolized his country and its will to resist. The new nation insisted upon endowing "His Excellency" George Washington with charismatic glamour.[20] He was able to sustain the role with remarkable modesty, all things considered, as well as with remarkable dignity. Like the French leader, he was a figure of exceptional strength of purpose. And like General Eisenhower, he was a coalition general for a large part of the war. A great proportion of his work went on in conference and in correspondence. Some of his activities were political or diplomatic rather than military, as when he had to deal with British offers to negotiate or with French military and naval chiefs. As with General Eisenhower, major strategic plans usually lay outside his scope; but their implementation often depended upon his advice. Despite his charismatic authority, he was more a mediator than a dictator. He communicated with governors of states, with Congress, with the Board of War, with the whole gamut of overlapping jurisdictions. In this respect, indeed, we might say that he was a dictator: a dictator of letters, not of decisions. If his charismatic symbols were those of the flag, the sword, the beautifully caparisoned horse, his day-to-day responsibilities were more appropriately symbolized by the chairman's gavel, the memorandum, the agenda, and the secretary's quill. It was his task and his talent to preside, to inform, to adjudicate, to advise, to soothe, to persuade, to anticipate, to collaborate. He had to weld the states together as far as he could: to co-operate with the French, harmonizing America's aims and theirs; to reconcile the competing claims of different theaters of war; to face the consequences in mounting pride and estrangement of having managed to create a professional army; to remember that though a master of men, he was the servant of his country and of Congress.[21] A co-ordinator, he had to learn how to stay near the scene of military action and yet not allow local problems to narrow his vision. A more mercurial figure might well have lost patience. A more genial one might have found his popularity was too cheaply purchased and so too rapidly dispersed. For most of the war he had to stand on the defensive, reacting to British pressures. But when the chance came in 1781, he showed that years of

---

[20] Seymour Martin Lipset, *The First New Nation: The United States in Historical and Comparative Perspective* (New York, 1963): 16-23.

[21] Edmund C. Burnett, *The Continental Congress* (New York, 1941), has some fascinating detail on Congress and the army. See, for example, pp. 442-67 for the period in 1780 when a committee of Congress visited Washington's headquarters.

parleying had not eroded his spirit. At a vital moment he seized the initiative, like an ideal coalition leader, in ensuring that he and the French for once acted in entire harmony. In earlier episodes he may perhaps now and then have picked the wrong alternative in what he called his "choice of difficulties." Should he, failing that, have retained the 3,000 men he sent to reinforce Schuyler and Gates? He made up his mind and acted, without vain regrets. He sent help to another army at the expense of his own immediate command. Can we imagine such a response from, say, General George B. McClellan?

What irony has accrued to those grudging judgments from *The Gentleman's Magazine*!

> *Now, though such a character may acquit itself with some sort of éclat, in the poor, pitiful, unsoldierlike war in which he has hitherto been employed, it is romantic to suppose he must not fail, if ever it should be his lot to be opposed by real military skill.*

If and perhaps. History can only answer that it was Washington who stayed the course; it was Howe and Clinton and Cornwallis who headed back home to their firesides and their extenuating speeches and memoirs.

BIBLIOGRAPHY

Burnett, Edmund C. *The Continental Congress*. New York, 1941. Explores the complicated relationships of the commander-in-chief with his civilian colleagues and mentors.

Cunliffe, Marcus *George Washington: Man and Monument*. Boston, 1958; rev. ed. 1982. Treats Washington's symbolic as well as military role.

Fitzpatrick, John C., ed. *The Writings of George Washington*, 39 vols. Washington, D. C., 1931-44. The best way of putting oneself in Washington's place is to read selected letters from these volumes. The portions dealing with the war years number some 10,000 pages.

Freeman, Douglas S. *George Washington: A Biography*, 7 vols. New York, 1948-54. The essential work on Washington. Volumes 4 and 5 relate to the Revolutionary War and they are thorough, dispassionate, and admirably indexed. Washington's military qualities are interestingly assessed at the end of Volume 5.

Frothingham, Thomas G. *Washington, Commander in Chief.* Boston, 1930. An older work that is laudatory in tone but still of some value.

Knollenberg, Bernhard *Washington and the Revolution: A Reappraisal,* New York, 1940. The most searching critical comment to be found on Washington.

Miller, John C. *Triumph of Freedom, 1775-1783.* Boston, 1948. A solid contribution as a general account of the war.

Sparks, Jared, ed. *Correspondence of the American Revolution, Being Letters of Eminent Men to Washington, 1775-1789,* 4 vols. Boston, 1853. Supplements the work of Fitzpatrick.

This essay appeared in *George Washington's Generals,* ed. George Athan Billias (New York, William Morrow and Co., 1964), 3-21.

Subsequent bibliographic titles include, among general interpretations, Don Higginbotham, *The War of American Independence* (New York, 1971); Charles Royster, *A Revolutionary People at War: The Continental Army and American Character, 1775-1783* (Chapel Hill, 1980); and John W. Shy, *A People Numerous and Armed* (New York, 1976). The British side of the conflict is presented in Piers Mackesy, *The War for America, 1775-1783* (Cambridge, Mass., 1964); and George A Billias, ed., *George Washington's Opponents: British Generals and Admirals in the American Revolution* (New York, 1969). On Washington himself, see Don Higginbotham, *George Washington and the American Military Tradition* (Athens, Ga, 1985), which draws a parallel with General George C. Marshall; and John Shy, "George Washington Reconsidered," in *The John Biggs Cincinnati Lectures in Military Leadership and Command,* ed. Henry S. Bausum (Lexington, Mass., 1986).

4

"They Will *All* Speak English": Some Cultural Consequences of Independence

This was originally presented as a paper in Washington, D.C., at the 1983 bicentennial conference on the Peace of Paris organized by the U.S. Capitol Historical Society, whose annual meetings have resulted in several volumes dealing with the era of the American Revolution. I contributed some related material, not reprinted here, to a 1984 conference held also in Washington under the auspices of the Woodrow Wilson International Center for Scholars and the Folger Institute's Center for the History of British Political Thought. This second paper bore the title "The Cultural Patrimony of the New United States": see Prosser Gifford, ed., *The Treaty of Paris (1783) in a Changing States System* (Lanham, Md., and London, 1985): 167-81.

———————————

The Scotsman Caleb Whitefoord was secretary to the British negotiating team empowered to work out peace terms in Paris in 1782. When his side and the Americans signed and exchanged documents on November 30, they rode outside the city to dine in celebration of the occasion. In Whitefoord's recollection, a French guest at the dinner held forth on the growing greatness of America," predicting that "the United States would form the greatest empire in the world." Whitefoord claims to have retorted: "Yes, sir, and they will *all* speak English; every one of 'em."[1]

This apparently chagrined response may seem an appropriate introduction for

———

[1] Richard B. Morris, *The Peacemakers: The Great Powers and American Independence* (New York, 1965), 378-85.

a discussion of the cultural, and more particularly *literary*, aftermath of the Peace of Paris. For in conventional literary histories of the United States, the early national period is supposedly full of British recrimination and condescension. The high (or low) point is often illustrated by the Rev. Sydney Smith's query in the *Edinburgh Review* of January 1820: "In the four quarters of the globe, who reads an American book?" Earlier in the same article, Smith had said:

> *The Americans are a brave, an industrious, and acute people; but they have hitherto given no indication of genius, and made no approaches to the heroic, either in morality or character. They are but a recent offset indeed from England; and should make it their chief boast for many generations to come that they are sprung from the same race with Bacon and Shakespeare and Newton. Considering their numbers . . . and the favourable circumstances in which they have been placed, they have yet done marvelously little to assert the honour of such a descent, or to show that their English blood has been exalted or refined by their republican training and institutions. Their Franklins and Washingtons . . . were born and bred subjects of the King of England. . . . And since the period of their separation, a far greater proportion of their statesmen and artists and political writers have been foreigners, than ever occurred before in the history of any civilised and educated people. During the thirty or forty years of their independence, they have done absolutely nothing for the Sciences, for the Arts, for Literature, or even for the statesmanlike studies of politics, or political economy.*

After asking "who reads an American book?" Sydney Smith had continued, "Or goes to an American play? Or looks at an American picture or statue? What does the world yet owe to American physicians or surgeons? What new substances have their chemists discovered? Or what old ones have they analysed? What new constellations have been discovered by the telescopes of Americans? What have they done in the mathematics?" And so on through commerce and manufacture, to the ultimate Smithian stab. At the close of his summary of the bare "annals of this self-adulating race," he queried: "Finally, under which of the old tyrannical governments of Europe is every sixth man a slave, whom his fellow-creatures may buy and sell and torture?"[2]

---

[2] Review of Adam Seybert's *Statistical Annals of the United States of America, Edinburgh Review* 65 (1820): article 3. Such review articles were anonymous. In this case, however, the authorship is confirmed by republication (see *Essays by Sydney Smith* [Reprinted from the *Edinburgh Review,*

Smith's severe interrogation, a standard item in the so-called War of the Quarterlies, seems of a piece with another notorious comment of the same era from the London *Quarterly Review* on "Republicanism, as it exists beyond the Atlantic, in all the glories of bundling, gouging, negro-driving, and dram-drinking; such poems as the Columbiad . . . and young ladies, who, when asked to dance, reply, 'I guess I have no occasion.'" The *Quarterly Review* said of Americans: "They have nothing original; all that is good or new is done by foreigners, and yet they boast eternally." Such pronouncements so infuriated the New York writer James Kirke Paulding that he produced several counterblasts, among them *John Bull in America, or the New Munchausen* (1825). *John Bull in America* parodied the gullible yet supercilious reactions of Tory travelers. Paulding's imaginary Briton follows the Smith line in asserting that since 1783 not one exceptional American has appeared. James Fenimore Cooper and Washington Irving "have, it is true, gained some little reputation; but I am credibly informed that the former of these gentlemen, has been once or twice in England, and that the latter never wrote English, until he had been long enough there to forget the jargon of his own country. So, after all, they furnish no exemption to my rule" — that post-Revolutionary America was a cultural desert (or as H. L. Mencken was to say much later of the American South, a "Sahara of the Bozart").[3]

So, in one common view, literature and other forms of culture in the new nation were treated with ignorant hostility by the bulk of British observers. Paulding's riposte, in the shape of a dialogue between his "John Bull" and an educated American, scores heavily for the American side. The sociocultural difference between the two countries, in the words of Paulding's spokesman, is that "our world is not quite ripe, and yours a little decayed. We think our world is the better for blooming in all the freshness of youth; while you appear to be of opinion that your world, like a cheese, is the better for being a little rotten." Paulding's fatuous John-Bullish narrator records that the American "bowed and

---

[London, 1848], 294-301). There is much useful information on publishing, authorship, and political coloration in David Paul Crook, *American Democracy in English Politics, 1815-1850* (Oxford, 1965). Two earlier studies by William B. Cairns still retain a little value: *British Criticisms of American Writings, 1783-1815*, University of Wisconsin Studies in Language and Literature, no. 1 (Madison, 1918), and *British Criticisms of American Writings, 1815-1833*, University of Wisconsin Studies in Language and Literature, no. 14 (Madison, 1922).

[3] James Kirke Paulding, *John Bull in America* (1825; reprint ed., Upper Saddle River, N.J., 1970), 164-65. The *Quarterly Review* piece (vol. 10 [1814]: 494-539) was a scathing gloss upon Charles Jared Ingersoll's *Inchiquin: The Jesuit's Letters* (1810). Paulding was particularly incensed by a comment in the same issue (p. 463) on his own work (see Cairns, *British Criticisms, 1815-1833*, 33-34). Paulding was angered too by the *Quarterly's* strictures on the United States contained in a review of William Faux's *Memorable Days in America* (1823) (vol. 29 [1823]).

left me, before I had time to make a cutting reply."[4]

Another familiar claim is that, given the relatively small population and resources of the infant nation, its cultural achievement was in fact impressive. No political writings? What of the intense constitutional debates of the 1780s and their outcome in the ingenious, lucid, and persuasive *Federalist* papers of Alexander Hamilton, James Madison, and John Jay? "Who reads an American book?" What of the poetry of Philip Freneau, Joel Barlow, and Timothy Dwight? What of the descriptions of America provided by the naturalist William Bartram, by the farmer-philosophe Crèvecoeur, and by Thomas Jefferson's *Notes on the State of Virginia*? Or, in fiction, of the psychological novels of Charles Brockden Brown? Again, Sydney Smith had asked, "Who looks at an American picture?" We can find positive answers in Kenneth Silverman's *Cultural History of the American Revolution*. The artist Benjamin West, resident in London from 1763 until his death in 1820, without disavowing his American origins, enjoyed high favor and even became president of the Royal Academy. The painter John Singleton Copley of Boston practiced his art in London for forty years after coming there in 1775. In December 1782 Copley was working on a portrait of the American merchant Elkanah Watson. After hearing of George III's speech acknowledging American independence, Copley added a Stars and Stripes flag to the background of Watson's portrait. "This was, I imagine," said Watson, "the first American flag hoisted in Old England." Gilbert Stuart, equally prominent as an American artist abroad, lived in England throughout the 1780s. Other Americans known in the London art world of the epoch included John Trumbull and Robert Fulton.[5]

We may cite additional evidence of American promise. The lexicographer Noah Webster, in the two decades after 1783, insisted on the need for and possibility of "a *national language*, as well as a national government." In the same essay (*Dissertations on the English Language*, 1789) he held out the prospect that "within a century and a half, North America will be peopled with a hundred millions of men, *all speaking the same language*." "They will *all* speak the same

---

[4] Paulding, *John Bull in America*, 196.

[5] Kenneth Silverman, *A Cultural History of the American Revolution: Painting, Music, Literature, and the Theatre . . . 1763-1789* (New York, 1976), is an excellent analysis. The Copley-Watson anecdote is cited in many books, for example, James T. Flexner, *America's Old Masters: First Artists of the New World* (New York, 1939), 156; also see Flexner's *John Singleton Copley* (Boston, 1948). General considerations are presented in Lillian B. Miller *Patrons and Patriotism: The Encouragement of the Fine Arts in the United States, 1790-1860* (Chicago, 1966), 1-23; in the early chapters of Neil Harris, *The Artist in American Society: The Formative Years, 1790-1860* (New York, 1966); and in J. Meredith Neil, *Toward a National Taste: America's Quest for Aesthetic Independence* (Honolulu, 1975).

language," he went on, but their vocabulary, phrasing, and pronunciation would constitute *American* English, not English English, and this standard *American* usage would be an essential element in unifying the new nation. In articles published in November 1783, Noah Webster sounded a note of patriotic euphoria. America was "the last resort of liberty and religion . . . where vice and despotism will be shrouded in despair, and virtue and freedom triumph in the rewards of peace, security and happiness." Religious toleration would help ensure for the United States a "greatness and lustre, before which the glory of ancient Greece and Rome shall dwindle . . . and the splendor of modern Europe shall fade into obscurity."[6]

Contemporaries of Webster and subsequent commentators have offered more cautious estimates, though usually dismissing British verdicts as ill-informed and resentful. These observers have put forward various explanations for the unexciting nature of American cultural accomplishments in the post-Revolutionary era. Moralists questioned whether a nation's true quality could be measured by its cultural products and pointed out that dazzling achievements in the fine arts tended to occur when a nation was past its prime and growing decadent. The Massachusetts historian and bluestocking Mercy Otis Warren argued that perhaps the plainness and simplicity of "republican institutions" were incompatible with the sophisticated elegance of aristocratic societies.[7] Others have maintained that no nation could expect to be preeminent in every art. Even the British had to look to Italy for lessons in opera or sculpture and to Germanic Europe for music or philosophy. It was thus unreasonable to expect that the young United States should immediately attain leadership in every field.

A third view held that a newly independent nation, occupied in settling and clearing its domain, could not give the highest priority to the fine arts. First things had to come first, and in the later 1780s problems of government filled the horizon. America, it was said, lacked the cultural resources — wealth, patronage, academies, galleries, libraries, printmaking, engraving — available in Europe; and others felt that the absence of an effective international copyright agreement was

---

[6] The most detailed biography of Noah Webster is still that by Harry R. Warfel, *Noah Webster: Schoolmaster to America* (New York, 1936); and Warfel was the editor of *Letters of Noah Webster* (New York, 1953). Webster's *Dissertations on the English Language* (1789) were reprinted in facsimile and edited by Warfel as well (Gainesville, Fla., 1951). Excerpts from his writings can be found in such selections as Russel B. Nye and Norman S. Grabo, eds., *American Thought and Writing*, vol. 2, *The Revolution and the Early Republic* (Boston, 1965), 281-88.

[7] William Raymond Smith, "Mercy Otis Warren's Radical View of the American Revolution," in Lawrence H. Leder, ed., *The Colonial Legacy*, vol. 2, *Some Eighteenth Century Commentators* (New York, 1971), 219-25.

a severe potential handicap to American authors. (Noah Webster and Thomas Paine, in the Revolutionary era, were among the keenest advocates of such protection, which was, however, not to be afforded to Americans until 1891.)[8]

A number of commentators contend that things were going well until the outbreak of the French Revolution plunged the world into a quarter century of warfare and ideological controversy, which served to disunite America and to delay the emergence of independent national styles in literature and the arts. Another view maintained that, despite Noah Webster's early high hopes, the American language was inevitably overshadowed by English English. English books continued to dominate the American market and to define American tastes. Not until the era of Washington Irving and James Fenimore Cooper could the United States begin to provide an adequate livelihood for professional authors.

A final line of argument suggested that even if Crèvecoeur or Barlow or Hugh Henry Brackenridge or Charles Brockden Brown were relatively unsuccessful in their own day or deficient in literary polish, their efforts initiated an American *tradition* (for example, of psychological introspection in Brown), even if later generations might not be aware that others had pioneered the modes they themselves were attracted to.[9]

Such views could be thought compatible with the criticism of national cultural pretensions delivered by certain Americans during the 1790s and the early nineteenth century. One of the most withering analyses was that of the New Englander Fisher Ames. "What geniuses have arisen among us?" he inquired:

> *This state of the case is no sooner made, than all the firefly tribe of our authors perceive their little lamps go out of themselves, like the flame of a candle when lowered into the mephitic vapor of a well. Excepting the writers of two able works on our politics, we have no authors. . . . There is no scarcity of spelling-book makers, and authors of twelve-cent pamphlets;*

---

[8]There is a condensed account of international copyright issues in Clarence Gohdes, *American Literature in Nineteenth-Century England* (Carbondale, Ill., 1944), 16-18; also see Benjamin T. Spencer, *The Quest for Nationality: An American Literary Campaign* (Syracuse, 1957), 67-68, 143-46.

[9] Views of this sort, some of them originating as articles in the important periodical *Early American Literature*, can be found in Silverman, *Cultural History of the American Revolution*; Emory Elliott, *Revolutionary Writers: Literature and Authority in the New Republic, 1725-1810* (New York, 1982), which contains detailed discussion of Dwight, Barlow, Freneau, Brackenridge, and Brown; various essays in Everett Emerson, ed., *Major Writers of Early American Literature* (Madison, 1972) and *American Literature, 1764-1789: The Revolutionary Years* (Madison, 1977); and William L. Hedges, "The Old World Yet: Writers and Writing in Post-Revolutionary America," *Early American Literature* 16 (1981): 3-18.

and we have a distinguished few, a sort of literary nobility, whose works have grown to the dignity and size of an octavo volume. We have many writers who have read, and who have the sense to understand, what others have written. But a right perception of the genius of others is not genius; it is a sort of business talent. . . . Nobody will pretend that the Americans are a stupid race. . . . But has our country produced one great original work of genius?

Ames is an eloquent polemicist. But he wrote as a conservative, a Federalist, a detester of Thomas Jefferson and of what he took to be the decline of the United States into demagoguery and commercialism. His argument can therefore be read as a party harangue, the expression of a person convinced that "unmixed democracy" will subvert American liberty. And Ames concludes with the rather perverse notion that when democracy in America yields to despotism, *then* the new "emperor . . . will desire to see splendor in his courts" and there will be a flowering of the arts. "Nature, never prodigal of her gifts," will then at last produce "some men of genius" in the United States. Does Ames welcome that outcome, or not? Such jaundiced utterances could be dismissed as proofs that Federalists were fundamentally undemocratic (or unrepublican), and therefore apt — consciously or not — to repeat the cultural assumptions of the Old World.[10]

Two centuries later it may still be impossible to offer an entirely objective assessment of the state of American literary culture during the ten or twenty years that followed the Peace of Paris. Old patriotic sensibilities are not completely inert; raw nerves may still be touched. Moreover, new techniques of literary discourse may unintentionally minister to the national pride by treating questions of literary merit as naively irrelevant; or historically disadvantaged groups may object that conventional modes of judgment are distorted. In such cases one encounters a dispute as to whether Americans were fundamentally the same as Europeans or importantly different; an assertion that Americans ought to be judged by special, perhaps self-established criteria, instead of by measures imposed by alien, uncongenial arbiters; a tendency to emphasize the hostility, incomprehension, and other handicaps that inhibit the flowering of a first-rate autonomous culture; and a contrary tendency, to claim that what was produced was first-rate, when seen in the proper light.

---

[10] Cited in Nye and Grabo, eds., *Revolution and Early Republic*, 295, 302-4, from Fisher Ames's essay "The Future of American Literature," published in his *Works* (1809) but written somewhat earlier.

Despite such difficulties of fair interpretation, it ought to be possible to restate some of the realities of the post-1783 American literary scene. First, the *anti-Americanism* of Europeans, and more particularly that of the parent country, was *not of primary significance.* Certainly there were elements of British disapproval and schadenfreude. The tone of the quarterlies could be disdainful in the extreme, and their anonymous contributors seemed to profess omniscience, objectivity, and absolute insight. But this was the tone they took about everything and everybody, including one another.

The Tory *Quarterly Review*, established in 1809, was the avowed opponent of the Whig *Edinburgh Review* (1802). They differed in tone from such older periodicals as the *Gentleman's Magazine*, the *London Magazine*, and the *Monthly Review* — and from newer monthlies such as *Blackwood's Edinburgh Magazine* (1817). Gifford's *Quarterly Review* and Jeffreys's *Edinburgh Review* reserved their harshest criticisms for British authors. The poet John Keats was among the victims. According to Lord Byron (another target), Keats's early death was hastened by a brutal attack on his *Endymion*:

> *Who killed John Keats?*
> *"I" says the Quarterly,*
> *So cruel and Tartarly,*
> *"Twas one of my feats."*

These regally opinionated periodicals were also in their day extremely readable — in part, of course, because of the readiness to express ridicule and scorn. Their tomahawk tendencies made them much read and reprinted in the United States. But, to repeat, anti-Americanism was not a principal feature of editorial policy. True, most of the British commentators were poorly qualified to discuss American affairs. The poet William Cowper, for example, wrote occasionally about the United States with only a vague grasp of American geography or government. So did the *Quarterly Review*'s contributor Robert Southey (who was to be poet laureate from 1813 to 1843). As befitted a Tory publication, the *Quarterly* reviewer no doubt infuriated Paulding by dismissing one of his would-be humorous pieces as follows (January 1814):

> *It was to be expected that in the process of time an American wag should make his appearance. In a nation derived from so many fathers it has justly been a matter of wonder that there should hitherto have existed so tame a uniformity, and that ... such varied elements should produce the*

merest monotony of character that the world has yet seen. It is not our business to inquire into the cause of this phenomenon. . . . We will only observe that when the vulgar and illiterate lose the force of their animal spirits they become mere clods; and that the founders of American society brought to the composition of their nation few seeds of good taste, and no rudiments of liberal science.

The writer paused to suggest that eventually an American art and literature would emerge. Reverting to Paulding's *Lay of the Scottish Fiddle*, a jocose imitation of Sir Walter Scott, the reviewer said it was inevitable that American wit should first manifest itself in parody: "Childhood is every where a parodist. America is all a parody, a mimicry of her parents; it is, however, the mimicry of a child . . . abandoned to bad nurses and educated in low habits."[11]

It is also true that even in commentaries professing admiration for the United States, a tinge of amused condescension creeps in. Praise bestowed in one clause is usually balanced with disparagement, as in these generalizations from an *Edinburgh Review* criticism (July 1803) of a British book of travels. The writer rebukes the author for expressing disdain for American publications, but does not muster more than two cheers for American culture (italics are mine): "Their party pamphlets, though *disgraced with much intemperance and scurrility*, are written with keenness and spirit, that is not often to be found in the old world; and their orators, though occasionally *declamatory and turgid*, frequently possess a vehemence, correctness, and animation, that would command the admiration of any European audience."[12]

[11] On British periodicals see Crook, *American Democracy*; and Cairns, *British Criticisms, 1783-1815* and *British Criticisms, 1815-1833*. The *Quarterly Review*'s scolding of Paulding is quoted in Cairns, *British Criticisms, 1783-1815*, pp. 33-34. William Cowper's limitations of knowledge and sympathy are discussed in Pat Rogers, "On the Edge of the Abyss," *Times Literary Supplement*, April 8, 1983. Cowper, who at one stage contributed an assessment of Barlow's *Vision of Columbus* to the *Analytical Review*, confessed in correspondence his indifference to public issues and foreign countries. According to Rogers, "Having regarded the American War at first with blithe confidence (there is no reference at all to the Declaration of Independence), he finds the news from Yorktown disconcerting, but chiefly because it means discarding two flag-waving poems 'that I was rather proud of.' He makes a vague reference . . . to the Peace of Versailles in 1783, without much sense of engagement. There is no allusion to the events in France of 1789. . . . As for *The Rights of Man*, 'I have not seen Payne's [*sic*] book, but refused to see it when it was offer'd me. No man shall convince me that I am improperly govern'd while I feel the contrary.'"

[12] *Edinburgh Review* 2 (1803): 448. The book in question was John Davis, *Travels . . . in the United States of America* (1803). The reviewer dismissed the author as "a pedagogue, who would be a wit and a fine gentleman" (p. 443), denying his claim to either condition and noting with astonishment that Davis had managed to obtain a commendatory preface "from no less a person that the President of the United States" (Thomas Jefferson). See also Herbert G. Eldridge, "The Paper War Between England and America: The *Inchiquin* Episode, 1810-1815," *Journal of American Studies* 16 (1982):

Nevertheless, anti-Americanism is not the key to such apparently unfavorable reactions. And some of the most prickly British remarks, especially those from the *Quarterly*, were made during the War of 1812. There was an actual armed conflict as well as a War of the Quarterlies. It would have been even more remarkable if the combat had not colored the effusions of journalists. On the other side of the story are the many signs of willingness among Britons, especially Whiggish ones, to welcome American publications. The New World was looked to even with eagerness for tokens of innovative literary genius. In this way, decades later, innovators on the order of Whitman and Dreiser were to receive a more enthusiastic welcome in certain British circles than in their own land. Again, while American themes became part of the repertoire of a sometimes xenophobic British pattern of humor, they took their place among a numerous company that included illiterate yokels, pedantic Germans, nervous curates, nouveau-riche nabobs, fantasizing Irishmen, and fatuous aristocrats. Sydney Smith, who had a brother in the United States, was in the main pro-American and wrote little or nothing about the country until 1815. The large, uncomfortable fact is that the first generation of American literati failed to produce the promised masterpieces. This was acknowledged, however sadly or reluctantly, by most of the old chroniclers of American literary history.[13] The admission would have been less painful for American patriots if their preliminary claims had been more circumspect. Prophecies of future greatness made during and just after the Revolution were in general grandiose and unspecific. Some of them implied that American cultural greatness was not only guaranteed but imminent. "Columbia,

---

49-68.

[13] Edwin P. Whipple, *American Literature and Other Papers* (Boston, 1887), contains a quite lively survey of writing between 1776 and 1876 (pp. 1-138). Whipple seeks to praise at least some aspects of Brown and Brackenridge. Barlow, however, aroused him to mirthful scorn: "Joel Barlow is fairly entitled to the praise of raising mediocrity to dimensions almost colossal. Columbia is, thank Heaven, still alive; 'The Columbiad' is, thank Heaven, hopelessly dead. . . . No critic within the last fifty years has read more than a hundred lines of it, and even this effort of attention has been a deadly fight with those merciful tendencies in the human organization which softly wrap the overworked mind in the blessedness of sleep."

William P. Trent et al., *The Cambridge History of American Literature*, 3 vols. (New York, 1917-21), 1: viii-ix, comments on the assumptions of works such as Charles F. Richardson, *American Literature, 1607-1885* (1887-89), and Barrett Wendell, *Literary History of America* (1900), which take for granted that little if any significant literature appeared in America before 1800 and, indeed, little before 1820. Such attitudes died hard. Russell Blankenship, *American Literature as an Expression of the National Mind* (New York, 1931), while expressing a general pride in the nation's cultural record, can muster little enthusiasm for most of the early products. Thus, on the author of *The Columbiad*, Blankenship comments, "The kindly thing is to remember Barlow as a lover of freedom and to forget his heavy-handed toying with poetry" (p. 189). Percy H. Boynton's text *Literature and American Life* (Boston, 1936) says of Charles Brockden Brown, with some severity, that while he possessed "certain native gifts," he lacked self-discipline. Brown "oscillated between being a Poe and a [Harriet Beecher] Stowe, and his pendulum came to a dead stop in the middle" (pp. 202-3).

Columbia," cried Timothy Dwight in 1777,

> *to glory arise,*
> *The queen of the world, and child of the skies!*
> *Thy genius commands thee; with rapture behold,*
> *While ages on ages thy spendors unfold.*

"We are called to sing a New Song," declared Nathaniel Appleton, "a Song that neither We nor our Fathers were ever able to sing before." In the words of John Trumbull:

> *This land her Swift and Addison shall view,*
> *The former honors equalled by the new;*
> *Here shall some Shakespeare charm the rising age,*
> *And hold in magic chain the listening stage.*

"Thy native land is big with mighty scenes," Mercy Otis Warren assured aspiring poets in 1782.[14]

Such rhetoric sometimes shaded into bombast. The praise of republican institutions, the confidence that these would generate an exemplary new culture, went along with denunciation of the tyranny, despotism, and corruption supposed to typify Europe. In the process the faults of the mother country, "that detestable place" in Freneau's phrase, were exaggerated, and the extent of previous American association with England was correspondingly minimized. Such assertions, more extravagantly xenophobic than a Freneau or a Barlow probably realized, served to provoke British counterinvective. The persistence of slavery in America's "piebald polity," as the Anglo-Irish poet Tom Moore called it, made the United States vulnerable to charges of hypocrisy.

So did the curious record of the Americans on the matter of republicanism. With the Revolution came the proud boast that the colonies had always been republican. Why then had colonists, with hardly any exceptions, sung the praises of George III until the very eve of the Revolution? Why during the Revolution

---

[14] The "Rising Glory" theme, as he dubs it, is discussed in Silverman, *Cultural History of the American Revolution*, 228-35; also see his treatment of *translatio studii* — a venerable notion, adapted to American circumstances, of a westward global transit of the arts (pp. 9-11). Predictions of American greatness in the arts are described also in Michael Kraus, *The Atlantic Civilization: Eighteenth-Century Origins* (Ithaca, N.Y., 1949), 216-307; and in Joseph J. Ellis, *After the Revolution: Profiles of Early American Culture* (New York, 1979), 3-21. My quotations are borrowed from Nye and Grabo, eds., *Revolution and Early Republic*, 366-67; and from Russel B. Nye, *American Literary History, 1607-1830* (New York, 1970), 179-80, 186.

did the Americans show so little embarrassment in paying ceremonial tributes to the French monarchy of Louis XVI? Joel Barlow, a chaplain in the Continental army, joined with fellow officers in celebrating the birth of Louis XVI's heir, the dauphin. And in 1786 Barlow was at great pains to secure the patronage of Louis XVI for his would-be epic poem, *The Vision of Columbus*. The French monarch graciously accepted the dedication of the *Vision* and got sales off to a handsome start by purchasing twenty-five copies. (Barlow, incidentally, gleaned much of the background information in the *Vision* from the *History of America* by the Scottish historian William Robertson, who had never been across the Atlantic.) Barlow went to Paris and lived there through the dramas of the 1790s, a friend of Thomas Paine and author of the (by then) antimonarchical *Advice to the Privileged Orders*. But it could be said of Joel Barlow, unkindly, that he was himself a member of the privileged orders, practicing what we have learned to think of as radical chic. At any rate, former chaplain Barlow took advantage of his international connections, his cosmopolitan charm, financial shrewdness, and a measure of luck, to build up a sizable fortune. He has acquired a recent new renown through the anthologizing of the last poem he ever wrote, a bleak depiction of the sufferings of Napoleon Bonaparte's army on the way back from Moscow. Had it taken Barlow so long to circle back to the antirevolutionary and anti-Napoleonic beliefs of his former associates, the conservatively minded Connecticut Wits? Understandably, his revised version of the *Vision*, now known as *The Columbiad* (1807), was no longer dedicated to Louis XVI, but to Barlow's friend Robert Fulton. It was also, however, a sumptuously bound and illustrated edition, selling at $20 a copy and looking gorgeous enough to adorn a royal library, if too magnificent for a republican one.[15]

Comparable complexities surround the stories of other figures in the early

[15] Theodore A. Zunder, *The Early Days of Joel Barlow . . . 1754 to 1787* (New Haven, Conn., 1934); James Woodress, *A Yankee's Odyssey: The Life of Joel Barlow* (Philadelphia, 1958); Elliott, *Revolutionary Writers*, 92-127; Robert D. Arner, "The Connecticut Wits," in Emerson, ed., *American Literature, 1764-1789*, 245-51. A. Owen Aldridge, *Early American Literature: A Comparatist Approach* (Princeton, 1982), 187-88, suggests a source for Sydney Smith's mockery in a much-ridiculed debate of December 1796, when the House of Representatives produced the assertion that the United States was, as "a whole nation, the freest and most enlightened in the world." Smith's 1820 article referred to the American "orators and newspaper scribblers [who] endeavour to persuade their supporters that they are the greatest, the most refined, the most enlightened, and the most moral people upon the Earth." On the readiness of the anti-monarchical American patriots to embrace the relatively absolutist French monarchy, see a letter from the *Nation* editor E. L. Godkin to the historian Francis Parkman (December 14, 1885), congratulating him on his new book *Wolfe and Montcalm*: "considering the fearful memories that war must have left in the colonies, and the horror of the French it must have inspired, was not the alliance with and liking of them twenty years — only twenty — later most extraordinary?" William Armstrong, ed., *The Gilded Age Letters of E. L. Godkin* (Albany, N.Y., 1974), 336.

history of American literary nationalism. It is not easy to set the record straight. Pietistic literary historians have sometimes portrayed arduous, frustrated pioneer efforts as clear-cut success stories — victories for the wholesome impulses of democratic patriotism. Richard Rollins and Joseph J. Ellis are, however, among the scholars who have recently explored the career of Noah Webster and show that his career involved even more tergiversation than that of Joel Barlow.

Webster began during the Revolutionary War as an ardent nationalist, insistent that "America must be as independent in *literature* as she is in *politics* — as famous for *arts* as for *arms*." He was also tirelessly ambitious; "a person of my youth," he added, "may have some influence in exciting a spirit of literary industry." This he had attempted by means of a projected three-volume set of publications, heralded by the *Spelling Book*.[16]

Webster's aim was to establish a single American standard of pronunciation, spelling, and usage, purged of what he regarded as British linguistic corruptions and errors (such as the eighteenth-century habit of adding a superfluous *k* to musick, Gothick and other *-ic* endings). His schoolbooks would inculcate these "American" rules and provide American instead of British specimen instances. He insisted that the acceptance of a universal, rational system would serve to bind the former colonies into nationhood.

Some of his proposals were indeed sensible. Several of his spelling reforms were eventually adopted, notably the change from *-re* to *-er* in words like *center* and the deletion of *u* from *colour, honour*, and the like. His small 1806 *Dictionary* was commendable as a one-man operation; the larger 1828 *Dictionary* was quite a heroic achievement, even if the immense *Webster's* of later decades was linked to the lexicographer in name only. He was right, too, to argue the importance for the United States of becoming or remaining a land of one common language.

In other respects Webster fails to fit the specification of far-sighted democratic innovator. By the 1790s he had begun to settle into a cranky Federalism, deploring what he took to be the follies and sins of such dangerous radicals as Jefferson and Paine. His dictionary definitions revealed increasing skepticism as to the desirability of *equality, democracy, republicanism*, and the like. One of the synonyms for *president* in Webster's 1828 dictionary — cynical, resigned, approving? — is *monarch*.

On the matter of language, Webster abandoned his early insistence that American English could or should differ radically from English English. He was

[16] Richard Rollins, *The Long Journey of Noah Webster* (Philadelphia, 1980); Ellis, *After the Revolution*, 161-212.

gratified to discover, on a trip across the Atlantic in 1826, that "good usage in England accords almost wholly with the good usage in this country." His final view? "Our language is the *English*; except for a "few peculiarities" in each, he declared it "desirable that the language of the United States and Great Britain should continue to be the same." What of the Websterian dream of a distinct American culture founded upon a purified language? Had it been properly thought out, any more than the brainwave of Brissot de Warville, who jotted down in his journal the notion that Americans ought to start speaking a sort of franglais in order to break loose from the thrall of the mother tongue? Conceivably, Webster was doing actual harm by denying the existence and utility of regional dialects. If Americans paid attention to Webster, did they not risk denaturing their native speech?[17]

Another man of letters much cited in accounts of America's literary evolution is Michel Guillaume St. Jean de Crèvecoeur, commonly known as J. Hector St. John de Crèvecoeur, who published *Letters from an American Farmer* in 1782. He is known above all for the third chapter of the book, entitled "What is an American?" Crèvecoeur is credited with being perhaps the first author to express the "American Dream," through his evocation of the American "new man," working as a yeoman farmer in an idyllic middle landscape. This picture is appealing and in some crucial sense true. But Crèvecoeur is a complicated case. Most of the *Letters* were written before the Revolution, when this French-born settler was a British citizen. The felicity he celebrates is that of British colonies under the protection of a benevolently remote yet powerful government. His "new man" is an Anglo-American and certainly free in ways denied to Europe's landless poor. However, "new man" is also a rendering of *novus homo*, the self-made figure who is frequently mentioned in Roman history. John Adams was one of the Americans who spoke of *novi homines*, using the Latin tag as an evident commonplace of eighteenth-century reference. The degree of newness of Crèvecoeur's new man is no more clear-cut than his nationality.

Nor was Crèvecoeur's own allegiance free from doubleness. He quit his farm in Orange County, New York, in 1780 and after some delay reached London

---

[17] Warfel, ed., *Letters of Webster*, 415. As for Brissot de Warville: "Americans must detest the English; they will try, if they can, to erase every trace of their origin. But since their language will always betray them, they must introduce innovations into their language as they do in their constitution. . . . What, then would stop them from adopting turns of phrase peculiar to the French language? Why would they make fun, as the English do, of Frenchmen who introduce gallicisms into their English? There is a double advantage . . .: Americans will be drawn closer to other nations and will be drawn father away from the English. They will create a language of their own; there will exist an American language" (J. P. Brissot de Warville, *New Travels in the United States* (1788), ed. Durand Echeverria [Cambridge, Mass., 1964], 78).

aboard a British ship. The British authorities appear to have concluded that he was a loyalist (and that is how he is regarded by historians of loyalism). His wife's family and some of his friends were associated with loyalism. The final part of *Letters from an American Farmer*, and the bulk of other material that remained unpublished until 1925 (*Sketches*), is at best lukewarm toward the American cause. Crèvecoeur returned to the United States in 1783, after a sojourn in Paris, but as French consul. He went back to France for several months in 1785 and left America for good in 1790. His volume of *Letters*, markedly more "patriotic" in the revised French editions of 1784 and 1787, when independence was an accomplished fact, enjoyed some popularity for a few years. But an American edition of 1793 was virtually ignored and, thereafter, *Letters from an American Farmer* remained out of print until 1904. For all that time the American Dream had to do without Crèvecoeur.[18]

There are other indications of a collapse of morale, from the élan of the 1770s to the worries of the 1780s, and the feuds and lamentations of the 1790s. Barlow's New England friends, the spry intellectuals of the war years, turned to the semidisenchanted light verse of the *Anarchiad* (1786-87). They had enthusiastically supported the American side in the War of Independence. By degrees these Connecticut, or Hartford, Wits became caustic. Indeed, "Christopher Caustic" was one of their pen names. "The Echo" (1805) sharply attacked Jefferson and his administration:

> *Sometimes We talk in hypocritic strain*
> *Sometimes we're hand in hand with atheist Paine,*
> *Sometimes Our style is mere bombastic sound,*
> *Sometimes 'tis mean and grovelling on the ground.*[19]

Philip Freneau was a skillful versifier and pamphleteer with a more deeply revolutionary or, at any rate, anti-British impulse. "That rascal Freneau" served

---

[18] Marcus Cunliffe, "Crèvecoeur Revisited," *Journal of American Studies* 9 (1975): 129-44; Elayne Antler Rapping, "Theory and Experience in Crèvecoeur's America," *American Quarterly* 19 (1967): 707-18; James C. Mohr, "Calculated Disillusionment: Crèvecoeur's *Letters* Reconsidered," *South Atlantic Quarterly* 69 (1970): 354-63; Everett Emerson's essay on Crèvecoeur in W. Fluck, ed., *Forms and Functions of History in American Literature: Essays in Honor of Ursula Brumm* (Berlin, 1981); A. W. Plumstead, "Hector St. John de Crèvecoeur," in Emerson, ed., *American Literature, 1764-1789*, 213-31. It should be said that Plumstead and some other recent commentators do not perceive Crèvecoeur as a deviously unhappy figure, but rather as a pioneer of literary Americanism.

[19] "The Echo," no. 20, a collaborative work mainly written by Theodore Dwight and Richard Alsop for *The American Mercury* (1792-1805). This, from the final section, was composed by Alsop. It is cited in Vernon L. Parrington's valuable edition *The Connecticut Wits* (1926; reprint ed., 1969), 509.

as a journalist for the Jeffersonians in the early 1790s. His animus against kings and aristocrats never abated. What did fade were his dreams that America might enable people of talent to live by the pen. In one of his personae Freneau as "the Late Mr. Robert Slender" offered wry advice to aspiring authors not to expect to find an audience for their literary wares. There were simply not enough Americans interested in such things.[20]

This was the discovery too of the novelist Charles Brockden Brown, often described as America's first professional author. He wrote six novels between 1798 and 1801. Twenty years later, in recommending Brown's fictions, James Kirke Paulding was obliged to confess that most Americans had probably never heard of them. The most Paulding could venture was a pious expectation that Brown's "future fame will furnish a bright contrast to the darkness in which he is now enveloped." In the years before his death in 1810, Charles Brockden Brown still did some writing but had to spend most of his time as a businessman.[21]

Freneau's Princeton classmate Hugh Henry Brackenridge had collaborated with him in a glowingly optimistic undergraduate poem, "The Rising Glory of America" (1772). After war service Brackenridge settled in frontier Pennsylvania to practice law, with strongly patriotic and democratic impulses. His major work was a long picaresque novel, *Modern Chivalry*, published in installments from 1792 to 1815. In the more perfunctory surveys of American literature *Modern Chivalry* is treated as rollicking backwoods comedy. There is indeed some humor of a semi-Jeffersonian sort, as in a mocking account of the self-importantly snobbish concerns of the Society of the Cincinnati. Brackenridge never became a high Tory. On the other hand, a principal theme is that men should remain in their proper stations, once these have been established. The two chief characters are Captain Farrago and his servant Teague O'Regan. Farrago's enterprises

---

[20] Elliott, *Revolutionary Writers*, 146-47; Lewis Leary, *That Rascal Freneau: A Study in Literary Failure* (New Brunswick, N.J., 1944); and "Philip Freneau: A Reassessment," in Leary, *Soundings: Some Early American Writers* (Athens, Ga., 1975), 131-60; Philip M. Marsh, *Philip Freneau: Poet and Journalist* (Minneapolis, 1967). Also see some acute remarks by Lewis P. Simpson, "The Satiric Mode: The Early National Wits," in Louis D. Rubin, Jr., ed., *The Comic Imagination in American Literature* (New Brunswick, N.J., 1973), 49-61. The most convenient excerpt from the views of "Slender" is to be found in Robert E. Spiller's fine compilation, *The American Literary Revolution, 1783-1837* (Garden City, N.Y., 1967), 5-12. Slender makes a lighthearted complaint against condescending literati from Britain and Ireland who "boast that they have introduced the Muses among us since the conclusion of the late war. . . . They are, however, excusable [*sic*] in treating the American authors as inferiors; a political and a literary independence . . . being two very different things — the first was accomplished in about seven years, the latter will not be completely effected, perhaps, in as many centuries" (Spiller, *American Literary Revolution*, 8).

[21] Paulding's comments on Brown, cited in Spiller, *American Literary Revolution*, p. 386, were originally published in the second series of *Salmagundi* (1819-20).

usually fail; he is a gentleman. The unschooled "bog-trotter" O'Regan succeeds in various adventures, such as being elected to the legislature. Despite his name, however, Farrago is no foolish Don Quixote or other absurd character; in the latter stages of the novel he has in fact become governor of his state. Nor is the illiterate, cloddish O'Regan presented as a shrewd peasant on the Sancho Panza pattern, still less a crafty manservant like Mozart's Figaro. O'Regan's Irish brogue is rendered half-phonetically, with every appearance of authorial disdain. *Modern Chivalry* is a peculiar back-to-front book, in its boisterous yet unjovial way arguably not less but more class-conscious than comparable European tales of the era.[22]

As a group, American writers were, like their artist colleagues, definite in their support for the Revolution. Crèvecoeur's complications of nationality and kinship made him unusual. So did the loyalist connections of Thomas Green Fessenden and of his friend Joseph Dennie, the editor of the Philadelphia *Post Folio*. It is nevertheless intriguing to consider how few of the new nation's literati bore any active combatant role. John Trumbull and Noah Webster were never in uniform. Brackenridge, Barlow, and Timothy Dwight secured relative comfort, privilege, and leisure in the commissioned rank of army chaplain. Of the three only Dwight had strong religious convictions, and his military service was quite brief. Chaplain Barlow devoted more time to writing poetry than to preaching or to pastoral duties. Brackenridge resigned from the Continental army in 1778 to launch a literary magazine. After the venture failed, Brackenridge did not reenter the military; shifting from theology to jurisprudence, he opened up a law practice in Pittsburgh in the spring of 1781, several months before the tide of war had swung decisively in favor of the United States.[23]

Philip Freneau's wartime record, given his fierce literary commitment to the patriot cause, is likewise equivocal. He spent the first years of the conflict in blissful tranquility, living with a well-to-do planter in the Virgin Islands. During the latter part of the war Freneau was still based in the Caribbean and still for the most part a gentleman of leisure, though involved in intermittent spells of

---

[22] On Brackenridge and *Modern Chivalry*, see Ellis, *After the Revolution*, 92-110; Elliott, *Revolutionary Writers*, 171-217, Gordon S. Wood, *The Creation of the American Republic, 1776-1787* (Chapel Hill, 1969), 480-82; Simpson, "The Satiric Mode," 58-61; and William F. Keller, *The Nation's Advocate: Henry Marie Brackenridge and Young America* (Pittsburgh, 1956), 22-27, 45-47, 177-78.

[23] Biographical details culled from standard biographies. On Barlow's chaplaincy, for instance, see Zunder, *Early Days of Joel Barlow*, 102-63. The complex circumstances of another author are explored in Peter Kafer, "The Making of Timothy Dwight: A Connecticut Morality Tale," *William and Mary Quarterly* 47 (April 1990): 189-209, which points out that Dwight's father and two brothers could be called Loyalists.

privateering — a form of legalized piracy whose dangers were offset by the possibility of large profits. Freneau never forgave the British for intercepting one of his voyages and locking him up for several weeks in the unhealthy confines of a prison ship. But his fury at such treatment was, it seems, prompted by his captors' disbelief in his cover story (that he was *not* a privateer) and by their refusal to show him the courtesies appropriate to a gentlemanly product of the College of New Jersey.[24]

One could augment the list of Americans with literary or intellectual ambitions who, though they may have been active after 1783, did not exactly flourish then, if *flourish* means "win fame and wealth." And there were others whose Americanness was qualified. There is, for example, the Vermonter Ethan Allen, who fell under the shadowy accusation of having engaged in treasonable correspondence with the British enemy; or Tom Paine, absent in Europe from 1787 to 1802, once an American hero but then assailed as an atheist and iconoclast, a man supposedly without a country and without gratitude either to the United States or to George Washington. Again, John Paul Jones, the naval officer, was no man of letters. Some, though, might discern parallels with the career of Tom Paine. Both of them were British by birth and upbringing, of artisan stock. Both were intelligent, restless persons, whose dislike of authority was probably compounded by awareness that poor, obscure men could only hope to win recognition by ingratiating themselves with powerful patrons. Jones and Paine were drawn accordingly to the American side, but being prickly characters then began to suspect that their Revolutionary services had been undervalued. Both, as if by preference, subsequently lived in France. John Paul Jones estranged himself further by transferring to the Russian navy, having accepted a rear admiral's commission from Catherine the Great. Paine ("the American Voltaire") offended nearly all his onetime American associates by appearing to reject formal Christianity in his *Age of Reason* (1794-96) and then by attacking President Washington in a ferocious open letter. Brackenridge alluded to *The Age of Reason* as the work of "an uncommon, but *uninformed* man." Even if theologians were wrong, he asked, "why dissipate the vision? Does it not constitute a great portion of our happiness? Are those men supposed to have done nothing for the world who have raised fabrics of this kind to the imagination *even upon false grounds*?" James Kirke Paulding, in *A Sketch of Old England* (1822), was at pains to disavow admiration for Paine:

I have no great regard to the memory of this person, although his early

24 Marsh, *Philip Freneau*, 67-72.

writings were serviceable to our cause in the time of the revolutionary war. All that he ever wrote in favour of freedom, is insufficient to atone for the indecent and arrogant manner in which he questions the authority of Holy Writ; nor can all the clearness of his reasonings in support of human liberty, counterbalance the injury he has inflicted upon it, by giving its enemies a plausible pretext for connecting the progress of political freedom with the spreading of religious indifference, if not absolute unbelief.[25]

The ambivalences in such biographies remind us that in Washington Irving's classic tale "Rip Van Winkle," the principal character sleeps right through the American Revolution. Returning to his native village after his twenty-year slumber, he is bewildered to find, for instance, that "the ruby face of King George" on the old inn sign has been "singularly metamorphosed." In the amended version, "the red coat was changed for one of blue and buff, a sword was held in the hand instead of a sceptre, the head was decorated in a cocked hat, and underneath was painted in large character, GENERAL WASHINGTON." Irving himself in a figurative sense held dual nationality. He was an American, named in honor of the Union's great hero. His family, on the other hand, was strongly Scottish, still with close family ties to Britain. Irving's fame was to be international and would rest chiefly upon *The Sketch Book of Geoffrey Crayon, Gent.* (1820) and *Bracebridge Hall* (1822) — volumes initially published in London and predominantly "English" in treatment.[26]

Even where an American author had no external ties to the former mother country, his handling of Anglo-American relations was often puzzlingly double-edged. William Wirt of Maryland and Virginia was the son of a Swiss immigrant. He prospered as a lawyer and married into the Virginia gentry. In 1803 he had considerable success with a batch of essays collected under the title of *The Letters of the British Spy.* They purported to have been written by an English member of Parliament who viewed the United States, and Virginia in particular, with condescending disapproval. Wirt presented character sketches of James Monroe, John Marshall, and other prominent Virginians, and used the British persona as a way of criticizing aspects of Virginia society, such as the state's low educational

[25] Brackenridge's comments on Paine occur in *Modern Chivalry,* ed. Claude M. Newlin (New York, 1937), book 4, 573. Paulding's strictures are in *A Sketch of Old England* (New York, 1822; reprint ed., London, 1822), 83-84.

[26] Stanley T. Williams, *The Life of Washington Irving,* 2 vols. (New York, 1935), is still the most amply detailed biography, but for the themes covered in this essay see especially William L. Hedges, *Washington Irving: An American Study, 1802-1832* (Baltimore, 1965).

standards. Wirt's approach is on the whole playful, imitating the geniality of Addison and the whimsicality of Laurence Sterne. He pretends to rebuke his supercilious narrator, and asterisked footnotes draw the reader's attention to the "author's" monarchist slurs upon American republicanism. Presumably Wirt himself wished to see reforms in Virginia education but if so, why risk weakening the impact of the criticism by attributing it to an unsympathetic British traveler? Perhaps readers of the *Letters* knew who was the real author. But then, why should they and Wirt conspire at so curious a simulation?[27]

Revolutions, it is said, devour their children. That drastic judgment may apply to the leading orators and intellectuals of the French Revolution. It would be too extreme a comment on the literati of Revolutionary America. None, not even avowed loyalists like the Boston poet-clergyman Mather Byles, perished on the scaffold. A handful subsequently hinted that independence had been a mistake. Such was the assertion made by Joseph Dennie in May 1800, in a letter to his parents. The "settled attachment to *Englishmen* and English principles" that he professed, and the contempt for America's "rascal populace," were, however, not proclaimed in print and may in their hyperbole represent a certain attitudinizing bravado.[28] Loyalists, high Federalists, and emphatic patriots all recognized that the Revolution was irreversible. Few if any genuinely hankered after a return to British suzerainty. Rip Van Winkle in Irving's tale appears happier under the American flag than he was before, once he recovers from the shock of his awakening. It is important not to exaggerate the malaise of American literature in the first decades after the Peace of Paris. One could, after all, produce any number of highly pessimistic verdicts on American culture, delivered during the latter part of the nineteenth century or indeed during the twentieth century. It would obviously not follow from these that their authors regarded American independence as a disastrous error.

Nevertheless, to recapitulate and conclude, the early era of American independence was, culturally speaking, a letdown. Excessive expectations of

---

[27] The best modern edition of *Letters of the British Spy* (Chapel Hill, 1970) carries an introduction by Richard Beale Davis. On Wirt himself, consult Jay B. Hubbell, *The South in American Literature, 1607-1900* (Durham, N.C., 1954), 236-37; and William R. Taylor, *Cavalier and Yankee: The Old South and American National Character* (New York, 1961), 70-80, 178-80.

[28] Dennie's rambling letter is reproduced in Harold Milton Ellis, *Joseph Dennie and His Circle: A Study in American Literature from 1792 to 1812* (1915; reprint ed., New York, 1971), 114-20. A private letter, similar in tone, was sent to Dennie's mother in April 1792 (see Lewis P. Simpson, *The Man of Letters in New England and the South* [Baton Rouge, 1973], 54-55). Young Dennie, in his tory-curmudgeon role, announced that if only the Revolution had been avoided, "I might now . . . in a Literary Diplomatic, or lucrative Situation [have] been in the service of my rightful King." See the crisp assessment, "Literary Opinions of Joseph Dennie," in Leary, *Soundings*, 253-70.

literary as of other forms of "rising glory" were announced at the outset of the Revolution. The expected outpouring of literary genius failed to occur during the next twenty or thirty years. British military, economic, and cultural power did not go into a decline, but on the contrary seemed more impressive than ever. West, Copley, and other American artists who had brought renown to their country by achieving fame in London tended to remain in Europe — as if to reinforce the depressing facts of life borne in upon their literary colleagues: that style, themes, milieu, and patronage were all still largely defined by the Old World.

American literature turned out, at least in the short run, to lack a distinctive vocabulary and idiom, or any markedly "democratic" ambience. Ironically, plain-folk imagery and attitudes were more evident in the literature of the supposedly aristocratic mother country. In Burns and Wordsworth, in the unheroic couplets of George Crabbe's *The Village* (1783), and painstaking accuracy of Robert Bloomfield's *The Farmer's Boy* (1800), or in the unabashed dialect of John Clare's *Poems Descriptive of Rural Life* (1820), Britain produced a literature that made contemporary American verse seem lifelessly genteel.

Why was this so? Several reasons have already been suggested, such as the absence of a sizable leisure native population; the time it would necessarily take to evolve distinctive, appropriate American modes; and the divisive, protracted tensions of the Revolutionary and Napoleonic wars. There were perfectly good reasons why the emergence of a major "American" literature proved slower and harder than had been forecast. But they sometimes sounded like excuses or recriminations against Britain, rather than sober explanations. On the matter of language, for example, the United States faced problems of cultural identity that could not be resolved in a decade or even a half century. The mistake was to underestimate the size of the task — and to misstate it —as Noah Webster did in hypothesizing the existence of an American English that would constitute both the purest, most authentic form of the language to be found anywhere in the world *and* a dynamic American variant such as befitted a separate new nation.

A second formidable difficulty lay in the ideological assumptions of the new nation. Literary expression was shaped, and in several ways inhibited, by democratic-republican imperatives. The American patriotic creed didactically imposed upon authors the duty to indicate the superior virtue of mankind in the New World. Villainy was the attribute of foreign or nonwhite persons, or of Americans who had succumbed to insidious temptation (drugs, alcohol, seduction, religious heresy). In ideal American circumstance, divisions by class or creed did not exist. The operation of such roles forced early American imaginative literature into moralistic simplifications or into idiosyncratic, covert evasion (as with a novelist like Charles Brockden Brown). Europe and

Europeans tended to be portrayed in censorious caricature.

The process was not entirely to be deplored. The United States was at least attempting to get to grips with some fundamental issues — of protest and restraint, novelty and tradition, nationhood and federalism, leadership and democracy. The challenge these presented during the 1780s (for example, over Shays's Rebellion) was intensified as a result of the French Revolution. Americans were entitled to take pride in the reflection that, if they had not finally resolved the crises of modernity, they had grappled more successfully with them than the ultras of either persuasion, conservative or radical, in Europe.

Nevertheless, a degree of disillusion marked the early history of literature in the United States. The ideological conflicts of the Revolutionary era turned a number of American authors toward social conservatism, so that their political opponents were prompted — somewhat unfairly — to portray them as sympathizers with monarchy and aristocracy. An awful question confronted Brackenridge and others. If the people were sovereign, and popular choice turned against the work of a particular author, should he accept the verdict as vox populi, vox dei? Political democracy must assume that people were collectively sensible and that majority decisions were decisive. But if so, given the poor sales of native American authors, few or none had any real function in the United States. Unwilling to accept such a deduction, men of letters looked for consoling explanations such as the argument that, in the absence of an international copyright agreement, unfair foreign competition was depriving them of a livelihood, or perhaps that things would improve in ten or twenty years with the growth of national wealth, numbers, and sophistication.

A horrid suspicion remained, forcing itself toward the surface in *Modern Chivalry* and other early works. If majority taste was fallible in literary or aesthetic matters, why should it be politically infallible? But if the mass of Americans were creatures of defective sense, why believe in republican or democratic principles — untried and, according to most political philosophers, unsound? Why have made a Revolution?

Such literary misgivings affected even the most emphatic spokesmen for American democracy. Philip Freneau more and more frequently expressed the view that solitude and public indifference were the lot of the American author. Democracy was all very well in the abstract, and greatly preferable (thought Freneau) to the snares and delusions of the old order. Yet he could not help looking back to a half-imaginary metropolitan golden era. In his wistful "Author's Soliloquy" he invoked:

Thrice happy DRYDEN who could meet

Some rival bard on every street:
When all were bent on writing well,
It was some credit to excel
While those condemn'd to stand alone
Can only by themselves be known.

Did the mainly conventional pathos of a Freneau poem of 1781 acquire a deeper meaning ten or twenty years afterward, when the image could be glossed as a pessimistic prophecy of conditions under independence?

So nightly on some shallow tide,
Oft have I seen a splendid show;
Reflected stars on either side
And glittering moons were seen below
But when the tide had ebb'd away,
The scene fantastic with it fled,
A bank of mud around me lay,
And sea-weed on the river's bed.[29]

This essay appeared in *Peace and the Peacemakers: The Treaty of 1783*, ed. Ronald Hoffman and Peter J. Albert (Charlottesville: U.S. Capitol Historical Society by the University Press of Virginia, 1986), 132-59.

[29] Quoted in Leary, *Soundings*, p. 143; also see Simpson, "The Satiric Mode," 58.

5

The Presidential Elections of 1789 and 1792

This appeared in a four-volume history of presidential elections, each by a different author and each accompanied by a selection of source-readings. My own, necessarily long contribution, set the scene for subsequent presidential contests and covered the two elections in which George Washington, a non-campaigning non-"candidate," received unanimous support within the newly created Electoral College.

The nature of the presidential office proved to be the most recalcitrant issue that confronted the delegates at the Philadelphia convention in 1787. There were, James Madison reported to Thomas Jefferson, "tedious and reiterated discussions" on whether the executive should "consist of a single person, or a plurality of co-ordinate members, on the mode of appointment, on the duration in office, on the degree of power," and on whether the President should be eligible for reelection. True, the delegates fairly soon reached agreement on the need for a single executive. Other problems concerning the office were more intractable. A key difficulty, Madison recollected, was that "of finding an unexceptionable process for appointing the Executive Organ of a Government such as that of the United States . . . ; and as the final arrangement of it took place in the latter stage of the Session, it was not exempt from a degree of the hurrying influence produced by fatigue and impatience in all such bodies."

The Philadelphia convention began on May 25, 1787. Within a week the delegates had declared themselves in favor of a single "Executive Magistracy" who was to be elected by the national legislature for a term of seven years and then to be "ineligible a second time." By July 26, having consumed the greater part of eight days in discussing the election and term of office of the President, the delegates were still on record (by the votes of seven states to three) as supporting the original broad method proposed in Edmund Randolph's resolution of May 29. Such harmony was, however, more apparent than real; it signified that they could see no ideal solution to the complexities they had explored.

Randolph's "Virginia plan" seemed to provide the only workable means of election. In 1787 only a few states, including Massachusetts, New Hampshire, and New York, relied upon the popular election of their governors. Arguing the point on July 17, Roger Sherman of Connecticut thought that "the sense of the Nation would be better expressed by the Legislature, than by the people at large. The latter will never be sufficiently informed of characters, and besides will never give a majority of votes to any one man. They will generally vote for some man in their own State, and the largest State will have the best chance for the appointment." In the same debate, George Mason of Virginia concurred: "It would be as unnatural to refer the choice of a proper character for chief Magistrate to the people, as it would, to refer a trial of colours to a blind man. The extent of the Country renders it impossible that the people can have the requisite capacity to judge of the respective pretensions of the Candidates." Charles Pinckney of South Carolina and Hugh Williamson of North Carolina were of the same opinion. Then and subsequently, certain delegates (Madison and Gouverneur Morris of Pennsylvania among them) preferred the idea of popular election. But they could not disguise their uneasiness at the prospect of an election on so diffuse a scale; their recommendation was not so much out of enthusiasm for the principle of popular suffrage, but resistance to other principles for which they felt still less enthusiasm.

Nor did alternative proposals immediately commend themselves. Elbridge Gerry of Massachusetts made no headway on June 9 with a resolution "that the National Executive should be elected by the Executives of the States whose proportion of votes should be the same with that allowed to the States in the election of the Senate." Replying to Gerry, Edmund Randolph of Virginia maintained that in such a method the big states would secure the appointment; that even so, bad appointments would result, "the Executives of the States being little conversant with characters not within their own small spheres"; that a President selected under state auspices would be unlikely to defend the national interest against state encroachments; and that state governors would not willingly support a national executive — "They will not cherish the great Oak which is to reduce them to paltry shrubs."

John Dickinson of Delaware found equally little support for a suggestion (July 25) that the people of each state should nominate a "best citizen. . . . [They] will know the most eminent characters of their own States, and the people of different States will feel an emulation in selecting those of which they will have the greatest reason to be proud — Out of the thirteen names thus selected, an Executive Magistrate may be chosen," either through the national legislature, or electors appointed by it. More attention was paid to sundry proposals for electors chosen by state legislatures. But these and other expedients failed to unite a convinced majority. "There are objections," said Madison (July 25), "against every mode that has been, or perhaps can be proposed." His fellow-Virginian, Colonel Mason, wearily echoed the observation (July 26): "In every Stage of the Question relative to the Executive, the difficulty of the subject and the diversity of the opinions concerning it have appeared. Nor have any of the modes of constituting that department been satisfactory."

At this phase, on the eve of a ten-day recess, the delegates exhibited a fatigued dullness. They seemed also to have become the prisoners of the initial formulation: election by the national legislature for a single seven-year term. Every time the executive came up for discussion this basic premise was reiterated and voted on. One reason for the frustration, as J. R. Pole explains, was that "the delegates wanted the new head of state to have some of the attributes of a prime minister but some of the attributes of a king; and they allowed themselves to be confused by their own terminology." British precedent both impressed and alarmed them. They did not fully understand the respective and changing, roles of the Crown and the chief minister in the British system — in part because of their own sensitivity to the charge that they might, deliberately or otherwise, saddle the United States with a monarchy or an aristocracy. They were groping for a means of establishing an executive element that was to be much more than a formal head of state.

Gradually, and thanks largely to the interventions of James Madison, the logic of their wishes disclosed itself. One of Madison's most persuasive speeches was delivered on July 25. The President, he said, must be elected either by some existing authority under the national or state constitutions, or by some special authority derived from or directly exerted by the people of the United States. Under the national constitution the two existing authorities would be the legislature and the judiciary. The judiciary was clearly unsuitable. As for the legislature, Madison continued, summarizing views already expressed in the convention and adding some of his own, it too was an unsuitable agency. The

election would seriously "agitate & divide the legislature." The effect upon a
presidential candidate would be equally undesirable. He would "intrigue with"
the legislators, would owe his appointment to "the predominant faction," and
would be "apt to render his administration subservient" to the controlling faction.
Moreover, as the cases of the Holy Roman Emperor and the elective Polish
monarchy showed, such a claustrophobic method of election would encourage
foreign powers to meddle: "No pains, nor perhaps expense, will be spared, to
gain from the Legislature an [appointment] favourable to their wishes."

If appointment within the national sphere would be unsatisfactory, what of the
state level? Neither governors nor the judiciary would be desirable. The state
legislatures were unreliable bodies with a propensity for "pernicious measures."
One purpose of a national legislature was to offset this. And one of the objects
of creating a national executive was to control the national legislature (through
the veto power), "so far as it might be infected with a similar propensity." But
such a check would be impossible if the executive were chosen by a legislative
body, at whatever level.

There remained the mode of popular election, either "immediately" or by
means of electors popularly chosen. Madison himself preferred a mass popular
vote, though he admitted that "the disposition in the people to prefer a Citizen
of their own State" would confer an advantage on the larger states. He was also
responsive to the idea of selection by specially chosen electors. But he admitted
that the device, having already been rejected by the convention, would probably
not win approval.

On this occasion Madison's reasoning did not prevail. But he stimulated a
fruitful discussion. Here was one of the days when instead of negating and
perplexing each other, the delegates seemed to think their way forward. Some,
it is true, reverted to the stale issue of whether ineligibility for reelection would
be an adequate safeguard against undue legislative influence upon the president
or whether that would not excessively hamper the executive freedom of
maneuver. But other delegates were more constructive. Williamson suggested
that if popular election were sanctioned, the claims of candidates from the
smaller states could be recognized by allowing every voter to choose three names.
One of the three would probably be a man from his own state; the other two
might be drawn from other states. Gouverneur Morris liked the idea, suggesting
as an amendment that "each man should vote for two persons one of whom at
least should not be of his own State." Madison also warmed to the amended
suggestion. A plethora of favorite sons would be likely to yield the election to
some universally admired second choice. There was the risk that each citizen
might throw away his second vote on some obscure figure, in order to improve

the chances of his favorite candidate. "But it could hardly be supposed," said Madison, "that the Citizens of many States would be so sanguine of having their favorite elected, as not to give their second vote with sincerity to the next object of their choice."

The decisive advance was still some way off. On August 24, when the delegates again scrutinized the executive provision of their draft constitution, they were still committed to election through Congress (as it was to be called). They wrangled about whether the President was to be chosen by one or both houses of Congress. Faced with the prospect of an interminable task, and increasingly restive, they agreed however to place all such unfinished business in the hands of a committee made up of one delegate from each state.

Now the leaven worked. The committee comprised some of the ablest members of the Philadelphia convention and some of those most firmly persuaded of the need for a strong executive. On September 4 they introduced a set of proposals in almost the form with which we are familiar. They had concluded that the principle of a separation of powers made it impossible to elect the executive entirely in the legislature. Once this was affirmed, there was no overriding need to limit the executive to a single term, since the president would be immune to excessive congressional influence. Nor need his term of office be lengthy if he could be reelected: four years would be preferable to seven. The method of election recommended, in line with previous suggestions, was via a body of presidential electors, to be chosen as each state legislature determined. The number of electors would equal the number of federal senators and representatives to which each state would be entitled. The electors would meet in their respective states (not in one central place, which might have exposed them to corruption and which would have been a laborious and expensive procedure). They would vote for two persons, "one of whom at least shall not be an inhabitant of the same State with themselves." Their votes would be transmitted to the presiding officer of the Senate, under whose chairmanship the Senate — balloting among themselves if there were no clear majority — would decide the outcome. The person coming second in number of votes should become the vice-president, and then would act as president of the Senate.

An intricate debate followed and continued next morning (September 5). "The greater part of the day," noted James McHenry of Maryland, whose appetite for constitution-making had become sated, was "spent in desultory conversation on that part of the report respecting the mode of chusing the president — adjourning without coming to a conclusion." He was too despondent. Except for the few who were uneasy over the whole tenor of the convention, opposition to the committee's proposals focused mainly on the prominence given to the Senate. By September 6 the draft had been amended to meet the chief objections.

In the event of a tie, or the absence of a clear majority of votes, the House of Representatives (one vote per state) was to choose a president by ballot. At last the convention had a formula commanding the assent of the majority of delegates. They probably assumed that the election would nearly always be determined in Congress; this had been their contention when the plan was to let the Senate be the arbiters. Still, they had hit upon a pattern that would in theory allow the voice of the people to be heard. If all went well, the principal persons nominated ("candidates" is perhaps the wrong word) would be characters of nationwide repute; they would not have been picked by any small conclave; and Congress would be choosing from among citizens already chosen by the citizenry.

An additional comment should be made on the invention of the vice-presidency, an office not mentioned in the Philadelphia proceedings until the committee report of September 4. It had previously been implied that the president would also act as president of the Senate, an unacceptable provision if the separation of powers was to be observed. Yet this was not the main reason for creating a Vice-President; indeed Elbridge Gerry and George Mason were among those who complained that "the office of vice-President [was] an encroachment on the rights of the Senate; . . . it mixed too much the Legislative & Executive, which . . . ought to be kept as separate as possible." Roger Sherman of Connecticut defended the innovation by remarking that if the vice-president were not to preside over the Senate, he would have nothing to do and that if some senator were to preside, he would automatically be deprived of his voting rights: a deprivation that would halve the voting strength of one state. The chief rationale for the vice-presidency was mentioned by Hugh Williamson, who thought it a superfluous office, "introduced only for the sake of a valuable mode of election which required two to be chosen at the same time." The genesis of the office appears to lie in Williamson's own proposal of July 25, as amended by Gouverneur Morris. They hoped to avoid jealousies between the states and a sense of impotence among the smaller ones, by permitting more than one vote for the presidency. Once the idea was implanted, duties could be found for the man who was runner-up; and there were equivalent figures (lieutenant-governors and the like) in the organization of state governments. So the vice-presidency was established, belatedly consequentially, and somewhat perfunctorily. Yet the comments of Madison and others on the niceties of plural voting indicated that American politicians would be quick to master the tactics appropriate to a dual vote.

At Philadelphia and in ensuing months, Americans of every viewpoint assumed there was only one man who could and would inaugurate the presidential office: General Washington. When the convention first broached the idea of a single executive on June 1, there was a "considerable pause" before the debate got under way. Among the reasons for this hesitation was embarrassment at discussing the proposal in the presence of the presiding officer: George Washington. Three days later, on June 4, Pennsylvania's venerable delegate Benjamin Franklin offered some gloomy predictions as to the eventual aggrandizement of the executive branch. He conceded however that "the first man, put at the helm will be a good one." Such observations crop up again and again in private correspondence, in pamphlets and in the newspapers. The Philadelphian Dr. Benjamin Rush, not present at the convention but alert to catch stray rumors that filtered through its closed doors, was optimistic. "The new federal government," he told Timothy Pickering on August 30, "like a new continental waggon will overset our state dung cart . . . and thereby restore order and happiness to Pennsylvania. . . . General Washington it is said . . . will drive the new waggon." An unidentified correspondent, also from Philadelphia, writing to Thomas Jefferson on October 11, 1787, in the same spirit as Rush, explained why the Constitution would and ought to be ratified. Thus, Washington was still vigorously alive, and "as he will be appointed president, jealousy on this head vanishes." The General's associates were writing to him in the same strain. David Humphreys, a Connecticut soldier-diplomat, and one of the General's devoted admirers, wrote, "What will tend, perhaps, more than anything to the adoption of the new system will be an universal opinion of your being elected President of the United States and an expectation that you will accept it for a while." Washington's wartime friend Lafayette chimed in from Paris, "You cannot refuse being elected President."

Even those with deep misgivings on the "new system" concentrated their criticism upon other features of the Constitution, or — like Franklin — upon the hazards that would befall America after Washington had gone. The Virginian Richard Henry Lee, a one-time president of the Continental Congress, was convinced that the Philadelphia document was fraught with danger. A reeligible President, he argued in January, 1788, "will have no permanent interest in the government to lose, by contests and convulsions in the state, but always much to gain, and frequently the seducing and flattering hope of succeeding. . . . [This] will be the case with nine tenths of the presidents; *we may have, for the first president,* and perhaps, one in a century or two afterwards . . .*a great and good man, governed by superior motives;* but these are not events to be calculated upon in the present state of human nature." Pierce Butler, a former delegate, admitted in

May, 1788 that the considerable powers entrusted to the executive would not
have "been so great had not many of the members cast their eyes toward General
Washington as President; and shaped their Ideas of the Powers to be given to a
President, by their opinions of his Virtue."

The expectation that General Washington would become President Washington
was voiced in the press within a few days of the adjournment of the convention.
Newspapers favoring the Constitution, such as the important *Pennsylvania Packet*,
repeatedly sang his praises. Washington, they assured readers, would not have
lent his name to the convention if its intentions had been dubious; and with him
at the head the new government's success was beyond doubt. The Fourth of July
celebrations in 1788 came at the climactic moment of the struggle over
ratification. Though the news took some time to reach every corner of the
Union, the necessary nine states (including Washington's Virginia) had already
ratified. At many places the national holiday was seized upon as an occasion to
pay tribute to the future President. Toasts and songs embroidered the sentiment:

> —*Farmer Washington — may he like a second Cincinnatus, be called
> from the plow to rule a great people.*

> —*May the Saviour of America gratify the ardent wishes of his
> countrymen by accepting that post which the voice of mankind has
> assigned him.*

> —*Great Washington shall rule the land / While Franklin's counsel aids
> his hand.*

Whatever the nation expected or friends urged upon him, George Washington
was far from reconciled to fate. Well-informed Americans were worried by what
Jefferson called Washington's "vast reluctance," though like Jefferson they clung
to the conviction that he "will undertake the presidency if called to it." Alexander
Hamilton was only the most persistent of several correspondents in pressing the
General to signify his willingness. They appealed to his pertinacity, his
patriotism, his personal sense of duty, his standing with posterity, the parlous
state of the country. Hamilton was subtle in his reading of Washington's
psychology; he never resorted to such overblown statements as that of the
General's old friend John Armstrong, who seemed to feel that divine providence
was in charge of the impending election.

George Washington's hesitations were understandable. Fifty-six years old in
1788, he felt he had already given up some of the best years of his life to the

service of his country. After eight and a half years as Commander-in-chief he had, at the end of 1783, resigned his commission with unfeigned relief. His own affairs, above all the management of his Mount Vernon estate, absorbed energies which he felt to be waning. In quitting public service he had stressed the finality of his retirement. If he now came back at the head of affairs he could, he wrote Alexander Hamilton, be accused of "inconsistency and ambition." He knew from the tenor of the Philadelphia convention and from the abundant subsequent criticisms of the Constitution that Americans were highly suspicious of the corrupting effect of high office.

As he frequently remarked, he dreaded the "new fatigues and troubles" of undertaking a new duty for which he did not think himself equipped. Soldiering had been onerous enough; the entire weight of executive responsibility would be almost unendurable.

One aspect of his uneasiness was thus propriety. Even if he were firmly to decide that he was ready to stand, he could see no way of making this known without seeming presumptuous. He could not declare himself or do more than make plain his support for the new Constitution as a whole, while its ratification remained uncertain: that would be to anticipate events to an unthinkable degree. And in the second half of 1788, when ratification had been assured (at least by eleven of the thirteen states: North Carolina and Rhode Island still held aloof), the delicacy of his position continued to preoccupy him. It was surely not his task to inform the nation that he would agree to be president, before or even after the meetings of the presidential electors in the various states. He may have reflected that it would be egotistical even to announce in advance that he would *not* serve; for that would indicate he saw himself as a likely occupant of the office. Other men might not have shown so much punctilio; Washington's situation was unique, and therefore — for him — uniquely painful. He was neither running for office nor able to run away from it.

A second cause for uneasiness shaded from the first. Almost nine months elapsed between the close of the Philadelphia convention and the knowledge that the Constitution had passed muster, in some instances by a narrow majority in state ratifying conventions. Prominent citizens in his own state — George Mason, Edmund Randolph, Patrick Henry — were outspoken in criticism of the new instrument of government. Nine more months were to elapse before the results of the first presidential election would be formally announced, though they had been unofficially bruited about several weeks earlier. In this hiatus the extent of opposition was a source of increasing dismay to Washington. He confided to Hamilton that he found a faint consolation in the hope that "the Electors, by giving their votes in favor of some other person, would save me from

the dreaded Dilemma of being forced to accept or refuse." Though Washington
was the only person being spoken of for the presidency, the actual operation of
the Electoral College was conjectural. No one could tell whom the electors
would be; they were not even to be chosen, so dilatory were the workings of the
old moribund Congress, until the first Wednesday in January, 1789.
Washington's consolation might instead prove a humiliation. In the same letter,
he asked:

> *If the friends to the Constitution conceive that my administering the
> government will be a means of its acceleration and strength, is it not
> probable that the adversaries of it may entertain the same idea? and of
> course make it an object of opposition? That many of this description will
> become Electors, I can have no doubt of. . . . It might be impolite in them
> to make this declaration previous to the Election, but I shall be out in my
> conjectures if they do not act conformably thereto — and from that the
> seeming moderation by which they appear to be actuated at present is . . .
> a finesse to lull and deceive. Their plan of opposition is systemised, and a
> regular intercourse, I have much reason to believe between the Leaders of
> it in the several States is formed to render it more effectual.*

   Such a development would be humiliating if it led to a spread of votes in which
some other man was preferred. That, however, was most unlikely unless by some
fluke distribution of electoral preferences; the only American who could be
ranked with George Washington in universal esteem was Benjamin Franklin, but
Franklin was eighty years old and in failing health. One gains the impression
that, for Washington, any semblance of a contest between him and some other
man or men would be abhorrent. He did not want to be president. Yet if he
must be president, he wanted to be chosen *nem.con.* He could not seriously have
supposed that someone else would get more votes than he. What perturbed him
was the possibility of any sort of competition. A challenge of that kind would
stigmatize his good name and indicate alarming dissensions within the country.
   Washington's perplexity was aggravated by the sluggishness of the newly elected
Congress.   The twenty-two senators and fifty-nine members of the House
converged on New York (the temporary seat of the federal government) with
agonizing slowness. The presidential electors duly met on the first Wednesday
in February, 1789, and the presidential inauguration had been set for March 4.
But the electoral votes could not be counted until there was a quorum of both
houses. By March 4 only eight senators and eighteen representatives had shown
up; and the last laggard legislator required to make the quorum did not arrive in

New York until April 5. Washington was still parrying the congratulations and importunings that each post delivered to Mount Vernon. In effect he had consented to stand and to become president. He must have been cheered to learn that "Federalists" (i.e., men ready to defend the Constitution) had secured a commanding position in the elections for the Senate and a sizeable share of the House of Representatives. But one of the few clues to his own acquiescence came when his followers consulted him on a suitable person for the vice-presidency. His answer amounted to a definite though hardly enthusiastic commitment on his own part. Washington intimated that any "true Foederalist" capable of commanding the votes of true Americans would not be "disagreeable" to him. Whoever the hypothetical person might be, "I would most certainly treat him with perfect sincerity and the greatest candor in every respect. I would give him my full confidence and use my utmost endeavors to cooperate with him, in promoting . . . the national prosperity; this should be my great, my only aim."

An assurance in a private letter was about the nearest that Washington came to a declaration of his readiness to serve if elected. Candidates in future presidential elections would make gestures toward the Washington style of stately, reluctant immobility. But never would a hat float so spectrally into the ring. Nor would any future putative president add, as Washington did in the same letter, his "fixed and irrevocable resolution of leaving to other hands the helm of the State, as soon as my services could possibly with propriety be dispensed with." He would serve, that is, but he would not bind himself for a full term if a chance of escape came his way.

Since none of the Anti-Federalists made any move to deny the presidency to General Washington, partisan calculations were confined to the vice-presidency. Even at this rudimentary stage of presidential electioneering, both sides were swift to see the utility of uniting around one name instead of allowing the scatter of choices envisaged by the Philadelphia delegates. (Perhaps this quick development owes as much to the primacy of Washington as to the controversy over the Constitution and the means by which it had been introduced. If more than one man had appeared exceptionally qualified for the presidency, the electors and politically active Americans might not have drawn any sharp distinction between the two people whom they desired to see in executive office.) With Washington as the universal nominee for the first office, the situation of the second office engrossed attention.

Among leading Federalists, the initial problem was to agree upon a suitable associate for General Washington. To name another Virginian would be to lose the 10 votes of the Virginia electors, who would be debarred from giving both their sets of votes to men of their own state. But in any case sectional strategy dictated the choice of a Northerner, presumably from the powerful state of Massachusetts (which also had ten electors), since the comparably powerful states of New York and Pennsylvania had no one of outstanding eligibility.

Massachusetts possessed an ample share of prominent citizens. Among those who had become associated with Washington during the Revolutionary War were Henry Knox and Benjamin Lincoln. Hamilton referred to both, though somewhat incidentally, in canvassing opinion.

Another man with a national reputation, Samuel Adams, was ruled out because of his brusque temperament and his supposed antagonism to the Constitution. He had remarked, on the occasion of the Massachusetts ratifying convention: "As I enter the building I stumble on the threshold. I meet with a National Government, instead of a Federal Union of Sovereign States." A more plausible candidate, certainly in his own eyes, was Governor John Hancock, who had appropriated much of the credit for his state's ratification. Hamilton seems to have been prepared at one point to back him. At length, though, Hamilton and his cronies concluded that John Adams was their best bet.

Adams had a long record of public service — a delegate to the First and Second Continental Congresses (1774-78), Commissioner to France (1778), delegate to the Massachusetts Constitutional Convention (1780); and under Franklin and Jay, a negotiator of the Paris Peace Pact (1783) — and a considerable if controversial reputation as a political theorist. The first volume of his *Defence of the Constitutions of the United States of America*, written while he was American minister in London, appeared just in time to be consulted by the Philadelphia convention. Returning home in 1788, Adams, now fifty-three years old, soon made it clear, in spurning an offer of election to the Senate, that he wished for a high office or none at all. He had not displayed ecstatic admiration for the new Federal Constitution, and he could never be said to possess a lovable disposition. But his assets far outweighed his disadvantages.

Did Hamilton scheme against Adams? Hamilton did express only a grudging readiness to recommend him and sought to reduce the vote for Adams. Replying to Theodore Sedgwick in October, 1788, Hamilton showed that he was not yet convinced that Adams should be the man. He mentioned theories that Adams was "unfriendly in his sentiments to General Washington" and might form an alliance with the Virginia Lees that would embarrass a Federal executive.

Once the selection had narrowed to Adams, Hamilton worked busily to ensure that Adams would poll appreciably fewer votes than Washington. The reason he gave was "that defect in the constitution which renders it possible that the man intended for Vice-President may in fact turn up President." The probability, he said, was that Washington would be the unanimous choice. But so might Adams.

Either through accident or "Anti-Federal malignity," the transfer of a handful of votes could place Adams in the Chief Magistracy. It was advisable to "throw away a few votes," say 7 or 8, that would have gone to Adams, and distribute them among "persons not otherwise thought of." Hamilton instructed at least two people along these lines — James Wilson of Pennsylvania and Jeremiah Wadsworth of Connecticut. The outcome was much as Hamilton had foreseen. In later years Adams got wind of Hamilton's intervention, and complained of the "dark and insidious manner" in which Hamilton "like the worm at the root of the peach" had intrigued against him.

There is no proof that Hamilton acted out of malice, though within a few years he and Adams were to become intensely suspicious of one another. Nor, on the scanty evidence, are we entitled to assert that his conduct was underhand, though it was staged — as it had to be — under cover. He was not alone in doubting the suitability of John Adams. James Madison, at this juncture a staunch supporter of the Constitution, provided a similar estimate of vice-presidential candidates in October 1788:

> *Hancock is weak, ambitious, a courtier of popularity, given to low intrigue, and lately reunited by a factious friendship with Samuel Adams. John Adams has made himself obnoxious to many, particularly in the southern states, by the political principles avowed in his book. Others, recollecting his cabal during the war against General Washington, knowing his extravagant self-importance, and considering his preference of an unprofitable dignity to some place of emolument . . . as a proof of his having an eye to the presidency, conclude that he would not be a very cordial second to the General, and that an impatient ambition might even intrigue for a premature advancement.*

Such opinions suggest that Hamilton may merely have been voicing reservations shared by a number of Adams' contemporaries. Hamilton's own ambitions, while they included president-making, probably did not run to making himself president. In this respect he was not a rival to Adams. Madison's comments are a reminder of how deep were the distrusts of the day and how sharp the memory remained of wartime "cabals." A further worry may legitimately have concerned Hamilton, as it seemed to concern Madison. Washington's dream of an early retirement was presumably known to all of his associates. They may have indulged him, in order to strengthen his resolve to submit to the electoral will. Suppose Washington, once in office, persisted in the idea? According to the somewhat hazy constitutional notions of succession held in 1788-89, John Adams would then merely be acting president. But he might be difficult to dislodge. Madison's letter suggests that he contemplated the possibility; so perhaps did Hamilton. In a memorandum of May, 1792, describing a conversation with Washington concerning retirement from office, Madison noted that he had in 1788 "contemplated, & I believe, suggested" to the General "a voluntary retirement to private life as soon as the state of the Government would permit," in order to demonstrate the sincerity of previous announcements about remaining a private citizen.

On the matter of "losing" votes that would have gone to Adams, Hamilton's intentions may likewise not have been "dark and insidious," and the problem may have been anticipated by others. At Philadelphia, Madison had speculated that in an undifferentiated two-vote system the second vote might be the winning one. Subsequent experiences revealed that Hamilton was correct in describing the two-vote mechanism as defective; the 12th Amendment recognized the fact. With so much at stake, and uncertain, there was a strong argument for making sure that Washington came first. If through mischance the General came second, the consequences might be appalling. Washington would not consent to fill the role of vice-president; whoever was installed as president would be regarded as an interloper, if not a usurper; and the new federal government might collapse under the strain. John Adams' son-in-law, William Stephens Smith, writing to Jefferson on February 15, 1789, showed no sign of believing that there had been any treachery: "It is Generally believed here [Boston] and in the middle states, that Mr. Adams will be the Vice President, he had the unanimous Vote of Massachusetts and New Hampshire and 5 out of 7 of the electors of Connecticut. That he had not the whole there, originated from an apprehension, that if the state of Virginia should not vote for General Washington that Mr. A. would be President, which would not be consistent with the wish of the country and could only arise from the finesse of antifoedral Electors with a view to produce confusion and embarrass the operations of the Constitution."

While Hamilton and other Federalists were at work, the "Anti's" were equally preoccupied with their own exercises in electoral arithmetic. They too, accepting that General Washington would be president, wanted a northerner as vice-president. The most conspicuous possibility was Governor George Clinton of New York, whose anti-constitutional onslaught had gone down to narrow defeat in the state ratifying convention. Like Governor Patrick Henry of Virginia, he talked of summoning a new national plenary convention to reopen the affair. "Mr. Henry," a Virginia correspondent told Madison in November 1788, "is putting in agitation the name of Clinton for vice-president." The main activity of behalf of Clinton went on in New York and Virginia, with feelers put out to other areas. Early in the new year, St. John de Crèvecoeur, the author of *Letters from an American Farmer*, then in New York as French consul and in outlook a rather bewildered Federalist, reported to Jefferson: "'tis proposed in Virginia to Vote for Govr. Clinton as a President, some back Counties in Pensilvania Will unite as well as this State." Henry was one of Virginia's presidential electors, and in fact gave his second vote to Clinton, who also collected 2 other Virginia votes. But this meager total of 3 was all that Clinton garnered in the electoral college. His New York enemy Hamilton discerned that Clinton's challenge was negligible. Clinton could nibble away a few votes in the South; a few more might have been forthcoming in New York, but a dispute over the method of selecting electors led to a failure to choose any, so that Clinton's own state had no say in the 1789 presidential election. Indeed, as Hamilton explained to Madison, Clinton's candidacy could actually benefit the federal cause: "if pains be taken the dangers of an Antifoederal vice President might itself be rendered the instrument of Union."

The New York electoral mess wrecked whatever hopes Clinton and his friends nourished. The "Federal-Republican" clubs they had founded and the circular letters they had sent counted for little at this juncture. Even with better fortune it is hard to see how the Anti-Federalism of 1788-89 could have been organized into a coherent opposition. There was a real case against some aspects of the Constitution, mixed up with fears and grudges. In ratifying, six of the eleven states had submitted lists of proposed amendments, and two other states had withheld ratification. Clinton was presented as a plain, hearty Republican who inside the new government would speak for the dissatisfied. But as yet the situation supplied no leverage. The new government could not be attacked until it had been given a reasonable opportunity to display itself and to honor the understanding that amendments would be incorporated in the Constitution. What could an Anti-Federalist vice-president hope to accomplish, especially when he dare not, and had no reason to, impugn the good faith of the man destined to be president?

The first part of the process, the choosing of electors, passed off smoothly in most of the states, though not without excitements (at the same time elections for Congress were also under way). Only in New York was there a total fiasco. In part this reflected the Clintonian-Hamiltonian division, in part the weaknesses of a method involving a bicameral legislature, when the two houses were of two minds. For in New York, as in Connecticut, Delaware, Georgia, New Jersey, and South Carolina, presidential electors were to be chosen by the legislature. The Assembly, the lower house, was Clintonishly Anti-Federalist; the Senate, the upper house, was predominantly though not overwhelmingly Federalist. The

Assembly proposed a joint ballot, the Senate a concurrent one. Each house calculated that its own method might yield the desired results in the shape of a batch of faithful Federalist (or Anti-Federalist) electors. Since neither would agree to compromise, New York deprived itself of its presidential ballots — and, incidentally, of its pair of senators during the first session of the new Congress.

A dispute of similar proportions threatened a similar outcome in New Hampshire. Here the nomination of electors was left to popular choice, but the actual appointment lay with the legislature. It had not been explained how the appointment should be determined. The lower house wanted a joint ballot; the upper house insisted on a veto power, on the same lines as its power to negate bills and resolutions emanating from the lower house. After prolonged contention the lower house gave way, under protest. New Hampshire ended up with five presumed Federalists for electors.

There was electricity in the atmosphere of two other states, Pennsylvania and Maryland, where the choice of electors depended directly upon a popular vote. Citizens of those states feared or hoped, according to temperament, that there would be an Anti-Federalist majority. Two "tickets" were disclosed in Pennsylvania. That of Lancaster, representing the sentiment of eastern counties, listed ten men known to be staunch supporters of Washington and the Constitution. The Harrisburg ticket, representing the suspicions of the western counties, listed a phalanx of men who had resisted the ratification of the Constitution. The Lancasterians triumphed: all 10 of the Pennsylvania electoral votes went to Federalists. In Maryland too there were rival tickets, addresses, accusations of fraud. A few electoral nominees in Baltimore, whose leanings were in doubt, issued cards declaring that if chosen they would cast their votes for Washington and Adams. The same thing was done in Philadelphia. As in Pennsylvania, Federalism — or at least Washingtonism — gained the victory.

There were some scuffles in Virginia, of the kind taken for granted on election day. Otherwise the first Wednesday in January 1789 went off tranquilly. No troubles were reported, for instance, in Massachusetts, where two electors were chosen at large and the eight others were picked by the legislature from twenty-four names produced by the state's congressional districts. In the nation as a whole, sixty-nine electors were chosen: with New York the number would have been seventy-nine and, of course, larger still if North Carolina and Rhode Island had come within the rubric.

The electors met a month later, cast their votes, and prepared to transmit the sealed figures to Congress as soon as there was an adequate Congress to count them. Their lips were less sealed. As we have seen, the verdict was accurately though unofficially tabulated long before the official announcement. The electors did not feel that their ballots were secret, and indeed there was no reason why they should, except out of courtesy to Congress.

None of the men who received an electoral vote had delivered himself of a manifesto or of a promise as to how he would act if elected. General Washington had scrupulously declined to commit himself, not only to being a candidate but also to considering the claims of those who wrote to him about possible federal appointments. Those who labored in support of particular candidates allowed themselves to think that loyalty would not go unrewarded. Benjamin Rush was actuated by more than simple benevolence when he wrote to John Adams in January, 1789:

> *You will perceive by the Philadelphia papers that your friends here have not been idle. You will I believe have every vote from this state, and pains have been taken to secure the same unanimity in your favor in several of the adjoining states. I assure you, sir, that friendship for you has had much less to do in this business . . . than a sincere desire to place a gentleman in the Vice-President's chair upon whose long-tried integrity, just principles in government, and firm opposition to popular arts and demagogues, such a dependence could be placed as shall secure us both from a convention and from alterations falsely and impudently called by some of our state governors amendments.*

A month later, Rush had the embarrassment of accounting to Adams for something less than the "unanimity" of which he had boasted. Two of Pennsylvania's vice-presidential votes had gone to John Hancock, although Adams acquired the other 8. All of Delaware's 3 votes had been diverted from Adams to John Jay, and Maryland's 6 to Benjamin Harrison.

Rush turned the difficulty to advantage. The conduct of Delaware and Maryland in "throwing away their votes for vice-president" revealed "a jealousy of the New England states, which has been revived . . . by their vote in favor of the meeting of the first Congress in New York." Philadelphia was the true "headquarters of federalism." The setback to Adams was thus explained and linked with a broad hint that his friends had rallied to him in the belief that he would be their champion. "There is an expectation here," Rush asserted, "that your influence will be exerted immediately in favor of a motion to bring Congress to Philadelphia."

A foretaste of interest politics? But in 1789, so far as Adams was concerned, there was no deal. Pennsylvanians like Rush and William Maclay supported him in the hope he would use his weight to bring the national capital to their state.

Philadelphia did become the temporary capital, but this was a mere sop. They were soon disabused. Like a second Washington, apparently, Adams supposed that votes would accrue to him as of right; he would not bargain for them.

So came April 6, when the electoral votes were opened in Congress, in the presence of both houses. The result gratified George Washington and chagrined John Adams. Every one of the sixty-nine electors, even the disaffected Patrick Henry, had given a vote to Washington. While Adams had no serious rival, he had gathered only 34 votes (Henry's other vote, it will be recalled, went to Clinton.)

TABLE 5.1

P R E S I D E N T I A L   E L E C T I O N   1 7 8 9

STATE	WASHINGTON	ADAMS	JAY	HANCOCK	OTHERS
New Hampshire	5	5			
Massachusetts	10	10			
Connecticut	7	5			2
New Jersey	6	1	5		
Pennsylvania	10	8		2	
Delaware	3		3		
Maryland	6				6
Virginia	10	5	1	1	3
South Carolina	7			1	6
Georgia	5				5
	—	—	—	—	—
	69	34	9	4	22

A few of the also-rans — Jay, Hancock, John Rutledge of South Carolina (who collected 6 of his state's votes) — were men of some stature. Others such as John Milton and Edward Telfair, whom fellow-Georgians gave 2 votes and 1 vote respectively, were in no sense national figures. However the verdict was interpreted — and Adams thought his own treatment "scurvy . . . an indelible stain on our Country, Countrymen and Constitution" — it was clear that in 1788-89 Washington was *hors de concours* and that any who stood against him would be placed *hors de combat*.

The final stroke of the electoral mechanism consisted of notifying Washington and Adams that they had been chosen. A messenger brought the summons to Adams on April 12, as he fidgeted in his Braintree home, his bags already packed.   Charles Thomson, the elderly Secretary of Congress, had a more difficult journey to Mount Vernon and did not arrive with the news until April 14:

> *I have now, sir, to inform you that the proofs you have given of your patriotism and of your readiness to sacrifice domestic separation and private enjoyments to preserve the liberty and promote the happiness of your country did not permit the two Houses to harbour a doubt of your undertaking this great, this important office to which you are called not only by the unanimous vote of the electors, but by the voice of America, I have it therefore in command to accompany you to New York where the Senate and House of Representatives are convened for the dispatch of public business.*

The formal notification, which old Thomson also delivered, while it was briefer and reminded the General that the support he commanded was that of "a free and enlightened people," was in the same mode of solemn compliment. The vocabulary of such addresses suggested that the first president had received an "election" almost more in the religious than in the political sense of the word.

THE ELECTION OF 1792

Four years after his first qualms about undertaking the office of President, Washington found himself embroiled in the same painful cycle. The renewed demands upon him were to lead to the same conclusion: unanimous reelection for a second term, and reelection by a divided vote of Vice-President John Adams.

Much had, however, changed in the meantime; and the changes both increased and made more illusory Washington's desire to liberate himself. He celebrated his sixtieth birthday in February 1792 and felt older than his years. He had survived serious illnesses in 1790 and 1791. He was, he complained, growing deaf; his eyesight was deteriorating; and his memory was beginning to be defective. The detailed and far from absentminded letters that he wrote on Sundays and sent to his agents at Mount Vernon on farm management reveal that he was perhaps not so much tired of life as tired of being president. The federal government had moved headquarters from New York to Philadelphia in the autumn of 1790, but though Washington was now less than a week's coach-ride away from Mount Vernon and managed to spend some time there in 1791 and 1792, it was still too far away to suit him. His concern for his plantations increased; in the summer of 1792 his nephew-manager George Augustine Washington fell into a wasting illness from which he was to die in February 1793. Uncle Washington knew that his nephew's decline and the decline of the estate would go hand in hand.

He was concerned too for his reputation. He had not yet overcome the scruples of four years before. In fact they were augmented. He had then fretted over the impropriety of taking office, despite previous declarations of a final retirement; he now feared that he might appear still more disingenuous if he did not decisively honor his old pledge. Moreover, the hope of resigning before the end of his first term had evaporated. But he had surely given enough of himself by enduring the weight of one whole term?

Nor could this first term be regarded as pleasurable. There were accomplishments in which he could take pride. Some Anti-Federalist grievances had been removed by the ten amendments to the Constitution that formed the so-called Bill of Rights. North Carolina and Rhode Island had entered the Union and so had two new states — Vermont and Kentucky. He had drawn some of the country's cleverest men into his Administration, notably Alexander Hamilton as Secretary of the Treasury and Thomas Jefferson as Secretary of State. Edmund Randolph, his Attorney-General, had become a supporter of the Constitution. The Secretary of War, Henry Knox, was staunchly loyal to his old military chief.

Yet there were fresh and growing dissensions. Opposition to Hamilton's financial measures — the funding and assumption of state and national debts, the establishment of a national bank under federal auspices, and excise tax — showed the persistence or the emergence of deep sectional and economic cleavages. His opponents maintained that the legislation he had pushed through Congress confirmed what they had long suspected: the move toward a "consolidated" government was a move toward dictatorship by a selfish, "aristocratic" minority. Such assertions filled the columns of "Republican" newspapers. The most truculent of these, the *National Gazette*, had begun publication in 1791 in Philadelphia under the very nose of the national government. Worse still for Washington's ease of mind, the controversy radiated from within his executive circle. Hamilton and Jefferson were, as Jefferson later remarked, pitted against one another like two fighting-cocks. Both men had a gift for friendship, and Jefferson in particular was temperamentally averse to personal quarrels. But their friends were more and more grouped in rival camps (they resorted to pseudonymous journalism to attack one another), and Jefferson was accused of having improperly established the *National Gazette* in order to undermine the administration. There was no denying that its editor, Philip Freneau, was on the payroll of Jefferson's State Department in a minor capacity.

Some of the worst feuding was still to come when in May 1792 the President summoned James Madison on a confidential matter. Madison, a member of the House of Representatives, was already a critic of Hamilton's financial policy and was to develop into a leading Jeffersonian. Washington, however, still relied upon Madison's political acumen and wanted to reopen a question on which he had hitherto sought Madison's advice: "the *mode* and *time*" for announcing to the nation that he would not again consent to be president. He had already consulted Jefferson, Hamilton, Knox, and Randolph, though apparently not John Adams. They had all "made pressing representations" to induce the President to reconsider his decision. What he wanted from Madison was a draft of a suitable Farewell Address and an opinion as to how he should deliver it. As in 1788, Washington was fretted by a logical paradox. He could not retire without saying so; but if he said so, he might seem to be "arrogantly presuming" that he would be reelected. The timing also was difficult. The opening of the next session of Congress, in November, would be "an apt occasion" in itself. But it would be perhaps too close to the election, and the reply that Congress would make to his Farewell Address "might entangle him in further explanations."

Apart from questions of protocol, Washington revealed to Madison something of the heavier burdens that oppressed him. Popular discontents were showing themselves more and more; and while "the various attacks against public men & measures had not in general been pointed at him, yet in some instances it had been visible that he was the indirect object." In spite of Madison's counter-arguments, the President gave no indication that he had relented or would do so.

As in 1788, a combination of gloomy reluctance and bashful *hauteur* inhibited Washington from making any direct statement, positive or negative, during the second half of this election year. His dismay at continuing in office was no doubt magnified by further evidence of the gulf between Hamilton and Jefferson and of factions throughout the nation. The stirrings of a "whiskey rebellion" in western Pennsylvania at the end of the summer could be taken as a symptom of a widespread unruliness. Washington and his associates were ready to believe that disaffection was being fomented by the enemies of the administration. Hamilton, in his pamphleteer-role, asserted that one of the principal enemies might be inside the administration — the Secretary of State. Edmund Randolph, writing to Hamilton early in September, was perturbed enough to begin his letter: "Persuaded as I am, that the last effort for the happiness of the United States must perish with the loss of the present Government." The President, in correspondence with Randolph, revealed his angry alarm at the effects of newspaper polemics — "those attacks upon almost every measure of government with which some of the Gazettes are so strongly pregnated; & which cannot fail, if persisted in with the malignancy they now teem, of rending the Union asunder. . . . In a word if the Government and the officers of it are to be the constant theme for Newspaper abuse . . . it will be impossible, I conceive, for any man living to manage the helm, or to keep the machine together." And while the abuse was only obliquely aimed at him (by comparison with the salvoes sent against John Adams, he was immune), he took it personally.

However, the worse things became, the more he was open to the insistence that he alone could save the nation. Randolph had not meant in his lament to Hamilton that the United States was doomed, but only that it would be if the federal government allowed the situation to get out of hand. The men whom the President consulted about his retirement all returned the same answer: it would be a black day for the country, at the present juncture. They also, perhaps inconsistently, reassured him that things were not so bad and could soon vastly improve. This time he might escape without having completed his term. The crisis was coming to a head, Jefferson told him in May 1792, and must shortly be settled. If so, Washington might retire "without awaiting the completion of the second period of four years. I cannot but hope" — Jefferson added a flattering flourish — "that you can resolve to add one or two more to the many years you have already sacrificed to the good of mankind." Two months later, in almost identical language, Hamilton begged the President to "make a further sacrifice. . . . I trust that it need not continue above a year or two more — And I think it will be more [eligible] to retire from office before the expiration of the term of an election, than to decline a reelection." But that there *was* a crisis Randolph direly insisted: "Should a civil war arise, you cannot stay at home. And how much easier will it be, to disperse the factions, which are rushing to this catastrophe, than to subdue them after they shall appear in arms? It is the fixed opinion of the world" — again an appeal to Washington's self-esteem — "that you surrender nothing incomplete."

The condition of the outside world, especially in western Europe, was in itself enough to demand continuity and stability in the American Government. The ferment of militant French republicanism might have grave consequences for the United States. But in the midsummer of 1792, as Washington sought the relative tranquility of Mount Vernon, domestic and personal factors were probably foremost in his imagination. One point developed by Madison may have struck home. Eventually there would have to be a successor to Washington; but who could succeed him at the moment? Madison reviewed the options, with a "Republican" emphasis that could not be entirely discounted. The three likeliest successors were Jefferson, Adams, and John Jay (who in a close-fought election had just been robbed of the governorship of New York by Clinton, in circumstances discreditable to Clinton). Of these, Jefferson wanted to quit public life for the peace of his Monticello home; and in any case he could not command enough support in the North. Adams was unacceptable because his views were too "monarchical" and he was unpopular in the South. "It would not be in the power of those who might be friendly to his private character, & willing to trust him in a public one, notwithstanding his political principles, to make head against the torrent." As for Jay, he had offended groups throughout the Union; "his election would be extremely dissatisfactory on several accounts." Washington could not deny that the estimate was essentially correct. He was the only person who could command a national following.

This was reinforced by the remarkable harmony of viewpoint expressed by Hamilton and Jefferson. Agreeing on almost nothing else, they were at one in wishing Washington to remain in office. Could he, though, expect that the rest of the nation would concur? Even if no one could come near him in electoral votes, might there not be a contest of sorts and of an ugly character? Hamilton reassured him, exactly as in 1788: "The dread of public indignation will be likely to restrain the indisposed few. If they can calculate at all, they will naturally reflect that they could not give a severer blow to their cause than by giving a proof of hostility to you. But if a solitary vote or two should appear wanting to perfect unanimity, of what moment can it be?"

Thus for Washington the wheel had come full circle. In 1792 as in 1788 he yearned to avoid the inevitable, while friends implored him to yield to it. Not knowing what else to do, he kept silent. By November 1792, when Congress reassembled and the President offered no indication of impending withdrawal, it was taken for granted that next March would witness his second inauguration. As in 1788, the political horoscope then shifted to a subsidiary yet highly intriguing question: who would qualify as vice president?

Those who were generally in sympathy with the development of American affairs, and approved of Hamiltonian policies agreed that John Adams should remain as the President's deputy. Though his office was, as he complained, relatively insignificant, it made him known to every member of Congress. Even overshadowed by Washington, he was a national figure. The warmest support, not surprisingly, came from his own section, New England. But he could count on the esteem of men throughout the Union, whether or not they shared his political opinions. He enjoyed a fluctuating but basically firm friendship with Thomas Jefferson, who thought that in the coming election "the strength of [Adams's] personal worth and his services will . . . prevail over the demerits of his political creed," and so actually recommended Adams to one of the Virginia electors. Leading Federalists such as Charles Carroll of Maryland, Oliver

Wolcott of Connecticut, and Rufus King of New York, gave him their imprimatur. Hamilton also bestowed a reluctant blessing; certainly he did not contemplate any other candidate within the Federalist persuasion.

Jefferson himself held aloof from electioneering in 1792. Others in the Republican camp made fitfully strenuous efforts to turn the vice-presidential contest to their advantage. When the struggle was over, the Federalist Theodore Sedgwick observed that the "Opposition has been as busy as the Devil in a gale of wind." One tack was to denounce Adams for monarchical leanings. He had made himself look silly in the first session of Congress by advocating semi-regal designations ("His Highness") for the President. His *Defence of the Constitutions*, written in 1786-87 and stretching to three volumes, made plain his conviction that the executive branch must be separate and powerful and that there was much to be said for a hereditary instead of an elective chief of state. He argued on the same lines in his *Discourses on Davila*, which he regarded as a sequel to the *Defence*. The *Discourses* were written as a series of letters in John Fenno's Federalist newspaper the *Gazette of the United States,* in 1791. They provoked so much "Jacobinical" protest that Adams terminated the series before he had exhausted his theme, though not before he had trailed his coat in thirty-two issues of the *Gazette*. Freneau's rival publication, the *National Gazette*, thundered against "those monarchical writers on Davila, &c., who are armed with long wigs, long pens and caitiff printers ready to disseminate their poisoned doctrines." Admirers of Adams countered, sometimes in dinner-table exchanges, by asking his critics whether they had read his works or merely heard about them. Patrick Henry was challenged in this way. So was the vehement Virginia Republican William Branch Giles, who was forced to admit that his knowledge of Adams' "monarchal" doctrines was confined to newspaper accounts and random extracts. Jefferson observed (in code) to Madison about Adams that the presidential title affair was "superlatively ridiculous. . . . It is a proof the more of the justice of the character given by Dr. Franklin of my friend, 'always an honest man, often a great one, but sometimes absolutely mad.'" Adams' idiosyncratic and skeptical ruminations weakened his popular appeal; yet their very idiosyncrasy prevented them from doing fatal damage, since his attitudes were complex and hard to interpret.

Thrusts at John Adams were incidental; the Republicans needed a candidate to set against him. As in 1788, George Clinton was the obvious person. His reputation suffered in a sordid quarrel over the vote-count in New York gubernatorial election of 1792 — an episode prefiguring in miniature the disputed presidential election of 1876. Jefferson feared it might weaken "the cause of republicanism." There were subsequent rumors that if Clinton succeeded in ousting Adams, he would remain Governor of New York while also acting as vice-president — a pluralism liable to cast contempt upon the federal government. The affair, again according to rumor, put Clinton at odds with New York's junior senator, Aaron Burr, who together with Senator Rufus King was asked to adjudicate in the controversy.

Nevertheless by June the Republicans were apparently agreed on Clinton. "You are I presume aware," Hamilton told Adams, "that Mr. Clinton is to be your Competitor at the next election. I trust he could not have succeeded in any event, but the issue of his late election will not help his cause." Hamilton added "Alas! Alas!" with mock sincerity. At the same time, the Republicans were making a determined effort to run strong candidates in the forthcoming congressional elections.

Adams' own reaction was an unhappy and incomplete detachment. News that reached him of maneuvers afoot heightened his old distaste for "electioneering" (a word which, incidentally, was already current). In his native Massachusetts, his cousin Samuel Adams and John Hancock were said to be promoting the Anti-Federalist interest. Fisher Ames, the Massachusetts Federalist — "The colossus of the monocrats and paper [money] men" in Jefferson's phrase — was being challenged. Ames in turn, urging New Englanders to give "zealous support" to Adams, expressed his regret at the tone of anti-Adams propaganda; it was sad that "a life of virtue and eminent usefulness should be embittered by calumny." Adams, who in selfrighteous moments felt the same way about himself, decided to remain in seclusion on his Quincy farm, and not expose himself to the factious atmosphere of Philadelphia until well after the beginning of the next session of Congress in November. Alarmed by the report, the tireless Hamilton, claiming it was "the universal wish of your friends," implored him to show himself "as soon as possible at Philadelphia."

> *I fear that this will give some handle to your enemies to misrepresent — and though I am persuaded you are very indifferent personally to the . . . election, yet I hope you are not so as it regards the cause of good Government. The difference . . . is in my conception between the success of Mr. Clinton or yourself; and some sacrifices of feeling are to be made.*

Others in Philadelphia, including the Vice-President's son Thomas Boylston Adams, wrote in the same vein. But John Adams did not set out from Quincy until the end of November. By the time he reached the federal capital the presidential electors had met and cast their votes. No one would be able to say John Adams had stooped to conquer.

In the meantime there had been a flurry of behind-the-scenes activity among the Republicans, especially between key men in New York, Pennsylvania, and Virginia. Two busy personages in Pennsylvania were Dr. Benjamin Rush and John Beckley, the clerk of the House of Representatives, who has been identified as a significant agent in the formation of a fully fledged Republican party. Rush, previously a good friend of Adams, had become temporarily hostile to what he thought Adams portended. Gripped in the emotions of a period when both America and Europe saw before them a tremendous drama of choices, Rush opted for the side of liberty and republicanism — as he interpreted it. With the knowledge of Madison and Jefferson, Beckley traveled to New York at the end of September. He bore a letter of introduction from Rush to Aaron Burr. Burr's own opinions had not hitherto seemed to place him firmly in one camp or the other. He was not on good terms with Hamilton, since he had captured the Senate seat of Hamilton's father-in-law, Philip Schuyler. Apparently he was now reckoned to be a Republican and a talented and promising one; for Rush wrote that his "friends everywhere look to you to take an active part in removing the monarchical rubbish of our government. It is time to *speak out* — or we are undone." Rush also encouraged Burr to extend the network into New England: "The Association in Boston augurs well. Do feed it by a letter to Mr. Samuel Adams." Apart from pseudonymous printed polemics, it would seem most of the speaking out was done in private, almost conspiratorially.

Beckley, back in Philadelphia, informed Madison that Burr was ready to "support the measure of removing Mr. A" and replacing him with Mr. C. But a Philadelphia Republican, John Nicholson, had already suggested a better candidate in the shape of Mr. B — namely, Senator Burr. "The people here," said Nicholson, understood that Clinton wished to withdraw. They thought Burr might prove a more popular candidate in some areas. They would back either man and would like "a communication with their Southern Brethren on the subject." Burr sent an emissary to Nicholson: and in the same crowded interval a letter signed by two New York Republicans arrived in Virginia, addressed to Madison and to James Monroe and delivered by hand to Monroe. The bearer, Monroe told Madison, "was intrusted with a similar [communication] from some [gentlemen] in Penn'a & elsewhere, particularly to the south." Monroe was not enthusiastic. He thought Burr too young and the scheme somewhat presumptuous and probably launched too late, although in a straight contest, he would not hesitate "to aid Burr in opposition to Adams." Madison wrote back to express general agreement, but proposed that he and Monroe should first meet in Fredericksburg, Virginia, and jointly "weigh the subject in every scale." When they were able to reply to the New Yorkers, they stated that "the Republican interest, so far as the voice of this State may be estimated, requires that things should be kept to the course which they have in manner spontaneously taken."

In short, Virginia preferred Clinton. "Warmly supported by sundry influential characters," he was more likely "to unite a greater number of electoral votes." When they wrote, a meeting had in fact already taken place in Philadelphia between Pennsylvania Republicans and one of the New York spokesmen, Melancton Smith. They had decided to "exert every endeavor for Mr. Clinton and to drop all thoughts of Mr. Burr." Smith volunteered to make the decision known and to take an immediate trip into New England to spread the word for Clinton. John Beckley, present at the meeting, begged Madison and Monroe to display similar energy in Virginia and other southern states. The chronology of the episode, which was squeezed into about a fortnight, indicates the sense of urgency of those involved and their capacity to move swiftly despite the handicaps of distance.

So ended the brief flare of Burr's candidacy. Clandestine though it had been, it soon came to the ears of Rufus King. He wrote in alarm to Hamilton: "If the enemies of the Government are secret and united we shall lose Mr. Adams." Burr was "industrious in his canvass." In Connecticut, Burr's uncle Pierpont Edwards, a prominent lawyer, was busy on his behalf; and maneuvers were in train elsewhere. The danger was not so much that Burr would win, but that he could get so many votes that Adams might out of pique "decline the Office." For a few weeks Hamilton seems to have lost his usual coolness, perhaps out of the personal antipathy to Burr that was to grow with the years and eventually to cost him his life on the dueling ground at Weehawken. He conveyed the gist of King's letter to several correspondents, including Charles Cotesworth Pinckney, a leading citizen of South Carolina, John Steele, a congressman from North Carolina, and — perhaps the clearest indication of his loss of composure — to President Washington, who may have thought Hamilton's letter indiscreet and best left unanswered. In nearly identical phrasing Hamilton, in his other letters also, offered a ferocious assessment of Burr. Clinton was bad enough — "a man of narrow and perverse politics, . . . steadily opposed to national principles." Burr was potentially far more dangerous — a man "whose only political principle is, to *mount at all events* to the highest legal honours of the Nation and as much further as circumstances will carry him."

Hamilton revealed himself, too, to be in the grip of an erroneous conviction about Jefferson. In the course of his *nom-de-plume* newspaper onslaughts against the Republicans he had asserted that Jefferson was scheming to become president through jealousy of Hamilton. In so doing he gave unwitting proof of his own jealousy of Jefferson. He speculated in this batch of letters as to whether

Clinton or Burr, or both, might be run by the Republicans "as a diversion in favour of Mr. Jefferson." Perhaps he was genuinely mystified by the Republican tactics. Perhaps he honestly believed that votes might be steered to Jefferson, though such a plan would not have made much sense. Even more than the clash of personality, however, Hamilton's reaction points to the intensity of the political divisions of the era. Each group assumed that the other group would act without scruple in order to secure an advantage. Hamilton and others of the Federalist "interest" watched their opponents like hawks. And Hamilton, for political as well as personal reasons, must have been vastly relieved when it was clear that the Burr candidacy had been abandoned. It could now be seen as evidence of Republican confusion rather than collusion. Once Hamilton had regained his composure, he was convinced that Adams would be safely reelected.

In March 1792, Congress approved a new law regulating the presidential succession and the method of establishing the electoral vote. The electors were to be appointed in the month preceding the first Wednesday in December, on which day they were to meet in their states and vote by ballot for two men — making no mark on their papers to disclose which of the two they preferred for president or vice-president. A certificate from each state was to be sent to the presiding officer of the Senate before the first Wednesday in January 1793; and the votes were to be counted in Congress on the second Wednesday in February. No elector was pledged in advance. Each camp read the signs — the trend in congressional and state elections, the political coloration of the men chosen as presidential electors, analyses published in the press or conveyed in private letters — and totted up provisional scorecards. The Republican interest gained appreciably in Congress, though they would not take their seats until the fall of 1793 and so could not influence the immediate pattern of events in Philadelphia. However, Republican morale was high, and Adams disclosed his uneasiness in a Christmas letter to his wife, Abigail. The Burr following had swung behind Clinton; Burr's New England uncle, Pierpont Edwards, had turned up in Philadelphia and closeted himself with Jefferson. Ready for the moment to think the worst of his friend, Adams professed to be "really astonished at the blind spirit of party which has seized on the whole soul of this Jefferson. There is not a Jacobin in France more devoted to faction." The public seemed to be carried away "with every wind of doctrine and every political lie." The Federalists must fight the enemy on every literary front: "reasoning must be answered by reasoning: wit by wit. . . ; satire by satire; . . . even buffoonery by buffoonery."

The war of pamphlets continued, with Hamilton as an army in himself. The votes came in slowly; corroboration of those from the new state of Kentucky apparently did not reach Philadelphia until March 1. But every sophisticated citizen knew before the close of 1792 that there would be no surprises. The only uncertainty was the exact margin of Adams' lead over Clinton. In mid-October Hamilton accurately forecast the outcome. Adams, he said, would have a "nearly unanimous vote" in New England. In New York, the Republican majority in the legislature would pick Clintonian electors. Adams would get all the votes of New Jersey, and probably sweep the board in Pennsylvania. Delaware and Maryland were fairly secure. Virginia and Georgia were Republican territory; North Carolina might be. Adams would get some votes in South Carolina, but Hamilton confessed he did not know how many. By December 18, he wrote of the election as a thing of the past. "The success of the Vice President," Hamilton informed John Jay, "is as great a source of satisfaction as that of Mr. Clinton would have been of mortification & pain to me." He protested that he would "relinquish my share of the command, to the Antifederalists if I thought they were to be trusted — but I have so many proofs of the contrary as to make me dread the experience of their preponderancy." When the tally was complete, it confirmed a unanimous vote for Washington: 132 in all. Adams had 77 votes, Clinton 50. The ghost-candidacies of Jefferson and Burr were commemorated in a couple of eccentric gestures; four for the former, the product of Rhode Island's obscurely wayward practices; and a single stray South Carolina vote for Aaron Burr. Otherwise the scatter of 1789 had disappeared, giving way to a more disciplined alignment. Each "interest" could draw some satisfaction from the result, although — a perhaps apocryphal story — Adams is said to have reacted to the news of the final vote with a furious "Damn 'em, damn 'em, damn 'em. You see that an elective government will not do." One Republican, writing to Madison on December 24, 1792, felt that their newspaper campaign against Federalist iniquities had started too late. A Massachusetts Federalist, David Cobb, described the result in his state in odd, perhaps jocular, language: "Our Elections are unanimous for the old King and his second." The Republicans had failed to make any real impact on Pennsylvania. On the other hand, they had swung obediently behind Clinton, for all the peculiarities of his candidacy; they had the makings of a solid southern bloc; and the link between New York and Virginia was emphatically pictured in the following voting table.

TABLE 5.2
PRESIDENTIAL VOTE 1792

STATE	WASHINGTON	ADAMS	CLINTON	JEFFERSON	BURR
New Hampshire	6	6			
Massachusetts	16	16			
Connecticut	9	9			
New Jersey	7	7			
Pennsylvania	15	14			
Delaware	3	3			
Maryland	8	8			
Virginia	21		21		
South Carolina	8	7			1
Georgia	4		4		
New York	12		12		
North Carolina	12		12		
Rhode Island	4			4	
Vermont	3	3			
Kentucky	4	4			
	132	77	50	4	1

The two presidential elections of 1788-89 and 1792 are the forerunners of a long and still flourishing sequence of such contests. They hold something of the pride of place, the nostalgic appeal that in the history of aviation is accorded to those few precarious seconds when the Wright brothers first became airborne over the dunes at Kitty Hawk. By analogy, we may say that in the first try-outs the federal electoral mechanism took wing. It *worked*, if not very well; optimists, of whom, on the whole, George Washington was one, could be reasonably confident that with time the machinery would work a good deal better. The electors were chosen — apart from the New York muddle of 1789 — just as the blueprint prescribed. Having been chosen, the electors chose; and their choices were nationally accepted. No elector was assassinated or kidnapped or browbeaten, though a certain amount of psychological pressure was doubtless brought to bear upon them. In this respect the Washington-Adams elections set the vital precedent.

In other respects they furnish only a shadowy precedent. Seen in the perspective of later elections, they may appear strikingly different, even aberrant. The events of 1788-92 were not "campaigns" in the familiar American understanding of the term. The lines were not clearly drawn, the performers were (by later standards) reluctant and uncommunicative, their supporters secretive and maladroit. Absent were the characteristic features of a campaign in any modern sense: the prolonged search for candidates, the nationwide activities of professional politicians, the crowded and ritualized conventions, the banners and songs and slogans and processions, the convergence of a mass electorate on the polling stations on a specified day in November. The profound divisions that existed in 1788-92 were not yet focussed and polarized. To the extent that they found a political outlet, they were expressed rather in state and congressional elections than in the presidential one. While this was most conspicuously evident in the states where the legislature picked the electors, it applied also in states where the electors had to submit to a popular vote. So we may argue that the subsequent presidential elections are linked to the first ones not so much by direct, as by a kind of collateral, descent.

The unique situation of George Washington is in itself enough to explain much that was atypical in 1792. Though James Monroe was to be unopposed in 1820 and to receive every electoral vote except one, he owed his elevation to the temporary disappearance of the party system, not to any widespread belief that he was a second Washington. Washington was the automatic and universal nominee, *pater patriae*, the father of his people, even if some grumbled privately at the dangers of excessive adulation and if these murmurings found their way into print toward the end of his second administration. Because he was above the battle, the presidency did not yet become the principal strategic feature of the political battleground. Because of this, the vice-presidency likewise did not serve as a genuine symbol around which to rally; for the office in its nature lacked an autonomous reality. Its meaning was conditional upon the meaning attached to the presidency. Adams understood this and once remarked, "I am nothing, but I may be everything." While Washington was President, Adams was a cipher, the occupant of what he termed "the most insignificant office that ever the invention of man contrived or his imagination conceived." No wonder that the effort to beat him in 1792 had a slightly half-hearted quality. He was blanketed, so to speak, by Washington's aura; while Washington was President, there was little point in mounting a large-scale operation to capture the post of vice-president.

Viewed thus, Washington inhibited and delayed the political evolution of the presidency, like a man who will not allow a match to be put to a fire that has been laid. If such a parallel had been suggested to him, he might well have replied that he had no intention of risking a conflagration before the house was fireproof. Washington's mere presence may have inhibited the growth of undesirable forms of electioneering. If there had been a free-for-all contest, there might have been vicious wrangling over the methods of choosing electors, and an overwhelming temptation to buy and sell them. John Adams, culling his examples from the sadly corrupt history of mankind in all epochs, insisted that this was the inevitable tendency of government by the few. "Awful experience," he said in 1790, had convinced him "that Americans are more rapidly disposed to corruption in elections than I thought they were fourteen years ago." Adams nourished a belief, which became more and more heretical in the American context, that it would be safer to appoint an executive and an upper house for life than to plunge the country into an elective system. "First magistrates [i.e., presidents] and senators had better be made hereditary at once, than that the people should be universally debauched and bribed, go to loggerheads, and fly to arms regularly every year." One does not need to accept the Adamsite thesis to concede that presidential elections were open to abuse. To the degree that Washington's reputation spared him such fevers, he provided his country with a beneficial lull, during which electioneering was muted. This, and the fact that the Presidency was not yet the major prize of political competition, may explain why there was so little discussion in the Washington era of the possibility that a handful of men would arrange the business between them, a point touched on, for instance, by historian James Schouler. The 1788-89 election, he writes, "showed that though [the] State colleges might act independently of the people, they were exposed to the yet greater danger of secret cabals among party leaders. In fact the machinery of this election, with all its simplicity of choice, was turned by a crank over which a few party Federalists presided."

Washington's primacy also minimized the serious inadequacy of the constitutional device of naming two men without separating the functions for which they were being named. True, the confusion was to produce an alarming deadlock in the 1800 election that had to be resolved by the twelfth Amendment. At any rate Washington's lead over all the other potential candidates postponed the crisis for a few years, until Americans were more habituated to their new government. Simply by being president, he saved the United States from the divisive confusion that could have been caused by competition between a multiplicity of candidates. Such a competition had been envisaged when the Constitution was drawn up. But one can imagine the delay, bewilderment and dissatisfaction that would have followed if the first presidential elections had had to be decided in the House of Representatives.

Suppositions of this kind ignore an equally crucial factor, the relative absence of national party politics during 1788-92. The matter may be put the other way round: without Washington, party politics might have emerged earlier, though admittedly it is hard to tell what men of the period meant when they used a word like "party." What are we to make, for instance, of the following statement?

In all public bodies there are two parties. The Executive will necessarily be more connected with one than with the other. There will be a personal interest therefore in one of the parties to oppose as well as in the other to support him. Much has been said of the intrigues that will be practiced by the Executive to get into office. Nothing has been said on the other side of the intrigues to get him out of office. Some leader of party will always covet his seat, will perplex his administration, will cabal with the Legislature, till he succeeds in supplanting him.

It occurs in a speech by Gouverneur Morris at Philadelphia in 1787. Is it a prescient vision of the future course of presidential politics, or merely Morris's version of English parliamentary tactics, with their alternation of "ins" and "outs"? The latter seems more likely; Morris seems to confine his notion of party behavior to what goes on inside the government.

What is clear is that though many Americans of the era expected parties to emerge, few rejoiced in the prospect and fewer still could perceive the shape that they would take. If by a "party" we mean an interconnected structure operating at national, state, and local level with a program of sorts, a self-conscious identity of name and sentiment, and a sustained determination to capture the federal executive branch, then such a phenomenon did not exist in the period under review. "Opposition" claimed but was not granted legitimacy. Party labels tended to be anachronistic ("Anti-Federal") and pejorative rather than honorific, terms of abuse rather than badges of identity. They have been loosely employed in this essay, with the partial justification that they were loosely employed at the time. The word "interest" perhaps comes closest to conveying both the limited, manipulative nature of political groupings and the conception that Madison, Hamilton, and others actually had of their own activities.

Yet such groupings — cliques, cabals, juntos, connexions, all with an eighteenth-century flavor of politics as a game played by family alliances — were not incompatible with a passionate if uneven and intermittent response to ideological issues. The presidential politics of the 1790s were, starting in 1793, to be powerfully swayed by ideology, though these heady emotions did not last. The elections of 1788-89 and 1792 mark a transitional zone. The elements that were to make the capture of the presidency a central aim of party politics were already in being, but not as yet brought together. Washington could still endeavor to conduct himself as a "disinterested" *head of state*; most of his successors would owe their election and their subsequent fortunes to the fact that they had also been designated *head of a national party*. Perhaps the process was inevitable, once a federal government was a going concern. *E pluribus unum*: the many depended upon some single focus; in unity was strength. The differences between these two primordial elections and the style of a fully developed presidential system are substantial. Most of the enduring precedents set by Washington belong to quite other realms of statecraft. Yet there are continuities to be discerned in the amorphous but coalescing affiliations between New York and Virginia and even in the various things that Washington and Adams did *not* do.

In children's drawing books are pages made up of apparently miscellaneous dots, each dot with a number. They are transformed into recognizable pictures — say of a donkey or an elephant — by joining up the dots in numbered order. From 1788 to 1792, so far as presidential elections were concerned, the dots were all there. The diagram, however, had not yet been completed, and only some of the dots bore numbers; others were puzzlingly blank. So, within the scope of the diagram, a different though not totally different pictures could have emerged.

BIBLIOGRAPHICAL ESSAY

Several editions exist of the writings of many major figures in early American political history, with new scholarly enterprises gradually replacing older collections. The most important source materials begin with *The Records of the Federal Convention of 1787*, ed. Max Farrand (4 vols., rev. ed., 1937). Useful collections include *Works of John Adams*, ed. Charles Francis Adams (10 vols., 1850-56); *Writings of Samuel Adams*, ed. H. A. Cushing (4 vols., 1904-08); *The Writings of George Washington*, ed. John C. Fitzpatrick (39 vols., 1931-44); *The Papers of Alexander Hamilton*, ed. Harold C. Syrett and Jacob E. Cooke (in progress, 1961-); *The Papers of Thomas Jefferson*, ed. Julian P. Boyd (in progress, 1950-); *The Writings of James Monroe*, ed. Stanislaus M. Hamilton (8 vols., 1898-1901; reprinted 1969); William Wirt Henry, *Patrick Henry: Life, Correspondence and Speeches* (3 vols., 1891). Biographical studies include Page Smith, *John Adams* (2 vols., 1962); Nathan Schachner, *Alexander Hamilton* (1946; reprinted 1957); Dumas Malone, *Jefferson and the Rights of Man* (1951); Irving Brant, *James Madison: Father of the Constitutions, 1787-1800* (1950); Douglas Southall Freeman, *George Washington* (6 vols., 1948-54) and John A. Carroll and Mary W. Ashworth, *George Washington: First in Peace*, (vol. 7, 1957). Broad perspective on the role of politics and political parties is provided by J. R. Pole, *Political Representation in England and the Origins of the American Republic* (1966); Richard Hofstadter, *The Idea of a Party System: The Rise of Legitimate Opposition in the United States, 1780-1840* (1969); Morton Borden, *Parties and Politics in the Early Republic, 1789-1815* (1968); Joseph E. Charles, Jr., *Origins of the American Party System* (1956); William N. Chambers, *Political Parties in a New Nation, 1789-1809* (1963); and Norman Risjord, ed., *The Early American Party System,* (1969). The last five titles have much to say regarding the elections immediately following 1792.

———————————

This essay appeared in *The Coming to Power: Critical Presidential Elections in American History*, ed. Arthur M. Schlesinger, Jr. (New York: Chelsea House in association with McGraw Hill, 1972) and was also published as part of *History of American Presidential Elections* (New York: Chelsea House Pub., 4 vols., 1971, 1972), 3-32.

Fitzpatrick's old edition of Washington *Writings* is being replaced by a comprehensive series of *Washington Papers* edited by W. W. Abbot and others. Newer biographical material includes James T. Flexner, *George Washington*, of which vols. 3 and 4 (1969, 1972) cover the presidential years; Forrest McDonald, *The Presidency of George Washington* (1974); Garry Wills, *Cincinnatus: George Washington and the Enlightenment* (1984); Barry Schwartz, *George Washington: The Making of an American Symbol* (1987), part 1; and John E. Ferling, *The First of Men: A Life of George Washington* (1988). Early political-presidential questions are examined in Michael J. Heale, *The Presidential Quest: Candidates and Images in American Political Culture, 1787-1852* (1982); Richard P. McCormick, *The Presidential Game: The Origins of American Presidential Politics* (1982); Ralph Ketcham, *Presidents Above Party: The First American Presidency, 1789-1829* (1984); and Merrill Jensen and Robert A. Becker, eds., *The Documentary History of the First Federal Elections, 1788-1790* (1976-).

6

Madison as Commander-in-Chief

The essays commissioned by Ernest R. May dealt with the success or otherwise of the handful of American presidents in acting as constitutional commanders-in-chief when they had a foreign war on their hands. My contribution was an assessment of James Madison's performance, more favorable in tone than that of some other commentators, including Henry Adams. In editing, I have struck out or altered infelicities here and there but left the essay basically intact.

Esteemed as a Founding Father and respected as a president, James Madison is not much celebrated for his performance as commander-in-chief in the War of 1812. Political opponents denounced his folly in having led the country into war at all, and his administration's mismanagement of the war once it was declared. Federalist critics in Congress charged that he had been pushed into the conflict by such Republican "war hawks" as Henry Clay and John C. Calhoun. Madison, they asserted, only *pretended* to be warlike during the summer of 1812 so that he could secure the Republican renomination as president. According to one of his senior generals, James Wilkinson, who writes with a heavy irony, the "meek and amiable republican," "the wise and virtuous President Madison," was dominated by the active members of his cabinet.[1]

Historians have reacted comparably. Less heavy-handed than Wilkinson but

---

[1] James Wilkinson, *Memoirs of My Own Times* (Philadelphia, 1816), 3: 359, 367.

no less ironical, Henry Adams explains Madison as a prim soul almost comically ill-equipped for his belligerent role. Most of Madison's biographers agree. To Sydney Howard Gay he is a man who "plunged the country into an unnecessary war" and who, when it was on his hands, "neither knew what to do with it nor how to choose the right men who did know." Gay speaks of "the remarkable incompetence which he showed in rallying the moral and material forces of the nation to meet an emergency of his own creation." Another biographer, Gaillard Hunt, agrees:

> In truth he was not an inspiring figure to lead in war. The hour had come, but the man was wanting. Not a scholar in governments ancient and modern, not an unimpassioned writer of careful messages, but a robust leader to rally the people and unite them to fight was what the time needed, and what it did not find in Madison.

Julius W. Pratt concurs that "despite his admirable qualities," he was "not the man to lead the country through such an ordeal." A fourth biographer, Abbot Emerson Smith, reinforces the indictment: "the real shortcomings of Madison as a war president . . . lay not in his ignorance of military affairs, nor in the misfortunes of his early appointments, but in his failure to exert a powerful moral and political leadership." Madison failed "because he did not understand either the necessity or the method of forcibly combining interests and ideals into a great national emotion. The War of 1812 was not a national crusade like that of 1917, but the difference lay not in the causes or justification, but in the manipulation of public opinion." In his administrative history, *The Jeffersonians*, Leonard D. White says of Madison:

> As commander in chief, the President was irresolute, weak in his judgement of men, unaware of his proper function, and incapable of giving direction to the course of events.

And an investigation of American civil-military relations leads Louis Smith to describe Madison as "a most inept war-time executive, who provided little energy or direction in the War of 1812."[2]

---

[2] Henry Adams, *History of the United States*, 9 vols. (New York, 1891), 6: 398-99; 7: 34; Sydney Howard Gay, *James Madison* (Boston, 1884), 325-28; Gaillard Hunt, *The Life of James Madison* (New York, 1902), 325; *Dictionary of American Biography*, 22 vols. (New York, 1928-1944), 12: 191-92; Abbot Emerson Smith, *James Madison: Builder* (New York, 1937), 308-9; Leonard D. White, *The Jeffersonians, 1801-1829: A Study in Administrative History* (Chicago, 1951), 221; Louis Smith,

One voice, it is true, has been raised in Madison's defense — that of his biographer, Irving Brant.[3] But there seems to be an almost unanimous conviction that little Jemmy Madison was a bad commander-in-chief. Is this justified?

Even at its narrowest, as a narrative of battles and campaigns, military history tempts us into too-positive assertions. How confidently we apportion praise and blame, pronounce upon the relative merits of a Grant or a Lee, consign the defeated to the dustbin of history and install the victorious in the halls of fame. But how do we *know*? How may we truly assess the part played by luck, superior numbers, better training, the talent of subordinates?

It may be answered that we must and do nevertheless make such judgments and that by their admittedly conventional and approximate standards Madison rates as a bad commander-in-chief. Even if we withhold blame for the pitiful outcome of the 1812 campaigns along the Canadian border, when three American forces (under William Hull, Stephen Van Rensselaer, and Alexander Smyth) were routed, little improvement was discernible in 1813; and in 1814, though some able American leaders came to the fore, Madison was fortunate to escape military disaster and the possible collapse of the Union.

Any useful evaluation must take into account the wider elements of the war. First, it was an extremely unpopular war. One might construct a rough graph of the degree of national unity underlying the various declared American wars of the nineteenth and twentieth centuries. On an unpopularity-scale the War of 1812 would appear as the highest mark in the graph, which would run steadily downward through the Mexican War, the Civil War (within the Union), the Spanish War, the First World War, and so down to the almost complete unanimity of national sentiment brought about in World War II by the Japanese attack on Pearl Harbor on December 7, 1941. The day after the attack, Congress declared war on Japan with only one dissenting vote.

Contrast the public reaction of December 8, 1941, to the spectacle in 1812. Madison sent his war message to Congress on June 1. It was wrangled over until June 18. In the final vote the Senate responded with a hesitant majority of only 19 to 13, while the House split 79 to 49 in favor of the declaration. At the very outset "Mr Madison's War" was resisted by some and disliked by many. For the next two and a half years, until the peace proposals reached America from Ghent in February, 1815, the war on the American side was attended with serious

---

American Democracy and Military Power (Chicago, 1951), 42.

[3] The latest volume so far (1959) of Irving Brant's biography is *James Madison: The President, 1809-1812* (Indianapolis, 1956). But see his article "Timid President? Futile War?" in *American Heritage* 10 (October, 1959): 46-47, 85-89.

disunity and uncertainty. What were Madison's war aims? To resist British maritime oppression? To wrest Canada from the enemy, or East Florida from the Spanish? If these aims eluded definition, how could any sensible strategy be devised?

And how should this factor be weighed? Irving Brant sees it as an extenuating circumstance. "Open sedition and silent resistance forced the United States to fight the war with one arm — New England — tied behind her back. That was more crippling than incompetent generals, raw militia, and an empty treasury."[4] Madison's supporters in Congress used the same argument. Felix Grundy, a "war hawk" from Tennessee, accused the Federalist bloc of "moral treason." New Englanders and New Yorkers, or a Republican such as John Randolph of Roanoke who also opposed the war, gave comfort to America's enemy every time they rose to speak. They crippled the nation's war effort, it was said, by advising constituents not to enlist or subscribe money. They warped the direction of strategy. If America were bent on seizing Canada, the major thrust should have been up Lake Champlain and on to Montreal. But since the northeastern states were so dissident, Madison was compelled to rely upon secondary attempts at invasion via Detroit or the Niagara front.

On the other hand, Madison's critics have echoed the complaint made by the Federalists. In the forceful language of Daniel Webster, who was then a young Congressman from Portsmouth, New Hampshire,

> *Quite too small a portion of public opinion was in favor of the war, to justify it originally. A much smaller portion is in favor of the mode in which it had been conducted. This is the radical infirmity. Public opinion . . . is not with you, in your Canada project. Whether it ought to be, or ought not to be, the fact that it is not should by this time be evident to all; and it is the business of practical statesmen to act upon the state of things as it is, and not to be always attempting to prove what it ought to be.*

Mere party support, Webster went on, "is not the kind of support necessary to sustain the country through a long, expensive and bloody contest; and this should have been considered before the war was declared. The cause, to be successful, must be upheld by other sentiments, and higher motives." From this, "the radical infirmity," flowed Madison's troubles — for instance, the poor response to his efforts to raise a sizeable army:

[4] Ibid., 47.

Unlike the old nations of Europe, there are in this country no dregs of population, fit only to supply the constant waste of war, and out of which an army can be raised, for hire, at any time and for any purpose. Armies of any magnitude can here be nothing but the people embodied — and if the object be one for which the people will not embody, there can be no armies.[5]

To Webster Madison's initial blunder was to take his country into war; and the mishaps which followed derived from this primary mistake. It is clear that Madison faced a task of exceptional difficulty, also that leaders of democracies are wise to make sure of the public's support before they commit themselves to warfare. Despite the comment by Abbot Emerson Smith, quoted above, there was a far greater difference between the war spirit of 1812 and that of 1917 than could be eliminated by any "manipulation of public opinion" on Madison's part.

A second complication lies in the fact that this was a "limited" war:

1. His war was traditional (and thus "limited") in style. It was diplomacy carried on by other means: a logical stage in a dispute, a final form of protest, to prove that America was in earnest and meant to have redress. The gigantic struggle in Europe, in contrast, was "unlimited": it could have no outcome except in the overthrow of Napoleon or in the downfall of Britain and her allies. This very contrast made it hard for Madison to refute the accusation that he had allowed the United States to fall into the Napoleonic orbit. It exposed him to the charge of greed and cynicism; and even at best, it lent an air of pedantry and futility to his protestations.

2. In their wars, Americans have not responded readily to a fight for "limited" objectives. Even if there had been no dissension, Madison would probably have failed to convince his countrymen of the need for taking the War of 1812 seriously. The British Orders in Council, a chief cause of friction, were revoked immediately before Congress declared war; and though this was not known at the moment of the declaration it was known soon after. A temporary and local armistice was agreed upon in 1812 by the British and American commanders on the Canadian front (Sir George Prevost and General Henry Dearborn). More ambitious efforts were initiated only a few

[5] *Debates and Proceedings in the Congress of the United States,* (hereafter cited as *Annals of Congress*), *13th Congress, First Session, May 24, 1813-Aug. 2, 1813,* 945-46. I have omitted a few commas from these and later quotations.

weeks after the war began, though they came to nothing. A Russian offer of mediation was accepted by Madison in March 1813. Although the British would not meet Madison's commissioners on that occasion, by the beginning of 1814 they were arranging with him for direct negotiation. The Anglo-American commissioners did not manage to sit down together at Ghent in Belgium until August 1814, and did not sign the peace articles until Christmas of that year. But peace terms ran together with war aims; and while that might be a sensible way of conducting war, it undercut the roaring oratory of the "war hawks."

Moreover, the War of 1812 was a peripheral affair. Whatever Madison might have accomplished in the way of victories, in the eyes of Europe his war was a sideshow. His army and navy, even if they had been as big as the administration presupposed, would have been tiny in comparison with the vast formations of the Napoleonic Wars. The War of 1812 had too little shape of its own. Whatever the Americans might say or do, the principal decisions — at any rate until the last months of 1814 — were reached in Europe. Even in American cartoons, let alone those drawn in England, Brother Jonathan or Uncle Sam were puny figures when set against burly John Bull or the Napoleon colossus. To an unsympathetic eye, the actual physique of little James Madison expressed all too accurately the secondary stature of the United States in a conflict of giants.

A third problem is that the Republicans claimed to be a party governed by principle. They had not always been consistent. Nevertheless they were associated with belief in a modest, minimal federal government and so with opposition to a national debt or to anything that would produce a national debt or a swollen administration, including a standing army and navy. War involved debt, a regular army, a federal navy. True, an army and navy had existed under the peacetime administrations of Jefferson and Madison, but these were vestigial — a few thousand men and a handful of frigates, with a scatter of smaller craft. In theory the army had been augmented in 1808 to something over ten thousand men. But enlistment lagged; in 1809 the actual strength was still under three thousand.[6] The Republican heritage proved an acute embarrassment for Madison. His own supporters in Congress grumbled at his war measures and did not hesitate to scale down the administration's proposals. They were joined by the Federalists in dwelling upon the anomalies of Republican doctrine.

In his annual message to Congress of November 5, 1811 — several months

---

[6] William A. Ganoe, *The History of the United States Army* (New York, 1942), 113.

before the declaration of war — Madison tried to put the nation on a war footing. He recommended that "adequate provision be made for filling the ranks and prolonging the enlistments of the regular troops; for an auxiliary force to be engaged for a more limited term; for the acceptance of volunteer corps, whose patriotic ardor may court a participation in urgent services; for detachments . . . of other portions of the militia, and for such a preparation of the great body as will proportion its usefulness to its intrinsic capacities."[7] But when this was translated into a legislative proposal it offered an irresistible target to a soured Republican like John Randolph. Reminding his party of their resistance to the army of 1798-99, raised at the time of the French crisis and under the command of George Washington, the enraged Randolph cried out:

> *Republicans were then unwilling to trust a standing army even to his hands who had given proof that he was above all human temptation. Where now is the revolutionary hero to whom you are about to confide this sacred trust? . . . Sir, you may raise this army, you may build up this vast structure of patronage, this mighty apparatus of favoritism; but . . . you will never live to enjoy the succession; you sign your political death-warrant. . . ."*[8]

As to the outcome of this particular debate, Madison wrote ruefully to his mentor Jefferson in February 1812:

> *The Newspapers give you a sufficient insight into the measures of Congress. With a view to enable the Executive to step at once into Canada they have provided after two months delay, for a regular force requiring 12 to raise it, and after 3 months for a volunteer force, on terms not likely to raise it at all for that object.*

Jefferson replied sympathetically, though his letter could not have brought much comfort to the President:

> *I have much doubted whether, in case of a war, Congress would find it practicable to do their part of the business. That a body containing 100*

---

[7] James D. Richardson, *Compilation of the Messages and Papers of the Presidents, 1789-1897*, 10 vols. (Washington, D.C., 1907), 1: 494.

[8] *Annals of Congress, 12th Congress, First Session, 1811-1812*, 441-42.

lawyers . . . should direct the measures of a war, is, I fear, impossible.[9]

A fourth problem in assessment is hinted at in such quotations: namely, the lack of precedents to guide even a more harmonious administration. Most countries begin a new war by seeking to refight the previous one. So it was not surprising that Republicans and Federalists alike should invoke the Revolutionary memory of George Washington; or that the moves against Canada planned in 1812 should recall Montgomery's endeavor of 1775; or that naval tactics should also harken back to the Revolutionary War. In the same vein, Madison's Secretary of War, summoning James Wilkinson north in 1813 to take up a command, told him: "If our cards be well played, we may *renew the scene of Saratoga.*"[10] Both men had been present at the victory of 1777. Perhaps it was natural, too, that when he headed away from Canada a year later in disgrace, to face a court-martial, Wilkinson should ask his old friend Van Rensselaer to join him in a last sentimental tour of the Saratoga battleground.[11] Unfortunately, though, these and other commanders were elderly men, past their prime.

Still more unfortunate, if the Revolutionary War yielded useful lessons, they had not been learned. George Washington furnished orators with an easy inspiration but — as Randolph's speech reveals — with not much else. What *could* be learned from one who was "above all human temptation?" There had been little serious discussion since the Revolution of military affairs. Commentators have been unrealistic in condemning the Founding Fathers for their failure to establish a substantial regular army and navy.[12] These would have been a grievous financial burden and were arguably not indispensable in the early years of the republic. And though warnings against the dangers of a standing army became empty rhetoric after the War of 1812, they were not baseless until the war was over. Artemas Ward of Massachusetts was not merely indulging in partisan prejudice when in March 1814, he invited the House of Representatives

to consider what has taken place in our time, and what they have read in

---

[9] Madison to Jefferson, February 7, 1812, in Gaillard Hunt, ed., *Writings of James Madison,* 9 vols. (New York, 1900-1910), 8: 176; Jefferson to Madison, February 19, 1812, in P. L. Ford, ed., *Writings of Thomas Jefferson,* Federal Edition, 12 vols. (Washington, D.C., 1896), 11: 226.

[10] John Armstrong to James Wilkinson, March 12, 1813, quoted in Wilkinson, *Memoirs,* 3: 342.

[11] James. R. Jacobs, *Tarnished Warrior: Major-General James Wilkinson* (New York, 1938), 307.

[12] The best-known example of this is Emory Upton, *The Military Policy of the United States* (Washington, D.C., 1904), a piece of special pleading by a regular officer who sought to ram home the lesson that only the regulars had saved America's military honor.

*the history of other times. We have seen the legislature of France, turned
out of the Hall of Liberty by a military force which it had nurtured. . . . We
have read in history that the same was done in England, in the days of
Cromwell. However secure gentlemen may feel in their seats, it is not
impossible that they may witness . . . the same scenes here, and that the
military force which they now vote to raise, without being able to render
any reason, may ere long put an end to their existence as legislators.
Executive patronage and executive influence are truly alarming.*[13]

Another negative precedent concerned the role of the militia. If nothing more
than a skeleton standing army was to be tolerated, then (as orators affirmed)
America's main reliance must be upon the militia. But to be effective the militia
would have to be equipped, trained, classified by age-group, with the main
obligation falling upon younger men. It would have to be available, in wartime,
outside state borders for periods longer than the usual ninety days. These steps
were never taken. They entailed conscription, inconvenience, expense. Here
Jefferson and Madison were fairly clear as to what was needed and that an
efficient militia was consonant with Republican doctrine. In repeated messages
they reminded Congress of the importance of the militia, without result except for
the meager enactment of 1808, which allotted the annual sum of $200,000 for the
arming of the "constitutional force" of a whole nation.[14] Jefferson was informing
Madison and his cabinet colleague James Monroe of what they already knew and
had relearned during the war, when he wrote to Monroe in October 1814 that

*we must prepare for interminable war. To this end we should put our
house in order, by providing men and money to indefinite extent. The
former may be done by classing our militia, and assigning each class to the
. . . duties for which it is fit. It is nonsense to talk of regulars. They are not
to be had among a people so easy and happy at home as ours. We might
as well rely on calling down an army of angels from heaven. I trust it is
now seen that the refusal to class the militia, when proposed years ago, is*

[13] *Speech of the Honorable Artemas Ward . . . on the Fifth Day of March, 1814, on a bill making
appropriations for the support of the military establishment.* . . . (Washington, D.C., 1814), 18.

[14] In the first five years, according to a report of July 8, 1813, only $94,792 out of a total of $1 million
was expended by the states. *American State Papers: Military Affairs*, 1: 337.

the real source of all our misfortunes in this war.[15]

Jefferson exaggerated. *Some* professional soldiers were required, and some were raised. The Military Academy at West Point had been established in 1802 under his administration. He and Madison approved of it, and though only about seventy cadets had graduated by 1812, Madison took steps in that year to fill it with 250 cadets.[16] In practice Madison depended upon a stiffening of regulars, enlisted for five years. But Jefferson was right that the solution did not rest with a regular army. Despite bounties and land grants, the regular ranks could not be filled during the war. Nor was it possible to improvise any large, reliable militia force. In between came the troops known as volunteers, who were neither regulars nor militia but something of both. Madison, in short, inherited an unsatisfactory military system which he could not reform overnight. Polk inherited essentially the same system. But by 1846 the regular army was in better shape, and the militia as a field force yielded almost entirely to the volunteer regiments.

Nor was Polk confronted with the constitutional issue that faced Madison when some New England governors denied his authority to call out the militia of their states and the right of any subordinate of the president to prescribe their duties when they were called out. Not until the war had been over for a dozen years did the Supreme Court rule (in *Martin v. Mott*, 1827) that the initial authority rested with the president. The issue was still not quite dead, as Jefferson Davis and even Lincoln to a lesser extent were to discover. Madison's tribulations in this matter as in others exceeded those of later commanders-in-chief.[17]

The authority of the commander-in-chief had not yet been determined in other

[15] Letter of October 16, 1814, *Writings of Jefferson*, 11: 436-37. In his first inaugural address (March 4, 1809, Richardson, *Messages & Papers*, 1: 468) Madison had declared his intention "to keep within the requisite limits a standing military force, always remembering that an armed and trained militia is the firmest bulwark of republics — that without standing armies their liberty can never be in danger, nor with large ones safe." In subsequent messages (Richardson, 1: 486, 494, 519, 538) Madison stressed the need for an improved militia. In his annual message of September 20, 1814 (Richardson, 1: 549-50), he recommended "classing and disciplining" the militia.

[16] In his second annual message (December 5, 1810; Richardson, 1: 486-487) Madison said: "The Corps of Engineers, with the Military Academy, are entitled to the early attention of Congress." He recommended the foundation of a second military academy. "In a government happily without the other opportunities seminaries where the elementary principles of the art of war can be taught without actual war, and without the expense of extensive and standing armies, have the precious advantage of uniting an essential preparation against external danger with a scrupulous regard to internal safety." The second academy was not established.

[17] Louis Smith, *American Democracy and Military Power*, 309-11; Leonard D. White, *The Jeffersonians*, 539-43.

areas. A minor uncertainty existed as to whether the president might take command in the field. It could be argued that Washington had done so or had been prepared to do so during the Pennsylvania Whiskey Rebellion of 1794.[18] Perhaps Madison had some such martial impulse when, immediately after the declaration of war, "he visited in person — a thing never known before — all the offices of the departments of war and the navy, stimulating everything in a manner worthy of a little commander-in-chief, with his little round hat and huge cockade."[19] When the war arrived on his doorstep in the shape of a British raid on Washington in August 1814, Madison rode out from the city to witness the fighting at Bladensburg. These instances do not indicate any real clash of interests on Madison's part. His place was obviously at the center of affairs; though if the war had continued to be waged close to Washington, as it was for Lincoln, he might have anticipated Lincoln in occasionally directing operations.

A more central uncertainty involved his relations with the Navy and War Secretaries. It was hard to distinguish them in career and temperament from some of the senior officers in the services, particularly where the army was concerned. Henry Dearborn, whom Madison appointed major general in February 1812 and so to the army's senior post, had indeed been Jefferson's Secretary of War. His military experience in the field had been no greater than that of Madison's first Secretary of War, William Eustis, who served as a surgeon in the Revolution. Eustis' successor, John Armstrong, likewise a Revolutionary officer, held a brigadier general's commission for several months before coming to the War Department. Before that he had acted as American minister to France. Another Revolutionary veteran and diplomatist, Thomas Pinckney, was appointed to the junior major-generalcy of the army in 1812. Madison's Secretary of State, James Monroe, had risen to a colonelcy during the Revolution; he eventually supplanted Armstrong at the War Department, while also remaining Secretary of State. A few other senior figures, notably James Wilkinson, had long years of continuous military service. But the majority had only civilian careers stretching between their memories of the Revolution and the new excitements of 1812.

In such a situation no nice line could be drawn between the civil and the military. There was nothing inherently absurd in Madison's suggestion to Monroe, in September 1812, that he might be given a senior commission and the

---

[18] James B. Fry, "The Command of the Army," in his *Military Miscellanies* (New York, 1889), 62-146.

[19] Richard Rush to Benjamin Rush, June 20, 1812, quoted in Henry Adams, *History of the United States*, 6: 229.

chance of leading the advance into Canada. In view of the dismal defeat of William Hull and the somnolence of Henry Dearborn, it was not absurd to suppose that the energetic Monroe might be made lieutenant general and commander of the American armies.[20] As it happened, none of these plans was implemented. But the lines between civil and military duty and between the administrative and command functions of Madison's cabinet remained vague. After William Eustis resigned his office in December, 1812, Monroe acted as Secretary of War *pro tempore*. He was immensely active in this part-time capacity, recommending a new organization for the army, drawing up plans for the 1813 campaigns, and not altogether relinquishing his dreams of personal military glory. When John Armstrong stepped into the War Department in February 1813, he was equally ambitious. Soon he was proposing to go himself to the Canadian front. Later in the year Armstrong did so, arriving at Sackett's Harbor (at the eastern end of Lake Ontario) on September 5 and not returning to Washington until November.[21] It was much more than a tour of inspection; Armstrong assumed control of operations, issuing detailed and sometimes peremptory orders to Wilkinson, Wade Hampton, and other commanders.

This conduct was criticized at the time by members of Congress and by Monroe. Monroe wrote to the President, on hearing of Armstrong's intended move, to question its constitutionality and propriety:

> *There ceases to be a check on Executive power as to military operations; indeed the Executive power, as known in the Constitution, is destroyed. The whole is transferred from the Executive to the General at the head of the army. It is completely absorbed in hands where it is most dangerous. It may be said that the President is Commander in Chief; that the Secry at War is his organ as to military operations, and that he may allow him to go to the army, as being well informed in military affairs, & act for himself. I am inclined to think that the President, unless he takes the command of the army in person, acts, in directing its movements, more as the Executive power than as Commander in Chief.[22]*

[20] Ibid., 419-26.

[21] James B. McMaster *A History of the People of the United States* 8 vols., (New York, 1883-1913), 4: 50, 53.

[22] February 25, 1813, in S. M. Hamilton, ed., *Writings of James Monroe*, 7 vols. (New York, 1898-1903), 5: 244-45. Daniel C. Gilman, *James Monroe* (Boston, 1892), 108, gives the date of this letter as July 25, 1813.

Madison later reprimanded Armstrong in detail for having exceeded his authority. But how did Madison feel in 1813? He had been ready to release his Secretary of State, Monroe, for a field command; and Monroe, though a stickler for constitutionality, never seemed to feel that his own ambitious schemes were open to criticism. Madison fell seriously ill in the early summer of 1813. During his long convalescence he could probably take no more than a languid interest in such problems. Yet he had long been aware of Armstrong's intentions and made no formal objection. Perhaps he shared the straddling views of his Secretary of the Treasury, Albert Gallatin. In April 1813, Gallatin wrote to Madison:

> *In a conversation with General Armstrong, he appeared disposed to make an excursion towards the scene of action on our northern frontier. I have, perhaps, more confidence in General Dearborn than almost any other person, and, for many reasons, have no wish to see General Armstrong unite the character of general with that of secretary.*

From this beginning we would expect Gallatin to proceed to a denunciation of Armstrong:

> *Yet from my knowledge of both, I think that the success of the campaign may be secured by General Armstrong's presence for a few days at the army. His military views are generally more extensive, and for this years's operations appear to me more correct, than those of General Dearborn.*[23]

Gallatin was keenly aware of the need to form American government on sound constitutional principles. But on this debatable ground of civil-military relations his thinking, like that of Madison, Monroe, Armstrong, and the rest, sounds uncertain. The precedents did not exist.

A fifth complexity concerns the clash of personalities in the armed forces and within Madison's administration. Here his difficulties differed rather in degree than in kind from those of later commanders-in-chief; but it is arguable that his difficulties were greater and that only in part were they of his own making. Within the army he had little initial choice, and the senior officers on whom he had to rely were often snarlingly at odds. As Winfield Scott (himself a Republican) reminiscently testified,

---

[23] April 22, 1813, in Henry Adams, ed., *The Writings of Albert Gallatin*, 3 vols., (Philadelphia, 1879), 1: 538-39.

> *Party spirit of that day knew no bounds, and, of course, was blind to policy.*
> *Federalists were almost entirely excluded from selection, though great*
> *numbers were eager for the field, and in the New England and some other*
> *states, there were but very few educated Republicans. Hence the selections*
> *from those communities consisted mostly of coarse and ignorant men. In*
> *the other States, where there was no lack of educated men in the dominant*
> *party, the appointments consisted, generally, of swaggerers, dependents,*
> *decayed gentlemen, and others . . . utterly unfit for any military purpose*
> *whatever.*[24]

Among the Republicans an intense antipathy developed between James Wilkinson and Wade Hampton, with their subordinates lining up one side or the other. Since these two held senior commands on the northern frontier in 1813, and the whole advance on Montreal depended upon their co-operation, the results were fatal. Each despised and blamed the other when the campaign collapsed. "*To General Hampton's outrage of every principle of subordination and discipline may be ascribed the failure of the expedition,*" Wilkinson told Armstrong in November 1813; "and that I have not yet arrested him must be attributed to my respect for you, and my desire that the arrest should proceed from the highest authority."[25] Recrimination became universal. Relieved of command, Wilkinson poured out his abuse on Armstrong. No one held aloof from controversy. This was true even of relatively uncontroversial figures like William Henry Harrison, the governor of Indiana Territory, who from the vantage point of 1840 seemed a respectable enough military hero to secure the Whig nomination for the presidency. In 1813 he was less widely admired. "This man's talents have been greatly overrated," W. H. Crawford of Georgia wrote to Gallatin. "He flatters the Kentuckians, and they tell the government he ought to be made a major-general, and he is made one. His official communications . . . are the most vague and puerile productions which I have ever seen. . . . For God's sake, . . . endeavor to rid the army of old women and blockheads."[26]

The worst clash of temperament and ambition, however, occurred within the cabinet, between Armstrong and Monroe. Madison's first Secretary of War, William Eustis, resigned in December 1812. Madison's mediocre Navy Secretary, Paul Hamilton, resigned at the same time. Jefferson described Eustis as "a

---

[24] Winfield Scott, *Memoirs* (New York, 1864), 1: 35.

[25] November 24, 1813, in *American State Papers: Military Affairs*, 1: 35.

[26] September 22, 1813, in *Writings of Gallatin*, 1: 582-83.

pleasant, gentlemanly man in society" and said that "the indecision of his character rather added to the amenity of his conversation." Gallatin commented that "his incapacity and the total want of confidence in him were felt through every ramification of the public service."[27] Eustis was overwhelmed by his sudden responsibilities. At the beginning of the war he had only eight clerks in his small department, and Congress rejected a proposal to provide him with two senior assistants. Like Simon Cameron in Lincoln's cabinet and Russell A. Alger in McKinley's, Eustis was made the scapegoat. His faults, like theirs, were exaggerated; or, as Josiah Quincy of Massachusetts stated it, Eustis was "hunted down."[28]

Gallatin, in the letter just quoted, went on to admit that "To find a successor qualified, popular, and willing to accept is extremely difficult." The main snag was that Monroe wished to be entrusted with the direction of strategy, either as secretary of war, or, preferably, at the head of the troops in the field. According to Josiah Quincy, who delivered a withering speech on the topic in January 1813:

> *Mr. Speaker, when I assert that the present Secretary of State, who is now acting Secretary of War, is destined by a cabinet of which he himself constitutes one third for the command of this army, I know that I assert intentions . . . which have not yet developed themselves by an official avowal. . . . The cabinet must work along by degrees, and only show their cards as they play them. The army must first be authorized. The bill for the new Major Generals must be passed. Then, upon their plan, it will be found necessary to constitute a Lieutenant General. "And who so proper," the cabinet will exclaim, "as one of ourselves?"*[29]

Quincy asserted that the scheme was in mind as early as June 1812. Madison, Monroe, and Gallatin, he continued, "are about to raise an army of fifty-five thousand men, invest one of their own body with this most solemn command, and he the man who is the destined candidate for the President's chair! What a grasp at power is this!" Though Quincy's interpretation of Madison's and Monroe's motives was partisan, there is little doubt that they did hope for some such

---

[27] Jefferson to William Duane, October 1, 1812, in *Writings of Jefferson*, 11: 268-69; Gallatin to Jefferson, December 18, 1812, in *Writings of Gallatin*, 1: 530-31.

[28] Speech in House of Representatives on the invasion of Canada, January 5, 1813, in Edmund Quincy, ed., *Speeches of Josiah Quincy* (Boston, 1874), 407.

[29] Ibid., 405-06.

outcome and that the criticism voiced by Quincy and others discouraged them. Instead, Madison appointed John Armstrong of New York, a man whose ambitions were as militant as those of Monroe. Monroe was disappointed. "Had it been decided," he told Jefferson, "to continue the command of the army under Genl Dearborn [whom Armstrong relieved of active command in the summer of 1813], and the question been with me, would I take the dept of War, . . . I would not have hesitated a moment in complying. But it never assumed that form." Monroe was doubly disappointed when Armstrong proceeded to outmaneuver him. In plans for an augmented army, drawn up while he was temporarily in charge of the War Department, Monroe had recommended several new senior posts. These were approved by Armstrong and sanctioned by Congress:

> On the day that the nomination of these officers was made to the Senate, the President sent for me, & stated that the Secretary at War, had placed me, in his list of major Generals, at their head, and wished to know whether I would accept the appointment, intimating that he did not think I ought to do it, nor did he wish me to leave my present situation.[30]

On the face of it, Armstrong had paid the Secretary of State a handsome compliment. But Monroe declined to serve in a subordinate capacity. And by the time that Dearborn was discarded, Armstrong was in control where Monroe had wished to be. "I suppose you are apprized," John Randolph wrote to Josiah Quincy in August 1813,

> of the deadly feud between [Monroe] and Armstrong. The partisans of the former keep no terms in speaking of the latter. There is no measure to their obloquy, if a great deal of truth mixed with some falsehood may pass by that name. It is however plain that the cabinet dare not displace Armstrong. He is now gone on to "organized victory" in Canada.[31]

The nature of the triangular relationship between Madison, Armstrong, and Monroe remains opaque. The President's two executive heads were men of exceptional ability. Armstrong was vigorous and decisive. Whatever his motives, he strengthened the war effort by ousting Dearborn and Wilkinson, and he was probably right to get rid of Harrison. Though Armstrong was self-seeking and

---

[30] *Writings of Monroe*, 5: 264-65.

[31] August 30, 1813, in William C. Bruce, *John Randolph of Roanoke* (New York, 1922), 1: 397.

sometimes disingenuous, so was Monroe, and his standing with the President was not improved by the accusations that Monroe made against him in correspondence with Madison. As it happened, Armstrong ruined himself by failing to produce a successful invasion of Canada; then, in an attempt to win favor with Andrew Jackson, by claiming the credit for promoting that warrior to a major-generalcy when the credit should have been at least shared with Madison; and finally, perhaps through pique, by doing almost nothing to prepare the defenses of Washington against the threat of a British raid. When the raid became a reality in August, 1814, Armstrong was hooted out of office without the need for a formal dismissal by Madison. Monroe at least had got what he wanted. By the test of success in the remaining months of the war, he was the better man.

We have listed five factors that inhibit judgment of Madison's performance as commander-in-chief. They are

—the unpopularity of the War of 1812
—the limited, ill-defined, and peripheral nature of the war
—the nature of Republican party doctrine
—the lack of precedents to guide the nation or the president in war
—friction between the principal figures involved in the war effort.

What Madison achieved has to be seen in the context of what was possible for him to achieve. In addition to the handicaps already outlined, Madison was unlucky. True, he might have expected to run into vehement opposition. But he knew that he could count on congressional majorities. It was not foolish to suppose that his war preparations would be approved by Congress. His explanation of what he hoped for, written in September 1813, accords with what he had said earlier. He believed the war to be just and unavoidable. He gambled on a quick blow:

As it was obvious that advantage ought to be taken of our chusing the time for commencing, or rather retorting, hostilities, and of the pains taken to make the British Government believe that they were not to be resorted to by the United States; and as it was foreseen that there would be great delay, if not impossibility, in raising a large army for a long term of service, it was thought best to limit our first attempts to such a force as might be obtained in a short time, and be sufficient to reduce Canada, from Montreal upwards, before the enemy would be prepared to resist its progress; trusting to the impression to be made by success, and to the time that would be afforded, for such an augmentation of the durable force as would be able to extend as well as secure our conquests.[32]

The British garrisons in Canada were small and could not be quickly reinforced. Neither Madison nor the overconfident "war hawks" were initially foolish in anticipating an easy victory. The British (and the Canadians) turned out to be tougher and more enterprising than during the Revolutionary War. Even so, if any of the American senior commanders in 1812 had shown the energy or initiative that Andrew Jackson or Winfield Scott or Jacob Brown were later to reveal, the campaigns against Canada might have fared very differently. A good deal of the unpopularity of Mr. Madison's War lay in the early setbacks. A successful start might have made it much less unpopular, even in New England. Under these considerations Madison's original scheme was sound enough. It acknowledged America's peculiar military situation. If he erred on the side of rash optimism, he himself — unlike Hull and the others — could not be convicted of timidity and inactivity.

Madison's administration asked Congress at the end of 1811 for a regular army to be built up to its existing establishment of 10,000 men and for 10,000 more with a shorter enlistment, together with a force of volunteers. Congress thwarted him, in part through the malice of the Republican leader, William B. Giles of Virginia, who insisted on a larger army than the country could hope to provide. Madison asked also for the establishment of two new "vital Departments, the Commissary's and Quarter Master's," within the army.[33] But Congress reacted so reluctantly that these essential administrative services were organized too late and never functioned properly during the war.

Despite these handicaps, Madison remained cool and determined. His new Secretary of War, John Armstrong, reflected this determination even though the appointment perhaps created more problems than it solved. Madison's new Secretary of the Navy, William Jones, seems to have been an admirable choice.[34] Jones and Madison both understood the importance of naval supremacy on the Great Lakes (a point which General Hull had also vainly emphasized); and Madison is entitled to recognition for the crucial victories on Lake Erie in 1813 and Lake Champlain in 1814.

[32] Letter to William Wirt, September 30, 1813, in *Writings of Madison*, 8: 262-63.

[33] Ibid., 8: 264.

[34] Kenneth L. Brown, "Mr. Madison's Secretary of the Navy," *U.S. Naval Institute Proceedings* 73 (1947): 967-75.

The President and his Navy Secretary worked harmoniously with the House Naval Affairs Committee; and even Madison's harshest critics paused in their diatribes to shower compliments upon the nation's seamen. They paid a more grudging tribute to Andrew Jackson for his bold operations in the Floridas against the Indians and to the soldiers who fought tenaciously on the Niagara front in the summer of 1814. Criticism was altogether silenced by Jackson's spectacular victory at New Orleans in January 1815.

If Madison was held responsible for the ignominies of 1812-13, then he may be given credit for the accomplishments of 1814-15. The more so in that he was not a mere cipher. No one, even at the height of the feud between Monroe and Armstrong, took the President to be a weakling at the mercy of strong-willed associates. He allowed them more latitude than some presidents would have cared to do, just as he left Congress more to its own devices than would subsequent presidents. In part these tendencies reflected his own and his time's view of the nature of the executive branch. Despite Federalist assertions that the President had been bullied into the war by Republican fire-brands, they knew that it *was* Mr. Madison's War.

Strategy was evolved inside the cabinet. Learning as he went along, Madison developed an increasingly focused picture of himself as commander-in-chief. To some extent the trend was a consequence of the character of the American federal government: in war, the president's powers grow almost despite himself. Madison's own conscious contribution can be seen in the long letter of rebuke he addressed to Armstrong in August 1814, which begins:

> *On viewing the course which the proceedings of the War Department have not infrequently taken, I find that I owe it to my own responsibility as well as to other considerations, to make some remarks on the relations in which the Head of the Department stands to the President, and to lay down some rules for conducting the business of the Department which are dictated by the nature of those relations.*

It is an incisive and not a petulant document. The same firmness and clarity are evident in a later communication discussing the Navy Department.[35]

So much for Madison's accomplishments. What of his deficiencies as commander-in-chief? Perhaps he was not a good judge of men. Anticipating

---

[35] *Writings*, 8: 286-87; Madison to Benjamin W. Crowninshield, June 12, 1815, in *Letters and Other Writings* (1865 ed.), 2: 603-6.

war, as he did, he might have been wise to replace William Eustis and the ill-qualified Paul Hamilton with more aggressive figures, before war came. The appointment of Brigadier General William H. Winder to command the Washington district in 1814 seems ill-advised, and Madison's handling of the British descent on the capital is open to criticism. At least he foresaw the likelihood of the attack and ordered that steps be taken to meet it, even if the appointment of Winder was one of the steps and if the chain of command became twisted at Bladensburg. He created difficulties for himself in encouraging Monroe's dreams of military glory and then in not satisfying them. In view of his subsequent strictures on Armstrong, Madison might have been more sensible not to have appointed him at all or at any rate to have kept a closer watch upon Armstrong's activities.[36]

In other respects he might have been more ruthless. It is impossible not to feel sympathy for Madison when one reads through the testimonies of Wilkinson, Armstrong, and the rest, with their sour flavor of recrimination and jealousy, their florid sentiments and hand-on-heart protestations of probity and zeal.[37] The road to Canada was paved with good intentions and bad faith. Madison could not but be perplexed by his far-off assortment of bickering, vain, ill commanders (half their letters are dictated from sickbeds; they are absorbed in their own symptoms). But one wonders whether an occasional explosion from Madison might not have had some effect — for example, in making Wilkinson and Wade Hampton either cooperate or resign.

The same reaction is prompted by some of Madison's messages to Congress. True, such messages are almost always couched in a tone of pious generality; it would not be easy to gauge the temperament of, say, Andrew Jackson by studying his annual messages. True, also, there is no defeatism in Madison's utterances. Nor did presidents in his era have the means or inclination to arouse the nation by bursts of oratory. Even so, Madison's messages are chilly and a little evasive. Unwilling to provide ammunition for his enemies, he glossed over defeats and financial woes, expatiating on the wickedness of the enemy, the prowess of America's soldiers and sailors, and the beneficial effects of adversity upon the formation of the American national character. This would have mattered less if he had not simultaneously asked for large-scale and expensive additions to the war establishment. His enemies pounced on the discrepancy. Elisha Potter of

[36] Madison, *Letters*, 3: 384 (comments made in 1824).

[37] In addition to Wilkinson's *Memoirs*, see John Armstrong, *Notices of the War of 1812* 2 vols., (New York, 1836-40); and the report on the causes of failure on the northern frontier, *American State Papers: Military Affairs*, 1: 439-88.

Rhode Island, in the House debate of January 1814 on the administration's five-year enlistment bill, said:

> *The President, in his Message to Congress of November, 1812, after stating what progress had been made in the war . . . , mentions the capture of General Hull and his army, and the surrender of the whole Michigan Territory, as but a partial calamity; and that even that calamity had been converted into a source of invigorated effort, so that it had become more necessary to limit than to excite the patriotic zeal of the people. . . . And, in his Message [Dec. 7, 1813] at the opening of the present session, . . . he seems to impute the failure of . . . the most sanguine . . . expectations, not to . . . the want of any human exertions, but to adverse weather. . . . Why then should we provide for raising more men, or giving such extraordinary encouragement to enlistments, not asked for nor recommended by the Executive authority?*[38]

We are back again at the tantalizing problem of whether Madison, the good Republican who disliked military establishments, the mild and decent scholar whose logic carried him into a command for which neither training nor temperament fitted him — whether, given all the circumstances of disunity and ill-preparedness, this man's capacities can be calculated without an excess of qualifications.

It is evident that he did not make an inspiring success of the task, though conceivably the task was impossible. It may also seem evident that he did not disgrace the office. His weaknesses — personal insignificance, attachment to Republican principles, a certain demureness and detachment — were also his strengths. Not a heroic figure, he was not a bully either; there was no Sedition Act under his administration, though his opponents might have been considered seditious. In failing to arouse Congress and the nation by feats of oratory, he also kept calm in moments of black crisis. British troops set fire to the White House and the Capitol in August 1814. When Madison summoned Congress to assemble, less than a month later, the legislators had to squeeze into the post-office building. His annual message of September 1814 betrayed no sense of dismay. Its prose was as circumspect, as faintly old-fashioned as ever.

Whatever scorn they might reserve for his executive heads or for his generals, most of Madison's political opponents recognized this quality in him. Elisha

---

[38] *Annals of Congress, 13th Congress, First Session, May 24, 1813-Aug. 2, 1813,* 1113.

Brigham of Massachusetts, after presenting the usual Federalist version of the war, said of the President: "Indeed, he has not seen much service — he has not had the experience of Bonaparte; but there is no doubt but he is hearty in the cause, and has conducted the war according to the best of his ability."[39] That is as good an assessment of his stature as commander-in-chief as we are likely to get.

After all, it is basically the same statement as the one made by his political supporters. Charles Jared Ingersoll, though writing a generation afterward, was a Republican Congressman in the War of 1812. According to Ingersoll, Madison

> went through the war meekly, . . . no doubt with anxious longing for the restoration of peace, but without ever yielding a principle to his enemies or a point to his adversaries; leaving a United States, which he found embarrassed and discredited, successful, prosperous, glorious and content. A constitution which its opponents pronounced incapable of hostilities, under his administration triumphantly bore their severest brunt. Checkered by the inevitable vicissitudes of war its trials never disturbed the composure of the commander-in-chief, always calm, consistent and conscientious, never much elated by victory or depressed by defeat, never once by the utmost exigencies of war, betrayed into a breach of the constitution.[40]

Neither opinion is an unqualified panegyric. An implication of Ingersoll's appraisal is that the United States was lucky to get off so lightly or that Madison slept more tranquilly than circumstances always warranted. But he and Brigham would agree that, for the United States, it is just as well that its commanders-in-chief have not "had the experience of Bonaparte"; and we may agree with them.

BIBLIOGRAPHICAL ESSAY

The best account of the period is still Henry Adams, *History of the United States during the Administration of Jefferson and Madison*, 9 vols. (New York, 1891). Irving Brant has a biography in progress, but the latest volume, *James Madison:*

---

[39] Ibid., 1065.

[40] Ingersoll, *Historical Sketch of the Second War Between the United States . . . and Great Britain* (Philadelphia, 1845), 1: 262.

The President, 1809-1812 (Indianapolis, 1956), comes up only to the outbreak of war. Theodore Roosevelt, *The Naval War of 1812*, 2 vols. (Boston, 1882), does not hold up as well as Adams' *History*, but it is still surprisingly valuable. Neither F. F. Beirne, *The War of 1812* (New York, 1949), nor Glenn Tucker, *Poltroons and Patriots*, 2 vols. (Indianapolis, 1954), is a distinguished contribution.

The major sources are the *Annals of Congress, American State Papers: Military Affairs*, and the papers and writings of participants, especially Gaillard Hunt, ed., *The Writings of James Madison*, 9 vols. (New York, 1892-1899); S. M. Hamilton, ed., *The Writings of James Monroe*, 7 vols. (New York, 1898-1903); and Henry Adams, ed., *The Writings of Albert Gallatin*, 3 vols. (Philadelphia, 1879). James Wilkinson, *Memoirs of My Own Times*, 3 vols. (Philadelphia, 1816); and John Armstrong, *Notices of the War of 1812*, 2 vols. (New York, 1835-40), are important, and so are the biographies of Wilkinson: James R. Jacobs, *Tarnished Warrior* (New York, 1938); T. R. Hay and M. R. Werner, *The Admirable Trumpeter* (New York, 1941); Henry Adams, *Albert Gallatin* (Philadelphia, 1879); and the sketch of William Jones by Kenneth L. Brown, "Mr. Madison's Secretary of the Navy," *U.S. Naval Institute Proceedings* 73 (1947): 967-75.

This essay first appeared in *The Ultimate Decision: The President as Commander in Chief*, edited with an introduction by Ernest R. May, (New York: George Braziller, 1960), 21-53.

In the thirty years since this piece was written, several sophisticated studies have appeared on Madison, the presidential years and the aftermath. Ralph Ketcham has followed up his skilful post-Brant biography (New York, 1971) with some judicious articles, such as "James Madison: The Unimperial President," *Virginia Quarterly Review* 54 (1978): 116-36. A formidably comprehensive interpretation is provided by J.C.A. Stagg, *Mr. Madison's War: Politics, Diplomacy, and Warfare in the Early American Republic, 1783-1830* (Princeton N.J., 1983), the work of a New Zealand scholar. Robert A. Rutland's treatment of Madison's presidential years (Lawrence, 1990) is a volume in the workmanlike American Presidency series published by the University of Kansas Press. Steven Watts, *The Republic Reborn: War and the Making of Liberal America, 1790-1820* (Baltimore, 1987) argues ingeniously that Republican Americans actually welcomed, and even longed for, the War of 1812. Drew McCoy, in a sensitive interpretation of Madison's later years — the span of Irving Brant's final volume — makes a case for feeling that Madison's unemotional calm was of enduring value to the young republic: see McCoy, *The Last of the Fathers: James Madison and the Republican Legacy* (Cambridge and New York, 1989). On the war itself, there are sound studies by John K. Mahon (1972), by Reginald Horsman (1972), and those in a collection edited by George R. Taylor (1980).   Federalist political maneuvers in Massachusetts are analysed in James M. Banner, Jr., *To the Hartford Convention. . . 1789-1815* (1970).

MONUMENTAL WASHINGTON

I cannot remember just how or when George Washington began to intrigue me. A main stimulus, certainly, was the invitation to write a short biographical account of his place in American life. The resultant book, *George Washington: Man and Monument* (1958), tried to explain a person whose symbolic importance, the "monumental" qualities ascribed to him even in his own lifetime, served to obscure the actual character and career of the "man." Although this was a principal emphasis of my book, I pointed out that balancing the "real" and the legendary has been a problem for Washington biographers of every stripe. In fact the very first of these chroniclers ran into difficulties: see my introduction to Mason Locke Weems's *Life of Washington* (John Harvard Library, 1962). The aim of "Parson" Weems, apart from making some money out of the project for himself and his publisher, was to humanize Washington by devising homely anecdotes, especially of the hero's childhood, in order to offset the habit of dwelling only upon Washington's supposedly superhuman virtues. The irony is that subsequent generations accused Weems of contributing to the idealization that — at least in part — he was endeavoring to modify.

Here in Part II, then, are various approaches to Washington the monumental. Two essays discuss biographies, by John Marshall and by Woodrow Wilson, produced at the beginning of the nineteenth century and at the century's end. Neither treatment, I argue, was altogether satisfactory, though the authors were Americans of exceptional caliber. The reasons for their relative failure include uneasiness over the right tone to adopt in avoiding deification on the one hand and disparagement (or what in the 1920s became known as "debunking") on the other.

The point is reinforced in this section's two intermediate pieces. One of these shows how often Washington's reputation has been expressed historically as a contrast to the negative, villain image of his British opponent and contemporary, George III. My argument is that this involved some distortion of the British George, who in truth shared a number of elements of character and circumstance with his transatlantic counterpart. The other essay in the quartet takes note of the upsurge of Abraham Lincoln in American esteem (following his assassination), until he is regarded as a complementary figure or even a superior alternative to George Washington in the patriotic pantheon. Has he displaced Washington, or has patriotic sentiment managed to rate them as different but essentially equal?

7

John Marshall's George Washington

This piece was intended (in 1980) as an introduction to a reprint of John Marshall's life of George Washington. The publisher, Chelsea House, dropped the plan. Why, I don't know: not, I imagine, because of pressure from some Jeffersonian latter-day mafia. One incidental benefit was that preparing the essay prompted me to read Marshall's tomes, a task hitherto evaded. The essay appears here in print for the first time, so I have modified the 1980 version.

In the twentieth century John Marshall's reputation as a constitutional lawyer has stood high. This cannot be said of his reputation as a historian; scholars are apt to treat his biography of Washington as a minor detour in Marshall's career or even as a venture not altogether honorable. It is worth considering why this should be so — given my view, which I shall explain later, that Marshall's *Washington* deserves more sympathetic attention than has been accorded.

Marshall's historical abilities have been defined for most subsequent commentators by Albert J. Beveridge's *Life of John Marshall* (4 vols., 1916-19), the third volume of which contains a substantial chapter on Marshall's toils as a biographer. Although, in general, Beveridge presents his subject as a great man, the account of Marshall the would-be historian is negative in tone. Thus, we gather that he undertook the work for mixed reasons, including the hope of a big financial return. George Washington had died in December 1799. A nephew, Bushrod Washington, came into possession of the President's papers. To Bushrod and to Marshall the opportunity may have seemed golden. They reckoned a full-scale history of Washington and his era, running to five volumes, would appeal to thirty thousand subscribers in the United States alone, not to mention Europe. They counted on an equal division of the profits, each man netting about $75,000. Marshall was not rich; additional revenue was important to him.

Mason Weems, book peddler and sometime clergyman, would himself try to cash in on General Washington's demise. "Pence and popularity," he urged a publisher, would await whoever hurried a biography into print. To all appearance, authors of his stamp did not stand a chance against Chief Justice John Marshall in partnership with Bushrod Washington, not only a nephew but also a Supreme Court Justice. Marshall, born in 1755, had served as an officer in the Continental Army. He had become a prominent lawyer and legislator in Virginia — playing an effective part, for example, in the state's convention to ratify the 1787 Constitution. An energetic supporter of the administrations of Washington and John Adams, he had been an American negotiator in Paris at the time of the "X.Y.Z." affair (1797-98). Before accepting the chief justiceship in 1801, he had for a short while been a member of the House of Representatives, and Adams's Secretary of State. Moreover, his court duties left him free for several months each year.

In Beveridge's account, however, Marshall's *Life of George Washington* was a disappointment to nearly everyone, including its compiler. The Chief Justice labored over his first volume for the best part of two years, not finishing until the end of 1803. The finish, though, was hardly even a beginning in relation to the youthful Washington, who received only two incidental mentions in a survey of North American settlement that moved at a measured pace from Columbus to the peace of 1763. Marshall's second volume was not quite so grandly impersonal, though its hero's early life was disposed of in a couple of pages. The initial pair of volumes was published — by C. P. Wayne of Philadelphia — in the summer of 1804. Pressing forward, Marshall managed to complete the third and fourth volumes for publication in 1805. The fifth volume, dealing mainly with the last decade of Washington's life, came out in 1807.

Beveridge's description brings out Marshall's lack of literary experience or of natural talent. His style verged on the ponderous and, writing in haste, he knew he had resorted to cliché. The proportioning was maladroit, not only in the first volume but later: an unduly terse allusion to the Philadelphia Convention of 1787 was followed by a detailed treatment of the ratification debates, and a cursory reference to Washington's election in 1789 opened into a leisurely account of the journey from Mount Vernon to New York and of the inauguration ceremony there. These idiosyncratic allotments of space bore no evident relation to Marshall's own participation in events or to any particular abundance or dearth of papers in the Washington archive.

Beveridge emphasizes too the dragging work schedule. Thomas Jefferson had heard of the project early in 1802 and expected the whole book to be brought out in 1804 so as to influence the presidential election campaign of that year. Beveridge draws upon letters sent to C. P. Wayne by his book agent Weems, full of grumbles at the difficulty of selling Marshall's turgid and unpunctual material to the citizenry of the Southern states. Weems's exasperation with the Marshall volumes may have stimulated him to expand his own breezy, inexpensive little *Life of Washington*.

Beveridge also cites contemporary comments ranging from boredom to anger. One of the most judicious was an analysis by the New England clergyman Samuel Cooper Thatcher, in the *Monthly Anthology and Boston Review*, spread over the summer issues of 1808. The reader, said Thatcher, finds "the history of North America, instead of the life of an individual." Washington was always depicted in an official role, "never in the ease and undress of private life." The same complaint was voiced by the *Edinburgh Review* (October 1808): "We look in vain, through these stiff and countless pages, for any sketch or anecdote that might fix a distinguishing feature of private character in the memory." "A great, heavy book," said *Blackwood's Magazine*. "One gets . . . sick of the very name of Washington before he gets half through these . . . prodigious . . . octavos." And John Adams, responding to a letter from Jefferson in July 1813, spoke of Marshall's work as "a Mausolaeum, 100 feet square at the base, and 200 feet high."

A voluminous flop, then? In that light, one could explain as mere gesture, perfunctory politeness, the presence of the book in so many gentlemen's libraries (as revealed for example in Richard Beale Davis, *Intellectual Life in Jefferson's Virginia*, 1964) or the compliments paid by colleagues of Marshall's such as Justice Story ("invaluable for . . . the accuracy and completeness of its narrative") or acquaintances such as the historian Jared Sparks ("able, accurate, and comprehensive"). More surprising, perhaps, is the praise bestowed in Charles A. Beard's 1913 *Economic Interpretation of the Constitution* ("a historian of great acumen," "masterly"). Had Beard read the whole work or only the parts that suited his own purposes?

Marshall's scholarly reputation was also undermined in an article by William A. Foran ("John Marshall as a Historian," *American Historical Review* 43, October 1937). Foran shows that Marshall borrowed extensively from other authors, especially in Volume 1. Sometimes his wording was almost identical with that of passages from George Chalmers's *Political Annals*, William Stith's *History of*

Virginia, Thomas Hutchinson's *History of Massachusetts*, and Jeremy Belknap's *History of New-Hampshire*. When his narrative reached the Revolution, of which he himself had firsthand knowledge, Marshall continued to lift material. His main sources included a history of the American Revolution by the Reverend William Gordon, an English supporter of the colonial cause, and the well-informed surveys published in the London *Annual Register*. His methods of citation were misleadingly unspecific. Foran concludes that Marshall's work was second-rate in being secondhand; in fact, by twentieth-century standards Marshall could be charged with plagiarism.

But there is more to be said. Marshall's *Washington* was actually not such a disaster for author or publisher as we have been led to believe. A slightly amended second edition appeared in 1805-07. The first volume was held in enough esteem to be issued separately in 1824 as a *History of the American Colonies*. The remaining four volumes, slightly abridged and revised, were brought out as a two-volume set (with the aid of a smaller typeface) in 1832. In drastically shortened form, bringing it closer to Weems's *Washington* in length if not in anecdotal brio, Marshall's book emerged in 1838 as a one-volume treatment. In this format it was adopted fairly widely to edify and instruct schoolchildren. There were foreign-language editions, and the entire work achieved publication in London in 1807. Marshall, Bushrod Washington, and C. P. Wayne, while not making a fortune, did secure a reasonable return over a period of nearly thirty years.

The most significant gauge of John Marshall's impact, however, is the reaction of the Chief Justice's kinsman Thomas Jefferson. Jefferson was already installed in the White House when he got wind of the proposed biography. He immediately assumed that it would be couched as and employed as Federalist propaganda, certain to be biased against the Jeffersonian Republicans. In the spring of 1802 he therefore urged the writer Joel Barlow, a fervent Republican, to produce a history of the era as an "antidote" to Marshall. He continued to press the suggestion though Barlow was living in Europe and busy with projects of his own. By 1808, not long after the appearance of Marshall's final, fifth volume, Barlow was back in America; his affairs were settled, and he agreed to undertake the task in collaboration with Jefferson, who during the next couple of years offered encouragement and advice — among the latter some notes on objectionable statements in Marshall's last volume. Barlow seems not to have got very far when, in 1811, he accepted an appointment from President Madison and returned to France as American minister. He died the following year.

The antipathy between Jefferson and Marshall was heightened during the administrations of Jefferson and Madison. The Supreme Court remained in

Jefferson's eyes the last surviving stronghold of Federalism, which he equated with covert or even open preference for socioeconomic inequality: in a word, or at least Jefferson's word, "monarchy." He regarded Marshall as a cunning and dangerous adversary whose behavior during such episodes as the Aaron Burr treason trial struck him as itself almost treasonable.

Jefferson transferred these emotions to his enemy's *Washington*, especially the fifth volume. He fretted that Marshall's version of the great dramas of the 1790s, in the absence of an antidote, was still able to poison the nation's mind. Marshall, he told John Adams in a letter of June 1813 (to which Adams replied less acidly with his "Mausolaeum" verdict), had written "libels on one side." Two years later, reverting in his correspondence with Adams to the need for a proper history of the Revolution, he commended a book by the Italian Carlo Botta, *Storia della guerra dell'independenza degli Stati Uniti*, which had first been published in 1809 and eventually came out in English translation. Botta's work, said Jefferson, was "more judicious, more chaste, more classical, and more true than the party diatribe of Marshall's." Unfortunately, though, Botta had "put his own speculations and reasonings into the mouths of persons . . . who . . . never made such speeches." Similar objections could be raised against William Wirt's biography of Patrick Henry (1817), for all its readability and "Republican" spirit; moreover, Henry in the 1790s had turned into a Federalist.

During his active career Jefferson had written a great many personal memoranda. In retirement he began to assemble these, under the suffix *ana* (Shakespeariana, Jeffersoniana), for what was to be posthumous publication in 1829. The preface to the *Anas*, as they are commonly known, was composed in 1818. Jefferson made plain his concern to answer Marshall's "five-volumed libel." His old notes could offer testimony "against the only history of the period which pretends to have been compiled from authentic and unpublished documents." The final volume in particular incensed Jefferson. What had been at stake, he insisted, was a fierce and fundamental struggle between republican democracy (his own side) and the selfish toryisim of the Federalists, with Washington an innocent front. Marshall's narrative, according to Jefferson, "represents us as struggling for office" out of mere party expediency, "and not at all to prevent our government from being administered into a monarchy."

We can now begin to put the Chief Justice's biography into perspective. One must admit that the book *is* prolix, sonorous, and lacking in psychological insight. It leaves a chilly impression, as if one were standing barefoot on a marble floor. Critics were correct to complain of the book's frigidity and of the author's failure to distinguish between the evolution of George Washington and the evolution of the United States. Marshall showed none of the imaginative vitality that infused

Wirt's life of Patrick Henry.

On the other hand, Marshall faced difficulties that few of Washington's biographers have entirely overcome. Washington's story *was* intertwined with that of his country. Most Americans held him in awe and wished him to be presented as patriot, warrior, statesman — a person well-nigh without blemish, far above reproach. Marshall himself shared this veneration. His prose was in consequence, marmoreally sincere. His own patriotism no doubt prompted him to envisage an American history on the grand scale. The first volume, all nine hundred pages, was in this respect an appropriately dignified prologue that would also serve to suggest the potential underlying unity of the colonies, even from the outset. Wesley Frank Craven (*The Legend of the Founding Fathers*, 1956) points out that other early historians yielded to similar impulses:

> *Jeremy Belknap and Ebenezer Hazard undertook in the 1790s an American biographical dictionary so ambitiously conceived that the two volumes that were published did not get beyond the seventeenth century. John Sanderson in the 1820s felt the same compulsion as had Marshall to preface his Biography of the* Signers to the Declaration of Independence, *a work completed in nine volumes, with an introductory volume devoted, except for the thirty-eight pages given John Hancock, to a review of colonial history.*

In Marshall's day the art of American historical biography was as immature as the nation itself. Jefferson, for example, had high hopes of William Johnson, raising him to the Supreme Court at the age of thirty-two as a sound young Republican. Johnson subsequently undertook a biography of the Revolutionary war hero Nathanael Greene, using family papers. Jefferson encouraged him in the endeavor, still hoping for antidotes to Marshall. Justice Johnson, however, fared no better than Marshall as a historian. His book (2 vols., 1822) took four years to complete. Only six hundred copies were sold during the next four years. The work was attacked as clumsy and partisan (in the Jeffersonian interest). John Quincy Adams called Johnson a "hotheaded, politician caballing Judge."

As for plagiarism, the Revolutionary historians David Ramsay and William Gordon both borrowed liberally from the *Annual Register*. Botta quarried Marshall — as Jefferson could not help noticing. Marshall's practices, in short, did not differ basically from those of his contemporaries. None objected, not even Jefferson, who owned two sets of the five-volume work and would have pounced upon any evidence of authorial incompetence or depravity. Nor could Jefferson complain of serious factual errors. Marshall had been reasonably conscientious in consulting printed and manuscript sources. Here and there, for instance in explaining Jefferson's views on the constitutionality of the proposed Bank of the United States, Marshall made public details not hitherto known.

He wrote as a Federalist, but then Jefferson was pressing Barlow and Johnson to argue the Republican case. Partisanship was in the eye of the beholder. Jefferson's bias was at least as strong as Marshall's. At the time when he was exercised about Marshall's version of the Washington administration, Jefferson began to take against David Hume's *History of England*, whose flowing style he had once admired. Convinced now that Hume was an insidious, reactionary influence, he cast about for a more wholesome substitute and thought John Baxter's *New Imperial History* (1805-7) might provide the antidote. Perhaps as an intellectual Jefferson was inclined to exaggerate the power of the printed word, especially when the word was expounded with urbane authority, as by Hume or Marshall. Indeed Jefferson seems more intemperate than John Marshall in accusing his opponents of being monarchists. Did he mean the charge literally? If so, he misread the situation. If he used the term loosely, then he may have been guilty of deliberate distortion for political advantage. At any rate, Jefferson seems to have sought to get his own back on Marshall by leaving the *Anas* for posterity. They have been quite effective in this regard.

Yet Jefferson's annoyance with Marshall appears excessive. That he and his followers were furious is clear, but there is a discrepancy between the claim that the Chief Justice had published a "diatribe" and the grumble that Marshall displayed a "cold indifference" to the arguments of the 1790s. Marshall would have been a prime target in any case, but the ultimate vexation, for Jeffersonians, was his air of magisterial impartiality. In the words of Henry S. Randall (*The Life of Thomas Jefferson*, 3 vols., 1858), Marshall's "mortal stabs, as Mr. Jefferson deemed them, at both his reputation as a statesman and a man . . . were probably rendered none the more palatable because they came from a dignified source, because they were clothed in dignified language, and because his assailant assumed many of the ceremonious forms of weighing the testimony and even of occasionally making some liberal concessions, before putting on the black cap to pass sentence." It was therefore not so much what Marshall said as how he said it, or simply implied it. The reader may judge: here is Marshall on Jefferson's resignation as Secretary of State at the end of 1793:

> *This gentleman withdrew . . . at a moment when he stood particularly high in the esteem of his countrymen. His determined opposition to the financial schemes which had been proposed by the secretary of the treasury, and approved by the legislative and executive departments of the*

government; his ardent and undisguised attachment to the revolutionary
part in France; the dispositions which he was declared to possess in regard
to Great Britain; and the popularity of his opinions respecting the
constitution of the United States; had devoted to him that immense party
whose sentiments were supposed to comport with his, on most, or all of
these interesting subjects.

Marshall went on to say that Jefferson's attitudes were openly avowed; that his essential patriotism was not in question; and that his resignation was probably right in view of the awkwardness of combining support for France with officially representing the American policy of neutrality.

Bias? Jefferson is not actually named: was that a slight? Seemingly not, since his enemy Hamilton, the Treasury Secretary, was not named either. What rankled, we may guess, was Marshall's very coolness. He did not engage in abuse or personalities. He was at some pains to summarize opposing views wherever a controversy arose. In fact, as Jefferson's ardent admirer Randall maintained, Marshall was acting the part of an appellate judge, like a Solomon or a Daniel. But his opinions had an unfair, quasi-legal weight. To Jefferson, Marshall was claiming the prerogative of judge *and* jury before the bar of history. So, to Marshall the Republicans were in error, though he was prepared to think them misguided rather than wicked. (But misguided by whom?) The Federalists were wiser: the Revolution was republican, with a small *r*; its fulfillment depended upon the establishment of an effective federal government. Samuel Thatcher felt that Marshall's narrative was indeed too coolly balanced; the Chief Justice behaved like a spectator instead of a person "who has himself descended into the arena."

Jefferson's irritation is understandable. Yet the more one considers the basis of his charges, the more Marshall begins to sound like a good proto-historian rather than a biographer. Omit the first volume; read the remainder, covering the years 1763-99, and one has a detailed chronicle from the viewpoint of a moderate Federalist.

This is the cheerful, plain-living citizen of Richmond, Virginia, who impressed a host of people as a kind, shrewd, unaffected person. He irritated or disappointed now and then — usually in declining to commit himself too hastily to any emphatic course of action. Some of the New England Federalists thought him almost a traitor to their party in 1798-99 when he would not endorse the Alien and Sedition Acts. He was not a stylist to compare with Jefferson or Adams. But he could express himself dexterously, which meant that sometimes he used words for general effect and possibly to avoid committing himself. He was aware that having had to compose a very long work in a relatively short period of time, he had not pruned and revised.

He was pleased to have the opportunity to do so for the 1832 edition. The body of the text remained the same. Apart from amplifying notes here and there, the changes he made were intended to shorten and clarify. The result is a distinct improvement. Thus, in the first edition Marshall remarked of the 1780s: "The discontents and uneasiness, arising in great measure from the embarrassments in which a considerable number of individuals were involved, continued to become more extensive." In revised form the disencumbered sentence read: "The discontents arising from the embarrassments in which individuals were involved, continued to increase." The effect was sometimes to soften the kind of pronouncement that had nettled Jefferson. In the 1832 edition, continuing with his analysis of the 1780s, Marshall omitted the following from a passage on the superior wisdom of the "friends of the national government," as against those who professed to be content with the weak control exercised under the Articles of Confederation:

> *According to the stern principles laid down for their government, the imprudent and idle could not be protected by the legislature from the consequences of their indiscretion; but should be restrained from involving themselves in difficulties, by the conviction that a rigid compliance with contracts would be enforced.*

But the account then continues as before. One suspects that the Chief Justice was concerned to improve his lumpish prose rather than to placate Jeffersonian critics.

The last section he left intact. Probably Marshall had taken pains over it on first composition and was still satisfied. If so he was right. A character sketch of George Washington, or perhaps more accurately a memorial tribute, it is a lofty piece of formal English that deserves to be remembered:

> *In him was fully exemplified the real distinction, which forever exists, between wisdom and cunning, and the importance as well as truth of the maxim that "honesty is the best policy." If Washington possessed ambition, that passion was, in his bosom, so regulated by principles, or controlled by circumstances, that it was neither vicious nor turbulent.*

Biographers are liable to reveal themselves as they would like to be, when ostensibly discussing the subject of the book. Perhaps this is true of another comment by John Marshall upon George Washington:

> *Taught to distrust first impressions, he sought to acquire all the information*
> *which was attainable, and to hear, without prejudice, all the reasons which*
> *could be urged for or against a particular measure. His own judgment was*
> *suspended until it became necessary to determine; and his decisions, thus*
> *maturely made, were seldom if ever to be shaken. His conduct therefore*
> *was systematic, and the great objects of his administration were steadily*
> *pursued.*

Such assessments have been made of Marshall the constitutional lawyer; he does, in lesser measure, merit them as a historian.

BIBLIOGRAPHICAL ESSAY

In addition to the books and articles referred to, there is an extensive comparative assessment of John Marshall, in William Raymond Smith, *History as Argument: Three Patriot Historians of the American Revolution* (The Hague, 1966) — the other two historians being David Ramsay and Mercy Otis Warren. Stanley I. Kutler's *John Marshall* (Englewood Cliffs, N.J., 1972) is a useful collection of sources and commentary. See also Richard Beale Davis, *Intellectual Life in Jefferson's Virginia, 1790-1830* (Chapel Hill, N.C., 1964). There are historiographical discussions of Marshall's *Washington*, of varying length and value, in Page Smith, *The Historian and History* (New York, 1964), 165-99; Daniel J. Boorstin, *The Americans: The National Experience* (New York, 1965); and Bert James Loewenberg, *American History in American Thought* (New York, 1972). There is material on Jeffersonian versions of history and reactions to them, in Merrill D. Peterson, *The Jefferson Image in the American Mind* (New York, 1960). *The Triumphant Empire* (New York, 1967), volume 13 of Lawrence Henry Gipson's *The British Empire Before the American Revolution*, pp. 315-26, contains an account of Jeremy Belknap and of William Gordon. There is a little information on Carlo Botta, in Durand Echeverria, *Mirage in the West: A History of the French Image of American Society to 1815* (Princeton, N.J., 1957), 234. William Johnson's flop as a biographer is described, in Donald G. Morgan, *Justice William Johnson: The First Dissenter* (Columbia, S.C., 1954), 148-53. The fifth volume of Dumas Malone's *Jefferson and His Time*, entitled *Jefferson the President: Second Term, 1805-1809* (Boston, 1974), is useful on Marshall, especially 356-

59. Fragments of Barlow's projected counterblast are printed in Christine M. Lizanich, "'The March of This Government': Joel Barlow's Unwritten History of the United States," *William & Mary Quarterly* 33 (April 1976): 315-30. There is a fine piece of special pleading, against John Marshall, in Henry S. Randall, *The Life of Thomas Jefferson* (New York, 1858), 2:34-41, which manages to drag in the *Edinburgh Review*'s thumbs-down on Marshall's *Life of Washington*.

John Marshall's papers are being comprehensively presented in a scholarly new edition. Volume 6, edited by Charles F. Hobson and Fredrika J. Teute, of *Correspondence, Papers, and Selected Judicial Opinions, November 1800-March 1807* (Chapel Hill, N.C., 1990) covers the writing of Marshall's *Life of Washington*, but was not available in time to incorporate its no doubt valuable material. Jefferson's attitudes to "correct" historical work are touched upon in an essay of mine not reprinted here: "The Earth Belongs to the Living: Thomas Jefferson and the Limits of Inheritance," in *Forms and Functions of History in American Literature: Festschrift for Ursula Brumm*, ed. W. P. Adams et al. (Berlin, 1981), 56-70. I have drawn references to his complaints against the illiberal implications of David Hume's *History of England* from Douglas L. Wilson, "Jefferson v. Hume," *William and Mary Quarterly*, 46 (January 1989): 49-70.

8

The Two Georges:
The President and the King

A brief version of "The Two Georges" was presented in 1976 at a bicentennial degree-giving ceremony at the University of Pennsylvania. The notion that the presidency was also in some ways a monarchy has occurred to many people ever since 1789. Apart from my "Invention of the Presidency," mentioned on page 175, n. 25, I have paid some attention to the theme in various editions of a work first published in 1968, appearing in its most recent guise as *The Presidency* (Boston: Houghton Mifflin, 1987) — for example, 382-86, and also in the essay reprinted in the present volume, "The Presidential Elections of 1789 and 1792."

George III, Tom Paine's "Royal Brute of Great Britain," received a great deal of abuse during his lifetime. In *Common Sense* Paine argued both that the king was a clod and that he was or aimed to be an autocrat. In the *Crisis* papers and in other writings Paine continued to jeer and fulminate. He would (*Crisis* I, December 1776), "make a whore of my soul" if he were to swear allegiance to the "sottish, stupid, stubborn, worthless, brutish" George III, who on the day of judgment would seek to flee in terror when confronted by "the orphan, the widow, and the slain of America." Paine repeated the notion (*Crisis* VI, October 1776) that at the final judgment George III would be consigned to hell.

Such violently accusatory language was typical of the war years. It was the theme of Jefferson's indictment in the Declaration of Independence ("A prince whose character is . . . marked by every act which may define a tyrant."). Benjamin Franklin, who delighted in hoaxes, concocted one in 1782, pretending to be John Paul Jones. There was however nothing playful in the remarks he directed at George III in this hoax:

> *Pensions, places, and hopes of preferment can bribe even bishops to approve his conduct; but when these fulsome, purchased addresses and panegyrics are sunk and lost in oblivion and contempt, impartial history will step forth, speak honest truth, and rank him among public calamities. The only difference will be, that plagues, pestilences, and famines are of this world, and arise from the nature of things; but voluntary malice, mischief, and murder, are from hell; and this King will, therefore, stand foremost in the list of diabolical, bloody, and execrable tyrants.*[1]

After the war Jefferson was among the Americans still convinced that George III had a personal hatred for the colonists. As he remembered the occasion in old age, he and John Adams received a sour reception from the king in London in 1786 when they were prepared to negotiate an Anglo-American treaty. Jefferson's years as an American diplomat in Europe served to confirm his belief that kings were vicious despots. In a letter of 1787 Jefferson referred to them as "this class of human lions, tigers, and mammoths." Like Paine, though, he viewed monarchs as both rapacious and incompetent, rascally and ridiculous, formidable and outmoded. As beasts of prey — lions and tigers — they were dangerous: as mammoths they were doomed to extinction. Paine's animus against monarchy never abated, except when in *The Rights of Man* he spoke with mild approval of the French king, Louis XVI; but that was at an early stage of the French Revolution, and Paine's argument was that French constitutionalism made the crown subordinate to the people, whereas the British maintained the fiction that the country belonged to the king. In general, however, Paine emphasized the foolishness rather than the ferocity of monarchs. "There is something exceedingly ridiculous," he had said in *Common Sense*, "in the composition of monarchy; it first excludes a man from the means of information, yet empowers him to act in cases where the highest judgment is required." Fifteen years later derision typified his comments in *The Rights of Man*. The nobility were creatures of "no-ability"; and "when we look around the world, and see that of all men in it, the

---

[1] "Supplement to the Boston Independent Chronicle," in Albert H. Smyth, ed., Writings of Benjamin Franklin, 10 vols. (New York: Macmillan, 1907), 8: 446-447. During and after the War of Independence, Hugh Henry Brackenridge of Pennsylvania used similar language against the "cruel, unrelenting, and bloody king"; see Joseph J. Ellis, *After the Revolution: Profiles of Early American Culture* (New York: Norton, 1979), 80-87. There are other references in William D. Liddle, "'A Patriot King, or None': Lord Bolingbroke and the American Renunciation of George III," *Journal of American History* 65 (March 1979): 951-70.

race of kings are [sic] the most insignificant in capacity, our reason cannot fail to ask us, What are those men for?" Jefferson's attitudes evolved in the same direction. In a letter of 1788 from Paris to George Washington, Jefferson observed that "there is not a crowned head in Europe, whose talents or merits would entitle him to be elected vestryman, by the people of any parish in America."

From stupidity to idiocy or insanity was only a short step for monarchs, in the view of Paine, Jefferson, and many American contemporaries. Writing to John Langdon in 1810, Jefferson explained that during his European stay he had "often amused myself with contemplating the characters of the then reigning sovereigns." Inbred and pampered, they had "become all body and no mind" — sensual and mentally deranged. "Louis the XVI was a fool, of my own knowledge. . . . The King of Spain was a fool, and of Naples the same. They passed their lives in hunting, and despatched two couriers a week, one thousand miles, to let each other know what game they had killed the preceding days. The King of Sardinia was a fool. All these were Bourbons." The Queen of Portugal and the King of Denmark were idiots, whose sons ruled for them as regents. "The King of Prussia, successor to the great Frederick, was a mere hog in body as well as in mind." And finally, "George of England, you know, was in a straight waistcoat" — or, as Jefferson had reported to George Washington in 1788: "The lunacy of the King of England is a decided fact."

George III was in fact deemed to be insane for several months in 1788-89. Though he recovered, he later became almost blind, senile, and seemingly mad. When he died in 1820, at the age of 81, his son George had been acting as Prince Regent for the previous decade. The radical poet Shelley alluded to him with merciless scorn:

> An old, mad, blind, despised and dying king,
> Princes, the dregs of their dull race, who flow
> Through public scorn — mud from a muddy spring,
> Rulers who neither see, nor feel, nor know,
> But leech-like to their fainting country cling

George Hanover, Brunswick, "Guelf" or "Guelph" as Jefferson sometimes called him, had been attacked in Britain, at various times, almost as baldly as in America. The set of officially commissioned "oval" portraits of George III and his family by Gainsborough were cruelly parodied by the architect-artist George Dance as "The Lillylip Family." Many prints by James Gillray caricatured the king — a figure with bulging eyes and mouth, a large nose and receding chin and forehead — as a ponderous, ungainly eccentric.[2] The versifier "Peter Pindar" (John Wolcot), whose doggerel was much appreciated in the United States, loved to poke fun at the king's oddities — inquisitiveness, garrulity, ignorance of ordinary facts, repetitive speech mannerisms such as "what, what, what?" In one of Pindar's poems the king, out of curiosity, enters the cottage of an old woman to find her making apple dumplings. He has never seen them before and is puzzled to know how the apple got inside the suet ("But, Goody, tell me where, where, where's the Seam?").

Another long "Birth-day Ode" describes the visit of the royal family to the famous brewery of Samuel Whitbread:

> *And now his curious Majesty did stoop,*
> *To count the nails on every hoop;*
> *And, lo! no single thing came in his way,*
> *That, full of deep research, he did not say,*
> *"What's this? hae, hae? what's that? what's this? what's that?"*
> *So quick the words too, when he deign'd to speak,*
> *As if each Syllable would break its neck.*[3]

Horace Walpole, the son of the "Robinarch" political leader Sir Robert Walpole and well placed to observe the life of the court, left some withering comments in his memoirs: "There were but four characteristics in the King's composition. He was unfeeling, insincere, cunning and trifling. Nature had given him the first quality and the last. His mother had taught him the second, and practice the third." Such verdicts seemed to support the view of Paine that George III was by turns sadistic and fatuous, sometimes both at once. Biographers were to decide that madness had threatened his whole adult life; the first attack, it was said, had come during an illness of the young king, as early as 1765.

George III's last years were certainly pitiful. Tourists now and then glimpsed him on the terrace at Windsor Castle. Otherwise he was secluded. The tall,

---

[2] On George Dance, see review by Jeffrey Daniels, The Times, April 2, 1973. The best account of Gillray is Draper Hill, *Mr. Gillray the Caricaturist* (London: Phaidon, 1965). For a broader survey see John Wardroper, *Kings, Lords and Wicked Libellers: Satire and Protest* (London: John Murray, 1973); and Vincent Carretta, *George III and the Satirists from Hogarth to Byron* (Athens: University of Georgia Press, 1990).

[3] The writings of John Wolcot (1738-1819), a doctor by training, were published as *The Works of Peter Pindar*, 5 vols. (London, 1812). These instances are taken from a modern selection, *Peter Pindar's Poems*, ed. P.M. Zall (Bath: Adams and Dart, 1972), 32-33, 36-37.

regally clad figure of early portraiture gave way to a shambling, haunted old man in loose clothes and long white beard. One of his sons, the Duke of York, said that in death the king had the air of a venerable rabbi. To others his appearance recalled King Lear; and some may have known that during his breakdown in 1788-89 he had in fact requested a copy of Shakespeare's terrible story of royal collapse and ungrateful children. He muttered to himself or to imaginary companions. He played themes from Handel, his favorite composer, on harpsichord or flute. A few days after George's death, Princess Lieven wrote to Count Metternich: "There is something poetic in the picture of this old, blind king wandering about in his castle among shadows, talking with them; for he lived his life among the dead. " W. M. Thackeray, writing anonymously in *Punch*, saw him as oblivious to the climactic drama of the Napoleonic wars:

> *My guns roar'd triumph, but I never heard;*
> *All England thrilled with joy, I never stirred.*
>
> *What care I of pomp, or fame, or power, —*
> *A crazy old blind man in Windsor Tower?*

There was not much pity, though, in Byron's long poetic epitaph, *The Vison of Judgment*: "A worse king never left a realm undone!" Byron begins with a contemptuous dismissal of George III's burial service:

> *Of all*
> *The fools who flocked to see or swell the show,*
> *Who cared about the corpse? The funeral*
> *Made the attraction, and the black the woe,*
> *There throbbed not there a thought which pierced the pall;*
> *And when the gorgeous coffin was laid low,*
> *It seemed the mockery of hell to fold*
> *The rottenness of eighty years in gold.*

In the poem, when the king arrives at the bar of heaven he is at first unrecognized. An old radical politician of the 1760s, John Wilkes, is one of the figures summoned to give testimony. The weight of the evidence against the king is damning. But allowing him finally to slip into heaven amid great confusion, Byron conveys that in the last resort George's existence has mattered little, one way or the other.[4]

A similar derisive hostility breathes out from an epigram of 1855, by Walter Savage Landor, on the whole House of Hanover:

> *George the First was always reckoned*
> *Vile, but viler George the Second;*
> *And what mortal ever heard*
> *Any good of George the Third?*
> *When from earth the Fourth descended*
> *God be praised, the Georges ended!*

Again the hint ("descended") that hell is their destination. And the same jeering response is found, though more genially expressed, in a twentieth-century clerihew by E. C. Bentley:

> *George the Third*
> *Ought never to have occurred.*
> *One can only wonder*
> *At so grotesque a blunder.*

Detested or laughed at during his lifetime, George III was thus no better treated by posterity. And despite much scholarship devoted to George III's era, and his political situation, he was not a popular subject for biographers until recent years. Two sound biographies, by John Brooke and Stanley Ayling, appeared in 1972. Though they treat him fairly, they are not disposed to make extravagant claims for George III. Brooke's introduction concedes that "King George was neither a great king nor a great man. . . ." Ayling's postscript asserts: "The only greatness he could have was that which birth thrust upon him."[5]

George Washington, on the other hand, was vastly admired as soldier, patriot, and president. Paine praised him from time to time, for example in *Crisis* I, and

---

[4] On the king's death, see Peter Quennell, *Byron: The Years of Fame and Byron in Italy* (London: Collins, rev, ed., 1974), 364-65; "The Georges," *Punch* 9 (1845): 159. *Punch* was harder on the other Hanoverians — for example, on George II:

> I had neither morals, nor manners, nor wit;
> I wasn't much missed when I died in a fit.

Thomas Hardy's saga of the Napoleonic Wars, *The Dynasts*, likewise sees George III as if through the wrong end of a telescope. Thackeray's *Punch* doggerel became the basis of his subsequent lectures and book on *The Four Georges* (1855).

[5] John Brooke, *King George III* (London: Constable, 1972), xviii; Stanley Ayling, *George the Third* (London: Collins, 1972), 460.

dedicated the first part of the *The Rights of Man* to him ("I present you a small treatise in defense of those principles of freedom which your exemplary virtue hath so eminently contributed to establish"). In the second part (chapter 4), Paine referred to the election of Washington as president, assuming (not quite accurately) that this paragon had refused to receive any recompense. "The character and services of this gentleman are sufficient to put all those men called kings to shame. While they are receiving from the sweat and labors of mankind a prodigality of pay, to which neither their abilities nor their services can entitle them, he is rendering every service in his power, and refusing every pecuniary reward. He accepted no pay as commander-in-chief; he accepts none as president of the United States." The criticism Washington had met in life was far outweighed by the plaudits. At his death in 1799, at the age of 67, he was "first in war, first in peace, first in the hearts of his countrymen." He was universally eulogized. No satirist, even in Europe, would have dreamed of querying his place in heaven. The cynical Byron revered him. Posterity has agreed. There are innumerable biographies of George Washington, nearly all deeply respectful, some running to several volumes.[6]

There is no need to linger on the contrast between the two Georges. In broad terms it stands as the difference between a corrupt, vainglorious monarchical system and an honest, modest, competent republicanism. For most Americans, George III is and was a symbol of the bad old days, superseded by George Washington as the symbol of the good new days. Washington Irving (named after

---

[6] Instead of receiving an outright salary (set by Congress at $25,000 per annum), President Washington submitted expense claims against this figure — occasionally drawing in advance and slightly in excess. This has been made the subject of joking comment by the humorist Marvin Kitman, *George Washington's Expense Account* (New York: Simon & Schuster, 1970); and Washington's supposed extravagance was indeed denounced by a few Republican journalists during his second administration. There was a temporary sag in his reputation in Washington's last years. Otherwise, the chorus of praise, on both sides of the Atlantic, remained almost unanimous for many decades: see Marcus Cunliffe, *George Washington: Man and Monument* (rev. ed., New York: Mentor, 1982). Respect for Washington's attainments is implicit in current scholarship — e.g., in the ambitious new project, *The Papers of George Washington*, (ed. W. W. Abbot et al., Charlottesville: University of Virginia Press, 1983-   ); and in such biographies and monographs as Forrest McDonald, *The Presidency of George Washington* (Lawrence: University Press of Kansas, 1974); George W. Nordham, *George Washington: Vignettes and Memorabilia* (Philadelphia: Dorrance, 1977); Richard H. Kohn, *Eagle and Sword: The Federalists and the Creation of the Military Establishment in America, 1783-1802* (New York: Free Press, 1975); Charles Royster, *A Revolutionary People at War: The Continental Army and the American Character, 1775-1783* (Chapel Hill: University of North Carolina Press, 1979); Robert F. Jones, *George Washington: A Biography* (1979; rev. ed., New York: Fordham University Press, 1986); John R. Alden, *George Washington and the American Military Tradition* (Athens: University of Georgia Press, 1985); and T. H. Breen, *Tobacco Culture: The Mentality of the Great Tidewater Planter on the Eve of Revolution* (Princeton: Princeton University Press, 1985). Some of these assessments are sophisticatedly detached. Royster, for instance, believes (p. 257) that praise of George Washington, during his lifetime, ran to excess. Nevertheless, the extent of that adulation, in his life and posthumously, is not in doubt.

the exemplary soldier-president) encapsulates the drama of this supersession in his tale of Rip Van Winkle. Rip awakes from a twenty-year sleep which lasts right through the War of Independence. Among startling novelties, the old inn of his village has become the Union Hotel. On the inn sign "he recognized . . . the ruby face of King George, under which he had smoked so many a peaceful pipe; but even this was singularly metamorphosed. The red coat was changed for one of blue and buff, a sword was held in the hand instead of a scepter, the head was decorated in cocked hat, and underneath was painted in large characters, GENERAL WASHINGTON." In New York City the base of a destroyed statue of George III was used to accommodate one of Washington.

In other words, we tend to think of George III, in the American context, as Washington's unfortunate, unimpressive predecessor, at the fag end of the old order. We do not think of him as the American's contemporary, though in truth he was six years younger than Washington. We do not instinctively pair the lives of the two men. They seem not only different but separated by time, space, and sympathy.

This is odd, for closer scrutiny reveals such a number of resemblances that Irving's tale can be read to suggest the metamorphosis was not peculiar after all. Thus, both Georges were left fatherless at a quite early age (Washington at 11, the prince at 13: his father Frederick Louis, Prince of Wales, was the son of George II and never reigned). They were brought up by narrow-minded, commonplace mothers for whom neither was able to feel more than dutifully lukewarm affection. They were considerably influenced in their teens by youngish substitute father-figures (Washington's half-brother Lawrence; the prince's Scottish mentor the Earl of Bute).

Their courtships and marriages also followed similar patterns. Both Georges became infatuated with attractive young women named "Sally" or "Sarah" (Sally Fairfax; Lady Sarah Lennox) who were considered unsuitable (Sally Fairfax, née Cary, was already married, to the brother of Lawrence Washington's wife; Sarah Lennox, sister of the Duke of Richmond, was not of royal blood, but in any case disqualified as a member of a politically active family, related to the ambitious and not over-scrupulous M. P. Henry Fox). They went on to make socially appropriate marriages (Washington to the propertied widow Martha Dandridge Custis, George III to a German princess, Charlotte of Mecklenburg-Strelitz).They were conspicuously faithful to their wives (unlike many men of their day, including Alexander Hamilton and Benjamin Franklin), wives who were said to be pleasant in appearance and manner yet hardly beautiful.

The two Georges shared many of the same interests and social pleasures. Both were countrymen by habit, early to bed and early to rise, with a genuine interest in farming (more practical, of course, in Washington's case; yet the king's nickname of "Farmer George" was not undeserved: both men, for instance, corresponded with the celebrated English agriculturalist Arthur Young). They enjoyed country pastimes, especially horse-racing, riding and fox-and deer-hunts (both were excellent horsemen, willing to ignore the weather and spend long days in the saddle). They liked to travel, but in adult life never left their own countries. Washington at 19 made one voyage to Barbados; the Prince of Wales was rumored to have traveled in Scotland incognito with Lord Bute, but as king confined himself to the southern counties of England). They enjoyed music, dances, cards (though neither was a gambler) and going to the theater; they may have had the same favorite play, Joseph Addison's *Cato*, which abounds in familiar and edifying "quotations," for example,

> *'Tis not in mortals to command success,*
> *But we'll do more, Sempronius, we'll deserve it*

and

> *From hence, let fierce contending nations know*
> *What dire effects from civil discord flow.*

Prince George had been given a small juvenile role in a private reading of the play at the age of 10 and recited a prologue written for the occasion to link "great Cato's name" with latter-day defenders of constitutional liberty:

> *What, tho' a boy! It may with truth be said,*
> *A boy in England born, in England bred,*
> *Where freedom best becomes the earliest state,*
> *For there the love of liberty's innate*

Washington knew *Cato* as an adolescent and once wrote wistfully to tell Sally Fairfax how much he would like to perform in the play with her as heroine.[7]

The two leaders held other traits in common. They often showed courage, especially in adversity and when those around them were nervous. There are well-known instances of Washington's bravery in battle, for example, in crossing

---

[7] Ayling, *George The Third*, 28; Cunliffe, *George Washington*, 63; Paul L. Ford, *Washington and the Theatre* (New York, 1889).

the Delaware and in the near-disaster at Monmouth. As Prince of Wales, George Hanover had begged his grandfather George II to be allowed to join the army in 1759. As king he remained remarkably cool during the Gordon Riots which terrorized London in 1780, and again in 1786 when a madwoman tried to stab him in the street outside St. James's Palace. According to the novelist Fanny Burney, who was lady-in-waiting to the queen, "the King, the only calm and moderate person then present, called aloud to the mob, 'The poor creature is mad! Do not hurt her! She has not hurt me!' Then he came forward, and showed himself to all the people, declaring he was perfectly safe and unhurt; and then gave positive orders that the woman should be taken care of, and went into the palace, and had his levee".[8]

Both Georges handled the social graces in similar style. They could talk easily when relaxed and impress listeners at formal ceremonies with the dignity of their utterances, although neither was by nature a spellbinding orator. They could appreciate wit and intellect in others without being sparkling conversationalists. The king's sometimes ponderous efforts at bonhomie were ridiculed by sophisticates. But he was considerably hampered by the paralyzing etiquette of such exercises. He was required to initiate any conversation, and the other person was usually too inhibited to go beyond polite platitudes. His "What, what?" mannerisms may have developed out of the pressure upon him to start the talk and to keep it going. Horace Walpole, waspish in his later memoirs, wrote much more appreciatively of the young king at the time. "This sovereign," Walpole remarked in a letter, "don't stand in one spot, with his eyes fixed royally on the ground, and dropping bits of German news: He walks around and speaks to everybody." Walpole was referring to the tedium of the court under the previous king, George II. Now he was agreeably "surprised to find the levee-room had lost so entirely the air of the lion's den." It may be salutary to compare such occasions with a levee held in May 1789 by the newly installed President Washington, as recorded by the dour Senator William Maclay of Pennsylvania: "The President honored me with a particular *tête-à-tête*. 'How will this weather suit your farming?' 'Poorly, sir; the season is the most backward I have ever known. . . .' 'The fruit, it is to be expected, will be safe; backward seasons are in favor of it, but in Virginia it was lost before I left the place.' 'Much depends on the exposure of the orchard. Those with a northern aspect have been found by us [in Pennsylvania] to be the most certain of producing fruit.' 'Yes, that is a good observation and should be attended to.' Made my bow and retired." Poor

---

[8] Brooke, *King George III*, 67-68, 218, 314; Ayling, *George The Third*, 181-182.

Washington, poor Maclay, we feel: trapped in banality. It seems only fair to add: poor George III, who was no worse at the game than President Washington).[9]

The comparison between the two Georges can be extended. Both

—were generous in assisting people in distress (Washington, for example, in sending money to Lafayette's wife when her husband was imprisoned; the king in dozens of instances, as in his unobtrusive offer of a pension to Jean-Jacques Rousseau)

—lived in fairly high style, but were careful with their money, and so now and then were accused of being parsimonious

—were copious letter-writers, often in their own hand

—were industriously methodical (the king even to the point of dating his correspondence to the hour and the minute)

—had a high idea of their sworn duty to lead their nations and uphold the respective constitutions

—knowing themselves to be virtuous and conscientious, were apt to resent criticism (Washington perhaps rather more than George III)

—were members of the Church of England (after the Revolution, the Episcopalian Church in America), sturdily approving of its rituals without being fanatically devout

—believed that the army and government were best directed by "gentlemen"

—found their responsibilities burdensome, and occasionally dreamed of stepping down from office (the king drafted announcements of his

---

[9] There are good selections of Walpole's *Letters*, edited by Wilmarth S. Lewis (New Haven: Yale University Press, 1973); and of his other writings, edited by Matthew Hodgart (London: Batsford, 1963). The discrepancy between his immediate and his revised opinions is brought out in Martin Kallich, *Horace Walpole* (New York: Twayne, 1971). On the Washington levee, see *Journal of William Maclay* (New York: Appleton, 1890), 42-43. In 1790 Maclay (*Journal*, 204) went to a bookseller. "I bought Peter Pindar, whose sarcastic and satirical vein will write monarchy into disrepute in Britain. His shafts are aimed personally at his present Majesty, but many of them hit the throne, and will contribute to demolish the absurdity of royal government." Maclay was a prickly republican.

abdication in 1782 and 1783; Washington, reluctant to become president in 1789, and still more to be re-elected in 1792, was assured each time by associates that it might be possible for him to resign the office before completing the full term)[10]

—were afflicted by serious illnesses (the king in 1765, 1788-89, 1801 and 1810; Washington in 1768, then notably in 1789, with a tumor on the thigh, and from a dangerous bout of pneumonia in 1790), and were tired men in their later years in office

—received much adulation, and probably enjoyed some of it, yet resisted the dangers of arrogance and conceit (Washington sensibly stayed clear of the fuss in Congress over whether the president should be styled "highness," etc.; the young king rebuked some senior churchmen who had "bedaubed" him with praise in their sermons, saying that he came to hear the praises of God, not of himself).[11]

We could add details that in fact make George Hanover sound more American than George Washington. There is no record of Washington having played baseball, a game usually associated with the United States in the nineteenth century, though he may have done so — perhaps under the old English name of "rounders." Prince George, however, is mentioned in a letter of 1748 by Lady Hervey as having diverted himself with the other royal children, "at baseball, a play all who are or have been schoolboys are well acquainted with. The ladies as well as the gentlemen join in the amusement."[12] George Washington never lived in the White House, or "President's Palace" as it was occasionally called in the early years of its occupancy; for the White House did not come into use until the federal government moved to "Federal City," Washington, D.C., shortly after Washington died. King George, on the other hand, lived from 1772 at a small palace at Kew, a few miles outside London, whenever he was not obliged to be in the capital. His country residence had various names (Kew Palace, the Old Palace) but was often known as the "White House." It was pulled down in 1802

---

[10] Brooke, *King George III*, 221, 239-40; Cunliffe in *History of American Presidential Elections, 1789-1968*, ed. Arthur M. Schlesinger, Jr., and Fred L. Israel (New York: Chelsea House, 1971) 1: 14, 21-22.

[11] E. Pierce, *A Concise Biographical Memoir of His Late Majesty George the Third* (London, 1820), 137.

[12] Ayling, *George the Third*, 27-28.

or not long after the American White House began existence.[13] A popular belief but mistaken is that this got its name when repainted after the British had damaged the building in their raid on Washington during the War of 1812. A plausible explanation is that the name was borrowed from George III's old home.

There is a further ironical parallel. Tom Paine, we have seen, heaped scorn upon the "Royal Brute" again and again. A poem by Philip Freneau, on *The Rights of Man*, expresses the importance of Paine as the demythologizer of monarchy:

> *From Reason's source, a bold reform he brings,*
> *In raising up mankind, he pulls down kings,*
> *Who, source of discord, patron of all wrong,*
> *On blood and murder have been fed too long. . . .*
>
> *Be ours the task the ambitious to restrain,*
> *And this great lesson teach — that kings are vain; . . . .*
>
> *So shall our nation, form'd on Virtue's plan,*
> *Remain the guardian of the Rights of Man,*
> *A vast Republic, famed through every clime,*
> *Without a king, to see the end of time.*

In *Common Sense*, Paine even muckraked to the extent of spreading a story that George while Prince of Wales had seduced a young Quaker, Hannah Lightfoot, whose complaisant husband emigrated to Philadelphia.[14] But in 1796 Paine turned his wrath on George Washington. Living in France, he had been jailed for nearly a year and felt the United States had ignored his plight. He also believed that Washington's administration, unduly hostile to France, was leaning monarchically toward Britain. Paine's response was a tirade. General

---

[13] Brooke, *King George III*, 283.

[14] Freneau's poem is in Russel B. Nye and Norman S. Grabo, eds., *American Thought and Writing*, vol. 2, *The Revolution and the Early Republic* (Boston: Houghton Mifflin, 1965), 400-402. In other versions of the Hannah Lightfoot *canard* (see Brooke, 72, 389), their child emigrates to the United States or South Africa, takes the surname of Rex, and raises a family. As Brooke observes, such legends flourish despite an entire lack of supporting evidence. At least Paine probably believed the story, which cannot be said of the similar stories spread by British propagandists about George Washington, by concocting and printing supposedly intercepted letters. Some of these maneuvers are discussed in a pamphlet by John C. Fitzpatrick, *The George Washington Scandals* (Alexandria, Va., 1929); and in an article by Cunliffe, "The Washington Scandals," *Northern Virginia Heritage* (October 1982).

Washington, he asserted, had been mainly a figurehead. "You slept away your time in the field till the finances of the country" — rescued by French subsidies — "were completely exhausted, and you have but little share in the glory of the final event." President Washington started his new career "by encouraging and swallowing the grossest adulation." His typical demeanor was a "chameleon-colored thing, called *prudence*. It is in many cases a substitute for principle." Paine ended his denunciation: "And as to you, Sir, treacherous in private friendship (for so you have been to me, and that in the day of danger) and a hypocrite in public life, the world will be puzzled to decide whether you are an apostate or an imposter; whether you have abandoned good principles, or whether you ever had any."

Paine wrote other letters to (and against) George Washington. They were published as a pamphlet by the American journalist Benjamin Franklin Bache, the grandson of old Ben. Bache, Freneau, and a number of Republicans were highly critical of the president during his second administration, accusing him of prejudice against France and "Anglomaniac" subservience to royal Britain. Such attacks serve to emphasize how far conventional history has determined the record. The quasi-regal stiffness some of his contemporaries objected to in Washington and the suspicion that he was not possessed of great intellect, were not widely voiced during his lifetime, and then for a long time were ignored or mentioned as outrages by his biographers. Even before he died, he was half-sanctified. In the year after his demise almost nothing but eulogy was heard. Thus Robert Treat Paine (no relation to Tom) joined the chorus with a pious tribute, blandly declaring that the dead leader had been "inaccessible to human weakness." He passed into legend as "the perfect man."[15]

In the opposite way, the dominant historiography of the nineteenth century, British as well as American, forgot many aspects of George III's long reign, presenting him as a hopelessly imperfect king. Recent scholars have redressed the balance. They have pointed out that his illness of 1765 revealed no symptoms of insanity and was not interpreted as such until several decades had passed. They note that, though under great strain during the constitutional crises that punctuated the first half of his reign, including the grievous disappointments of

---

[15] Paine's *Letter to George Washington* (Paris, July 30, 1796) is reprinted in Harry Hayden Clark, ed., *Thomas Paine* (New York: Hill and Wang, 1961), 387-408, 434-436. His relation to Republican diatribes is analyzed in James D. Tagg, "Benjamin Franklin Bache's Attack on George Washington," *Pennsylvania Magazine of History and Biography* 100 (April 1976): 191-230. Paine's 1800 eulogy is mentioned (p. 53) in "The Flawless American: The Invention of George Washington," a chapter in Lawrence J. Friedman, *Inventors of the Promised Land* (New York: Knopf, 1975), 44-78. Friedman's chapter is admirable; but in this instance he has mixed up the two Paines. Tom Paine never recanted his hostile comments of 1796.

the War of Independence, George showed no sign of mental infirmity. It has been argued that his illness of 1788-89, which made him appear unhinged, was caused by a hereditary disease of the blood known as porphyria. When the disease struck again, he was becoming an old man. His blindness and senility were probably the product of age and not of insanity. If he had died at the same age as George Washington — that is, in 1805, and like Washington, still in possession of his faculties —our image of the "old, mad, blind, despised and dying king" might be different.[16]

Again, posterity tended to discount the obvious truth that "Farmer George" had been popular with most of his subjects for most of his reign. Especially when faced with war against France and the threat of invasion, the nation rallied to him as the symbol of patriotic unity. A broadside ballad of *c.* 1778 urged:

> *Now let's nobly advance,*
> *And crush the pride of France,*
> *Honour 'twill bring,*
> *Those who back the rebel's cause,*
> *Can never gain applause,*
> *Enemies to all laws,*
> *And George our king.*

Each stanza ended with "George our king." John Wilkes evolved, according to his lights, into a supporter of George. In the 1790s Gillray abandoned his caricatures of the royal household and started to jeer at the French (he too, poor man, was mentally unhinged during his last years). Peter Pindar, whose humor began to pall, also changed his tack. "The King," he confessed, "has been a good subject to me, but I have been a bad subject to his Majesty." John Adams disagreed with Jefferson on the reception given them by George III. He found the king open and manly, and not at all stupid. George's conversation was "agreeable and instructive. . . . His Majesty said as many things which deserved to be remembered as any Sage I ever heard." Adams's opinion was borne out by

---

[16] See Ida MacAlpine and Richard Hunter, *George III and the Mad-Business* (London: Allen Lane, The Penguin Press, 1969). A French-born American, whose English wife was the niece of Wilkes, was fascinated by the London print-shops in 1810. The French, he ruefully observed, were depicted as "diminutive, starved beings, of monkey-mien, strutting about in huge hats, narrow coats, and great sabres; an overgrown awkward Englishman crushes half a dozen of these pygmies at one squeeze." He also noted, however, that the English caricatured their own royal and other dignitaries, "often with cleverness . . . and a coarse sort of practical wit." Louis Simond, *An American in Regency England: The Journal of a Tour in 1810-1811*, ed. Christopher Hibbert (London: Pergamon, 1968), 28. He records (p. 124) seeing George III, apparently mad, on the terrace at Windsor.

all kinds of people who encountered George III, whether at court or informally. Samuel Johnson, one of a number of scholars given access to the magnificent library collected for George III, was charmed and impressed by a long talk with the monarch, whom he found well-informed and unassuming. Fanny Burney, despite the ceremonial tedium of court life, was grateful to the king and queen for their kindness to her and her musician-father, Dr. Burney; and she has left record to show that George's knowledge of literature was not negligible. His supposed comment to her that Shakespeare was "sad stuff" has been misquoted to imply a total indifference or ignorance. He was genuinely interested in astronomy, providing handsome support for William Herschel, the discoverer of the planet Uranus. The king once took the Archbishop of Canterbury to see Herschel's large telescope, which he had paid for, remarking with characteristic affability: "Come, my Lord Bishop, I will show you the way to heaven." George III founded the Royal Academy and amply rewarded its first two presidents, Sir Joshua Reynolds and the American-born Benjamin West.

Plenty of ordinary people thought well of George III: the citizens of Windsor, or those of Weymouth and Cheltenham who were hailed by him on his vacations, or folk who never saw him. A small church in Yorkshire still bears this inscription: "In the year of Our Lord 1809 when the People of the United Empire grateful for the Security and Happiness enjoyed under the Mild and Just Government of their Virtuous and Pious Monarch returned Solemn and Public Thanks to Almighty God that by the Protection of Divine Providence His Majesty King George the Third had been preserved to enter the fiftieth year of his Reign." Anecdotes stressed his decency, his bravery, his concern for the poor and oppressed, his lack of bigotry, and unaffectedness.

No doubt some of this praise was sycophantic, but hardly more so than in the case of George Washington. After Washington's death, Mason Weems produced his ingratiating *Life*, replete with stories about his hero and the cherry tree and so on. There was no exact equivalent in England to commemorate the supposed doings of George III. Yet in format and tone E. Pierce's *Biographical Memoir . . . of George the Third* (1820) is quite similar to Weems and to some of the eulogies hastily prepared in honor of the late president. The title-page of Pierce's modest compendium promised the reader *A Copious Collection of Royal Anecdotes, Respecting his Virtues, Religious Qualities, Talents, Munificence, Patriotism, &c.* — a pitch not unlike that of the enterprising "Parson" Weems, who told a publisher in 1800 that he meant to reveal Washington's "Great Virtues," such as "His . . . Religious Principles," "His Patriotism," and "His Magninimity" [sic]. Both chroniclers wished to humanize their heroes. "The glory of the MONARCH," Pierce's preface claimed, "was eclipsed by the goodness of the MAN; and his subjects loved to talk of him in his fireside enjoyments, rather than in his regal splendours." Pierce's compilation is in fact copiously anecdotal and more trustworthy than Weems. He quotes the comments of John Adams and Samuel Johnson and many other examples of royal generosity or bluffness. An example:

> *The king, some years ago, having purchased a horse, the dealer put into his hands a large sheet of paper, completely written over. "What's this?" said the King. "The pedigree of the horse which your Majesty has just bought," was the answer. "Take it back, take it back," said the King, laughing. "It will do just as well for the next horse you sell."*[17]

What is more, the notion of a friendly comparison of the two Georges did occur to at least one writer, the English poet-laureate Robert Southey. On the death of George III he was required to compose an appropriate elegy. His solution was a long poem on the apotheosis of the monarch, who arrives at the gate of heaven and is duly admitted, after the Devil has failed to find anyone willing to bear witness against the king. Southey called his poem *The Vision of Judgment*. Byron eventually gave the same title to a parody of Southey. Southey's *Vision*, a labored exercise, has been obliterated by Byron's scurrilous riposte. Perhaps Southey's poem deserves to be forgotten. Yet in it he contrives an intriguing encounter between George III and George Washington, who had never met on earth. Though no one will speak against the king, Washington with "Magninimity" speaks for him, saluting a former enemy:

> *And here, the witness I willingly bear thee, . . .*
> *Here, before Angels and Men, in the aweful hour of judgment. . . .*

> *Thou too didst act with upright heart, as befitted a Sovereign*
> *True to his sacred trust, to his crown, his kingdom, and people.*

> *Heaven in these things fulfill'd its wise,*
> *though inscrutable purpose,*
> *While we work'd its will, doing each in his place as became him.*

---

[17] Details of George III's tastes and temperament in Ayling, *George the Third*, 175-209; and Brooke, *King George III*, 260-317. The Yorkshire church inscription is noted in Asa Briggs, *The Age of Improvement* (London: Longmans Green, 1959), 183. On Mason Weems, see the introduction to his *Life of Washington*, ed. Cunliffe (Cambridge, Mass.: Harvard University Press, 1962). The horse anecdote is in Pierce, *Concise Biographical Memoir*, 146.

Twentieth-century historians might deem this a fair estimate of one head of state by another, whose problems as president were not entirely dissimilar to those of George as limited monarch — and whose opponents to his fury hinted that the behavior of the American George too closely followed that of the English one.

We should not of course make too much of the resemblances. The Hanoverian was reared as a prince, and before he was in his teens knew he was almost certain to become king, while the Virginian had to rely on his own exertions. As royalty, George III was set by protocol apart from and above the rest of his people. Everyone not of the immediate family was expected to remain standing in his presence, even senior ministers for discussions that might last for over an hour. Fanny Burney (Fanny D'Arblay, after her marriage) conveys in her memoirs the bone-weary boredom endured by court attendants, for example during a royal luncheon in Oxford, at which the dons in obedience to protocol assumed that only royalty must be seen to consume any food.[18]   George Washington never attempted or was accorded such a degree of deference. George III had fifteen children. He was a somewhat dictatorial parent, severely restricting their choices in matrimony. His daughters had almost no freedom of movement. So far as he could, he kept a tight rein on his sons; and, in the habitual manner of European royalty, was on increasingly bad terms with his eldest son and heir. As Prince of Wales he had himself conformed to the pattern: as king he continued it. Despite his domesticity, he was a disappointed and rather disappointing father, at least in the view of his male offspring. Washington, on the other hand, was childless, though he had a stepson and stepdaughter, both of whom died before their prime.[19]

Nevertheless, given that the two Georges had a surprising number of things in common, why have their historical reputations been so different?

Some of the answers are plain. In the eyes of posterity George Washington stands out as one of the world's few complete, satisfying, and deserved successes: a winner, superior by far to the monarchs of his era, yet putting the seal on his

[18] Brooke, *King George III*, 292. There are various editions of the diary and letters of Fanny D'Arblay, a respectful yet intelligent observer of court life. On Oxford, see, for example, *The Diary of Fanny Burney*, ed. Lewis Gibbs (London: Dent/Everyman, n.d.), 136-43. This royal visitation took place in 1786.

[19] See Bruce Mazlish, "The Psychological Dimension," in *Leadership in the American Revolution* (Washington: Library of Congress, 1974), 117-28. He argues that Washington was not a "revolutionary ascetic" (cf. Robespierre or Lenin); also that the loss of his father and of siblings may have induced a certain coolness or coldness of temperament; and that his identification with an older half-brother may be significant.

greatness by spurning any suggestion that he himself become an American king. By contrast, George III figures in the historical record as a maladroit loser, though not a born loser since he starts in front. Despite every advantage, somehow he loses America, he loses his mind, he loses all proper claim to posthumous admiration.

There is truth in Byron's charge that the king seemed invariably to stand on the *wrong* side of important questions, which according to progressive interpretations of history must ultimately be losing sides. His actions, being refusals to contemplate change, made him (in this light) a reactionary.[20] "Consecrated obstruction" defined his role — in relation to both the preliminary and the closing stages of the Revolutionary War, or, say, to the disabilities suffered by Catholics, which were removed without trouble in 1829, only nine years after his death. Paradoxically, George III may have failed to pursue enlightened policies because he was *not* an absolute monarch in the continental mold. If he had been he might have inclined to play the part of "enlightened despot." As it was, he obeyed his perceived duty to uphold the British constitution. Being the constitutional defender of the Protestant faith and remembering the fate of James II, how could he sanction Catholic emancipation? Likewise, he felt obliged to take a firm stand against the American colonies because Parliament had so decided. Some of his disparagers indirectly conceded that he was curbed by the constitution; after the Revolutionary War, in guying his alleged stupidity or insanity, they implied that he was a "limited" monarch, if only because his intellect was so limited.

His posthumous reputation, in Britain as in America, would have been higher if he had died ten or twenty years sooner, instead of lingering on as apparent proof that inbred royalty were mentally deficient or deranged. Though George III was vastly more respectable than his sons, their extravagances and marital follies effaced rather than heightened his own good name. The Prince Regent (George IV) was a battered old roué when he at last reached the throne in 1820 and did little to mend matters during his ten-year reign. The death of his succeeding brother William IV in 1837 ended the span of Hanoverian rule. By then monarchy appeared to have only a precarious hold in Britain. George III was lumped together with the primal George I, with his grumpy grandfather George II, and with his flabby son George IV. Writers such as Thackeray treated the "Four Georges" with irreverent disapproval.

---

[20] Byron, (see Peter Quennell, *Byron in Italy*, 364-65), while radical in some respects, retained the snobbery of an aristocrat. He regarded reformers like Henry Hunt as "low, designing, dirty levellers, who would pioneer their way to a democratical tyranny." Thistlewood and his little band of fanatics, who in 1820 plotted to assassinate the cabinet and proclaim a British republic, were scorned by Byron as "desperate fools."

Historians of the dominant Whig school in nineteenth-century Britain, in tune with their scholarly contemporaries in the United States, decided that parliamentary critics of George III like Edmund Burke had been correct. The king, that is, had deliberately and ominously attempted to reverse the flow of British history. He had used bribery and coercion in trying to recover royal prerogatives no longer sanctioned by the constitution. These charges have been refuted or diminished by twentieth-century historians.[21] They are, however, an important factor in explaining how George III's symbolic role became that of booby and/or monster, while George Washington's reputation as exemplary republican leader soared still higher.

If Americans needed corroboration that they were well rid of George III, they could thus get it from British sources. In American folklore he was established almost like the villain in popular melodrama, booed or hissed whenever he came on stage, or even when his name was mentioned. For example, in 1854 Walt Whitman wrote an angry poem about the arrest in Boston of the fugitive slave Anthony Burns. He was appalled that such a scene should have taken place in Boston, the cradle of the Revolution. Whitman imagines a seemingly patriotic parade through the streets of the city, attended by the ghosts of the old Yankee warriors of the 1770s. But it is actually a parade of "the President's marshal," come to seize Anthony Burns under the federal Fugitive Slave Law. The phantom veterans are bewildered and dismayed. Whitman suggests they do not belong at a spectacle of this nature:

[21] The controversy is usefully laid out in E. A. Reitan, ed., *George III: Tyrant or Constitutional Monarch?* (Boston: D. C. Heath, 1964), which provides excerpts from such hostile scholars as Thomas Erskine May and W.E.H. Lecky, together with a reasoned defense by Sir Lewis Namier and some in-between opinions. See also Richard Pares, *King George III and the Politicians* (Oxford: University Press, 1953); and Herbert Butterfield, *George III and the Historians* (London: Collins, 1957), which is critical of Whig assumptions but also regards George III as ambitious and pigheaded. The issue is still not quite dead: see John Brewer, *Party Ideology and Popular Politics at the Accession of George III* (Cambridge: University Press, 1976). But the cruder contentions of the Whig case have been abandoned. The king's conduct and outlook are carefully analyzed in Bernard Donoughue, *British Politics and the American Revolution, 1773-1775* (London: Macmillan, 1964), at one crucial period. He concludes (p. 163) that by 1774 George III was quite closely acquainted with American issues. The king spoke self-righteously of "doing my Duty" (p. 278) — a favorite word, incidentally, with George Washington also. Donoughue believes the king's smugness was unattractive: "Yet it was allied with a concern for his true duty as Monarch, and with the courage to carry out that duty as he saw it. Responsibility, loyalty, courage, complacency and priggishness were probably the five main ingredients of George III's character. None of them . . . caused him to lose his American Colonies. The forces at work there were much wider than a King or Government could master. But these royal qualities were certainly factors influencing the manner in which Britain faced up to the colonial crisis." See also Carl B. Cone, "George III — America's Unknown King," in Lawrence S. Kaplan, ed., *The American Revolution and "A Candid World"* (Kent, Ohio: Kent State University Press, 1977), 1-16.

> *But there is one thing that belongs here. . . . Shall I tell*
> *you what it is, gentlemen of Boston?*
> *I shall whisper it to the Mayor . . . he shall send a*
> *committee to England,*
> *They shall get a grant from the Parliament, and go with*
> *a cart to the royal vault.*
> *Dig out King George's coffin . . . unwrap him quick from*
> *his graveclothes . . . box up his bones for a journey*

George III's coffin is brought to Boston and another grand parade arranged:

> *Look! all orderly citizens . . . look from the windows women.*
> *The committee open the box and set up the regal ribs and*
> *glue those that will not stay,*
> *And clap the skull on top of the ribs, and clap a crown on*
> *top of the skull.*
> *You have got your revenge old buster! . . . The crown is*
> *come to its own and more than its own.*

A year later, in a worried comment on the moral wrong of chattel slavery, Abraham Lincoln recalled the time "when we were the political slaves of King George, and wanted to be free." The "self-evident truth" of human equality proclaimed in the Declaration of Independence had become a "*self-evident lie.*" Strictly speaking, Whitman and Lincoln were, of course, unjust to George III. But the injustice went back to Jefferson's draft of the Declaration which, focusing blame upon the king, had charged him not only with maintaining the slave trade but with inciting American slaves to rise against their masters. The inconsistency in the colonists' position — asserting that the king wished to "enslave" them, yet affirming their own right to retain chattel slavery — returned to bedevil them. In the 1850s, however, and for long afterward, George III, "old buster," continued mainly to supply a convenient rhetorical antithesis to the vaunted national values of republican democracy.[22]

---

[22] I am grateful to Hubert J. Cloke of Georgetown University for drawing my attention to Whitman's poem, untitled in the 1855 edition of *Leaves of Grass*, later (in slightly revised form) known as "A Boston Ballad." For the ruminations of Lincoln, see Roy P. Basler, ed., *Collected Works of Abraham Lincoln*, 9 vols. (New Brunswick, N.J.: Rutgers University Press, 1953). For a brilliantly quirky investigation of Jefferson's ideas in 1776, see Garry Wills, *Inventing America: Jefferson's Declaration of Independence* (Garden City, N.Y.: Doubleday, 1978). The "old buster" still has his uses for America. As a semiradical criticizing official America, Justice William O. Douglas said in 1971: "We must realize that today's establishment is the new George III. Whether it will continue to

What he was "really" like was therefore irrelevant. History in this respect is what posterity prefers to think happened. In retrospect, and with varying degrees of enthusiasm, British liberal opinion approved both of the American Revolution and the institution of monarchy. Washington, the Virginia soldier-statesman, was likewise approved — indeed wholeheartedly in Britain, as if he represented the constitutional monarch of an ideally reformed British system. These interpretations distinguished, so far as Britain was concerned, between the institution of monarchy and the actual sovereigns. The former was seen as good — a traditional office, making for stability in a topsy-turvy world in which the crash of thrones led (as in France) merely to chaos and new despotism. The latter, in the shape of the Hanoverian line, were regarded as deplorable and barely tolerable — with the result that the young Queen Victoria and her German consort Prince Albert were by no means instantaneously and universally acclaimed in Britain.

There were many ironies in history's treatment of the two Georges.[23] As in life, still more in death, their manifold similarities of characters and even of role were distorted. What was lauded as coolness in Washington was taken for dullness in George III. The president's firmness was contrasted with the king's obstinacy. To some extent Washington was felt by Americans to have replaced George III. The king had been their parent: now Washington was venerated as *Pater Patriae*, the father of his people. Being childless, his hagiographers hinted, he took on paternity for all America, and of course removed any temptation to consider the presidency as a hereditary office entrusted to the Washington family. This was fortunate for the young nation. The very idea that George Washington *was* a superior surrogate for George III implied that the presidency itself was a semi-regal office. Washington's way of conducting it, with levees, official birthdays, and "royal" progresses to various regions of the United States, aroused the suspicion of men like Maclay and Bache that the transition to republicanism was

adhere to its tactics we do not know. If it does, the redress, honored in tradition, is also revolution." Another example of mid-nineteenth-century rhetoric occurs in the melodramatic, fictionalized *Legends of the American Revolution . . . Or, Washington and His Generals* (1847) by George Lippard, in one scene in which George III is transported in a vision of 1780 to Washington's suffering yet defiant encampment at Valley Forge. The suggestion is that the monarch's madness is induced by the sight of this misery and the knowledge that he is himself to blame. The king's craziness is contrasted to the solemn dignity of Washington.

[23] Some of these ironies were belatedly recognized in the United States — for instance, in a Thomas Nast cartoon showing the amusement of old King George at America's failure to remove the abuses of which he had been charged; and in the later writings of Mark Twain, such as "The Secret History of Eddypus," revealing Twain's pessimistic conviction that, as George Washington anticipated, the nation would one day relapse into despotic monarchy. See, e.g., David Ketterer, ed., *The Science Fiction of Mark Twain* (Hamden, Conn.: Archon Books, 1984), 184-85.

incomplete and reversible. It was therefore the more necessary, after Washington's retirement (abdication?) in 1797, and still more after his death in 1799, to insist on the gulf between him and George Guelf. The need to define a separate national identity demanded that America's first president be absolutely differentiated from her last king. Washington must be as exalted as George III was execrated.[24] Still other ironies, however, present themselves: such as whether George Washington was nevertheless in a way the first elective monarch of the new United States.[25]

This essay appeared in *American Studies International* 24 (October 1986): 53-73.

[24] Friedman, *Inventors of the Promised Land*, 44-78; Cunliffe, *George Washington*; Daniel J. Boorstin, *The Americans: The National Experience* (New York: Random House, 1965), 337-56; James T. Flexner, *George Washington: Anguish and Farewell, 1793-1799* (Boston: Little, Brown, 1972); Robert P. Hay, "George Washington: American Moses," *American Quarterly* 21 (Winter 1969): 780-791; Tagg, "Bache's Attack on George Washington"; James H. Hutson, "John Adams' Title Campaign," *New England Quarterly* 41 (March 1968): 30-39. The equivocalness of Washington's place in American affection, even before he became president, is indicated in a letter of January 1785 from Jefferson in Paris to Governor Henry. The state of Virginia had resolved to commission a statue of Washington; Jefferson and Franklin were to choose the artist. Jefferson recommended Houdon, who was "resorted to for the statues of most of the sovereigns of Europe." Houdon "was so anxious to be the person who should hand down the figure of the General to future ages, that . . . he offered to abandon his business here, to leave the statues of kings unfinished, and to go to America to take the true figure by actual inspection and mensuration" — which he did. William Wirt Henry, *Patrick Henry: Life, Correspondence and Speeches* (1891, reprint, New York: Burt Franklin, 1969), 2: 263. The notion of Washington as a novelly nonauthoritarian leader is imaginatively presented in Jay Fliegelman, *Prodigals and Pilgrims: The American Revolution against Patriarchal Authority, 1750-1800* (Cambridge: Cambridge University Press, 1982); and in Garry Wills, *Cincinnatus: George Washington and the Enlightenment* (Garden City, N.Y.: Doubleday, 1984).

[25] Recent scholarly speculation along these lines includes M. J. Heale, *The Presidential Quest: Candidates and Images in American Political Culture 1787-1852* (London and New York: Longman, 1982), as well as work by Ralph Ketcham and Richard P. McCormick. See also Marcus Cunliffe, "The Invention of the Presidency," *The Great Ideas Today* (Chicago: Encyclopaedia Britannica, Inc., 1987), 157-221.

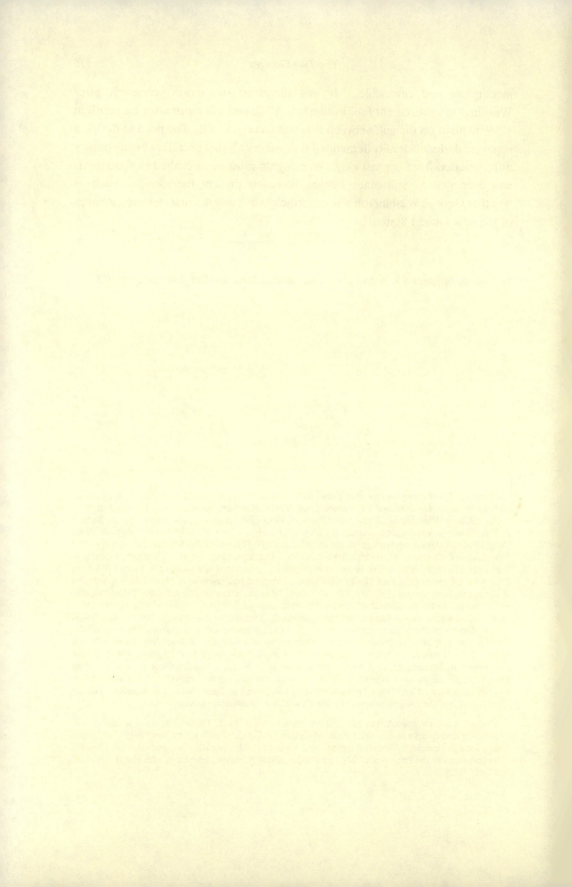

9

The Doubled Images of Washington and Lincoln

Each year on the anniversary of Abraham Lincoln's beautiful little Gettysburg battlefield dedication, Gettysburg College now offers a Fortenbaugh Lecture dealing with Lincoln's involvement in the Civil War or in other matters. My contribution was delivered there in November 1987. The lecture was illustrated with about fifty slides. I hope it does not suffer unduly in print when deprived of this quantity of visual support.

Two identical nuclear-power aircraft carriers are currently under construction at Newport News, Virginia, at a conjectured cost of $3.5 billion apiece. They are proclaimed to be the biggest and the best of their kind. It seems altogether appropriate that they are to be named the *Abraham Lincoln* and the *George Washington*.[1] For, to all appearances, Lincoln and Washington (or Washington and Lincoln? In many contexts the order is reversible) loom over the rest of American history and even today are omnipresent images. Washington is on the dollar bill and on the twenty-five cent coin. Lincoln has pride of place on the lowly penny and the modestly substantial five-dollar note. Theirs are the monuments, lined up along the same axis as the Capitol, that greet the visitor to the District of Columbia — itself named in honor of the nation's first President. The recent Vietnam Memorial is deliberately angled to point in one direction to the shrine of Lincoln and in the other to the soaring obelisk of the Washington Monument.

---

[1] *Washington Post*, September 26, 1987, A11.

A few years ago they were represented together in profile on a postage stamp, Washington in pure white and Lincoln in complementary black (Photo 1). Their primal duality is emphasized in a mass of earlier visual renderings and inscriptions. Sometimes these renderings allotted different yet equal roles to the two men: Washington as father of his country, Lincoln as the nation's noblest son; Washington as founder of the Union, Lincoln as its savior. Sometimes the point was to suggest that they were incomparable except in their resemblance to each other. In fairly typical vein, a 1941 issue of *Lincoln Lore* declared: "No two names in American history are more often associated than those of Washington and Lincoln. When you hear one name pronounced, you expect to hear the other in almost the same breath. When you see a portrait of one, you expect to see a profile of the other facing it." The article goes on to list evident parallels, such as English ancestry, lack of regular or advanced education, youthful athletic prowess, experience as surveyors, deserved reputation for honesty, military and presidential involvements, and — needless to say — the closeness of their birthdays. "The period between February 12 and February 22," said *Lincoln Lore*, "has now become somewhat of a Festival of Patriotism, and more emphasis is being placed on the interval each year." Similar notions were voiced by Theodore Roosevelt in a presidential address at Arlington National Cemetery, on Decoration Day, 1902: "Washington and Lincoln . . . stand head and shoulders above all our other public men, and have by common consent won the right to this pre-eminence." Their birthdays were public holidays. But there should be "few such holidays. To increase their number is to cheapen them." In a further address at Valley Forge in June 1904, where Roosevelt's main subject was George Washington, he remarked: "I am not here to say anything about Lincoln, but I do not see how any American can think of either of them without thinking of the other too, because they represent the same work." Roosevelt went on to draw matching lessons from the twin "landmarks of history," Gettysburg and Valley Forge, the first signifying a "single tremendous effort," the other a "long-sustained" endurance.[2]

The nearness has even led to a further tendency to collapse the two heroes into a single composite persona. Charlie Brown's sister, in a *Peanuts* cartoon, sets out

---

[2] *Lincoln Lore*, no. 621 (March 3, 1941); *Address and Papers of Theodore Roosevelt*, ed. Willis Fletcher Johnson (New York: Unit Book Publishing, 1909), 48-49, 147-48, 208-10. *Lincoln Lore* has raised its contributions to a significant scholarly level under the editorship of Mark E. Neely, Jr., director of the Louis A. Warren Lincoln Library and Museum, Fort Wayne, Indiana, which houses an excellent collection of visual and other research material. There are some paired Washington-Lincoln prints in *The Lincoln Image* by Harold Holzer, Gabor S. Boritt, and Mark E. Neely, Jr. (New York: Scribner's, 1984).

1. U.S. Postage Stamp, 1984.

to tell her class about George Washington, turns out to have sketched Lincoln instead, but carries on as if the mistake hardly matters. The writer Mary McCarthy recalls how, at school in the 1920s, teachers expected students to declare a preference for one man over the other — to determine, that is, whether "Mount Vernon [would] outshine a log cabin and a powdered wig a scraggly set of chin whiskers."[3] In grade school, twenty years later, the budding poet Sylvia Plath also encountered and was bewildered by the supreme figures of the American pantheon:

> *Every morning, hands on hearts, we pledged allegiance to the Stars and Stripes . . . and sang songs full of powder smoke and patriotics to impossible, wobbly, soprano tunes. One fine, high song, "For purple mountain majesties above the fruited plain," always made the scampi-sized poet in me weep. In those days I couldn't have told a fruited plain from a mountain majesty and confused God with George Washington (whose lamblike granny-face shone down at us . . . from the schoolroom wall between neat blinders of white curls).*[4]

Commerce and Congress have added to the confusion by merging the two anniversaries into one super-sale event, the "Presidents' Birthday," in order to reawaken the American consumer from possibly unpatriotic post-Christmas torpor (Photo 2). For American children, the blurring may have another and quite old element. Little Sylvia Plath perceived George Washington as a sort of androgynous "granny", thanks to his spotless wig. "She is very sleepy, George Washington," Gertrude Stein oracularly remarked in her *Four in America* (1947). The bewhiskered Lincoln could hardly be mistaken for a woman. Yet he is commonly described as covering his shoulders with a shawl and as displaying a grandmotherly tenderness for youngsters in trouble. The duo are not merely

---

[3] Mary McCarthy, "Personal History," *New Yorker*, July 14, 1986, 34-36.

[4] Sylvia Plath, *Johnny Panic and the Bible of Dreams* (New York: Harper & Row, 1980), 52-53. I owe this reference, with other interesting material, to Mary V. Dearborn, *Pocahontas's Daughters: Gender and Ethnicity in American Culture* (New York: Oxford University Press, 1986), 87-88. And see Edmond S. Meany, *Lincoln Esteemed Washington* (Seattle: Frank McCaffrey, 1933), 5: "The American People love to honor Lincoln and Washington above all their National Heroes — not least in the annual ceremonies of commemoration in our second month's precious fortnight, containing the pair of birthday anniversaries."

2. Presidents' Day at Safeway, advertisement, *The Washington Post,* February 10, 1978. Courtesy of Safeway Inc.

fathers but parents.[5]

Are Washington and Lincoln then the only significant American heroes? Obviously not. For one thing, two other mammoth aircraft carriers, of the same "Nimitz" class, have been budgeted for. Washington D.C. is a city of monuments. In addition to our pair, Thomas Jefferson has his lavish marble rotunda, and dozens of other figures (nearly all male) are commemorated there. The earliest post-Revolutionary epic poem, Joel Barlow's *Vision of Columbus* (1787), placed the great explorer at the center of his drama. He was, so to speak, the guest of honor, preceding Washington and Lincoln, in the "Columbian Ode" recited by Harriet Monroe in October 1892, to mark the four-hundredth anniversary of Columbus' landfall, and the opening of the World's Columbian Exposition in Chicago. A juvenile biography of the same epoch, *Abraham Lincoln: Plough-Boy, Statesman, Patriot*, began by announcing: "The names of three men — Christopher Columbus, George Washington, and Abraham Lincoln — stand apart in the history of America. The first of the three . . . was an Italian, who discovered the New World. The second was an Englishman, who founded the United States. And the third was an American, who saved the Union and gave freedom to the slave."[6] No doubt 1992 will be another big occasion for the sailor from Genoa.

Benjamin Franklin too has exercised a powerful hold over the American imagination, symbolizing North American rather than hemispheric characteristics. Franklin, we are told, came a close second to Washington as an exemplary figure in the nation's nineteenth-century schoolbooks; and he is still far from negligible in the reckoning.[7] Parson Weems's famous *Life of Washington* (the one that introduces the story of the hatchet and the cherry-tree) has Ben Franklin on hand

---

[5] Looking back on his boyhood in upstate New York, the novelist Henry James recalled a venerable great aunt, "a model of antique spinsterhood" who bore a "striking resemblance to the portraits, the most benignant, of General Washington. She might have represented the mother, no less adequately than he represented the father, of their country." *Notes of a Son and Brother*, chapter 13 (1914; reprinted in Henry James, *Autobiography*, ed. Frederick W. Dupee, New York: Criterion Books, 1956), 508. A print to commemorate the 28th annual convention of the National American Woman Suffrage Association (1896) shows five etherealized figures, mantled in skirtlike robes. George Washington is in the center, with Susan B. Anthony and Elizabeth Cady Stanton on either side, and flanking females to represent Utah and Wyoming (first to confer womanhood suffrage). See Martha Banta, *Imaging American Women: Idea and Ideals in Cultural History* (New York: Columbia University Press, 1987), 547-548. The Stein quotation is from *Four in America* (1947) in Karal Ann Marling, *George Washington Slept Here* (Cambridge, Mass.: Harvard University Press, 1988), 336. Stein is referring to the standard Gilbert Stuart portrait of Washington.

[6] Wlliam G. Rutherford, *Abraham Lincoln: Plough-Boy, Statesman, Patriot* (London: Sunday School Union, n.d.), 9.

[7] Ruth Miller Elson, *Guardians of Tradition: American Schoolbooks of the Nineteenth Century* (Lincoln: University of Nebraska Press, 1964), 190-91.

3. Charles Shober, *Behold Oh America, Your Sons. The Greatest among Men*, Chicago, 1865. Lithograph. Library of Congress, Prints and Photographs Division.

to greet Washington on arrival in heaven — Franklin having got there ahead of him — as if to indicate that Washington, "first in war, first in peace, and first in the hearts of his countrymen," was not quite first in *every* such competition. Among conspicuously prominent presidents are Jefferson; Andrew Jackson, who forever tips his hat to the West in Clark Mills's bold equestrian statue within full view of the White House; another soldier-president, Ulysses S. Grant; Theodore Roosevelt; his Democratic rival, Woodrow Wilson; and Teddy Roosevelt's distant cousin, another Democrat, Franklin D. Roosevelt. One could name also-rans, who in their day had thousands of devoted admirers. The "godlike" orator, Senator Daniel Webster, for example, appealed to the biographer George Ticknor of New England as second only to George Washington in his soaring dedication to the "great institutions of the country," which reciprocally "have inspired and called forth the greatest efforts of his uncommon mind." Webster was for Ticknor like the mythical giant Antaeus, who maintained his strength through renewed contact with his native soil.[8]

Jefferson and Teddy Roosevelt make a foursome with Washington and Lincoln in the epic heroes' gallery blasted out of a cliff by Gutzon Borglum and his workmen at Mount Rushmore, South Dakota, between the world wars. General Grant's prestige stood extraordinarily high up until his death in 1885 and beyond. If Washington had founded and Lincoln preserved the Union, Grant was the warrior who safeguarded it. A design for a medallion celebrating Grant's elevation to the presidency showed him profiled with Washington and Lincoln as the TRIUMVIRI AMERICANI (PATER 1789, SALVATOR 1861, CUSTOS 1869). Grant's funeral was staged as an event of awesome significance, on a scale to match the obsequies for his two great predecessors. When the coffin arrived by train in New York, according to Grant's popular biographer William Makepeace Thayer, the city "was arrayed in mournful emblems so elaborate that the market of black fabrics was exhausted. Nothing like it was ever witnessed in that city." Thayer estimated that several hundred thousand people must have filed past the coffin while the dead man lay in state.[9]

Thayer, who also produced biographies of Washington and Lincoln (in addition to *Benjamin Franklin: From Printing Office to the Court of St. James*), strove to prove that Grant belonged from childhood with the other two. He retailed an

---

[8] David B. Tyack, *George Ticknor and the Boston Brahmins* (Cambridge, Mass.: Harvard University Press, 1967), 213-16.

[9] William M. Thayer, *From The Tan-Yard to the White House*, (London: Hodder & Stoughton, 1885), 402.

anecdote of the ardently American ten-year old Ulysses feeling obliged to fight (and overcome) a no less ardently pro-British Canadian cousin who had dared to call Washington a "rebel" and a "traitor." Thayer depicted young Grant as a lover of sports, who had little formal learning, like Washington and Lincoln, and found "no school great enough to educate him," save the school of hard knocks. As late as 1899, when the Hall of Fame was opened in Brooklyn, Grant tied with Lincoln in second place, just behind Washington, when Americans were invited to vote for their favorite heroes.[10]

In addition to this uplifting trilogy, Thayer churned out a juvenile life of James A. Garfield, *From Log Cabin to White House*, likewise a bestseller, described in promotional literature as "pre-eminently suitable for presents, prizes, and school libraries." Horatio Alger, another prolific rags-to-riches author, included among his self-help homilies *Abraham Lincoln, the Young Backwoods Boy; or, How a Young Rail Splitter Became President* (1883) and a companion treatment, *From Canal Boy to President; or, The Boyhood and Manhood of James A. Garfield* (1891) — the latter of these echoing the title of Thayer's already published *George Washington: His Boyhood and Manhood*.[11] Garfield not only shared with Lincoln early poverty and a yearning for self-betterment: he died from an assassin's bullet in 1881. Twenty years later the same fate caused the death of President William McKinley. He, Garfield, and Lincoln were bracketed as the trio of Republican martyrs. At his death, McKinley too received the accolade of a grand funeral and a mass of eulogies. The assassination of John F. Kennedy in 1963 brought something of the same shock, anger, and upsurge of communal emotion. Americans could all recall what they were doing when they first heard of the shooting of President Kennedy, in the same way their ancestors would always remember how the news from Ford's Theatre had crashed upon them. Little Jane Addams in Illinois, four-year-old daughter of a founding member of Lincoln's Republican party, recounts in her autobiography her father's grim

---

[10] William M. Thayer, *From the Tan-Yard to the White House*, 32-38. In July 1865 old Winfield Scott sent a telegram to Grant, "from the oldest general to the ablest." Grant's biographer, William S. McFeely (*Grant: A Biography*, New York: W. W. Norton, 1981, 235) justly calls this a graceful tribute. It may however also carry another allusion, rather more in keeping with Scott's reputation for vanity. In apocryphal legend, Frederick the Great once presented a sword to the comparatively youthful George Washington, with the same inscription. If, as seems likely, Scott was drawing upon this well-known old story, he was paying a double compliment: to Grant as a second Washington, and to himself as another Frederick the Great. The Hall of Fame information comes from Barry Schwartz, *George Washington: The Making of an American Symbol* (New York: Free Press, 1987), 197 — a book full of instructive comments.

[11] John G. Cawelti, *Apostles of the Self-Made Man: Changing Concepts of Success in America* (Chicago: University of Chicago Press, 1965), 96, 266; Richard M. Huber, *The American Idea of Success* (New York: McGraw-Hill, 1971, reprint Pushcart Press, 1987), 50-52.

intimation that "the greatest man in the world had died." Henry James, beginning his author's career in Boston, confesses long afterward to a memory of "shame": the "dawn of April 15th," when Lincoln died, was also the dawn of James's twentieth birthday.[12]

The caisson that bore John F. Kennedy's coffin had been used for Franklin Roosevelt in 1945. In the sequence of American presidential heroes, F.D.R. is frequently ranked today with Washington and Lincoln: by some criteria he even stands above them.[13] If Borglum's Mount Rushmore were being executed after 1945, we may presume that a place would have been found for the second Roosevelt.

Nevertheless Lincoln and Washington do still stand apart from all others in the American pantheon, with the arguable exception of F.D.R.   Franklin is undoubtedly famous and admired.   Inventors and authors — Edison, Emerson, Whitman, Twain — are certainly accorded a place.   But they do not quite attain the front rank.   That, apparently, is reserved for political-cum-military leaders, who unlike Webster (or Lincoln's idol Henry Clay) actually reach the White House. Assassination, it is claimed, greatly enhances their placement; but, unlike Garfield and perhaps Kennedy, they must hold office for a reasonably long span.

---

[12] Chapter two of Addams's autobiography, *Twenty Years at Hull-House* (1910), where this memory is preserved, is entitled "The Influence of Lincoln." See Allen F. Davis, *American Heroine: The Life and Legend of Jane Addams* (New York: Oxford University Press, 1973), 163-64; and Henry James, *Autobiography*, 490-91. Kennedy's funeral procession passed near to the Lincoln Memorial on the way to Arlington National Cemetery. The marchers could catch sight of Daniel Chester French's seated figure of Lincoln: "many ... [looked] upward to the brooding head of stone. The band fell silent as it rounded the shrine; only the drums were heard." United Press International and American Heritage Magazine, *Four Days: The Historical Record of the Death of President Kennedy* (New York, American Heritage, 1964), 117.   A cartoon by Bill Mauldin (p. 133) showed French's Lincoln huddled forward, hands over eyes in grief.

[13] Two polls of presidential greatness, conducted in 1948 and 1962 by Arthur M. Schlesinger, Sr., ranked the top figures in the same order:
1. Abraham Lincoln
2. George Washington
3. Franklin D. Roosevelt
4. Woodrow Wilson
5. Thomas Jefferson

A subsequent, more elaborate ordering asked questions about prestige, strength, activity, idealism, practicality, and flexibility. The combined scores of these rated the top five as 1. Lincoln; 2. F. D. Roosevelt; 3. Washington; 4. Jefferson; 5. Theodore Roosevelt, in Gary M. Maranell, "The Evaluation of Presidents: An Extension of the Schlesinger Polls," *Journal of American History* 57 (June 1970): 104-13; and see Dale Keith Simonton, *Why Presidents Succeed: A Political Psychology of Leadership* (New Haven, Conn.: Yale University Press, 1987). In 1982, Robert K. Murray and Tim H. Blessing devised a full and carefully weighted questionnaire and continued to analyze data: see their *Greatness in the White House: Rating the Presidents, Washington through Carter. Final Report, The Presidential Performance Study* (University Park: Pennsylvania State University Press, 1988). Some assessments, though not Murray-Blessing, place Washington in a somewhat artificial "presidential" category and so disguise his standing on a more generalized "hero" level.

Other positive factors include, it is said, holding office during wartime, tallness (an obvious plus for Washington, Jefferson, Lincoln, and F.D.R.), pre-presidential authorship, energetic use of the the veto power, and a high rate of cabinet turnover.[14] However, these comparative presidential ratings, no matter how ingeniously calibrated, fail to fit the special case of George Washington and may tend to underpraise other figures, women among them.[15]

Among non-presidential candidates, military service alone is not enough. Some heroes, such as Robert E. Lee, have too sectional an appeal, though they may be revered in their own part of the country. Some, like Webster and Grant, are held to fall from grace, during or after their own lifetimes.

As for our Washington-Lincoln pair, it is worth noting that Borglum's original design, to be carved out of granite "needles" near to Mount Rushmore, was for two and only two gigantic standing figures — those (need we specify?) of Washington and Lincoln. Theodore Roosevelt vehemently disapproved of certain predecessors, among them Jefferson (this "scholarly, timid, and shifting doctrinaire" — the right person, one might think, to be on the never-quite-accepted $2 bill). Roosevelt's primary division was between the "weak" presidents, among whom he singled out James Buchanan and William Howard Taft, and the "strong" (Lincoln, Jackson, and Washington, plus himself by implication). After Theodore Roosevelt's death his widow gently discouraged talk of a monument to be erected in his memory in the nation's capital. They had always felt, she said, that the city belonged to Washington and Lincoln, whose basic primacy should remain unchallenged.[16]

We may note parenthetically that this virtuous, self-denying stance was more honored by politicians in the breach than in the observance. However, a more important issue is to explain the stages by which Lincoln attained parity with Washington, and then came to be even more idolized by most Americans than his great predecessor.

---

[14] Simonton, 188-195.

[15] Oddly enough, not a criticism to be leveled against W. M. Thayer. His publications encompassed one called *Women Who Win* and one based on the life of Mary Lyon, founder of Mount Holyoke College.

[16] Theodore Roosevelt, *An Autobiography* (New York: Macmillan, 1913; reprint New York: Da Capo, 1985), 378-79; and letter to G. O. Trevelyan, June 19, 1908, cited in John P. Roche and Leonard W. Levy, *The Presidency* (New York: Harcourt Brace, 1964), 20-22. The Mrs. Theodore Roosevelt anecdote (for which reference, thanks to Peter Thompson) occurs in a lecture, "The City of Washington and Lincoln," delivered by Charles Moore at the Cosmos Club, Washington D. C. (minutes of the 206th meeting of the Columbia Historical Society, February 1923).

The initial apparent puzzle is that Lincoln and his administration were often ridiculed and execrated. True, President Washington also met with criticism, especially in his second term, when he was accused of becoming a figurehead for Alexander Hamilton and other ambitious and unscrupulous Federalists.[17] True also, a good deal of the abuse aimed at Abraham Lincoln was partisan. It is not astonishing that he was attacked by Southern spokesmen, by some Democrats and by Confederate sympathizers, as well as by Radical Republicans who charged that he was weak and indecisive, especially in handling slave emancipation and plans for Southern Reconstruction. (Is it so surprising that foreign magazines and newspapers such as *Punch* and the influential London *Times* should have echoed the diatribes of Lincoln's own countrymen?) Henry Watterson, wartime editor of a Confederate army newspaper, naturally enough resorted to invective — calling the Union chieftain, for example, "a man without mind or manners," a "shapeless skeleton in a very tough, very dirty, unwholesome skin . . . born and bred a rail-splitter . . . and a rail-splitter still." Politically hostile Northern editors could be counted upon, perhaps, to label Lincoln a "half-witted usurper," or "the head ghoul in Washington." The historian-Democrat George Bancroft, no friend of Republicans, understandably if uncharitably called Lincoln "ignorant" and "incompetent." The impatient abolitionist orator Wendell Phillips, again understandably, could complain in 1862 that the President was a mere procrastinating politician or, as Phillips put it in a much-quoted phrase, a "first-rate *second-rate* man."

In retrospect such denunciations tend to cancel one another out, and so not to constitute fundamental criticism. How could the same man be both closet Copperhead *and* "an abolition orang-outang," a tyrant *and* "a weak-kneed man, a poor . . . horse that *must be led*"? Harder to deal with, though, are reactions to Lincoln from people whom one might have expected to be warmly appreciative. Lincoln's last Treasury Secretary Hugh McCulloch did admire the President and said so in his memoirs. He also, however, described Lincoln as "unprepossessing, in manners ungraceful, in taste unrefined, or at least peculiar." The novelist Nathaniel Hawthorne, visiting the capital in 1862 and having a chance to observe Lincoln, wrote an article for the *Atlantic Monthly*, portions of which the editor suppressed or Hawthorne amended. Hawthorne initially referred to the "uncouthness" of "Uncle Abe." In print this appeared as "the Western plainness of the President." The future philosopher William James, living in a genteel

---

[17] See, for example, Tom Paine's "Letter to George Washington" (Paris, July 30, 1796); and James D. Tagg, "Benjamin Franklin Bache's Attack on George Washington," *Pennsylvania Magazine of History and Biography* 100 (April 1976): 191-230.

boarding-house in Cambridge as a Harvard undergraduate, spoke of a Miss Upham, the proprietress, as "declaiming against the vulgarity of President Lincoln." This was in 1862. A year later, Ralph Waldo Emerson confided to his journal:

> *Lincoln. We must accept the results of universal suffrage, & not try to make it appear that we can elect fine gentlemen. We shall have coarse men, with a fair chance of worth & manly ability. . . . You cannot refine Lincoln's taste, or extend his horizon; he will not walk dignifiedly through the traditional part of the President of America, but will pop out his head at each railroad station & make a little speech, & get into an argument with Squire A. and Judge B.; he will write letters to Horace Greeley, and any Editor or Reporter or saucy Party committee that writes to him, & cheapen himself. But this we must be ready for, & let the clown appear, & hug ourselves that we are well off, if we have got good nature, honest meaning, & fidelity to public interest, with bad manners, instead of an elegant roué & malignant self seeker.*[18]

This rather equivocal reaction is manifest too in the diary of George Templeton Strong, a high-minded New Yorker who served as a volunteer official of the

---

[18] Watterson's attacks are cited in Michael Davis, *The Image of Lincoln in the South* (Knoxville: University of Tennessee Press, 1971), 162. For other criticisms quoted here, see Roy P. Basler, *The Lincoln Legend: A Study in Changing Conceptions* (Boston: Houghton Mifflin, 1935), 52-57; David H. Donald, "Died of Democracy," in Donald, ed., *Why the North Won the Civil War* (Baton Rouge: Louisiana State University Press, 1960), 86; Dixon Wecter, *The Hero in America: A Chronicle of Hero Worship* (New York: Scribner's, 1941; reprint, Ann Arbor: University of Michigan Press, 1963). 243 — a work that has retained much of its sparkle; Don E. Fehrenbacher, "The Anti-Lincoln Tradition," in *Lincoln in Text and Context: Collected Essays* (Stanford University Press, 1987), 197-213. Contemporary references to Wendell Phillips' jibe ("first-rate *second-rate* man") include Karl Marx's 1862 article, (see footnote 28; Sideman, p. 205), and remarks by the visiting English journalist Edward Dicey, whose *Six Months in the Federal States* (1863) did not stint criticism of Lincoln (see Dicey, *Spectator of America*, ed. Herbert Mitgang, London: Gollancz, 1972, 90-97). McCulloch's comments are in his *Men and Measures of Half a Century* (New York: Scribner's, 1889), p. 188. Hawthorne's remarks on Lincoln in 1862 are discussed in Nathaniel Hawthorne, *The Letters, 1857-1864*, ed. Thomas Woodson et al. (Columbus: Ohio State University Press, 1987), 456-462. "I should not wonder at many mistaking Abe Lincoln the first two or three years in Washington": Whitman's reminiscence of the confusing wartime atmosphere, in Horace Traubel, *With Walt Whitman in Camden*, vol. 5, *April 8-September 14, 1889* (Carbondale: Southern Illinois Press, 1964), 361-62. William James's boarding-house conversations are recorded in Henry James, *Notes of a Son and Brother* (1914), reprinted in *Autobiography*, ed. Frederick W. Dupee (New York: Criterion Books, 1956), 328. Comments by Radical Republicans are cited also in Allan Nevins, *The War for the Union*, vol. 2, *War Becomes Revolution* (New York: Scribner's, 1960), e.g., 169, 301; and in T. Harry Williams, *Lincoln and the Radicals* (Madison: University of Wisconsin Press, 1941, reprint 1960), *passim*; June [?] 1863, *Emerson in His Journals*, ed. Joel Porte, (Cambridge: Harvard University Press, 1982), 511, and see p. 526 for an April 1865 verdict rather more positive.

Sanitary Commission and became fairly well acquainted with the President. An entry for January 1862 says of Lincoln: "He is a barbarian, Scythian, yahoo, or gorilla in respect of outside polish (for example, he uses "humans" as English for *homines*), but a most sensible, straightforward, honest old codger." By September Strong had decided that the "honest old codger" (he again used the phrase) was a failure: "His only special gift is fertility of smutty stories." On December 18, 1862, after the bungled battle of Fredericksburg, Strong was even more depressed: "A year ago we laughed at the Honest Old Abe's grotesque genial Western jocosities, but they nauseate us now." In May 1864, along with some words of praise, Strong again characterized Lincoln as a "poor old codger." In September, disagreeing with someone that the President has "neither ability or honesty," Strong still could not summon up overwhelming enthusiasm: "Lincoln is an honest man, of considerable ability (far below the first grade)." Again, as with Wendell Phillips, the notion that Lincoln is at best a good second-rater. And in March 1865, as Union victory drew near, the emphatically self-assured Strong revealed himself nevertheless unable to form a judgment on Lincoln's Second Inaugural address — now universally regarded as a wise and moving utterance:

> *It is certainly most unlike the inaugurals of Pierce, Polk, Buchanan, or any of their predecessors; unlike any American state paper of this century. I would give a good deal to know what estimate will be put on it ten or fifty years hence.*

On April 11th, immediately after the news of Lee's surrender at Appomattox, Strong was more ready to reach a high valuation, but still with hesitations. Many people, he said, "hold Lincoln a sensible, commonplace man, without special talent, except for story telling, and it must be admitted that he sometimes tells stories that [do] . . . not become a gentleman and the holder of the exalted place. But his weaknesses are on the surface, and his name will be of high account fifty years hence." Fifty years! Would it take so long for Lincoln's virtues to shine out over his deficiencies?[19]

In 1865, Washington's pre-eminence was beyond dispute, although it has been ingeniously suggested in recent years that Lincoln and men of his generation may have resented and sought to emulate the heroic primacy of the Founding Fathers,

[19] *Diary of George Templeton Strong*, ed. Allan Nevins and Milton Halsey Thomas, 4 vols. (New York: Macmillan, 1952), vol. 3, *The Civil War, 1860-1865*, 204, 256, 281-82, 442, 484, 561, 580.

Washington above all.[20] In the 1860s and for long after, Washington's was *the* supreme standard of reference. Edward Everett, principal orator at the Gettysburg dedication in November 1863, had stumped the country in the previous decade, delivering a celebrated lecture on "The Character of Washington" to raise funds for the restoration of Mount Vernon. Public figures of every stripe, North and South, invoked his name, as did the advocates of temperance and other good causes. Washington's was the exalted standard for Americans to match. Often their fall from grace was expressed as a contrast: a plunging descent, it was said of Grant's administration, from Washington who could not tell a lie to Gilded Age politicians who could not tell the truth or who could not tell the difference.[21]

In the predominant nineteenth-century picture, Washington embodied not only modesty and integrity, but dignity and poise. He was and in legend looked the part of officer-and-gentleman. Literally as well as figuratively, his was a commanding presence. Nathaniel Hawthorne, visiting the studio of the sculptor Hiram Powers, in Florence, Italy, noted Powers' observation that European royalty "have a certain look that distinguishes them from other people, and is

[20] The principal speculative presentations along these lines are: George B. Forgie, *Patricide in the House Divided: A Psychological Interpretation of Lincoln and His Age* (New York: W. W. Norton, 1979); Dwight G. Anderson, *Abraham Lincoln: The Quest for Immortality* (New York: Knopf, 1982); and Charles B. Strozier, *Lincoln's Quest for Union: Public and Private Meanings* (New York: Basic Books, 1982). All three build upon the suggestion of Edward Wilson's *Patriotic Gore* (1962) that Lincoln's early Springfield Lyceum address (1838) revealed his own unconsciously inordinate ambition in the guise of warning the nation against the dangers of tyrannical rule. To a varying extent, all are likewise intrigued by the notion that Lincoln may have been led to ponder the Washington legend by a youthful reading of Mason Locke Weems's *Life of Washington* (1800; enlarged in further editions to incorporate the famous hatchet-and-cherry-tree anecdote). These theories have appealed to some scholars: see, for example, John P. Diggins, *The Lost Soul of American Politics* (Chicago: University of Chicago Press, 1984), 303-12. Forgie's interpretation has found more favor than that of Anderson, and rather more than Strozier's. Somewhat skeptical comments on these versions of psychohistory are offered in Don E. Fehrenbacher, "The Deep Reading of Lincoln," in *Lincoln in Text and Context: Collected Essays* (Stanford: Stanford University Pres, 1987), 214-27; Richard N. Current, "The Myth of the Jealous Son," in his *Arguing With Historians: Essays on the Historical and the Unhistorical* (Middletown, Conn.: Wesleyan University Press, 1987), 52-60; Marcus Cunliffe (on Anderson) in Gabor S. Boritt and Norman Forness, eds., *The Historians' Lincoln: Pseudohistory, Psychohistory, and History* (Urbana: University of Illinois Press, 1988); and in *Lincoln Lore*, nos. 1776 and 1777 (February and March 1987).

[21] The same ironic humor was applied to the Nixon administration. And the contrast has not quite lost its force in 1987. Calvin Trillin, poking fun at the "spin-control" manipulators of our era, imagines a new version of the cherry-tree legend: "I cannot tell a lie," says little George. "A cherry-tree was chopped down." Calvin Trillin, *If You Can't Say Something Nice* (New York: Ticknor & Fields, 1987). Washington's renown is analyzed by numerous historians, including Marcus Cunliffe, Daniel J. Boorstin, Lawrence J. Friedman, Peter Karsten, and Michael Kammen. Among recent contributions, see Garry Wills, *Cincinnatus: George Washington and the Enlightenment* (New York: Doubleday, 1984); and Barry Schwartz, *George Washington: The Making of an American Symbol* (New York: Free Press, 1987).

seen in individuals of no lower rank." But Powers then commented that Washington had it, and Hawthorne added: "I, too, recognize this look in the portraits of Washington, . . . a mild, benevolent coldness and apartness." Washington was to his countrymen not just a gentleman, but a sort of prince among gentlemen.[22] His contemporaries, while suspicious of overweening arrogance, expected a certain gravity of demeanor from the president. The chief magistrate must epitomize, said John Adams, the "dignity of the commonwealth." James Madison believed that a great man in office would "refine and enlarge the public views."[23]

Gentlemen, in Washington's and in Lincoln's time, did not indulge in colloquialisms or other familiarities. Geniality was approved on appropriate occasions, but not vulgar jocosity. Wit as an attribute of cultivation was desirable: humor, in the sense of cracking jokes, was not. Indeed, suspicion of levity among public men lingered on until after Lincoln's demise. Robert M. LaFollette of Wisconsin was greatly impressed by the seriousness of James A. Garfield, whom he heard speak in 1880:

> He was . . . of fine presence, dignity, and power; splendid diction and rather lofty eloquence. I do not remember a suggestion of humor. . . . I remember he impressed me more as a statesman and less as a politician than any of the men I had heard up to that time.[24]

Lincoln, on the other hand, did not look the part, particularly to people who were bookish, cosmopolitan, or affluent. Even Walt Whitman and Nathaniel Hawthorne considered him ugly, at least when first glimpsed, and ungainly. Lincoln lacked "dignity" and "refinement." His eloquence was not immediately apparent, perhaps because he did not assume the manner deemed correct for public performance. His comicality gave offense, especially when the President was alleged to have cracked jokes among the dead and dying. Worse still, Lincoln's jokes were rumored often to be "coarse" or "smutty." Whitman, living

---

[22] Nathaniel Hawthorne, *The French and Italian Notebooks*, ed. Thomas Woodson, Centenary Edition (Columbus: Ohio State University Press, 1980), 312-13. The meeting took place in June 1858. On Washington and gentry standards, see Robert H. Wiebe, *The Opening of American Society* (New York: Knopf, 1984), 41-47.

[23] Wiebe, 42.

[24] Robert M. LaFollette, *Autobiography* (1911), 16-17, cited in Marcus Cunliffe, *The Presidency* (3d ed., Boston: Houghton Mifflin, 1987), 200. As late as 1987, Representative Morris K. Udall, well known for his repartee and a 1976 candidate for the Democratic presidential nomination, suggested the disadvantages of humor by producing a book with the title *Too Funny to be President*.

in Washington in 1863, tried to reassure friends that the President was actually an admirable person "underneath his outside smutched mannerism, and stories from third-class country barrooms (it is his humor)." In later years Whitman grew to adore Lincoln. He reminisced on how stories about the President were invented and disseminated in the wartime capital by government clerks, "full half of whom had nothing to do. All day long these boys would loaf about, talk together, invent stories — invent filthy stories: their minds ran upon such themes. . . . Then in a day or two the story would turn up in the papers foisted on Lincoln . . . thenceforth to take a place among the 'facts' of his life."

But there is evidence that some of the stories *were* in Lincoln's repertoire and that sometimes they were deemed not suitable for polite company. A staff officer at McClellan's headquarters, where Lincoln dined in March 1862, informed his father that the President "told a story at our mess-table, which was very funny, but too broad to repeat here."[25] On the whole this officer, Harvard-educated and a supporter of General McClellan, did not care for Lincoln. Nor, as we have seen, did other Boston Brahmins such as Wendell Phillips. Charles Francis Adams, Jr., and his son Henry passed on rather negatively one-sided recollections of the conduct of President Lincoln, whom Henry Adams portrayed at the inaugural ball as a maladroit figure as worried by social etiquette as the self-made businessman at a Boston dinner party in William Dean Howells's novel *The Rise of Silas Lapham.*[26]

George Templeton Strong, who knew Lincoln better than these people, was increasingly disposed to admire the President for honesty, perseverance, and a certain shrewdness he could not quite define. Strong's recurrent epithet, "the old codger," like the widespread nicknames "Old Abe" and "Honest Abe," seems to combine affection with disparagement or at least a vein of mockery, of which

[25] Cunliffe, *Presidency*, 201; Marcus Cunliffe, "Humor as an American Political Style: The Case of Abraham Lincoln," *Jahrbuch für Amerikastudien* 11 (1966): 29-40; Horace Traubel, *With Walt Whitman in Camden*, vol. 5, *July 16-October 13, 1888,* (reprint, New York: Rowman & Littlefield, 1961), 542-43; *War Diary and Letters of Stephen Minot Weld, 1861-1865* (1912; Boston: Massachusetts Historical Society, 2d ed., 1979), 83; and George B. Hutchinson, *The Ecstatic Whitman: Literary Shamanism and the Crisis of the Union* (Columbus: Ohio State University Press, 1986), 1-21. Some fairly broad instances of Lincoln humor are provided in Charles B. Strozier, *Lincoln's Quest for Union: Public and Private Meanings* (New York: Basic Books, 1982), 214-18; and see the entry on "Humor" in Mark E. Neely, Jr.'s excellent *Abraham Lincoln Encyclopedia* (New York: McGraw-Hill, 1982; reprint, New York: Da Capo Press, 1984), 153-55.

[26] "Abraham Lincoln and the Adams Family Myth," *Lincoln Lore* no. 1667 (January 1977); Martin Duberman, *Charles Francis Adams, 1807-1886* (1961; reprint Stanford University Press, 1968), 256-57, 387-88; Henry Adams, *The Education of Henry Adams: An Autobiography* (Boston: Houghton Mifflin, 1918), 106. At the ball, Henry Adams saw "a long, awkward figure; a plain, ploughed face; a mind, absent in part, and in part evidently worried by white kid gloves ... above all, a lack of apparent force."

Lincoln himself was well aware. "Abe" was an undignified contraction. "Honest Abe" could be taken for a tradesman's slogan. "Old" suggested decrepitude as much as sagacity. The gradual spread of "Father Abraham," we may think, represented a deepening approval of the man Hawthorne visualized as a Yankee schoolteacher.[27]

The murder of Lincoln, stunning and horrifying though it was, did not immediately persuade the entire population that they had lost a great leader, still less that he was on a level with Washington. Some prescient observations were made by Karl Marx, in an article contributed to a Vienna newspaper in 1862, following the Emancipation Proclamation: "In the history of the United States and in the history of humanity, Lincoln occupies a place beside Washington."[28] But the great mass of reaction and reinterpretation naturally came after the assassination in April 1865. Some of the Radical Republicans were almost cynical. In what was supposed to be a eulogy, Wendell Phillips declared that "God . . . has withdrawn [Lincoln] at the moment when . . . the nation needed a sterner hand for the work God has given to do." For Phillips and his associates, "the removal of a man too great and too trusted is often a natural gain in times like these." Zachariah Chandler, writing to his wife a week after Lincoln's death, spoke of Andrew Johnson's accession as "a godsend to the country." God had retained Lincoln as long as he had a use, then "put a better man in his place."[29] Charles William Eliot, nephew of George Ticknor and future president of

[27] "Unquestionably, Western man though he be, and Kentuckian by birth, President Lincoln is the essential representative of all Yankees. . . . There is no describing the lengthy awkwardness nor the uncouthness of his movement; and yet it seemed as if I had been in the habit of seeing him daily, and had shaken hands with him a thousand times in some village street. . . . If put to guess his calling . . . I should have taken him for a country schoolmaster as soon as anything else." Hawthorne's draft version of his 1862 Atlantic Monthly article. This excerpt is quoted in Henry Steele Commager, ed., *The Blue and The Gray: The Story of the Civil War as Told by Participants* (Indianapolis: Bobbs-Merrill, 1950), 1079-81. See also Nathaniel Hawthorne, *The Letters, 1857-1864*, ed. Thomas Woodson et al. (Columbus: Ohio State University Press, 1987), 462 n.3.

[28] Marx, living in London, nonetheless acted as Civil War correspondent for *Die Presse*. An English version of his October 12, 1862, article was published in Belle Becker Sideman and Lillian Friedman, eds., *Europe Looks at the Civil War* (New York: Orion Press, 1960), pp. 189-91. It is also referred to in David Brion Davis, *The Emancipation Moment* (Twenty-second Fortenbaugh Memorial Lecture, Gettysburg College, 1983), 21. The Washington-Lincoln comparison may be a mere rhetorical formula. Arrestingly speculative, though, is this statement by Marx: "In his day, Hegel remarked that in reality, comedy is above tragedy, the humor of the mind above its pathos. If Lincoln does not possess the gift of the pathos of historic action, he does as an ordinary man, coming from the people, possess the gift of the humor of that action."

[29] James Brewer Stewart, *Wendell Phillips: Liberty's Hero* (Baton Rouge: Louisiana State University Press, 1986). Chandler cited in T. Harry Williams, *Lincoln and the Radicals* (Madison: University of Wisconsin Press, 1941), 374.

Harvard, was touring in Europe with a family party. He wrote home to express his shock at the murder and produce a slightly grudging epitaph:

> *I don't like to hear Lincoln's name put too near Washington's, but his character seems to me a rough and ungraceful but truly noble growth of republican institutions. You can count on your fingers the names which History will rank with his. . . . He did not lead the people — he rather followed the wisest and best thought of the people, and his successors will do likewise.*

Henry Adams, also going round Europe with a family party, sent a peculiarly flippant letter from Italy to his brother Charles Francis Adams, Jr. (May 10, 1865):

> *I have already buried Mr. Lincoln under the ruins of the Capitol, along with Caesar, and I don't mean this merely as a phrase. We must have our wars, it appears, and our crimes, as well as other countries. I think Abraham Lincoln is rather to be envied in his death, as in his life somewhat; and if he wasn't as great as Caesar, he shows the same sort of tomb.*

Ellen Sturgis Hooper came with her sister Marian (the future Mrs. Henry Adams) to Washington, D.C. in May 1865 to see the "Grand Review" of troops. Neither young woman seems to have written about Lincoln, except for Ellen's mention of a talk with a devoutly religious ex-slave, whose feelings she seems to respect rather than wholeheartedly to share: "like an old prophetess . . . her direct vision of this army that was coming — her faith that warmed your heart. There was . . . an intense feeling about Lincoln — and Faith that, though he was taken, the Lord never did his work by halves."[30]

Some such reservations persisted. Not surprisingly, a few Southerners continued for a while to vilify Lincoln. As late as 1871, the South Carolina poet Paul Hamilton Hayne could refer to the dead President as a "gawky, coarse, . . . whisky drinking . . . Blackguard."[31] The English critic Matthew Arnold, discussing

[30] Eliot to his mother, from Rome, April 27, 1865, in Henry James, *Charles W. Eliot*, 2 vols. (Boston: Houghton Mifflin, 1930), 1: 139-41.; *Letters of Henry Adams, 1858-1891*, ed. Worthington C. Ford (Boston, Houghton Mifflin, 1930), 119-20; *Letters of Mrs. Henry Adams*, ed. Ward Thoron (Boston: Little, Brown, 1936), 470-71.

[31] Quoted in Dixon Wecter, *Hero in America*, 243.

the lack of "distinction" in the United States of the 1880s, allowed that Washington and Alexander Hamilton possessed that quality. But they, he maintained, belonged to the "pre-American age." Lincoln, while "shrewd," "humorous," "honest" and the like, indeed, "a man deserving the most sincere esteem . . . has not distinction."[32] Arnold's ruling exasperated some Americans, Mark Twain among them: was humorousness a sign of ordinariness? Others however agreed with the verdict, if not always openly. A review of Henry Cabot Lodge's new biography of George Washington in *Harper's Monthly* (October 1889; "Editor's Study," presumably by the novelist-critic William Dean Howells, who had in 1860 produced a campaign biography of Lincoln) warned readers, "if we would be just, not to regard even Lincoln as the peer of Washington; for Washington was all that Lincoln was . . . with a vast breadth of military . . . achievement beside and beyond. Both men centered in themselves the national love, but Washington was as the father where Lincoln was the brother of his country." This may be regarded as a transitional formulation, carrying also the rather conservative verdict that while Washington (the opposite of Lincoln) was "a thorough republican, he was not socially a democrat."

Henry Adams's brother Brooks, a friend of Theodore Roosevelt, continued to think Washington the ideal American leader; he explained this view in two 1903 lectures at the Naval War College. Up to his dying day in 1893, the Brahmin historian Francis Parkman deplored Lincoln's displacement of Washington as a hero for schoolboys. The California novelist Gertrude Atherton, who wrote with gushing admiration of Alexander Hamilton (in *The Conqueror*), confessed she did not extend this emotion to Lincoln: indeed, "I hate the sight of him." Woodrow Wilson, eventually a professed devotee of Lincoln, took some time to arrive at this position. In 1894, offering his opinion on "great Americans," he said that Lincoln's mind never quite lost "the vein of coarseness that marked him grossly when a youth."[33]

---

[32] From Arnold's *Civilization in the United States* (1888); excerpt in Ray Ginger, ed., *The Nationalizing of American Life, 1877-1900* (New York: Free Press, 1965), 122.

[33] *Harper's New Monthly Magazine* 79 (October 1889): 800-02; Arthur F. Beringause, *Brooks Adams: A Biography* (New York: Knopf, 1955), 251; on Parkman, Alfred Kazin, *American Procession* (New York: Knopf, 1984), 112, and see pp. 112-27 for other comments, mainly by Whitman, on Abraham Lincoln. Atherton's visions of true distinction are brought out in Charlotte S. McClure, *Gertrude Atherton* (Boston: Twayne, 1979), in her high-toned novel *The Aristocrats* (1901), and in her autobiography, *Adventures of a Novelist* (New York: Liveright, 1932), in which she explains her refusal to write a book about Lincoln. Wilson's article appeared in the February 1894 issue of *Forum*. Peter Karsten, *Patriot-Heroes in England and America* (Madison, University of Wisconsin Press, 1978), 89, suggests that "as time passed, the veneration of Washington was increasingly an elite phenomenon," with a strongly "WASP" tinge.

However, Lincoln's own reputation began to soar. As soon as they got word of his death, people almost unconsciously associated his memory with that of Washington — and not to Lincoln's detriment (Photo 4). George Templeton Strong, on hearing of the assassination, instinctively looked up the records of Trinity Church, where he was a vestryman, to find what procedure had been followed when Washington died. A Presbyterian minister in another New York church asserted: "No-one since Washington is so enshrined in the hearts of the people." Henry George, working in San Francisco as a young typesetter, reacted immediately, describing the dead president as "the martyr of Freedom. . . . the Proclamation of Emancipation signed with the name and sealed with the blood of *Abraham Lincoln* will remain a landmark. . . . His memory will be cherished with that of Washington." Colonel Selden Connor (later Governor of Maine) was in a Washington hospital, recovering from wounds, at the moment of Lincoln's funeral. In a letter to his sister he said: "the sound of minute guns booming a hoarse requiem for the nation's highest, most loved and honored man, now cold in death, comes in at my open window. . . . President Lincoln was a great and good man, and not even the great and good Washington deserved more of the country." Connor added the consolatory epitaph that was in the minds of admirers as well as detractors: "the impression prevails, and it is certainly my own, the nation will benefit by the martyrdom of her great son."[34]

There is an element of ritual hyperbole in such declarations. *De mortuis nil nisi bonum*: the impulse is to cover the memory of the deceased in fragrance, to pretend that he had been as loved in life as the obituaries said. In Lincoln's case several separate factors converged to ennoble his reputation. His violent death at the war's very end, coming on Good Friday, solemnized and almost sanctified him. The insistence of the sermonizers (and more particularly of the Radical

---

[34] Strong, *Diary*, 584 (April 15, 1865). On Easter Sunday (April 16; p. 587) Strong wrote that Lincoln's death had opened the eyes of the many who despised or at best tolerated him as a "well-meaning, sagacious, kind-hearted, ignorant, old codger." The *Oxford English Dictionary* defines *codger* as a "fellow" or "chap" and in colloquial use, "a term applied irreverently to an elderly man, with a whimsical application". It offers as an illustration a reference in Washington Irving to "a gouty old codger of an alderman." A month later, however (May 19; p. 599), Strong reported a story of a Georgetown clergyman anxious to go to a parish further North, "because the ladies of his congregation are carrying about little card photographs representing [John Wilkes] Booth's head crowned with a laurel." On Henry George's piece, contributed anonymously to the *Alta California*, see Henry George, Jr., *Life of Henry George* (1900; reprint, New York: Schalkenbach Foundation, 1960), 163. Selden Connor is quoted in Reinhard H. Luthin, *The Real Abraham Lincoln* (Englewood Cliffs, N.J.: Prentice-Hall, 1960), 668. In leaping down to the stage at Ford's Theater, after he shot Abraham Lincoln, John Wilkes Booth — with a weird symbolism — caught his spur upon a framed portrait of George Washington that had been used to embellish the presidential box. See George S. Bryan, *The Great American Myth* (New York: Carrick and Evans, 1940), illustration opposite p. 212.

4. Max Rosenthal, *The Last Moments of Abraham Lincoln, President of the United States*, after design of Joseph Hoover, Philadelphia, 1865. Hand-colored lithograph. Library of Congress, Prints and Photographs Division.

Republicans) that the death was opportune, sounds perhaps insincere or perfunctory. But Lincoln's passing had in fact a curiously profound utility for Americans, at least those in the North, seeking to justify the war, which had at times seemed a shapeless, interminable contest. Bishop Matthew Simpson of the Methodist Episcopal Church, delivering the invocation at the White House funeral ceremony on April 19, 1865, produced a compelling if abstract reason for Lincoln's passing: "Thou hast shown that our Republican government is the strongest upon the face of the earth." The historian John Lothrop Motley told a friend: "I have got over my grief for [Lincoln's] murder in the conviction that he has gained in this sudden departure. His work was done. His wise cheerfulness which the vulgar mistook for vulgarity, his patience and his magnificent simplicity and truth are no longer absolutely indispensable to us."[35] Lincoln, apparently, perished in order that the Union might live. In Selden Connor's words: The survived republic is his . . . monument." He had gone to Heaven, there to be greeted by Washington. He had also achieved a type of spiritual metamorphosis, vanishing into the American body politic. Somehow this mysterious apotheosis accounted for his death, explained the war, concluded the dreadful bookkeeping of that conflict, and aligned him with the nation's other *Pater Patriae*. "Old Abe" was in more ways than one now Father Abraham. On Washington's death too, his memorialists had been almost unanimous in stressing the greatness of his accomplishment and that his task was done.

To this tally we may add the consideration, already referred to in connection with Theodore Roosevelt, that as the role of the presidency began to be reinterpreted in the direction of activist leadership, Lincoln, once perceivable as a "despot", emerged, along with Washington (and a newly reassessed Andrew Jackson) as hero-models for chief magistrates of the Roosevelt and Wilson stamp. Ambitious, politically minded Americans endeavored now to "get right with Lincoln" as they (Lincoln included) had hitherto claimed kinship with Washington. John Hay, Lincoln's one-time private secretary, had given McKinley a ring containing a lock of Washington's hair to wear at McKinley's 1897 inauguration. In March 1905, at his own inauguration, Teddy Roosevelt wore a ring incorporating a strand of Lincoln's hair, presented to him by the same adroit John Hay, who was by now secretary of state. "Dear Theodore," Hay wrote, "The hair in this ring is from the head of Abraham Lincoln. Dr. Taft cut it off the night of the assassination, and I got it from his son. . . . Please wear it tomorrow; you

---

[35] Simpson quotation in Carl Sandburg's biography of Lincoln, cited in Paul M. Angle, ed., *The Lincoln Reader* (New Brunswick: Rutgers University Press, 1947), 534. Motley's letter to his friend William Amory is mentioned in *Proceedings, Massachusetts Historical Society* 92 (Boston, 1981): 105.

5. John Sartain, *Abraham Lincoln, The Martyr Victorious,* after design of W. H. Hermans, New York, 1865. Engraving. Library of Congress, Prints and Photographs Division.

are one of the men who most thoroughly understand and appreciate Lincoln. I have had your monogram and Lincoln's engraved on the ring."[36] The Republicans displayed a large Lincoln portrait at every "sizeable campaign rally." But the Democrats also sought to align themselves with Lincoln as well as Washington as early as Grover Cleveland's 1884 campaign. Free-silver Populists laid claim to Lincoln, with Washington and Jefferson, in electioneering material of 1896. Wilson, Roosevelt and Taft all did so in the 1912 presidential election campaign — the Democrats, like the Populists, emphasizing too their affiliation not just with Washington but with Thomas Jefferson.

Lincoln appealed to Theodore Roosevelt as a "strong" president, then, and that vitalized image allured Woodrow Wilson as well. But even while he was alive, Lincoln began to symbolize another and profounder side of America, that of the common man. The message had indeed already been spread by the followers of "Old Hickory" Jackson and "Old Tip" Harrison. "Abe" the "Rail-Splitter" was assumed to prove attractive to a sizeable proportion of a mass electorate — to more, that is, than would be repelled by such maneuvers. But the contrary assumptions of loftiness, almost of regality, remained strong so far as the White House was concerned. Politics was one thing, statesmanship another and higher matter. While Lincoln held office, his behavior did not entirely please upright people such as Emerson, who in theory were wholly committed to democracy, but who wanted it to be "refined" not "vulgar" democracy.

Expectations were altering, and Lincoln's conduct helped the process along. The formulae of Washington-Lincoln equivalence sometimes sought to "gentrify" Lincoln and sometimes to "popularize" Washington. Lincoln's son Robert strenuously objected to the statue of his father by George G. Barnard (completed in 1917) which portrayed a gangling figure inelegantly clad. Biographers sought to present George Washington as a fiercely "human" being, fond of wine, women

---

[36] Lloyd Lewis, *Myths After Lincoln* (1929; reprint, New York: Grosset & Dunlap, Universal Library, 1957), has fascinating material: for example (p. 59), on the near-lynching of a man in New York City who asked jocularly, "Did you hear Abe Lincoln's last joke?" Chapeter 10, "The Dying God" (pp. 92-105) includes some Washington-Lincoln allusions. See also the historiographical essay in G. S. Boritt, *Lincoln and the Economics of the American Dream* (Memphis: Memphis State University Press, 1978), 289-311. David H. Donald discusses "Getting Right With Lincoln" in his *Lincoln Reconsidered*, chapter 1. Theodore Roosevelt, *An Autobiography*, 400. Uses of Lincoln imagery are instanced in Lloyd Lewis, *Myths After Lincoln*, 342-43. Sundry recourses to Washington and/or Lincoln are mentioned in John Milton Cooper, Jr., *The Warrior and the Priest: Woodrow Wilson and Theodore Roosevelt* (Cambridge: Harvard University Press, 1983). The Hay-Roosevelt connection is presented with tart insight in Gore Vidal's novel *Empire* (1987): see chapter 15 for an account of the Lincoln ring. There are amusing examples of Republicans as well as Democrats "working the Jefferson angle," in Merrill D. Peterson, *The Jefferson Image in the American Mind* (New York: Oxford University Press, 1960), e.g., 370-71.

and song and capable of profanity when under stress.[37] But these never wholly pleased the public. Instead, a doubling of compatible unlikes emerged. It was signalled in "Abraham Lincoln, a Horatian Ode," composed soon after the assassination by Richard Henry Stoddard. Stoddard spoke of Lincoln as his "country's father" and as a man of the "People" — "No gentleman, like Washington." Many another comparison, not seeking to defame either man, is nevertheless offered as a contrast. In a 1928 synagogue address, Washington is "the statesman, the scholar, the gentleman, the aristocrat and patrician, the scion of the blue-blooded hierarchy of the South," while "Father Abraham" figures as "farm hand, boatman, poor country lawyer with no family connections." But "both were needed . . . God-sent and divinely ordained." The country was "founded by Washington, and recemented and saved by Lincoln." A 1942 pamphlet reiterates the contrast and the double need for the "aristocrat" and the "commoner." Young Henry George had caught this sense of a "democratic" Lincoln, as distinct perhaps from a "republican" Washington, back in April 1865: "No other system would have produced him; through no crowd of courtiers could such a man have forced his way; his feet would have slipped on the carpets of palace stairs, and Grand Chamberlains ordered him back."[38]

Even where the circumstances are clearly different, a basically similar rhetoric of public-spirited, patriotic, incorruptible, ultimately exhausting service is evoked, together with images of reconciliation. The Georgia journalist and orator Henry W. Grady, editor of the *Atlanta Constitution*, delivered a sensationally popular speech in New York in 1886, hailing the re-united North and South and lauding Lincoln as "the first typical American, the first who comprehended within himself all the strength and gentleness, all the majesty and grace of this republic. . . . He was the sum of Puritan and Cavalier, for in his ardent nature were fused the virtues of both, and in the depths of his great soul the faults of both were lost." The subject of this panegyric may not have recognized himself in it, any more than George Washington might have concurred with the occasional efforts of the Wisconsin historian Frederick Jackson Turner to recast him as a frontier

---

[37] Roy P. Basler, *The Lincoln Legend* (Boston: Houghton Mifflin, 1935), 288-93; Marcus Cunliffe, *George Washington: Man and Monument* (1958; New York, Mentor, 2d ed., 1982), 146-49.

[38] Emanuel Hertz, *Washington and Lincoln: The Two Master Builders of the Union* (New York, 1928); Edward F. Schewe, *Washington and Lincoln: A Comparison and Contrast* (Los Angeles: Lincoln Fellowship of Southern California, 1942); *Life of Henry George*, 164-65.

expansionist.[39] But it picks up a notion advanced as early as July 1865, by James Russell Lowell. His Harvard Commemoration Ode recalled the memory of "our Martyr-Chief," shaped by Nature from the "sweet clay" of the "unexhausted West," owing nothing at all to Europe:

> *Sagacious, patient, dreading praise, not blame,*
> *New birth of our new soil, the first American.*

Though a cosmopolitan Easterner, Lowell was proud of his nationality, especially when he felt it impugned by foreigners. His vision of Lincoln is someone as far removed as possible from Europe and its hierarchies — a man necessarily of humble origins, self-made, irreverent on many subjects, and therefore of the West.

If Lincoln was the "first" true American, what of Washington, "first in war, first in peace, first in the hearts of his countrymen"? In some respects the Lincoln claim supersedes that of Washington. Washington's primacy, it might seem, is temporal. In fact, if Lowell and Grady (and Matthew Arnold) are correct, Washington is not fully an American: he is half-English. Or he is untypical, unrepresentative because he is an "aristocrat." Or his great stature has perhaps been equalled, even surpassed, by subsequent epoch-making circumstances. This has undeniably happened in relation to Lincoln. Over the years, the illustrations that showed Lincoln a newcomer to Heaven, brought into elysium by a benevolently omnipotent Washington, yield to depictions of equal status, and by degrees to scenes in which Lincoln holds the foreground. Washington's presence, in such compositions, is commonly suggested by a shadowy head-and-shoulders bust, as if to suggest that the prominent, "living" Lincoln pays dutiful tribute to an honored ancestor, yet is his own master. Another formula avoids a direct comparison. Washington is assumed to be the unchallenged leader of his *own* era, the eighteenth century: Lincoln, for instance in an essay by Charles R. Brown, dean of the Yale Divinity School, is singled out as *The Greatest Man of the Nineteenth Century* (1922).

George Washington the man has been characterized as one of the three chief American wonders — the others being Niagara Falls and the Brooklyn Bridge. Not everyone would accept that estimate or confine the tally to three. Other wonders have been created or discovered with the passage of time. Lincoln's

---

[39] Joel Chandler Harris, *Life of Henry W. Grady, including his Writings and Speeches* (New York: Cassell, 1890), 85-86; *America's Great Frontiers and Sections: Frederick Jackson Turner's Unpublished Essays*, ed. Wilbur R. Jacobs (Lincoln: University of Nebraska Press, 1969), 109-15.

friend William Herndon once told him how awed he had been by Niagara and asked Lincoln for his opinion of the Falls. Lincoln supposedly answered: "The thing that struck me most forcibly . . . was, where in the world did all that water come from?" The humorous expression is characteristic and pleasing to us, for we are more inclined to appreciate habitual joking than were public figures of the Washington era. Equally characteristic is Lincoln's concealment from Herndon that he had actually himself been stirred by the sight of Niagara, above all by the thought that the water had been flowing and falling since long before Columbus, or Christ, or Moses, or Adam. He had reflected that the physical aspects — the tonnage of water, the noise and spray and rainbows — were not what drew people in their millions to gaze upon Niagara Falls. What people made of the spectacle, their inner responses and emotions, provided the real meaning.[40]

He would have considered that in the time-span of Niagara, neither he nor Washington loomed very large; also that there is something subjective, fluctuating, almost factitious about the making and unmaking of historical reputations. If he were able to listen in on today's evaluations of himself and of Washington, F.D.R. and other heroes, from the perch above the clouds provided by the printmakers — if, that is, he had not better things to do — he might conclude, with a wry smile, that there is nothing substantial or permanent in the usual palaver about myths, images, legends, ratings, and so on.

But he would be wrong, though endearingly so. Despite the contriving and commercialism, and sometimes the cant and corniness of the image-makers, there is a genuine substance to the nation's leading heroes. Washington and Lincoln are with good reason first equal, although with varying emphasis on what constitutes firstness. There is certainly a place in America's appreciation for "aristocrats," in the White House as elsewhere, provided that they are "democratic aristocrats." There is a place too for "aristocratic democrats" — the natural aristocracy, the representative men, the uncommon people of common origins whom Jefferson and Emerson struggled to identify.[41] George Washington was a gentleman, yes, but never an aristocrat in the full European understanding of the word. Aristocrats do not keep meticulous accounts of expenditure in their own handwriting and submit them to their legislative superiors as Washington did with a bourgeois punctilio worthy of Ben Franklin. Nor of course was Lincoln the

---

[40] Strozier, *Quest for Union*, 124; Elizabeth McKinsey, *Niagara Falls: Icon of the American Sublime* (Cambridge: Cambridge University Press, 1985), vii, 1-3.

[41] W. C. Brownell, *Democratic Distinction in America* (New York: Scribner's, 1927), 38-44.

"uncouth" yokel pictured by contemporaries. His qualities of modesty, sadness and sensibility, and his extraordinary gift of language, have proved profoundly appealing. In both cases this appeal transcends national boundaries. If Lincoln figures as the Great Emancipator, Washington's decision to free the Mount Vernon slaves is an honorable prelude.

The Washington-Lincoln images are doubled because in the final analysis we perceive a substantial overlap, after allowing for the obvious large generational differences. The pairing indicates a tradition of American reverence for dead heroes (less for live ones) that has been modified over the decades, but that does not really entail a repudiation of old demigods. Lincoln and Washington jointly serve to remind Americans of cherished beliefs in country, courage, continuance.

This essay was published as the Fortenbaugh Lecture 1987, Gettysburg, Pa., by Gettysburg College, 1988.

In assembling visual representations, I am much indebted to Mark Neely and the Warren Library and Museum; to Gabor S. Boritt; for research assistance to Nan Thompson Ernst and for photographic work to Sarah Brown. I am indebted too to Keith Melder, National Museum of American History, and to Mary Ison, Prints and Photographs Division, Library of Congress.

10

Woodrow Wilson's
George Washington

I was asked to supply an introduction for a 1969 reprint of Professor Woodrow Wilson's 1896 biography of George Washington. I may still have had in mind a review I had written (*Encounter*, July 1967) of the bizarrely hostile and suppositious "psychological study," *Thomas Woodrow Wilson* (1967), a collaboration of sorts between Sigmund Freud and William C. Bullitt. Though I had never particularly warmed to Wilson, the Freud-Bullitt analysis seemed to deny to their subject any and every benefit of the doubt. My comments, while not highly laudatory, are I trust not devoid of sympathy for America's twenty-eighth president as he was in his Princeton chrysalis.

Woodrow Wilson's life of George Washington is no masterpiece. Yet apart from what it tells us about the first president of the United States, it also, unwittingly, reveals something of Wilson, the twenty-eighth.

The great work Wilson dreamed of during his academic years, on "The Philosophy of Politics," remained unwritten. Instead, having won an early success with *Congressional Government* (1885), he came dangerously close to being a hack author. He produced a flow of magazine articles, collected subsequently as *An Old Master* (1893) and *Mere Literature* (1896). His historical books were written at the suggestion of various editors; unlike his friend Frederick Jackson Turner, he was hardly a historian's historian. A harsh verdict would be that he published not because he had something to say, but because he felt he had to say something. An as-yet unfocussed ambition drove him on. Editors warmed to Professor Woodrow Wilson of Johns Hopkins (1883-85), Bryn Mawr (1885-88), Wesleyan (1888-90), and Princeton (1890-1902) for good editorial reasons: he was fluent, he was industrious, he was amenable to advice, and he was becoming a "name." So he wrote a textbook, *Division and Reunion, 1829-1889* (1893), for Albert Bushnell Hart's series on "Epochs of American History." Well-received, it stimulated other editors to approach him. His most ambitious endeavor, *A History of the American People* (1902), was serialized in *Harper's Magazine.* He earned $12,000 from the magazine installments and considerably more from sales in book form. Wilson refused several invitations to contribute unpaid reviews to the *American Historical Review.* "I know you will deem me a churl," he candidly admitted, "but really the thing is impossible, honorable as I should feel to find a place in the *Review* to be. The fact is, that the editors of the popular monthlies offer me such prices nowadays that I am corrupted." No wonder that a Princeton colleague later dismissed the *History of the American People* as a "gilt-edged potboiler."[1]

A similar epithet could be applied to Wilson's treatment of George Washington, also serialized in *Harper's Magazine* in 1895-96 and published as a book in 1896. Working under pressure and during vacations, he had no opportunity and no particular impulse to pursue original research. He drew upon secondary material. His portrait of Washington was conventional. To judge from later references, he did not even go closely enough into his hero's career to discover that it was Thomas Jefferson, not Washington, who spoke of "entangling alliances."[2] And while serial publication may have obliged him to chop his book into narrative blocks of equal length, the result is curiously disproportionate. Too much preliminary space is devoted to an evocation of Virginia colonial life. Throughout the work there is an excess of general narrative, a dearth of genuine biography. The last ten years of Washington's life are perfunctorily handled; the chapter contains little indication that one future president had meditated upon the presidential office.

---

[1] Henry Wilkinson Bragdon, *Woodrow Wilson: The Academic Years* (Cambridge, Mass., 1967), 247, 251. Much of my material has been drawn from Mr. Bragdon's study; see especially chapter 12, "Literary Historian." There are briefer accounts of Wilson's historical work in Arthur S. Link, *Wilson: The Road to the White House* (Princeton, N.J., 1947), 29-35; and Arthur Walworth, *Woodrow Wilson* (Boston, 2d ed., 1965), 63-66. An older discussion by Louis M. Sears in William T. Hutchinson, ed., *Marcus W. Jernegan Essays in American Historiography* (Chicago, 1937), 102-21, is still of value. Marjorie L. Daniel, "Woodrow Wilson — Historian," *Mississippi Valley Historical Review* 21 (December, 1934): 361-74, is of less use and does not deal with Wilson's *George Washington.*

[2] "We still read Washington's immortal warning against 'entangling alliances' with full comprehension and an answering purpose": speech in New York, September 27, 1918. There is a similar allusion in a Wilson address of September 19, 1919. See Donald Day, ed., *Woodrow Wilson's Own Story* (Boston, 1952), 287, 347.

Critics have been especially irritated by his overindulgence in archaisms. Dozens of sentences begin with "'Twas"; he uses "but" for "only," "ere" for "before," awkward inversions, superfluously picturesque adjectives. A couple of examples show Wilson at his stylistic worst:

> *But with Washington it was a different matter. There was that in his proud eyes and gentleman's bearing that marked him a man to be made friends with and respected. A good comrade he proved, without pretence or bravado, but an ill man to scorn, as he went his way among them, lithe and alert, full six feet in his boots, with that strong gait as of a backwoodsman, and that haughty carriage as of a man born to have his will.*

> *[Contrecoeur] was staking everything, as it was, upon this encounter on the way. If the English should shake the savages off, as he deemed they would, he must no doubt withdraw as he could ere the lines of siege were closed about him. He never dreamed of such largess of good fortune as came pouring in upon him. The English were not only checked, but beaten. They had never seen business like this. 'Twas a pitiful, shameful slaughter — men shot like beasts in a pen there where they cowered close in their scarlet ranks. Their first blazing volleys had sent the craven Canadians scampering back the way they had come.*

Costume-prose of this sort makes one sympathize with the plea of a cinema owner to his distributor: "Don't send me no more pictures where the hero signs his name with a feather." Wilson, according to one estimate, "only added to the steel-engraving status of the Father of his Country"; "rather fourth-state stuff," concluded another.[3]

Such criticism, however, requires qualification. Woodrow Wilson was quite highly esteemed by most of his academic contemporaries. They did not feel he was merely churning out historical pablum for the sake of the money. J. Franklin Jameson, the editor who kept pressing him to write for the *American Historical Review*, was a man of rigorous standards. Jameson and others had seen from *Congressional Government* and from some of Wilson's book reviews in the monthly magazines that, given a suitable subject, he could be an incisive commentator. The chapter that Wilson undertook for Lord Acton's *Cambridge*

---

[3] William E. Dodd and William Allen White, quoted in Sears, *Jernegan Essays*, 112.

Modern History, on "State Rights, 1850-1861," so pleased the editors that they tried to persuade Wilson to do three more chapters of United States history.

A second mitigation is that Washington biography has always posed problems for biographers. Until recent years, relatively little has been known about the Virginia of his day. One way of overcoming the absence of personal material was to indulge in supposition or to stretch out apocryphal anecdotes — as was notoriously done by Parson Weems of "cherry tree" fame. Alternatively, the biographer is led into a broad survey of the "times" in which Washington is apt almost to disappear from view. Later periods of Washington's life, as commander-in-chief and as president, carry a similar tendency, because his existence and that of his country seem inseparably intertwined. Again, every Washington biographer for a very long period has endeavored to avoid hero worship, to disclose the real man behind the chorus of adulation. The effort gained fresh impetus toward the end of the nineteenth century, encouraged by the emergence of professionalism in historical writing. A typical title, of a book published in the same year as Wilson's, was Paul Leicester Ford's *The True George Washington*. Henry Cabot Lodge, who produced a two-volume life of Washington in 1889, had been trained in Harvard's postgraduate school with Germanic strictness. His biography took a severe attitude to the sentimental inventions of Weems, " a man destitute of historical sense, training, or morals." Yet every biographer, except for a small minority of soured debunkers, found himself reproducing the traditional Washington portrait, in the conviction that this must after all be the "true" George Washington.[4] The more readable the treatment, the less professionally sound it was apt to be: *The Seven Ages of Washington* (1907) by the novelist Owen Wister is an example. Conversely, the more scholarly, the less readable: witness is the substantial yet colorless two-volume life of Washington (1900) by Worthington C. Ford. Henry Cabot Lodge's attempt was on the whole no better than Wilson's. Lodge tackled the task earnestly and possessed a vigorous style. But he presented Washington very much as a Federalist politician; and his confident analysis of Washington's military career rested on a shaky grasp of tactics and strategy.[5] The historical

---

[4] For an analysis of the problems of Washington biography, see the introduction by Marcus Cunliffe to *The Life of Washington* by Mason L. Weems, John Harvard Library (Cambridge, Mass., 1962). On Lodge, see esp. pp. xxxii-xxxiv.

[5] Senator Lodge's bitter enmity to President Wilson is a matter of common knowledge and indeed of great importance in the shaping of American foreign policy. Their rivalry began as early as the 1880s, when they were two ambitious young academics, competing for eminence in the same field and sometimes in the same magazines. *Harper's Magazine* ran a Lodge article in one of the 1896 issues that also contained an installment of Wilson's *Washington*.

profession of the 1890s, while fond of the notion that history was or might become an exact science, was still markedly patriotic and literary in outlook. In his 1898 presidential address to the American Historical Association, George P. Fisher, the author of a much-admired work on *The Colonial Era* (1892), maintained that if a choice had to be made, hero worship was preferable to iconoclasm. There was nothing to be gained from searching out the flaws (if any) in the character of George Washington; every nation needed at least one sacred personage "justly enshrined in popular veneration."[6]

The style in which Wilson garbed his narrative has not worn well. But his biography was written in a period when historical romance and glamorous make-believe were in vogue. Realistic and naturalistic prose was confined to a handful of writers such as Stephen Crane and Frank Norris, and even they were not entirely consistent. The most widely praised fiction of the decade leaned toward the tinted and the exotic. The taste of readers was formed upon such novels as Anthony Hope's *The Prisoner of Zenda* (1894), Frances Hodgson Burnett's *A Lady of Quality* (1896) and *His Grace of Osmonde* (1897), and S. Weir Mitchell's story of the American Revolution, *Hugh Wynne, Free Quaker* (1898). Mitchell's was one of a number of historical novels that deferentially introduced the personage of George Washington. So it would be wrong to suppose that Woodrow Wilson was guilty of any worse literary sin than writing in the idiom of his time, at least that approved by the educated middle class. This will be apparent to anyone who glances through the issues of *Harper's Magazine* which contain Wilson's *Washington*. Wilson's style differed little from that of Theodore Roosevelt, for example, whose account of the winning of the West was being featured at the same period. More surprisingly perhaps, there were certain affinities in the prose of Mark Twain. Twain's serialized *Personal Recollections of Joan of Arc*, a book in which he himself took considerable pride, is couched in a "historical" vocabulary, with deliberate archaisms:

> *It was vexatious to see what a to-do the whole town, and next the whole country, made over the news!*

That sentence could easily have come from Wilson's *Washington*.[7]

---

[6] Herman Ausubel, *Historians and Their Craft: A Study of the Presidential Addresses of the American Historical Association, 1884-1945* (New York, 1950), 268.

[7] Grant C. Knight, *The Critical Period in American Literature* (Chapel Hill, N.C., 1951), 95-98, 124-45. The Twain quotation is to be found in *Harper's Magazine*, 92 (December, 1895): 135. The same issue included, together with the first installment of Woodrow Wilson's *George Washington*, a short

Like Twain, Wilson was casting about for an appropriate narrative method. It is arguable that, unlike Twain, he never found one. An early attempt at a "psychoanalytic study" of Wilson, William B. Hale's *The Story of a Style* (1920), interpreted the increasing pomposity and obscurity of Wilson's prose as evidence of a progressive deterioration of intellect:

> *Mr. Wilson does not concur, he entirely concurs; he is seldom gratified, he is profoundly gratified; he does not feel pleasure, he experiences unaffected pleasure; he seldom says anything, but he is always privileged to say, or, speaking from his heart, says, or in all frankness says.*[8]

Yet before he entered politics, Woodrow Wilson was preoccupied with words and their uses. "I have imagined a style," he wrote to his fiancée Ellen Axson in January, 1884, "clear, bold, fresh, and facile (W.B. Hale might have said that "facile" gave the game away); a style flexible but always strong, capable of light touches or of heavy blows; . . . a style full of life, of colour and vivacity." He added: "Is it any wonder that I am disgusted with the stiff, dry, mechanical, monotonous sentences in which my meagre thoughts are compelled to masquerade?" Eleven years later, insisting to his wife that he was still no true man of letters, he lamented: "If I could only write prose that was delicate, imaginative, full at once of grace, force, and distinction, that would be something: my thoughts would at least go clad like aristocrats. But alas! I shall but wear my soul out trying." In 1897 he dwelt on the deficiencies of his literary essays in a letter to a friend. The phrasing, he said, was "too elaborate"; it lacked the "easy pace of simplicity."

Despite Wilson's capacity for self-criticism, there was a basic flaw in his desire to improve his prose. His real aim was oratorical rather than literary. He wanted to achieve glory, victory, immortality; he dreamed of great occasions and instantaneous acclaim. Indeed, oratory sometimes yielded him such triumph,

---

story entitled "The Last Sonnet of Princivalle di Cembino."

[8] Hale, a well-known journalist, was a former friend of Wilson. His tract against Wilsonian rhetoric is described by his son William Harlan Hale, "President Wilson, Dr. Freud, and 'The Story of a Style,'" *The Reporter*, June 26, 1958, 28-30. Freud's comments to William B. Hale are interesting in the light of his subsequent collaboration with William C. Bullitt (*Thomas Woodrow Wilson . . . A Psychological Study* [Boston, 1967]). Freud admitted to Hale his detestation of Wilson, but also said: "Mr. Wilson is a living personality and not a product of political phantasy. . . . In my opinion, psychoanalysis should never be used as a weapon in literary or political polemics. . . . Psychoanalysis should not be practiced on a living subject . . . unless he submits to it. I am not in the habit of killing my own patients."

notably in a commemorative address delivered at Princeton in 1896. *Belles lettres* and historical writing could hardly bear such a burden of expectation, especially since (he informed Ellen Axson in 1885) he had "no patience for the tedious toil of what is known as 'research'."[9]

Yet he had a point, in the historical milieu of the late nineteenth century. The emphasis on professionalism, the belief that history was or might become a science, led to a marked improvement in the technical competence of American historical writing. Johns Hopkins University furnished a dignified entry to the life of scholarship for Wilson as for Frederick Jackson Turner and many another budding professor. But Wilson clung stubbornly to an older ideal — of history as an art, a branch of literature. "Style is not much studied here," he informed his fiancée in October 1883. At Hopkins, "*ideas* are supposed to be everything — their vehicle comparatively nothing. But you and I know that there can be no greater mistake."[10] Whatever may be said in dispraise of Wilson's historical work, it is considerably more readable than most of the monographs produced according to the dictates of the new professionalism. Missing in Wilson was the dedication, the passion for facts, the intellectual curiosity of some of his academic contemporaries. Missing in them was the imaginative excitement, the determination to make history *live*, that linked Wilson with such amateurs as Theodore Roosevelt. He was a historian in the mould of Roosevelt or perhaps of Sir Winston Churchill. He wrote, in other words, not as the culmination of arduous research, but rapidly, fluently, for ulterior though not necessarily unworthy motives: to stimulate patriotic enthusiasm, to reach the ear of the public, to gratify concealed autobiographical impulses, to arm himself for future activity in some larger, public sphere.

The main value of Wilson's *George Washington* lies therefore in the clues it offers to the prepolitical stage of his development. Certain of the clues are negative. They hint either at limitations that were to persist throughout Wilson's career or at conventional opinions he was later to revise or repudiate.

The book confirms that up to the age of forty Woodrow Wilson was still orthodoxly conservative. George Washington figures as a "thoroughbred gentleman" of Virginia. Washington's Americanness is that of the good sturdy

---

[9] Donald Day, ed., *Woodrow Wilson's Own Story*, 25, 30; R. S. Baker, *Woodrow Wilson: Life and Letters*, 1: 109-14.

[10] Day, *Wilson's Own Story*, 24. These ideas are most fully expressed in "On the Writing of History," an 1895 contribution to *Century Magazine*: see Bragdon, *Woodrow Wilson: The Academic Years*, 243. Lodge and Roosevelt expressed almost identical views: see John A. Garraty, *Henry Cabot Lodge* (New York, 1953), 57.

sort of Englishman who took Wilson's intermittently Anglophile fancy. By contrast, Thomas Jefferson is too Frenchified, too affected by "demagogues and philosophers," to be altogether reliable. Wilson had decided in 1894 that while Washington was truly a great American, Jefferson could not quite qualify on account of "the strain of French philosophy that weakened and permeated his thought." As a Democratic political leader Wilson subsequently overcame such doubts. His initial response had been, as it chanced, quite close to that of Theodore Roosevelt.

Wilson's cordial adoption of Turner's idea on the importance of the American West, noticeable in his previous book *Division and Reunion*, finds little outlet in *George Washington*, where heroism is still the central concern. In his Turnerian "Calendar of Great Americans" (1894), Wilson proclaimed that "the typical Americans have all been western men, with the exception of Washington." Rather than seek to explain how the exceptional could be also the typical, he falls back in the biography upon a conventionally genteel admiration for Washington, the exemplary aristocrat-leader (with an occasional hint at "backwoodsman's" qualities).

The brief, trite summary of Washington's presidency shows that in the 1890s Wilson's conception of the role of the nation's chief executive and of practical politics while clear enough, was too simple and theoretical. He offered various Emersonian observations on leadership — for example, an address at the University of Tennessee in June 1890: "I do not conceive the leader a trimmer, weak to yield what clamor claims, but the deeply human man, quick to know and to do the things that the hour and his nation need." At the age of forty-five, in 1902, shortly before he became president of Princeton University, Wilson wrote to Frederick J. Turner, "I was born a politician and must be at the task for which, by means of my historical writing, I have been all these years in training."[11] The task he referred to, however, was that of settling down to compose his *magnum opus* on the "Philosophy of Politics." His destiny was vaguely conceived: he might sway men by means of oratory or eloquent printed arguments, but he had as yet gone no further than commencement commonplaces. The actual mechanisms of politics were remote to him and in a way would always remain so.

Some have traced Wilson's vision of a powerful executive further back than 1900. Even in his first published article of 1879, and more fully in *Congressional*

---

[11] Note the echo ("must be at the task") from the New Testament: "Young Jesus was found by his parents in the temple, sitting in the midst of the doctors, both hearing them, and asking them questions. And all that heard him were astonished at his understanding. When his worried mother chided him, Jesus replied: wist ye not that I must be about my Father's business?" (Luke 2:49).

Government (1885), he had stressed the importance of bold, efficient direction of national affairs. In an *Atlantic Monthly* article of July 1897, pointing to the examples set by Andrew Jackson and Abraham Lincoln, he demanded a new "national leadership"; and in a lecture delivered shortly afterward to a group of lawyers he deplored the American system as a "Leaderless Government." But in such pronouncements Wilson was still thinking of a partnership, more or less on the British model, between the president, his cabinet, and Congress. Power, he seemed to assume, resided in Congressional committees or among the executive officers. The president could not master enough of the complex mass of business, even with a reformed method of federal administration to be more than a kind of board chairman. In short, "leadership" appeared in practice to be a collective activity, not that of one man; by "executive" he understood the whole executive branch, rather than the president as "chief executive." The introduction he wrote in 1900 for a new edition of *Congressional Government* proved that he had begun to take note of a fresh political climate, involving a dramatic extension of presidential power. It was, however, a fact to be recognized, not a transformation he had predicted or urged. True, in the 1880s and 1890s he admired the courage of the Democratic president Grover Cleveland. But it cannot be demonstrated that Professor Wilson foretold the resurgent presidency that started to emerge after the Spanish-American War of 1898.[12]

On the other hand, there are in Wilson's *George Washington* generalized clues to his own inchoate visions of greatness. Washington had been drawn into public life by the demands of the age. So might that other Virginian, Woodrow Wilson, who in 1885 complained in an intimate letter that he had been "shut out from my heart's *first* — primary — ambition and purpose, which was, to take an active, if possible a leading part in public life, and strike out for myself, if I have the ability, a *statesman's* career." Washington as a young soldier displays the "haughty carriage . . . of a man born to have his will." Compare Wilson's avowal to Ellen Axson, on the acceptance of his first book (December, 1884): "I feel as I suppose a general does who has gained a . . . foothold in the enemy's country. . . . My rejoicing . . . has in it a great deal that is stern and sober, like that of the strong man to run a race." Washington's firmness of purpose and his ability to meet

---

[12] See August Heckscher, ed., *The Politics of Woodrow Wilson* (New York, 1956), 40-48; Woodrow Wilson, *Congressional Government* (Cleveland, 1965), with an introduction by Walter Lippmann which maintains that as early as 1884, when he was writing the book, Wilson began to take a new view of the presidency under the inspiration of Grover Cleveland. James M. Burns, *Presidential Government* (Boston, 1956), 94-95, shows that Lippmann's theory is unsound: Wilson sent the manuscript of *Congressional Government* to the publisher in October 1884, before Cleveland had even been elected president.

additional responsibilities are stressed in the biography. We hear too of his "old passion for success" and of the ardent, almost violent emotions held under control by the Mount Vernon planter-aristocrat. Compare again Wilson's confession to his fiancée (December 1884): "It isn't pleasant or convenient to have strong passions. I have the uncomfortable feeling that I am carrying a volcano about with me."[13]

Other parallels could not have been anticipated by Wilson the academic. It is reasonable, though, to assume that within Wilson the president, toward the end of his heartbreaking White House years, there may have stirred the memory of things he had once written about the nation's first chief executive. The picture of Washington coolly withstanding the clamor for war in 1793 might seem to prefigure Wilson's own insistence on high-minded neutrality. There is the sense of a parallel sequence thereafter. Washington faces controversy ("Strong measures bred strong opposition"). Congressional opponents stir up trouble ("the opposition slowly pulled itself together . . . to concert a definite policy of action"). Washington remains serene (confident that "the right view will prevail; that the 'standard to which the wise and honest will repair' is also the standard to which the whole people will rally at last, if it be but held long and steadily enough on high to be seen of all"). He suffers terrible abuse, until at length the nation perceives he was in the right and his enemies were wrong. But the abuse has taken its toll ("they had alienated his great spirit forever"), and so at the end of his second term he insists on resigning the office.

Prophetic utterances, the more oddly so when we recall that one of Wilson's inveterate enemies was his early rival in Washington scholarship, Senator Henry Cabot Lodge. It was young Lodge who once, while a magazine editor, turned down an article submitted by young Wilson, with the laconic notation "R.R.R." — received, rejected, returned. There was nothing uncanny in these unconscious anticipations. When Woodrow Wilson wrote *George Washington* he had no idea that he himself might one day be president. He had only a hazily lofty notion of the scope and responsibilities of the office. What he did have was a burning though obscure ambition for statesmanlike fame. He employed the metaphors of battle to describe his yearning, because he saw himself thwarted and challenged. In cheerful moments he felt irresistible; in not infrequent moments of depression he was conscious only that he would be resisted. Chronicling the career of George Washington, he unwittingly — as biographers usually do — disclosed his own buried hopes and fears. He revealed his strengths: energy,

---

[13] Donald Day, ed., *Woodrow Wilson's Own Story*, 29-30.

determination, integrity, intelligence, a kind of courtly charm. And he revealed something of his potential limitations: obstinacy, imperiousness, a disinclination to compromise, a fundamentally traditionalist outlook, a kind of glib superficiality. On balance his gifts were formidable. Among them, even with reservations, must be counted the stream of writings of his professorial years. Very few of his academic compeers managed to be so remarkably productive. But then Woodrow Wilson was no ordinary academic.

———————————

This essay appeared as the "Introduction," to Woodrow Wilson's *George Washington*. (New York: Schocken Books Inc., 1969, first published 1896), v-xviii.

VICTORIAN AMERICA
AND AFTER

The half-dozen essays assembled here address themselves to cultural and literary themes, running in chronology from roughly 1830 to 1930. I wish there had been room for various additional essays which bring us closer to modern or postmodern times. The bibliography at the end of the book indicates where readers can turn for such material in my writings.

Still, I realize upon reflection that over the years I have felt especially at home with those elements of American thought and behaviour that are often described as "Victorian." The term may seem a misnomer, applied to a society whose polyglot, republican inhabitants tended to evince either indifference or outright hostility to whatever British monarchy connoted to them. However, even if nineteenth century Americans may not commonly have spoken of themselves as "Victorian," historians in the twentieth century find it a useful label for the period covered by the present sample of essays.

During those decades the United States and Great Britain maintained a complexly antagonistic parallelism whose balancing features have largely disappeared since about 1930. Early rivalrous resentments are sketched in the essay on Frances Trollope's *Domestic Manners of the Americans* (1832), which aroused more attention in the United States than in Mrs. Trollope's own country. Some not dissimilar emotions are sketched in the account of London's "Great Exhibition" of 1851. This essay deals with American involvement in the first of what was to be a series of international extravaganzas during the Victorian era, including the Philadelphia centennial in 1876, and the Chicago World's Fair of 1893. Like its successors, the pioneering London venture was an international competition masquerading as a love-feast. Whether the United States intended a direct challenge to the host-nation or was a merely peripheral entrant, was not clear at the outset. Yet when the Great Exhibition closed and Paxton's prefabricated "Crystal Palace" was removed from Hyde Park to another site on the outskirts of London, the American presence had certainly made itself felt in that census year, 1851.

Of the remaining essays, only the one on Mark Twain directly stresses the Anglo-American relationship. The other three examine various aspects of literary and scholarly life in the late nineteenth and early twentieth centuries. All the pieces in this section locate their American material within a "genteel" or mainstream milieu which some recent cultural historians have been apt to disparage and minimize, but which I believe constituted a genuine if inevitably somewhat derivative cultural center.

Ralph Waldo Emerson may serve here as a spokesman. He could be sternly critical of Britain, finding its own cultural life rather heavy and conventional. On the other hand, Emerson more than once inscribed in his topical notebooks the thought that "America is England seen under a magnifying glass." The insights and possible limitations of such a dictum help to indicate the sphere of American Victorianism — a cultural more evidently than a political or economic phenomenon, though those elements also deserve consideration. What may be done with comparative and perceptual history in the transatlantic setting is more broadly suggested in the essays comprising Part IV.

11

Frances Trollope

This was written as one of twenty-nine essays on foreign visitors to the United States, to accompany an exhibition at the National Portrait Gallery in Washington, D. C. The volume that resulted was embellished with portraits and prints from the exhibition, including the cuckold caricature of Mr. Trollope referred to in my article. This book was one of several excellent bicentennial productions that, perhaps because of excessive competition with one another, did not receive the attention they merited.

I do not like them. I do not like their principles, I do not like their manners, I do not like their opinions.

— Domestic Manners of Americans

Frances Trollope (1780-1863) had just reached her fifty-second birthday when her first book, *Domestic Manners of the Americans*, was published in London in March 1832. She was to produce a spate of novels and travel books during the next couple of decades. Two of her five children, Thomas Adolphus and Anthony, became established authors. At her death in 1863, Mrs. Trollope could look back on a richly busy life which had also been financially rewarding.

Before the publication of *Domestic Manners*, however, things had been very different. She was married to a querulous lawyer with a dwindling practice. The Trollopes lived beyond their means, in the illusory hope of inheriting a fortune from a rich uncle. Mrs. Trollope's journey to the United States at the end of 1827, with three children and a manservant, looked like yet another stage on the family road to disaster. (Her husband remained in England for a time to look after the education of their two older sons.) She traveled in company with Frances Wright, a wealthy young radical who had persuaded her to spend some time at the new community of Nashoba, which Miss Wright had established near Memphis. Nashoba proved to be a wretched chaos. Mrs. Trollope's second scheme was to continue upriver to Cincinnati, which she had heard was a flourishing new city, and open an emporium to be called the Bazaar, where she would tap the flow of dollars by selling European novelties. This venture was a dismal failure. She managed to survive in Cincinnati for two years, supported by the efforts of a young French artist-protégé Auguste Hervieu.

In poor health and with ailing children, she headed eastward, wintered in the vicinity of Washington, D.C., visited the Middle Atlantic States, and sailed for home in the summer of 1831. Her one hope was to make a book out of her experiences. Even to this strong-willed woman the prospects could not have seemed bright. She had never appeared in print. Her education was haphazard — a governessy smattering of poetry, French and Italian, botany, and general romanticism. She had spent only a few days in New Orleans on arrival; she had merely passed through Baltimore and Philadelphia; and New England remained unknown to her. A recent English account, Captain Basil Hall's *Travels in North America in the Years 1827 and 1828,* which may have stimulated her to try her own hand, was also discouragingly — in her eyes — knowledgeable, ambitious, and complete. She regarded Captain Hall as a deep thinker; her own narrative, she confessed, amounted to "gossiping."

To her surprise and delight, the manuscript of *Domestic Manners* was accepted by a London publisher, largely on the recommendation of Captain Hall. The two volumes of the first edition included twenty-four lithographs by Hervieu, who was to illustrate several more of her books. To her still greater delight, *Domestic Manners* brought some cash, some fame, and a good deal of notoriety. She followed up immediately with a novel, *The Refugee in America* (1832). Things continued to go wrong within her family — she was not able to ward off bankruptcy for her feeble husband, and then he and two of her children died — but at last, after a half-century of scrabbling frustration, Frances Trollope could enjoy the solace of success. She wrote three more novels about America: *The Life and Adventures of Jonathan Jefferson Whitlaw; or Scenes on the Mississippi* (1836), *The Barnabys in America* (1843), and *The Old World and the New: A Novel* (1849). Americans took offence at *Domestic Manners*; and it cannot be denied that the "old woman" Trollope gave cause. The Americans, she announced, exhibited a "total and universal want of manners, both in males and females." They were inquisitive, boring, uncultivated, uncouth, humorless, and self-satisfied. Public behavior was appalling. She saw a woman suckling a baby at the theater; men there sat on the edge of boxes, their backs to the audience, or sprawled with their feet propped up. American women, when young, were "the handsomest in the world" and yet "the least attractive"; they held themselves badly and had scrawny figures. The males were similarly unappealing: "I never saw an American man walk or stand well. . . . They are nearly all hollow chested and round shouldered." Table manners were particularly repugnant:

> *The total want of all the usual courtesies of the table . . . the loathsome spitting, from the contamination of which it was absolutely impossible to protect our dresses; the frightful manner of feeding with their knives, till the whole blade seemed to enter into the mouth; and the still more frightful manner of cleaning the teeth afterwards with a pocket knife, soon forced us to feel that . . . the dinner hour was to be any thing rather than an hour of enjoyment.*

Except for Negroes, Americans had no ear for music: "I scarcely ever heard a white American . . . go through an air without being out of tune before the end of it." She was shocked by the casual treatment accorded to President Andrew Jackson when he came to Cincinnati in 1829:

> *I was at his elbow when a greasy fellow accosted him thus: "General Jackson, I guess?"*
> *The General bowed assent.*
> *"Why they told me you was dead."*
> *"No! Providence has hitherto preserved my life."*
> *"And is your wife alive too?"*
> *The General, apparently much hurt, signified the contrary, upon which the courtier concluded his harangue, by saying, "Aye, I thought it was one or the t'other of ye."*

In spite of her avowed emphasis on mundane detail — what she called in her preface "the daily aspect of ordinary life" — Mrs. Trollope did not hesitate to generalize. She noted the contempt for law: "Trespass, assault, robbery, nay, even murder, are often committed without the slightest attempt at legal interference." She commented on American indifference to the rights of slaves and Indians:

You will see them with one hand hoisting the cap of liberty, and with the other flogging their slaves. You will see them one hour lecturing their mob on the indefeasible rights of man, and the next driving from their homes the children of the soil, whom they have bound themselves to protect by the most solemn treaties.

She singled out Thomas Jefferson for particular criticism. He was responsible for the foolish and dangerous proposition that all men were created equal — and yet he kept slaves. With typical American hypocrisy, "Mr. Jefferson is said to have been the father of children by almost all his numerous gang of female slaves." She pictured America as "a vast continent, by far the greater part of which is still in the state in which nature left it, and a busy, bustling, industrious population, hacking and hewing their way through it" with scant regard for natural beauty. "This country," she asserted, "may be said to spread rather than to rise."

In her final chapter, Mrs. Trollope declared that apart from a "small patrician band" of well-bred and congenial people, the American population was dull, brutal, and arrogant. By the test of prosperity, the principles of equality and system of government no doubt suited the Americans. But the result was distressing for a European. "A single word indicative of doubt, that any thing, or every thing, in that country is not the very best in the world, produces an effect which must be seen and felt to be understood." How could a person of sensibility, especially a foreigner, be happy in such an environment? If Americans should ever mend their ways, "if refinement once creeps in among them, if they once learn to cling to the graces, the honours, the chivalry of life, then we shall say farewell to American equality, and welcome to European fellowship one of the finest countries in the world." But Mrs. Trollope did not seem to feel this was a likely change. In her portrayal Americans, endowed with a fine country, were destroying it, and wrecking themselves morally in the process.

There are two opposite ways of interpreting Mrs. Trollope's book and the impact it had in the United States. The first reaction, the commonest in the 1830s, is to dismiss *Domestic Manners* as a potboiler, written by an ill-informed woman who, having done badly in America, resorted to supercilious Toryism. This view is supported by passages in her book (and in her later novels about America) in which she appears to be upset not so much by bad manners as by the absence of social deference. She is shocked by the brusque behavior of household help, or by the discovery that men in public life are often not "gentlemen." Her preface, rather different in tone from first-draft versions, warns England against the "jarring tumult and universal degradation which invariably follow the wild scheme of placing all the power of the state in the hands of the populace." As the Whig *Edinburgh Review* observed in 1832, *Domestic Manners* was "an express advertisement against the Reform Bill." The book was published while Britain was locked in argument over electoral reform, which Tory sentiment opposed. The United States was cited as a dreadful warning of what might happen if "the mob" gained political power. Basil Hall had recommended Mrs. Trollope's manuscript because it bolstered his own more cautious analysis of the weaknesses of American democracy. Mrs. Trollope's revised preface and her final chapter may have been composed on her return to England with the Reform Bill controversy directly in mind. *Domestic Manners* may also be seen as a standard English reaction of the time to the humiliations of the War of Independence and the War of 1812. In these decades, and indeed to the end of the century, Americans felt they detected a jealous, disdainful resentment on the part of the mother country. So it could be said that *Domestic Manners* ministered to a British willingness to believe that in achieving independence the United States had gone astray. On their side, Americans would naturally resist a rendering of themselves so impressionistically prejudiced.

The alternative possibility is that Frances Trollope angered Americans not by propagandizing but by telling the truth. There is evidence in favor of this theory. After all, Americans such as James Fenimore Cooper sometimes offered similar strictures, and made themselves unpopular by doing so. Foreign visitors were expected to pay compliments. The young nation was touchy in the extreme. Americans castigated the author of *Domestic Manners*. But perhaps the shout of "Trollope!" at a man with his feet up in a theater was admission that there was in fact room for improvement in such matters. With the passage of time, at any rate, certain Americans were prepared to admit that Mrs. Trollope's testimony had in previous decades not been altogether inaccurate. In passages of *Life on the Mississippi* deleted by the author for its first printing, Mark Twain said that "poor candid Mrs. Trollope . . . lived three years in this civilization of ours; in the body of it — not on the surface of it, as was the case with most of the foreign tourists of her day. She knew her subject well, and she set it forth fairly and squarely, without any weak ifs and ands and buts. She deserved gratitude — but it is an error to suppose she got it." In 1908, John Graham Brooks's dispassionate study *As Others See Us* cited Frances Trollope as one of the foreign visitors whose criticisms had had a salutary effect.

The America of Twain and Brooks was a maturer, worldlier place than the America of Mrs. Trollope. When the sting had long departed from her words, it was possible to concede that she had actually lived in middle America. She had not arrived by the front door, armed with letters of introduction to the polite society of the seaboard. Though she showed only a cursory acquaintance with American literature, there was in truth, except for Irving and Cooper, not a vast amount of it to discuss in 1830. The glories of American art and architecture likewise lay in the future. To her credit, she did express warm admiration for the young sculptor Hiram Powers and subsequently found an English purchaser for his "Greek Slave" statue.

Then should Mrs. Trollope's reputation be reevaluated, as one who was not afraid to draw attention to the less rosy features of American life? Ralph Waldo Emerson praised England as the land of plain speaking, whose creed was: "Let us know the truth. Draw a straight line, hit whom and where it will." Was Mrs. Trollope a Tory snob, garrulous and sometimes spiteful, or a lively indomitable woman who had the wit and the courage to say what she thought?

Several factors must be taken into account. Probably without realizing so, she was a contributor to a dispute over the New World which, as Antonello Gerbi has shown, had already been in train for over three centuries. The issue was whether the American continent marked an advance on Europe or was a backward hemisphere. Many Europeans, other than potential emigrants, were conditioned almost from birth to believe in American degradation and to demand proofs to the contrary. Most Americans, of course, upheld the opposite view, and were correspondingly prejudiced against Europe. In this regard, *Domestic Manners* falls into place as another exhibit in a very long line.

The relations between the United States and Britain were especially complex. As Emerson remarked in *English Traits*, "English believes in English." Most of the people Mrs. Trollope liked in America seemed to be English by birth. There is something in the tone of the book liable to irk Americans and lead them to question her credentials. Her style has been called "clever." It is, however, clever mainly in being "smart." She scores points off people in dialogues that she recounts. She is breezy rather than funny. Her persona is that of the well-bred Englishwoman confronted with vulgarities and absurdities. She operates from within a fortress of assumed impregnability. She is almost always sure of her opinions, and intimates that — since they are based upon a superior upbringing — no appeal is possible from her judgments. She disclaims expert knowledge or wisdom but implies that her own grounding in common sense is thoroughly adequate. Such Englishry, also noticeable in her son Anthony Trollope's *North America* (1862), does not amount to blatant prejudice. But it can be annoying when it confuses candor and condescension.

The American response to this tinge of proprietary disapproval tended to be sharp. The mother country was attacked as moribund and aristocratic. From Tom Paine's ridiculing of George III in *Common Sense*, American reactions to the mother country had a sort of myth-destroying element. It was psychologically necessary to deny the parental bond. It is intriguing to consider the forms of abuse that greeted Mrs. Trollope in the America of the 1830s. Why, for example, was there so much exaggeration of the ugliness and elderliness of "Dame Trollope?" In squibs of the day she was the "old woman"; in waxwork effigy she was caricatured as an ancient crone. True, in *Domestic Manners* she tells of being referred to as "old woman" by unceremonious neighbors. But the taunt may have seemed particularly fitting for American contemporaries who wished to deny the legitimacy of any criticism emanating from England. A hostile American lithographer of the 1830s, showing the Trollope menage in Cincinnati, hints that her husband was wearing cuckold's horns — the guilty party being the young artist Hervieu.

On the other hand, her book is not wholly defined by the Anglo-American context. It is liberally sprinkled with allusions to French and Italian literature and music. Her faithful friend and companion during her entire American stay was the Frenchman Auguste Hervieu. She treasured a meeting with Lafayette in Paris in 1824. There was a romantic radicalism in her makeup of a continental European variety that we miss if we write her off as an English Tory. Indeed, how could she have been a friend of Frances Wright, whose freely expressed atheistical and socialist views scandalized American audiences, if her notions had simply been those of the London *Quarterly Review* — the only British periodical which wrote appreciatively of *Domestic Manners*? The creditors drove her to live in Belgium. Her own choice of domicile, when she was able to indulge her fancy, was Florence in Italy. Some of her most trenchant comments on America, to the effect that it was boring and materialistic, are remarkably close to the conclusions of certain French intellectuals. Victor Jacquemont, a young French naturalist who had visited the United States in 1827, read *Domestic Manners* in India in 1832, and gleefully discovered that it confirmed his own observations. Jacquemont's friend, the writer Stendhal, who also read Mrs. Trollope in 1832, thought too that she was right about the heaviness of American life.

Domestic Manners of the Americans is not a subtle book. It is a fairly artless mixture of several possible books, written by a woman of uncommon energy and aspiration, yearning for an existence that had so far eluded her. At any given point, her attitudes are sincere, and usually transparent. They do not make a perfect fit. The desperate, impoverished matron with an ineffectual husband coexists with the creature who would like to read soul-stirring literature on a mountain top and with a third lady who would love to be a *grande dame* instead of Dame Trollope. There is a moralizing streak, that led her a few years later to indict British industrialism in *The Life and Adventures of Michael Armstrong, the Factory Boy* (1839-40) — "almost as shocking," in the sarcastic riposte of the American Charles Edwards Lester, "as anything Mrs. Trollope found in the Domestic Manners of the Americans." There is too a Tory presence in the offing. Stendhal described her as "un sot ultra avec de l'esprit," which might be rendered as "a conservative fool with spirit." An irony which offers a further insight is that for Stendhal the English somewhat resembled the Americans. In castigating the Americans for being solemn, materialistic, and graceless, the English were unconsciously convicting themselves.

The unevenness, the innocent multiplicity of the book helps to explain why it exasperated American readers of the 1830s. Frances Trollope was not really ensconced within a fortress. She was herself a vulnerable witness. The Canadian humorist Stephen Leacock once wrote that "half truths, like half bricks, go further in argument." That may be the best summary of *Domestic Manners*. Its author, not quite knowing who she was, did not quite know what she meant to say. It was a half brick of a book, with an half unintended wallop.

This essay appeared in *Abroad in America: Visitors to the New Nation 1776-1914*, ed. Marc Pachter (Reading, Mass.: Addison-Wesley in association with the National Portrait Gallery, Smithsonian Institution, 1976), 33-41.

The following titles are of bibliographic interest. Donald Smalley's edition of *Domestic Manners of the Americans* (New York, 1960) is a fine guide to Mrs. Trollope's most famous book. Her experiences in the United States are carefully examined in Monique Parent Frazee, *Mrs. Trollope and America* (Publications de la Faculté de Lettres et des Sciences Humaines, University of Caen, France, 1969). On European attitudes see Antonello Gerbi, *The Dispute of the New World: The History of a Polemic. 1750-1900*, translated by Jeremy Moyle (Pittsburgh, 1973). Ralph Waldo Emerson's *English Traits* (1856) was based on two visits to Britain and a set of lectures on his findings that he delivered in 1848. Mrs. Trollope's friendship with Frances Wright is set in context in Celia Eckhardt, *Fanny Wright: Rebel in America* (Cambridge, Mass., 1984). On *Michael Armstrong, The Factory Boy*, and Charles Edwards Lester's comment on it and *Domestic Manners*, see Marcus Cunliffe, *Chattel Slavery and Wage Slavery: The Anglo-American Context, 1830-1860* (Athens, Ga., 1979).

12

America at the Great Exhibition of 1851

The centennial of the 1851 Great Exhibition gave rise to the Festival of Britain in 1951. This essay, which I have slightly revised, was also a modest centennial contribution. If it were being completely rewritten, I would look for American domestic reactions not available to me at the time and take note of initial English criticism of the role of Albert, Prince Consort, and his unmonarchical, "German" involvement in conceiving and organizing the Exhibition as a testament to the "visibility of progress."

The Great Exhibition of the Works of Industry of all Nations, which opened at Paxton's Crystal Palace in London's Hyde Park, on May 1, 1851, used to be portrayed as a collection of amusing Victoriana, running in scale all the way from the "colossal" statue of the Queen (in zinc) to a set of carved fruit-stones submitted by the Prince Consort's brother, Ernest of Coburg-Gotha. More recently, the Exhibition has come to be admired for its embodiment of an age which may have been lacking in taste but certainly had no lack of gusto. Or the Exhibition can be considered as a technological display, not the least interesting item of which is Joseph Paxton's nineteen-acre "Crystal Palace" in which it was housed. By contemporaries it was often taken as a gauge of the relative prowess, cultural and technological, of the exhibiting nations. It is this last aspect that I wish to discuss, in relation to the United States.

Before an answer can be attempted, something must be said of British opinions of the United States. In the 1840s Britain was not so much ignorant of America as unsympathetic. She did not ignore what went on across the Atlantic; the newspapers of 1851 devoted almost as much space to America as do those of the later twentieth century. The United States was subjected to a sometimes uneasy or scornful, but nevertheless constant, scrutiny. A new popular weekly, the *Illustrated London News* (1842), sent a writer-engraver to Washington D. C. in 1845 expressly to cover the inauguration of President James K. Polk. The British press naturally reported what it thought would most appeal to its readers, and the picture presented was in most cases unfavorable. Americans were either slaveholders, or connived at slavery. They were crude and boastful: a fact proved by continual quotation from James Gordon Bennett's *New York Herald*. They were lawless; Queen Victoria, examining Sheffield's wares at the Exhibition, was shown a quantity of bowie knives, which — she noted in her Journal — were "made entirely for Americans, who never move without one." Worse still, Americans were dishonest. British investors lost their money when several states in 1841-42 suspended payment on their debts. Wordsworth composed a sonnet on the faithlessness of Pennsylvania; and Sydney Smith, with the same state in mind, wrote that:

> *A great nation, after trampling under foot all earthly tyranny, has been guilty of a fraud as enormous as ever disgraced the worst king of the most degraded nation of Europe.*[1]

Equal and more lasting indignation was aroused by the pirating of British books, since Congress declined to subscribe to an international copyright agreement. Under the heading of *American Contributions to the Exhibition*, the humor magazine *Punch* said:

> *We understand that amongst other curiosities brought over by the St. Lawrence, there is a cheque sent by a distinguished American publisher to a no less distinguised English author — a cheque in payment of his book, originally produced in England, and immediately reprinted in New York — it is said that, [so] as this cheque may be seen to the very best advantage, LORD ROSSE'S telescope will be brought to bear upon it.*[2]

It would seem that middling and upper-class Englishmen agreed with Sydney Smith's view of the United States as a nation "unstable in the very foundations of

---

[1] A letter to the London Times, May 19, 1843, quoted in Leland H. Jenks, *The Migration of British Capital to 1875* (New York: Knopf, 1927), 105.

[2] Punch 20 (1851): 134. Lord Rosse, one of the royal commissioners for the Great Exhibition, was a prominent scientist.

social life."[3] They did not regard "Red Republicanism" as a serious threat to their institutions, but did fear that the looseness of American social structure might have bad effects upon their own country. The appearance of the female dress reform known as "Bloomerism" in 1851, while treated facetiously, was cited as a further evidence of American folly.

America was always in the news. The London *Times*, pontifical and bland, never tired of offering advice to "our American cousins." "Cousins" implied friendliness, but also the intrinsic complications of a familial relationship, with the right — one might almost say duty — to criticize which is recognized within families. But though the *Times* was an extremely influential organ, not all British newspapers and periodicals adopted its debonair approach to the United States. Sober-minded Englishmen were aware that by 1850 America's population was two-thirds that of Great Britain and that it was growing even more rapidly. How soon might American manufactures rival those of Britain? The *Economist*, noting how few American exports for the year ending June 30, 1850, were manufactured goods, concluded with some relief that there was nothing to worry about:

> Every symptom of increasing prosperity in the United States should, therefore, be hailed only as a new security for the trade and industry of our own people; and not viewed with that narrow jealousy which we regret to observe has become too much the fashion among a class of antiquated ... politicians of the day.[4]

This was the orthodox opinion of Free Traders, to whom the Crystal Palace Exhibition was a triumphant vindication of Free Trade principles. Britain was the world's great manufactory; let others come and marvel. Whatever the rest of the world could bring to the Exhibition would serve to emphasize British supremacy. It was therefore to be expected that Englishmen should be pleased if the United States, as a potential rival, made a poor showing. Some British comment on this score was fairly polite and restrained. Thus, the *Illustrated London News*:

> *There are very few of their manufactures which they could hope to sell here. American manufactures of the same kind as those exported from*

[3] Letter to the London Times, May 19, 1843.

[4] "American Prosperity the Best Security for English Trade," reprinted in Manchester *Guardian*, June 25, 1851.

Europe could only be sent as a matter of curiosity by a Government organization. Private individuals seldom take such useless trouble.[5]

Other comment, however, was gleefully hostile and somewhat illogical. It was occasioned by long-standing prejudices and by the particular events of the year.

The arrangements for the Exhibition were that each country should be responsible for its own contributions. Half the floor-space was to be occupied by the United Kingdom; the rest was to be applied for by the other nations according to their own estimates. America followed the usual pattern by forming a committee to organize exhibits. The committee grew out of the National Institute, whose President was Peter Force. Other distinguished committee-members were Levi Woodbury, Associate Justice of the Supreme Court; Commander Charles Wilkes, later known for his leading role in the *Trent* incident when he removed the Confederate commissioners Mason and Slidell from the British mail-steamer; Senator Jefferson Davis, since he was on the Board of Regents of the Smithsonian Institution; and the oceanographer Matthew Maury. As the *Illustrated London News* suggested, the American government played no active part in the proceedings, in accordance with a *laissez-faire* conviction which has perhaps placed America at a disadvantage in other expositions also. Misled by enthusiasm, the committee overestimated its requirements and applied for a greater floor-area than any other nation except France. However, this error did not become apparent until it was too late.

Gradually the American contributions were assembled at New York and put aboard the frigate *St. Lawrence*, which arrived at Southampton on March 15, 1851. With only six weeks to go before the Exhibition opened, there was an intensely excited, competitive spirit in the air. This seems to have communicated itself to the *St. Lawrence*, which "immediately commenced discharging her interesting freight for transmission to the Great Exhibition. . . . Three cheers were given by the crew when the first case (containing a carriage) was landed."[6] Taken by itself, the American list of exhibits is impressive. One's eye is caught by the name of Cyrus McCormick, with his Virginia grain reaper; by that of Mathew Brady, with a collection of daguerreotypes; by Charles Goodyear, who had a display of India-rubber goods; and by Samuel Colt, with his "formidable revolving charge pistols."[7] There were other firearms, locks, clocks, plows, carriages, piano-

---

[5] *Illustrated London News*, May 17, 1851, 432-3. To be cited as I. L. N.

[6] I. L. N., March 29, 1851, 252.

[7] *Great Exhibition: Official Descriptive and Illustrated Catalogue* (London: W. Clowes & Sons, 1851), part 5, p. 1454. To be cited as *Catalogue*.

fortes; there was a cotton-gin (made in Bridgewater, Conn.); and there was a sewing-machine (Lerow and Blodgett's: the one patented by Isaac Singer in 1851 was not shown). On a different level of achievement, there were chairs with patent centripetal springs, "constructed in a style peculiarly American"; a "patent double grand piano, upon which four performers at a time can execute compositions arranged for eight hands and two pianos";[8] an air-exhausted coffin, to preserve the dead from putrefaction; "transparent soaps, intended to represent stained glass";[9] many dental appliances; and a model of a floating church built for the Churchman's Missionary Association of Philadelphia:

> *The superstructure is firmly fastened on two of the New York clipper-ships,*
> *with a promenade all round the outside: the boats are about 90 tons each.*
> *The exterior is painted to represent brown stone, and the style throughout*
> *is Gothic: the tower and spire are at the west end, and are suitable features*
> *in the structure. . . . The interior is painted in fresco to resemble stone, with*
> *a groined Gothic ceiling, supported by cornice and pillars of the same style.*
> *The side windows are of stained glass, which greatly heighten the effect.*[10]

No paintings were hung in the Great Exhibition; American sculpture was represented by Hiram Powers's *Greek Slave* and Peter Stephenson's *Dying Indian*. Other Americana included a buck-eyed squirrel (stuffed, from Columbus, Ohio), a bookmark made by a little Choctaw girl, and a gossamer wig from Boston.

Altogether there were 600 exhibits. Those with a tinge of absurdity were no more extraordinary than the aberrations of other nations, while the more important contributions surely merited serious attention. Yet at the beginning the American section, surmounted by a huge pasteboard eagle, attracted little but ridicule. The exhibits filled up only a fraction of the room allotted. The majority consisted of raw materials and humdrum objects which were of little interest to spectators who had been gazing at silks and jewelry or at the vast contrivances in operation in the Machinery Room. Sections of the British press were quick to comment. One journalist dismissed McCormick's reaper as "a cross between an Astley's chariot, a flying machine, and a treadmill." The *Illustrated London News* mentioned some chewing tobacco "which bears the following noteworthy inscription:"

[8] *Catalogue*, 1438-39.

[9] *Catalogue*, 1453.

[10] *Catalogue*, 1457.

> *To be presented, after the World's Fair, to Lord Wellington, by Wiley J.*
> *Stratton, Glasgow, Haward county Missouri. No doubt, if the Duke chews,*
> *this will turn out a delicious article.*[11]

Punch thoroughly enjoyed itself:

> *The Americans say, that the reason they have sent nothing to the*
> *Exhibition is, that the productions of their industry are . . . too gigantic to*
> *be brought over; and . . ., the reality is so impossible to be understood or*
> *described, that the only way to give us any idea of it was to leave it all to*
> *our imagination.*"[12]

Three pages later it returned to the attack, with the suggesion that, London being crowded out with visitors, the "American Non-Exhibitors" should provide lodgings in the empty part of their area:

> *By packing up the American articles a little closer, by displaying* COLT'S
> *revolvers over the soap, and piling up the Cincinnati pickles on the top of*
> *the Virginia honey, we shall concentrate all the treasures of American art*
> *and manufacture into a very few square feet, and beds may be made up to*
> *accommodate several hundred in the space claimed for, but not one-*
> *quarter filled by, the products of United States industry.*
>
> *We would propose, therefore, that the Yankee Commissioners be*
> *empowered to advertise America as affording accommodation to those*
> *who wish to spend a week in visiting the Great Exhibition. . . . By an*
> *arrangement with the Commissioners, whose duties must be rather light,*
> *breakfast could no doubt be provided for the lodgers before starting on their*
> *rounds; and the sign of the Spread Eagle would be an appropriate one to*
> *adopt, for the hotel department of the speculation.*

Punch's suggestion was in fact accepted to the extent of giving up some of the space for seating: by which device the American section gained the rather jaded patronage of foot-weary visitors.

Not all press-comment was as acid as that of *Punch*. Colt's revolvers were highly praised, and so was the *Greek Slave* (Photo 6),

---

[11] I. L. N., August 23, 1851, 250.

[12] *Punch*, 20 (1851): 243.

deprived of her clothing, and exposed for sale to some wealthy eastern barbarian, before whom she is supposed to stand, with an expression of scornful dejection mingled with shame and disgust. Her dress, which is the modern Greek costume, on the column, and the cross implies her religion and country. The chains on her wrists are not historical, but have been added as necessary accessories.[13]

Yet even here *Punch* had its say, in speaking of the lack of American exhibits:

Why not have sent us some choice specimens of slaves? We have the Greek Captive in dead stone — why not the Virginian slave in living ebony?[14]

Horace Greeley, editor of the New York *Tribune*, who was in Europe during 1851 and acted as American juror on the Exhibition award-committee, acknowledged that "the hit in this case is certainly a fair one."[15] *Punch* thought so too, and printed a cartoon on the subject by John Tenniel (Photo 7).

It seemed that the United States had failed lamentably to impress Europe with its products, with the exception of some pistols and a statue carved in Florence which belonged to a British collector. It was all very well to explain that America was a young country; that it had had no time to produce fine arts or costly objects; or that more exhibits could have been brought over if arrangements had been more efficient. The sting remained. *Punch* compiled a list of "American Contributions" which were alleged to be still on the way. The items included:

> *The Leg of a Multiplication Table* . . . .
> *The tremendous Wooden Style that separates the American from the English Fields of Literature.*[16]

Even outside the Crystal Palace, elsewhere in London, the United States was a figure of fun. No wonder that cartoonists sometimes represented America by the figure of a Red Indian, when the painter George Catlin enlivened his American Indian Collection, off Regent Street, with "Promenade Lectures . . . with War-

---

[13] *Catalogue*, 1466.

[14] *Punch* 20 (1851): 209.

[15] Hints Toward Reforms, 2d ed. enlarged, with *The Crystal Palace and Its Lessons* (New York, 1857), 408. To be cited as *Lessons*.

[16] *Punch* 20 (1851): 218.

6. The Greek Slave by Hiram Powers, from *Illustrated London News,* August 9, 1851.

7. The Virginian Slave, from *Punch,* May 1851.

songs, War-whoops, &c., at 2 in the day, and half-past 8 in the evening."[17] Nor
did a play called *Apartments to Let*, then running in London, do anything to
modify Europe's idea of the typical American:

> *The master of the house, returned from his travels, finds it in possession*
> *of foreigners. One, "the American," is the tenant of a chair, while the*
> *disconsolate owner of all the chairs and tables is compelled to turn one of*
> *the latter into a four-post bedstead, and to couch thereunder as he best*
> *may. Fain would he sleep, but the go-ahead Yankee smokes, and*
> *impudently puffs his cigar under the board into the host's face.*[18]

However, before the Exhibition closed to the public on October 11, the United
States won a number of spectacular successes. Samuel Colt's revolvers were
acknowledged to be the most interesting firearms on display. Hiram Powers's
marble stature ranked in popularity with *The Lion in Love* from Belgium and a
Prussian group of an Amazon on horseback attacked by a tiger. Charles
Goodyear was awarded one of the 170 Council medals. Another of these, from
the five given to the United States, went to Gail Borden, Jr., of Galveston, for his
concentrated meat biscuit (five years later Mr. Borden found his true métier with
the invention of condensed milk). Yet these were small victories; as against the
five American awards, France secured no less than 56. The first resounding
American coup was that of Alfred Charles Hobbs.

Hobbs was a Massachusetts man, representing the New York firm of Day and
Newell, locksmiths, who were exhibiting a patent "parautoptic" permutating lock
(Photo 8). The foremost British locks were those of Messrs. Chubb and Bramah,
each of whose patents was believed burglar-proof. Convinced of their limitations,
Hobbs put the matter to trial, beginning with a Chubb lock on one of the vaults
of the State Paper Office, in the presence of several witnesses. What happened
is described by the *Morning Chronicle*:

> *The lock having been examined and found to be fairly locked, Mr. Hobbs*
> *produced from his waistcoat pocket two or three small and simple-looking*
> *tools — a description of which, for obvious reasons, we forbear to give —*
> *and proceeded to work. Within 25 minutes . . . the bolt of the lock flew*
> *back and the door was opened. It was then suggested by one of the*
> *gentlemen present that Mr. Hobbs should turn the bolt back again, and*

---

[17] *Catalogue Advertiser*, part 1, 67.

[18] I. L. N., May 31, 1851, 483.

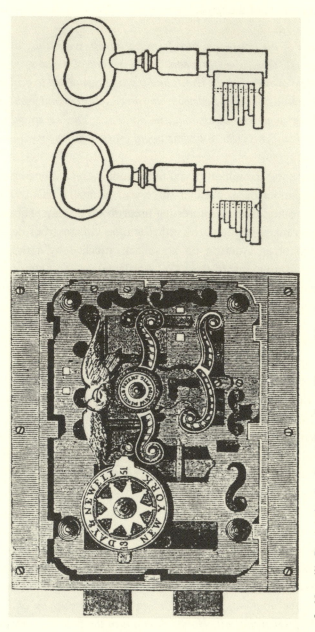

8. Newell's Permutation Lock and Key, from *Illustrated London News*, July–August, 1851.

lock the door; it being a "detector" lock, it was considered that he would be unable to accomplish this feat. In less than ten minutes, however, the door was again locked — no injury whatever was done to the interior of the lock — and no traces were to be seen of its having been picked.[19]

The feat created a sensation. Public interest was redoubled when the enterprising Mr. Hobbs immediately turned his talents to the overthrow of the Bramah lock, which had been on view for forty years in Bramah's Piccadilly store-window, with the proffered reward of 200 guineas to anyone who could pick it. One month was allowed to Hobbs in which to defeat the lock. He set to work on July 24, offering a similar reward to anyone able to master the parautoptic lock. There were no takers. Meanwhile, step by step, Hobbs drew nearer his goal, under the embarrassed eyes of Bramah's foremen. Finally, on August 23, after fifty-one hours of work, he opened it and claimed the reward. It was paid; and though his own lock may have been slighted — it was not given a prize — the British were forced to agree that Mr. Hobbs had fairly beaten them.

At the same time, the McCormick reaper, which looked so ungainly in the Crystal Palace, was demonstrating its value in the open fields where the agricultural jury watched its performance in amazement. Obed Hussey's reaper was also impressive, but McCormick's machine prompted a British commissioner to write:

It is certainly strange that we should not have had it over before, nor indeed should we have it now but for the Great Exhibition, to whose Royal originator [Prince Albert] the English farmer is clearly indebted for the introduction of the most important addition to farming machinery that has been invented since the threshing-machine first took the place of the flail.[20]

After winning a Council medal, the reaper was sent on a tour of agricultural districts where it seems to have had an astonishing effect upon men famous for their stolidity:

On its first successful trial at Tiptree the agriculturalists present raised a cheer. At Farningham the enthusiasm manifested was even greater.[21]

---

[19] Reprinted in the Manchester *Guardian*, July 26, 1851.

[20] Extract from the *Journal of the Royal Agricultural Society*, by Philip Pusey, F. R. S.; reprinted *Catalogue*, 1437-8.

[21] Manchester *Guardian*, August 27, 1851 (quoting the London *Times*).

Colt, Powers, Hobbs, McCormick: and now the clipper-yacht *America*, which had nothing to do with the Exhibition but a great deal to do with British opinion about the United States. The *America* was built specially in New York to take part in the first race for the International Silver Trophy (later known as the America's Cup) around the Isle of Wight. It was the only American entry of a large field, and when it arrived off the Isle at the end of July, its unusual design interested, but hardly alarmed, the rival British yachtsmen. *Punch* predicted defeat for the *America*, in a jocular poem. Nevertheless, the race was a great sporting event, and Queen Victoria was among the spectators who gathered at Cowes on August 28 to see the outcome of the contest. There were fifteen starters; as the yachts disappeared from view, the *America* was lying in a modest position. But when after some eight hours the first yacht reappeared, it was the *America*, twenty-four minutes ahead of its nearest competitor. *Punch* could not resist one more fling at the copyright piracy practiced by some of the more unscrupulous American publishers:

> *We are informed that the America yacht is about to be purchased by a distinguished bookselling firm in New York, for the purpose of running between that city and London. This is characteristically wise of publishing JONATHAN. If you will live by robbing the brains of others, it is only the more prudent to outstrip all competitors in the earliest possession of the stolen goods.*[22]

However, this was the last splenetic reference of the year; for, to underline the nautical achievement of the *America*, in the words of the London *Times*,

> *the Baltic, one of Collins's line of steamers, has "made the fastest passage yet known across the Atlantic," and, according to the American journals, has been purchased by British agents "for the purpose of towing the Cunard vessels from one shore of the ocean to the other." Finally, as if to crown the triumph of the year, Americans have actually sailed through the isthmus connecting the two continents of the New World, and, while Englishmen have been doubting and grudging, Yankees have stepped in and won the day.*[23]

Punch likewise made generous amends, in what it fondly imagined to be the

---

[22] *Punch* 21 (1851): 114.

[23] London *Times*, September 2, 1851 (a long editorial on the results of the Exhibition).

genuine American idiom:

> *YANKEE DOODLE sent to Town*
> *His goods for exhibition,*
> *Everybody ran him down,*
> *And laugh'd at his position;*
> *They thought him all the world behind;*
> *A goney, muff, or noodle;*
> *Laugh on, good people — never mind —*
> *Says quiet YANKEE DOODLE . . .*
>
> *Your gunsmiths of their skill may crack*
> *But that again don't mention;*
> *I guess that COLTS' [sic] revolvers whack*
> *Their very first invention.*
> *By YANKEE DOODLE, too, you're beat*
> *Downright in Agriculture,*
> *With his machine for reaping wheat*
> *Chaw'd up as by a vulture . . .*
> *You also fancied, in your pride,*
> *Which truly is tarnation,*
> *Them British locks of yourn defied*
> *The rogues of all creation;*
> *But CHUBBS' and BRAMAH'S HOBBS has picked,*
> *And you must now be viewed all*
> *As having been completely licked*
> *By glorious YANKEE DOODLE . . .*[24]

The year 1851, which had seemed humiliating for the United States, thus ended in jubilation (Photo 9). One American author asserted that his nation had conclusively shown its supremacy over the British in mechanical skill.[25] Horace Greeley gave a more balanced judgment:

> *Our share in the Exhibition was creditable to us as a nation not yet a century old, situated three to five thousand miles from London; it embraced many articles of great practical value, though uncouth in form*

---

[24] *Punch* 21 (1851): 117.

[25] Charles T. Rodgers, American Supremacy at the World's Fair (Philadelphia, 1852).

9. "The Great Exhibition of 1851," from the c. 1851 lithograph by N. Currier.

and utterly unattractive to the mere sight-seer; other nations will profit by it and we shall lose not credit; but it fell far short of what it might have been, and did not fairly exhibit the progress and present condition of the Useful Arts in this country. We can and must do better next time, and that without calling on the Federal Treasury to pay a dollar of the expense.[26]

In fact, both Britain and America could feel well pleased by the results of the Great Exhibition. The latter had recovered from a bad start; the former had accomplished what it set out to do, in acting as both host and hero in a superbly planned entertainment, which attracted six million visitors. The sense of her own primacy encouraged the journalists of Great Britain, "the Workshop of the World," to temper their observations on the United States. At the same time, it had to be admitted that America had compelled respect. And, like all good entertainments, this one concealed a number of moral lessons. One was that emotion played as great a part as rational thought in determining Anglo-American relations; heat seemed easier to generate than light. From the British point of view, the moral was that Free Trade was the golden rule of commerce (though even ardent Free Traders could not help wondering if they might not have failed to perceive the element of truth in American boasts). For the United States, Horace Greeley's argument that his country must expand her manufactures found a ready audience. For, despite his vulnerabilities of temperament, he had a shrewd reporter's eye, and saw that the typical American at the Great Exhibition was perhaps not an exhibitor but an observer: the

Yankee Manufacturer [who] passes rapidly through the Machinery-room, until his eye rests on a novel combination for weaving certain fabrics, when, after watching it intently for a few minutes, he claps his hand and exclaims in unconscious, irrepressible enthusiasm, "That will pay my expenses for the trip!"[27]

This essay appeared in the *American Quarterly* 3 (Summer 1951): 115-27.
Further reading takes note of the following. The technological innovations of the Crystal Palace are sketched in L.T.C. Rolt, *Victorian Engineering* (London: Allen Lane, 1970), chapter 5. See also Robert F. Dalzell, Jr., *American Participation in the Great Exhibition of 1851* (Amherst, Mass.: College Press, 1960); and Marcus Cunliffe, *Chattel Slavery and Wage Slavery: The Anglo-American Context, 1830-1860* (Athens:

[26] Preface, Horace Greeley, *Glances at Europe* (New York, 1852).

[27] *Lessons*, 414.

University of Georgia Press, 1979), 36-37. Encouraged by the British response, Samuel Colt opened a small-arms manufactory in London. New York City reacted to the Great Exhibition by holding one of its own in 1852, in a glass-and-wrought-iron structure imitating Paxton's "Crystal Palace" — the nickname conferred on his invention by *Punch*. The intricacies of copyright in this period are carefully explored in James J. Barnes, *Authors, Publishers and Politicians: The Quest for an Anglo-American Copyright Agreement, 1815-1854* (London: Routledge & Kegan Paul, 1974). In one of his notebooks Ralph Waldo Emerson compiled a list of twenty-five "Americans," starting with Franklin, Washington, and John Adams. Among these special people he included "George Steers, New York, born 1821, died 1856. Built the yacht 'America.'" *The Topical Notebooks of Ralph Waldo Emerson*, ed. Susan S. Smith (Columbia, Mo.: Univeristy of Missouri Press, 1990), 1: 212. As for Alfred Charles Hobbs, who became associated with Bridgeport, Conn. (see D.A.B), I have wondered whether he could have been one of the inspirations for Hank Morgan in Mark Twain's *Connecticut Yankee*. He lived on in Bridgeport, which Morgan initially thinks is Camelot, until 1891 as an engineer-inventor.

13

Mark Twain and
His "English" Novels

This piece was first printed in the London *Times Literary Supplement* of December 25, 1981. That helps to account for references in it to the Christmas trade. Publishers would bring out some choice item such as Dickens's *Christmas Carol* a few days before the holiday and count upon an astonishingly swift response where the author was already a household name.

Samuel L. Clemens (or "see *Mark Twain*," as indexes and enclyclopedias shunt us to the more famous pen-name) was born in 1835 and died in 1910. It is generally felt that Twain's best work was done in his fourth and fifth decades, ranging from *The Adventures of Tom Sawyer* (1876) to *The Tragedy of Pudd'nhead Wilson* (1894), with *Life on the Mississippi* (1883) and *Huckleberry Finn* (1884) the central summit of his achievement. Sam Clemens quit Hannibal, Missouri before he was a grown man and later on went back there only to gather notes for the autobiographical *Life on the Mississippi*. By then he was a well-established resident of New England, living in Hartford, Connecticut in prosperous proximity to such other celebrities as Harriet Beecher Stowe. However, it is also said that Twain was a deeply *American* writer, drawing his truest inspiration from the great Mississippi valley of boyhood and youth — the realm of his remembered, inmost heartland.

If so, what of his two "English" novels? *The Prince and the Pauper* was published in December 1881. *A Connecticut Yankee in King Arthur's Court* came out eight years after, at the end of 1889. They belong chronologically to Twain's most productive period. Do they belong in more important respects? Are they a closely related pair?

A common assertion is that the further Twain departed from America, in time, space and theme, the less sure his touch. *The Prince and Pauper* and *A Connecticut Yankee* were set not merely in England but in the past, one in the mid-16th century and the other in a semi-mythical Arthurian kingdom of around 600 A.D. Twain liked to read about the past, whether in the Waverley novels of Sir Walter Scott, the diary of Samuel Pepys, or Thomas Carlyle's fulminations on *The French Revolution.* He boned up on English history, looking for local color and for clues to how people generally spoke. But he was not a historian by instinct. Precise chronological accuracy was unimportant to him. Sometimes he attributed to one era behavior he knew of in connection with a different period. He defended himself by arguing that if the behavior (usually brutal) were a feature of a later, supposedly more civilized time, it was reasonable to infer that such conduct existed earlier.

At any rate, Twain scholars are apt to brush aside *The Prince and the Pauper.* They may grant that the novel is tighter in construction and more consistent in tone than much of Twain's fiction, including *A Connecticut Yankee.* Otherwise, they tend to classify it with *The Personal Recollections of Joan of Arc* (1896), Twain's subsequent venture into historical romance, as peripheral to his deepest concerns. *The Prince and the Pauper* is, in this view, not "American" or too obliquely so to carry conviction. We are told that Twain yielded to Hartford neighbors who begged him to put his talents to higher use than mere slapstick. He did indeed endeavor to present a reasonably authentic picture of the England of Henry VIII and Henry's heir, Edward VI, imparting (in the slightly coy claim of the subtitle) moral lessons for "young people of all ages." The publication date fitted in with the Christmas gift season. The "historical" narrative style Twain concocted was almost free from Americanisms. He considered publishing the book anonymously; and a reviewer in the *Atlantic Monthly* in fact remarked that "not even a critical expert" would attribute *The Prince and the Pauper* to Mark Twain "if his name were withheld from the title-page." Twain did do this with *Joan of Arc*, introducing it as a *Harper's Magazine* serial with his own authorship concealed — as if to deny an essential identity.

The *Connecticut Yankee* has been far more thoroughly worked over by critics, yet often with the intent to account for the book's uncertainty of touch. Back in 1889 the London *Spectator* disparaged the novel as "coarse and clumsy." An Edinburgh newspaper said it was "a 'lecture' in dispraise of monarchical institutions and religious establishments, and in praise of Yankee cuteness and Wall Street chicanery as compared to the simple fidelity . . . of the knightly ideal." Though such dismissals have been commoner in Britain than in the United

States, we can trace a recurrent notion that when Twain strayed too far from home, literarily, he lost his way.

A second approach is to maintain that while the *Yankee* is a more interesting work, both novels fit into the Twain canon. *The Prince and the Pauper* reveals the author's life-long fascination with doubles, twins and reversed identities. The accidental exchange of roles between the boy-prince, England's future king Edward VI, and Tom Canty, a lad from a London slum, anticipates the switching in *Pudd'nhead Wilson* of a light-hued slave baby and a white infant. The reversal of fortunes that exposes Edward, Prince of Wales, to rags, to hunger and to danger, likewise anticipates the plight in *A Connecticut Yankee* of King Arthur, sold into slavery through error when he accompanies Hank Morgan on an incognito tour of his domain. "Boss" Morgan, former superintendent of the Colt arms factory in Hartford, is projected back into mediaeval England. Twain portrays him as the quintessential American — irreverent, laconic, shrewd, and versatile. He may start out as a New England Yankee; yet as the book goes on, Morgan's skills reach out to embrace the West also: he proves to be a good horseman, a dead shot, and handy with a lariat.

So *A Connecticut Yankee* can be thought of as a novel about Twain's America rather than about mediaeval England. That was the interpretation put forward by Twain's close friend, the critic-novelist William Dean Howells, reviewing *A Connecticut Yankee* with almost uncritical amity. Twain, "our arch-humorist," in Howells's words, transcended mere humor. "At every moment the scene amuses, but it is all the time an object-lesson in democracy. It makes us glad of our republic and our epoch; but it does not flatter us into a fond content with them" — for, Howells suggested, the noble of King Arthur's day was shown to be basically identical to the exploitative entrepreneur of nineteenth-century Britain or America. Certainly the parallels with his modern world were specified, to Twain's hearty approval, in the illustrations supplied by the American artist Dan Beard for the first edition. (Tennyson, the Poet-Laureate and author of the Arthurian *Idylls of the King*, appeared as the wizard Merlin. The American "robber baron" Jay Gould was caricatured as a mediaeval slavemaster.)

Much of this commentary is concerned with the complexities of Clemens/Twain. Henry Nash Smith and Justin Kaplan have analysed Twain's increasing difficulty in completing any book. *The Prince and the Pauper* was four interrupted years in the making. *A Connecticut Yankee* involved a still more distracted struggle. Twain was preoccupied with the Paige typesetting machine, on which he staked his and his wife's resources in the expectation that the perfected invention would revolutionize printing and bring him a vast fortune.

The Paige machine, however, remained intricately imperfect.   Its failure bankrupted Twain, forcing him to sell his Hartford home and live abroad in Europe during most of the 1890s. Hence, some biographers surmise, the gradual turn in *A Connecticut Yankee* from pride in nineteenth-century know-how to the grim finale of "The Battle of the Sand Belt." Twenty-five thousand knights perish in vain assaults upon an electrified defense system manned by a handful of "Boss" Morgan's technicians; but the Boss and his followers are themselves trapped and doomed inside their cave. The dream of glorious modernity goes awry. So did the author's own fantasy of becoming a tycoon — greater than Jay Gould, on a par with the multimillionaire Andrew Carnegie, with whom Twain was delighted to be on first-name terms.

Justin Kaplan detects an additional link between the novel and its creator's experiences. In 1887, Twain dropped work on it temporarily to deliver a comic-confessional lecture to some Civil War veterans. "The Private History of a Campaign that Failed" was Twain's version of how for a few weeks in 1861 he and some Missouri acquaintances had formed a rebel or Confederate unit: a Tom Sawyerish prank except that Sam Clemens was by then 25 years old and that the gang shot an isolated stranger they mistook for the vanguard of a Union attack. In the lecture Twain facetiously referred to the killing as "the only battle in the history of the world where the opposing force was *utterly exterminated*." Having then decided to quit the war, seceding from the seceders, he in hindsight called his decision wise, the United States being the "sole country nameable in history or tradition where a man *is a man* and manhood the only royalty." The democratic ethos is undeniably a major element in *A Connecticut Yankee*. In the book, Twain's farcical-horrible "battle" - memory is reversed, becoming a conflict between the modern Union and the feudal Confederacy of aristocracy-and-church.

The blend of criticism and biography has been a conspicuous feature of Twain scholarship. Not surprisingly: his writing is, to a degree unusual among authors, personal in tone and at least implicitly autobiographical. Twain's unevenness, his abrupt shifts of plot, the jump from joke to sobriety, and from one level of humor to another, prompt us to seek explanations in the contrarieties of Clemens the man.

For instance, one may interpret his ambivalent judgments on rulers and ruled, elites and mobs, as signs of an innate dualism. Clemens/Twain was descended on one side of the family from the Lambtons — Earls of Durham who even up to his day professed a strong attachment to visions of mediaeval chivalry. On the other side he claimed descent from a regicide judge: a man associated with sending King Charles I to the scaffold in 1649.

This dualism has been charted by Howard D. Baetzhold (*Mark Twain and John Bull: The British Connection*) as an alternating dislike of and admiration for Great Britain, with admiration eventually coming out on top. Twain's final visit to England, to receive an honorary doctorate from Oxford University, was for him a marvelous accolade; and it brought his Atlantic crossings to a grand total of thirty-one. The figure is a reminder that he was an enthusiastic traveler and that he often turned toward England. He stayed for several months in 1872 and again twice in 1873-74. He toured the Continent in 1878-79, winding up with another English visit.

During the 1870s Twain was on the whole an emphatic anglophile. What he cherished and what he missed in his own country was the honest efficiency of government, local and national, and the enduring appeal of tradition. During the 1873 visit he told an American friend, with lyric wistfulness, of his emotion at Portsmouth in glimpsing Admiral Nelson's *Victory* — "that colossal & superb old ship, all beflagged . . . & her old historical signal flying at her masthead once more. . . . God knows I wish we had some of England's reverence for the old & great."

Not long afterward, in 1875, Twain contributed an anonymous satire, "The Curious Republic of Gondour," to the *Atlantic Monthly*. The essay amounted to a condemnation of American-type universal suffrage and a definite preference for a society graded through education and traditional wealth like that of Britain. In his imaginary paradise of Gondour, every citizen had one basic vote. But a person could receive up to nine votes; the additions were reckoned on an ascending scale of educational attainment plus affluence. In a letter of 1877 Twain, probably without any tinge of irony, asserted that "Republican Government, with a sharply restricted suffrage, is just as good as a Constitutional monarchy with a virtuous & powerful aristocracy; but with an unrestricted suffrage it ought to . . . perish because it is founded in wrong & it is weak & bad & tyrannical."

By 1881, when he finished *The Prince and the Pauper*, Twain's estimate of republican democracy was more favorable, at least by the negative gauge of Reformation England. Edward as prince and monarch, hitherto utterly ignorant of the miseries of the poor, begins to learn only when thrown among beggars and thieves. The lesson takes a while to sink in: "Carve me this rabble to rags!" is his imperious cry on being rescued from a mob. Still, Edward does eventually realize that "kings should go to school to their own laws . . . , and so learn mercy." All ends happily enough. Tom Canty the pauper and other worthy persons are suitably rewarded for their loyal services. Though Edward VI died after only a few years on the throne, Twain concedes that his reign was "singularly merciful for those harsh times." Edward's courage is never in doubt; nor are his innate intelligence and decency.

Anglophilia, we are told, gave way during the 1880s to irritability and then to fury. One stimulus was *The People's History of the English Aristocracy*, a book sent to Twain in 1887 by its radical English author, George Standring. Standring edited a magazine called *The Republican* and insisted that hereditary privilege was a fatal impediment to the development of democracy in Britain. The same argument colored *Triumphant Democracy* (1886), a hymn of praise to America by the Scottish-born magnate Andrew Carnegie. Twain, thanking Carnegie for the book in 1890, misnamed it "The Triumphant Republic," and claimed it "helped to fire me up" for the writing of *A Connecticut Yankee*.

Twain's pendulum-swing toward anglophobia, if that is what it was, can also be inferred from his touchy response to various pronouncements by the distinguished English critic Matthew Arnold, who unlike Howells was not Twain's chum. In various articles and lectures of the 1880s, Arnold decided that the United States was not distinguished or "interesting." Americans lacked reverence: a deficiency manifest in their "addiction to the 'funny man.'" Twain had at the outset conceived *A Connecticut Yankee* as a deliberately anachronistic burlesque, poking fun at outworn chivalric and superstitious modes: in short, an up-to-date equivalent of Cervantes' *Don Quixote*. This approach is still evident in the opening chapters, and intermittently thereafter.

But Twain's anger, fueled by other books like W.E.H. Lecky's *History of European Morals*, then impels him to denounce the past from the vantage-point of modern America. Countering "reverence" with caustic irreverence, he adopts the unsophisticated Yankee mechanic Hank Morgan as his spokesman. Twain-as-Morgan heaps abuse upon "king, nobility and gentry, idle, unproductive, acquainted mainly with the arts of wasting and destroying, and of no . . . use or value in any rationally constructed world." They are abetted in his tale by a priesthood (mostly symbolized by Merlin) that is both credulous and unscrupulous: a Twainian composite, embodying his prejudices against Roman Catholicism as well as the established Church of England, not to mention Mormonism and Christian Science.

His principal conscious target was privileged, supercilious, parochially narrow England, his principal intended contrast an America of vigorous freemen. Scholars offer various theories to account for his renewed subsequent politeness toward England. How could such an outright republican find himself paying lavish tribute to Queen Victoria — a unique monarch, he said, surpassing the virtuous young Edward VI in her dedication to "lofty ideals" — on the occasion of her Diamond Jubilee in 1897?

One theory is that with old age Twain became more radical and more focused, that his new targets — Russia's Tsarist régime, the horrors perpetrated in the Congo by Leopold of the Belgians — made the offenses supposedly committed by a Matthew Arnold appear negligible. This thesis can be restated to stress Twain's mounting pessimism — a deterministic bias so bleak that almost all human activities, virtuous or otherwise, shrank into microscopic insignificance. Twain's final, posthumous novel, *The Mysterious Stranger* (1916), is also "historical" in that it is set in mediaeval Austria. Its message, however, is that human history is neither comic nor tragic, neither progressive nor reactionary, but fundamentally unreal.

Pieces of evidence can be produced in support of all such propositions. As he grew older, Mark Twain wavered in his ideas as to the role of humor. Was "fun" mainly a method of amusing, and so winning a mass audience? He cared a great deal about the techniques of comedy, spoken and written: the deadpan delivery, the seeming *non sequitur*, the exact timing of the "clincher." On the other hand, he sought to justify himself, oxymoronically, as a serious entertainer, maintaining that his brand of humor, at least, was inherently humanitarian and reformist. Howells put the point by remarking that except for political humorists, notably J. R. Lowell, American funny men before Twain "chose the wrong side . . . ; they were on the side of slavery, of drunkenness, and of irreligion; the friends of civilization were their prey; their spirit was thoroughly vulgar and base."

Commentators have contended that Twain's temperament and his circle of friends imposed impossible strains. Certainly we cannot help noticing his lapses into sentimentality, especially in writing about women and children. There is also Twain the entrepreneur, an aspect that led him to attribute to the superintendent-mechanic Hank Morgan talents and ambitions (e.g. running a stock exchange) more appropriate to the banking magnate J. P. Morgan. This was the Twain who from time to time announced his imminent retirement from the drudgery of authorship, on the calculation that he could live off royalties and investments.

However valid these explanations, more remains to be said, emphasizing the cultural context rather than his own idiosyncratic biography. Howells saw that Twain signalled the arrival of some new force in literature which had to do with mood, style, versatility in genre and breadth of appeal. One of the questions in Twain's story is how by the early 1870s he was able to gain recognition, at home and in Europe, as an important man of letters. At that stage Twain's *curriculum vitae* included little more than the "Celebrated Jumping Frog" story, popularity as a platform humorist, *The Innocents Abroad* (1869), and *The Gilded Age* (1873), written in collaboration with C. D. Warner. The record itself is not big enough to account for his astonishing reception in the Anglo-American literary realm. The acclaim came, I think, because he filled a gap — the need hitherto met by W. M. Thackeray and Charles Dickens, who died in 1863 and 1870 respectively. Thackeray and Dickens both began as humorists (with comic pseudonyms), yet evolved into more serious art. Both were versatile, and prolific. Both lectured, Dickens with especial histrionic flair and with a strong theatrical instinct. In 1846 both brought out travel narratives, Thackeray the *Notes of a Journey from Cornhill to Grand Cairo* and Dickens the *Pictures from Italy*, which combined solemn art-appreciation with passages of facetious swagger. Both as professional authors produced December fictions aimed at the Christmas market. They tried their hand at historical novels (Thackeray's *Henry Esmond*, Dickens' *A Tale of Two Cities*). And, to repeat, both died in mid-career, leaving a vacuum that no-one else seemed quite equipped to fill. By default, in came the American claimant, Samuel Langhorne Clemens, a.k.a. Mark Twain.

Twain followed in the path of the acclaimed English pair. We recall, for instance, that he wrote a play and a novel entitled *The American Claimant* (1892), probably inspired by the case of the Tichborne Claimant, an English real-life drama of the early 1870s which Twain had followed with avid interest. The claimant to the Tichborne family fortune was deemed to be a fraud, and so was Colonel Sellers, the American "heir" of Twain's *Gilded Age*. At no conscious level, however, did he think that he had stepped into someone else's shoes, or that he was inferior in quality. We do know that Twain said he had never been able to laugh at *Pickwick Papers*, the book that brought early fame to Dickens. Moreover, he came to detest his one-time friend Bret Harte and counted among Harte's faults a tendency to plagiarize from Dickens. In 1879, too, he was bruised by a clipping from a London newspaper which preferred Harte's humor as "more English and less thoroughly Yankee" than Twain's, and added that the crude lack of taste in *Innocents Abroad* would prevent such humor from ever reaching the heights occupied by Dickens and Thackeray.

Consciously or not, Mark Twain did achieve an Anglo-American renown almost as great as that of Sir Walter Scott, more popularly based than that of the gentlemanly Thackeray, and possibly equivalent to that of the spectacularly self-made entertainer-moralist Dickens. Scott was the only one of the three Twain publicly disparaged — and this (from *Life on the Mississippi*) mainly in the guise of an indictment of the false chivalry of the American South, which he blamed on an excessive appetite for reading Scott's romances. Twain studied Scott, however, in preparation for his own ventures into historical fiction; and there is clear evidence that he felt such an endeavor was fitting for important authors on the plane of Scott, Thackeray, Dickens, and perhaps another prolific, well-known British novelist, Bulwer Lytton.

In other words, Twain regarded historical fiction as a genuine challenge. It sold well, on either side of the Atlantic (and with both of which authors as famous as Dickens and Twain must win approval: hence their passionate interest in improving international copyright protection). Some of this work was designed for the increasingly large juvenile market. Twain admitted that he had picked up notions for *The Prince and the Pauper* from Charlotte M. Yonge, whose tales of English history for young folks included *The Little Duke* and *The Prince and the Page*. He convinced himself that his own book had stimulated Frances Hodgson Burnett to write her best-selling *Little Lord Fauntleroy* (1886). Twain's *Prince and the Pauper* was intended to sell, to readers of all ages and as many countries as possible (he was eager to be published in other languages). But on some higher plane, *The Prince* like *Joan of Arc* and (more confusedly) *A Connecticut Yankee*, was visualized by Twain not as a hasty commercial offering, but as a demonstration of his full literary armament.

Despite mock-humorous disclaimers, Twain felt he could speak to a worldwide audience as Dickens had done. In part this was because of the universality of humor. In part it derived from his own unvarying certainty that the best English was now being written by Americans and that the very best came from his pen. And, hostile reviewers aside, a multitude of people agreed with him.

Twain devoted an extraordinary intensity of effort to denouncing the stylistic errors of *bêtes noires* such as Matthew Arnold and James Fenimore Cooper, as if their literary sins were forms of moral depravity. To be made an Oxford D.Litt., in 1907, was almost to suggest that the republic of letters was better understood as a kingdom. "King" was in fact the nickname given to Twain by his court of intimates in these last years.

This is not to say he was ultimately an anglophile. On the contrary: he resented the overlordship of English literature and exulted in the belief that the Americans had taken "the bulk of the shares" in the "joint stock company" of their common language, with himself the chief speculator in cornering the market. He felt the process was an Americanizing one, but also that slang or hyperbole were by no means the only American modes. Pure diction and universal/historical material were available to every master of the British or American culture.

In the process, Twain was a prominent figure but only one of several; and like them he was influenced by more than purely personal concerns. In a literary sense it is doubtful whether any author directly "influenced" him. He was entitled to take pride in his wayward originality. Nevertheless, a quantity of novels and stories in the Anglo-American literary domain are close enough to his to show that certain problems and plots were in the common air. Some of these parallels are familiar: for instance, the dual personality theme in Robert Louis Stevenson's *Dr. Jekyll and Mr. Hyde* (1886). Another much-read novel, Rider Haggard's *King Solomon's Mines* (1885), anticipates Hank Morgan: Haggard's hero, in peril among savages, overawes them through foreknowledge that a solar eclipse is about to occur. The exchange of roles in *The Prince and the Pauper* can be compared to F. Anstey's comic English novel *Vice Versa* (1882), in which a wretched schoolboy is delighted to change places with his father, Mr. Bultitude, a pompous businessman. In 1889, the same year as *A Connecticut Yankee*, another American humorist, the whimsical Frank Stockton, published *The Great War Syndicate*, an ingenious fantasy of future technological combat.

One other fascinating anticipation deserves attention. Several novels by Edward Bulwer Lytton were in Twain's Hartford library, among them *The Last of the Barons* (1843). It deals with the fifteenth-century Earl of Warwick, the "Kingmaker," at whose castle the story of Hank Morgan is introduced. Warwick is a brave leader, though finally killed in battle, and for his day unusually open-minded. A subplot involves a scientist-inventor named Adam Warner. Warner at one moment applies his intelligence to improving the design of the primitive cannon of the period. His main task however is to perfect his "Eureka" machine, a kind of steam engine. When Warner explains the project to the Earl, Warwick is worried that if actually put into service the machine would "turn this bold land of yeomanry and manhood into one community of griping traders and sickly artisans. *Mort Dieu!* we are over-commerced as it is." Even so, the Earl is sensible enough to grasp that "if thou canst succeed in making the elements do the work of man with equal precision, but with far greater force and rapidity, thou must multiply eventually, and, by multiplying, cheapen, all the products of industry; that thou must give to this country the market of the world, — and that thine would be the true alchemy that turneth all to gold." The Kingmaker determines to encourage the inventor, for the good of mankind and especially of England. He warns his assembly not to accuse Adam of black magic: "For ye wot well that the commons, from ignorance, would impute all to witchcraft that passeth their understanding."

But there is a cleric-villain, Friar Bungey, as envious, ignorant, bigoted and vicious as Twain's Merlin. Bungey contrives the destruction of the "Eureka" machine and a painful death for the hapless inventor.

Perhaps Twain read *The Last of the Barons*. Perhaps the tale lodged in his subconscious, surfacing when he began the saga of Hank Morgan. What is important is that in the last third of the nineteenth century, dozens of authors, British and American and some from other countries, drew eclectically upon a large available stock of genres and motifs. Some, including R. L. Stevenson and Rudyard Kipling, went beyond Twain in at least one respect: they were fluent versifiers where he had to content himself with notebook doggerel. Some, such as Stockton the American and Jerome K. Jerome the Englishman, never quite broke out of the limiting conventions of middlebrow entertainment. Some engaged themselves in the relatively new field of detective fiction. Several — Jules Verne, Edward Bellamy, H. G. Wells — addressed themselves to what has become known as science fiction, as Twain did in his later years.

Several others looked back, often to Tudor or Plantagenet England. A few hinted at burlesque, perhaps remembering the absurd fiasco of the Eglinton Tournament of 1839 — an actual neo-mediaeval pageant in Scotland washed out by rain. Most, though, were in earnest. The American Charles Major, for example, sold many thousand copies of his historical romance *When Knighthood Was in Flower* (1898). It and similar novels prompted Howells to complain that in current literature "nothing of late has been heard but the din of arms, the horrid tumult of the swashbuckler swashing on his buckler." William Morris (e.g. *A Dream of John Bull*, 1888) was among those who resorted to the past in order to create fables of an alternative future.

The more ambitious a writer, the more diversely experimental as a rule and perhaps the more restless. Bulwer Lytton had a go at almost everything, even a novel of the future (*The Coming Race*). Arthur Conan Doyle, unhappy at being confined to the exploits of Sherlock Holmes, ventured both into historical fiction and into stories of ultramodern combat.

Mark Twain was shaped by this Anglo-American milieu. He also helped to shape it, being more gifted and no more erratic than a number of his contemporaries. As an American who had started out as a "funny man," he was perhaps under exceptional pressure to prove himself equal to Thackeray and Dickens. Dickens in particular was the figure whose humor, pathos, range and renown Twain had to absorb and outperform. On his first date with his wife-to-be, Clemens/Twain took her to a prestigious social event, a Dickens recital. The rivalrous junior author noted that "this puissant God seemed to be only a man. . . . I was a good deal disappointed in Mr. Dickens's reading . . . a great deal disappointed." Or challenged?

We may still feel that his very best work was located in the Mississippi Valley. But he *was* versatile. He wished to prove himself so. He did genuinely share the complex enthusiasm of his age for historical romance. He had, he told Howells, felt "jubilant" in the writing of *The Prince and the Pauper* — at ease, confident in his power to bring the past alive in the present. Mark Twain's forays into English and European history were in his own estimation as justified as, perhaps finer than, all his other writings. Whatever our reservations as to Twain's skill at historical pastiche, a glance at the efforts of other authors in the same vein helps to bring out his decisive superiority. Gadzooks, what he could have done if he had set out to dissect the "literary offenses" of *When Knighthood was in Flower* or of *The Last of the Barons*!

SELECTED BIBLIOGRAPHY

Biography and Criticism

Anderson, Frederick, ed. *Mark Twain: The Critical Heritage*. New York: Barnes & Noble, 1971.

Anderson, Frederick, et al., eds. *Mark Twain's Notebooks & Journals*. Berkeley: University of California Press. *Vol. 2 (1877-1883)*, 1975; *vol. 3 (1883-1891)*, 1979.

Andrews, Kenneth R. *Nook Farm: Mark Twain's Hartford Circle*. Cambridge, Mass.: Harvard University Press, 1950.

Asselineau, Roger. *The Literary Reputation of Mark Twain from 1910 to 1950*. Paris: Didier, 1954; reprint, Westport, Conn.: Greenwood Press, 1971.

Baetzhold, Howard G. *Mark Twain and John Bull: The British Connection*. Bloomington: Indiana University Press, 1970.

Budd, Louis J. *Mark Twain, Social Philosopher*. Bloomington: Indiana University Press, 1962.

Cox, James M. "*A Connecticut Yankee in King Arthus's Court*: The Machinery of Self-Preservation," *Yale Review* 50 (Autumn 1960), reprinted in Henry Nash Smith, ed. *Mark Twain: A Collection of Critical Essays*. Englewood Cliffs, N.J.: Prentice-Hall, 1963.

DeVoto, Bernard. *Mark Twain's America*. Boston: Houghton Mifflin, 1932.

Hansen, Chadwick. "The Once and Future Boss: Mark Twain's Yankee," *Nineteenth-Century Fiction* 28 (June 1973).

Howells, William Dean. *My Mark Twain: Reminiscences and Criticism*. New York & London: Harper, 1910.

Kaplan, Justin. *Mr. Clemens and Mark Twain*. New York: Simon & Schuster, 1966.

Kasson, John A. *Civilizing the Machine: Technology and Republican Values in America, 1776-1900*. New York: Grossman, 1976; Penguin, 1977.

Lynn, Kenneth S. *Mark Twain and Southwestern Humor*. Boston: Little, Brown, 1959.

Salomon, Roger B. *Twain and the Image of History*. New Haven, Conn.: Yale University Press, 1961.

Scott, Arthur L. "Mark Twain Looks at Europe," *South Atlantic Quarterly* 52 (1953).

————, ed. *Mark Twain: Selected Criticism*. Dallas: Southern Methodist University Press, 1955.

Smith, Henry Nash. *Mark Twain: The Development of a Writer*. Cambridge, Mass.: Harvard University Press, 1962.

————. *Mark Twain's Fable of Progress: Political and Economic Ideas in "A Connecticut Yankee"*. New Brunswick, NJ: Rutgers University Press, 1964.

Welland, Dennis. *Mark Twain in England*. London: Chatto & Windus, 1978.

This essay appeared as the introduction to a double volume of Mark Twain's *The Prince and the Pauper & Connecticut Yankee in King Arthur's Court* (New York: New American Library, Signet Classsic, 1982), v-xvi.

If time allows, I would like to pull together material for a book on great popular authors of the nineteenth century, starting with Sir Walter Scott, and bringing out comparable themes in the international sphere: publishing circumstances, audiences, copyright, translations, adaptions of the novel to theatre and opera. Twain as an Anglo-American or "international" writer is a splendid exhibit. When my essay was written, I was unaware of Joseph H. Gardner's article, "Mark Twain and Dickens," *PMLA* 84 (1969). Since the essay first appeared, some useful studies should be added to the bibliography: Alan Gribben, *Mark Twain's Library*, 2 vols. (Boston: G. K. Hall, 1980); Robert Weisbuch, *Atlantic Double-Cross: American Literature and British Influence in the Age of Emerson* (Chicago: University of Chicago Press, 1986); David Ketterer, ed., *The Science Fiction of Mark Twain* (Hamden, Conn.: Archon Books, 1984); J.C.B. Kinch, ed., *Mark Twain's German Critical Reception, 1875-1986: An Annotated Bibliography* (Westport, Conn.: Greenwood Press, 1989); and John Lauber, *The Inventions of Mark Twain* (New York: Hill & Wang, 1989).

14

Stephen Crane and the American Background of *Maggie*

In part this essay owes its origin to an hour spent in the basement of a secondhand bookstore in Manchester, England, back in the early 1950s. There I came across well-thumbed, cheap English editions of the American sermons of DeWitt Talmage, a celebrity in his day of whom I had never heard. The essay has been cited here and there and reprinted in a couple of collections of writings on Crane's *Maggie*. As reprinted here, it excludes material from the beginning and end which now seems inessential. Feminist scholarship has reinterpreted some of the older attitudes, moral and economic, to the role of prostitution in American life. Some of this work amplifies and modifies the kinds of argument and evidence presented here. See, for example, Laura Hapke, *Girls Who Went Wrong: Prostitutes in American Fiction, 1885-1917* (Bowling Green, Ohio: Bowling Green State University Press, 1989).

I wish to take Stephen Crane as an example of an author who has been classified with a fallacious neatness. He is a difficult figure to deal with. His work is uneven, his talent precocious and dazzling. Largely on the strength of his first novel, *Maggie: A Girl of the Streets* (1893), Crane has been labeled as a naturalist. As such, he is supposed to have borrowed from other naturalists. Whatever he did not borrow from them, Crane is thought to have got from his own direct experience or to have absorbed at second-hand from the experiences of others (in the case of his *Red Badge of Courage*, from the experiences of Civil War veterans). Naturalistic *influences* and personal experiences would seem to fill out the picture completely. But they leave out a great deal of knowledge and atmosphere that Crane must have absorbed, even if half-consciously, merely through living in America at a certain time, under certain circumstances.

A look at *Maggie* serves to bring out this element. When Crane published it, pseudonymously and at his own expense, he was just twenty-one. The few who read the book on its first appearance found it a grim document. Maggie, its "heroine," grows up in a Rum Alley tenement of New York, her mother a drunken harridan, her brother a lout. Miserable at home, miserable in her sweatshop job, Maggie is delighted when a bartender named Pete begins to notice her. Seduced and then contemptuously abandoned by him, Maggie (whose family self-righteously disowns her) becomes a prostitute. Finally she drowns herself one night while Pete is entertaining some more resilient ladies of the town. The theme of the novel, as Crane expressed it in more than one dedicatory inscription, is that "environment is a tremendous thing in the world and frequently shapes life regardless."[1] Welcomed by William Dean Howells and Hamlin Garland (whom Crane once acknowledged as his "literary fathers"), *Maggie* falls into place for literary historians as a prime exhibit in the history of naturalism. The struggling young author offers his work for publication; timid publishers refuse it; genius is overlooked, "sincerity" beaten by "hypocrisy." Howells himself saw the situation in this vivid light, as part of the saga of realism, which runs on in turn to Theodore Dreiser and *his* struggles to have *Sister Carrie* published in 1900. It was perhaps because *Maggie* could be fitted into such a pattern that Howells preferred it to Crane's much better book, *The Red Badge*; for Howells, in his deceptively mild way, was more of a doctrinaire "revolutionary" theorist than appears on the surface. Howells was widely read in European literature and had caught the European habit of looking for sharp trends and movements in literature.

Moreover, *Maggie* seemed to have a European antecedent in Zola's novel *L'Assommoir*. Crane's English contemporaries thought he owed a debt to the French. When he met English men of letters, in 1897, he complained that they

> *let fall my hand and . . . ask me how much money I make and from which French realist I shall steal my next book. For it has been proven to me fully and carefully by authority that all my books are stolen from the French. They stand me against walls with a teacup in my hand and tell me how I*

---

[1] These words occur in inscriptions to Hamlin Garland, Dr. Lucius L. Button, and the Reverend Thomas Dixon. See Robert W. Stallman, ed., *Stephen Crane: An Omnibus* (New York: Knopf, 1952), 594. Hereafter, Stallman.

have stolen all my things from De Maupassant, Zola, Loti and the bloke
who wrote — I forget the book.[2]

Despite Crane's protests, he was typed as a follower of French naturalism — as
this comment by Robert E. Spiller reveals:

> *There is no doubt that [Crane] took direct inspiration from these French*
> *realists [Maupassant and Flaubert], and even more certainly from Zola,*
> *for* L'Assommoir *probably provided the plot for* Maggie, *and* La Débâcle
> *bears a close resemblance to* The Red Badge of Courage, *though he*
> *denied ever having read it. His work shows the stamp of European*
> *naturalism and contributed to the break of American literary history with*
> *the English tradition.*[3]

With or without reservations, most other literary historians have linked *Maggie*
with *L'Assommoir*. John Berryman notes some differences between the two
books but goes on to say that, even so, Crane "probably read *L'Assommoir* and
was influenced by it."[4] The Swedish scholar Lars Åhnebrink is also confident of
the connection and makes a close parallel examination of the two novels.[5]
Another student of Crane, Robert W. Stallman, is more cautious:

> *It is impossible to say where Crane got the stuff and craft of* Maggie.
> *Either he invented the plot or he took it from Zola's* L'Assommoir. *It is*
> *not certain, however, that he read that book.*[6]

Stallman brings out an important fact about *Maggie*: that Crane wrote the first
draft of the book in 1891, when he was a college student at Syracuse and "knew
very little about the Bowery, slum life, and prostitutes."[7] *In conception* the novel

---

[2] A letter to James G. Huneker, quoted in John Berryman, *Stephen Crane* (New York: William Sloan,
1951), 199 (hereafter, Berryman); and in Stallman, 674-75. The date is conjectural.

[3] *Literary History of the United States* (New York: Macmillan, 1948), 2: 1022.

[4] Berryman, 63.

[5] In *The Beginnings of Naturalism in American Fiction* (Uppsala: American Institute, 1950), 249-64.

[6] Stallman, 6.

[7] Stallman, 5.

precedes personal knowledge of the subject; and so we can say that Crane either invented it or borrowed from other writers.

But was Zola one of them? Crane *could have* read *L'Assommoir*. Two translations were available in America within a couple of years of its first publication in 1877. (One of these retained the original title: the other was known as *Gervaise*, after the principal character.) Admittedly, too, Crane's novel does have something in common with Zola's. Both demonstrate the overpowering effect of environment (though *L'Assommoir*, as part of the *Rougon-Macquart* series, was also conceived as a study in heredity). Both novels deal frankly and gloomily with human experience. They take for their characters the city poor, whose idiom they reproduce; in both, alcoholism helps to wreck a family; and the daughter of the family (Maggie, Nana) becomes a prostitute. Both books end in death, though in Zola it is Nana's mother, Gervaise, on whose death the story closes.

Yet none of these resemblances is strikingly close nor are the particular instances cited by Mr. Åhnebrink. On the contrary, they are less convincing than the dissimilarities also discussed by Åhnebrink. Let us assume (a) that Crane had never read *L'Assommoir* when he wrote *Maggie* and (b) *Maggie* was, however, not a complete invention of Crane's. If we put aside *L'Assommoir* for a while, we can start to look for other possible "influences."

The sensible place to search is not Europe but America: not Zola's Paris but Crane's New York. Little in fiction can be regarded as a lead. But a clue is provided by two sketches of the Bowery, "An Experiment in Misery" and "The Men in the Storm," that Crane wrote in 1893, not long after *Maggie* was published. They are documentary pieces, although the former is presented as a story. The latter was printed in B. O. Flower's *Arena*, a periodical that devoted much space to social problems of the day. It is here, surely, that Crane's sources might lie, not necessarily in the *Arena* itself, but in the mass of literature produced by Americans on the evils of slum-life: ill-health, intemperance, immorality and the like. Investigative literature was in being long before the muckrakers; it can be traced back as far as the 1830s and to the writings of such reformers as Edwin Chapin and John R. McDowall, who grappled with the question of poverty and vice in New York. In 1872, for example, five years before *L'Assommoir*, Charles Loring Brace published *The Dangerous Classes of New York*, a study that was the fruit of twenty years of philanthropic work. Like Zola, Brace believes that "inheritance" is a crucial factor — that "certain appetites" (especially "the appetite for liquor and of the sexual passion"), "if indulged abnormally and excessively through two or more generations, come to have an almost irresistible force, and, no doubt, modify the brain so as to constitute almost an insane condition."[8] Brace has a chapter on "Street Girls"; like Zola again, he has no illusions as to the beginning of the street-girls' career:

> *They usually relate, and perhaps even imagine, that they have been seduced from the paths of virtue suddenly and by the wiles of some heartless seducer. Often they describe themselves as belonging to some virtuous, respectable, and even wealthy family. Their real history, however, is much more commonplace.... They have been poor women's daughters, and did not want to work as their mothers did; or they have grown up in a tenement-room, crowded with boys and men, and lost purity before they knew what it was; or they have liked gay company, and have had no good influences around them, and sought pleasure in criminal indulgences; or they have been street-children, poor, neglected, and ignorant, and thus naturally and inevitably have become depraved women.*[9]

This account is embellished with an engraving called "The Street-Girl's End," in which a dejected prostitute stands at the end of a quay, peering down into the river-waters below, literally and metaphorically on the brink (Photo 10). If Crane had read Brace's book (there is, alas, no evidence that he did), he could have got from it more, except for the fictional form, than from *L'Assommoir*. It could have supplied him with details of the New York *milieu* — and also, of course, with the idea for Maggie's suicide. Brace has quite as close a grasp on his subject as Zola; in fact, the passage just quoted could serve as a description of Zola's *Nana*, as she appears in *L'Assommoir* and as she is in the sequel, *Nana*. Some years after he wrote *Maggie*, Crane was to comment with equal *expertise*. He said of *Nana*, indeed:

> *this girl in Zola is a real streetwalker. I mean, she does not fool around making excuses for her career. You must pardon me if I cannot agree that*

---

[8] Coupeau's horrible death in *L'Assommoir* is presented by Zola as the result of a hereditary weakness for liquor which induces insanity. Unlike Zola, however, Brace takes comfort from "the action of the great law of 'Natural Selection,'" which, "in regard to the human race, is always toward temperance and virtue," since "the vicious and sensual and drunken die earlier," or produce fewer children, "and so yield place to the sober elements of society." *The Dangerous Classes of New York* (New York, 1872), 43-44.

[9] Brace, 117-18.

10. "Street Girl's End," from *The Dangerous Classes of New York*, by Charles Loring Brace, 1872.

every painted woman on the streets of New York was brought there by some evil man.[10]

But this is not what Maggie is like. Crane's view of her differs entirely from that of Zola or Brace. For the implication of *Maggie* is that "some evil man" is directly responsible for the fallen woman's plight. Maggie *is* "seduced from the paths of virtue . . . by the wiles of some heartless seducer" (Pete). Her brother Jimmie has also seduced a girl, only to abandon the unfortunate creature. If Crane later came to think otherwise, at this time he imagined Maggie as essentially the victim of circumstance. Nana is "dans le vice comme un poisson dans l'eau" (in vice like a fish in water).

Maggie, on the other hand, is pure: "None of the dirt of Rum Alley seemed to be in her veins." In part, Crane's treatment of her is naturalistic — "Say, Pete, dis is great" is a sample of her conversation — but in other respects it is not. Altogether, Maggie is a somewhat unreal creature, and her life as a prostitute is handled by Crane with a marked lack of certainty. In chapter 17, which culminates in her death, we see Maggie as

> *a girl of the painted cohorts of the city. She threw changing glances at men who passed her, giving smiling invitations to those of rural or untaught pattern and usually seeming sedately unconscious of the men with a metropolitan seal upon their faces.*

For Crane, this is a peculiarly heavy-handed passage. At any rate, it presents Maggie as an experienced prostitute, who has apparently overcome her initial scruples. Moreover, she seems to have been reasonably successful, since she is wearing a "handsome cloak" and has "well-shod feet." Why, then, does she commit suicide?

Even less convincing is "Nellie," the "woman of brilliance and audacity" to whom Pete returns after he has grown tired of Maggie. Nell, when we first see her, speaks like the others, "Well, hello, Pete, my boy, how are you?" But before long, trying to show that she has a certain vulgar sophistication, Crane overdoes it and allows her to describe Maggie as: "A little pale thing with no spirit. . . . Did you notice the expression in her eyes? There was something in them about pumpkin pie and virtue. . . . Dear, dear, Pete, what are you coming to?" And when Pete disclaims interest in Maggie, Nell replies (almost like a character in

---

[10] Quoted in Stallman, 675.

Henry James), "Oh, it's not of the slightest consequence to me, my dear young man."

This is the writing of an inexperienced author who only knows his subject from hearsay or from reading. And the tone is not quite that of Zola, nor of the matter-of-fact Mr. Brace. There is an added ingredient: a moral, didactic motive, a slight preachiness. In the dedicatory inscriptions which state that "environment . . . frequently shapes lives regardless," Crane continues: "If one proves that theory one makes room in Heaven for all sorts of souls, notably an occasional street girl, who are not confidently expected to be there by many excellent people."[11] These could nearly be the words of a clergyman; and several clergymen of the period might nearly have uttered them.

For instance, there was Thomas DeWitt Talmage (1832-1902),[12] who came of a New Jersey family, and who — after holding ministries at Belleville, N. J., Syracuse and Philadelphia — was appointed in 1869 to the Central Presbyterian Church of Brooklyn. Here he rapidly acquired a fame which verged on notoriety. His sermons drew as many as five thousand people (the vast Brooklyn Tabernacle could hold them all); his words were reprinted, not only in book-form but also in newspapers throughout the English-speaking world. Talmage well understood the advantage of publicity on such a scale:

> *next to the Bible, the newspaper — swift-winged, and everywhere present, flying over the fences, shoved under the door, tossed into the counting house, laid on the work-bench, hawked through the cars! All read it: white, black, German, Irishman, Swiss, Spaniard, American, old and young, good and bad, sick and well, before breakfast and after tea, Monday morning, Saturday night, Sunday and week-day!*[13]

The newspapers, on their side, were glad to feature Talmage's sermons and lectures. As the above excerpt suggests, they were vivid and racy; and they dealt with alluringly newsworthy topics. They managed to be both moral and sensational. Collections of them sold widely under such titles as *The Abominations of Modern Society* (1872), *The Night Sides of City Life* (1878) and *The Masque Torn Off* (1880). Sometimes, as when he attacks the theatre, in

---

[11] Quoted in Stallman, 594.

[12] See *Dictionary of American Biography*, 18: 287-88; and *Life and Teachings of Rev. T. DeWitt Talmage* (n.p., 1902), with an introduction by Russell H. Conwell: a memorial volume.

[13] *Abominations of Modern Society* (London, 3d ed., 1873), 138.

Sports That Kill (1872), Talmage admits the charge that he is fulminating like an old-time Methodist:

> *My religion is not a jelly-fish, but a vertebrate. It has backbone, and tells of God's justice as well as God's mercy; and I have not in anywise, as you know, made a compromise of public iniquities.*[14]

In the *Night Sides*' "Sabbath morning discourses," he recounts how "I, as a minister of religion, felt I had a *divine commission to explore the iniquities of our cities.*"

Yet he tours the night-haunts of New York with a certain scientific detachment, "*as a physician goes into a small-pox hospital or a fever-shed.*" He goes as a social reformer as well as a clergyman. He has evidently read his Charles Loring Brace;[15] the police who pilot him around the brothels and saloons do so with a professional aplomb; and if Talmage draws moral lessons, they are not narrow or fanatical. He condemns the pleasure-seeking male rather than the purveyors of pleasure. In the sermon called "The Gates of Hell," after expatiating on "impure literature," "the dissolute dance," "indiscreet apparel," and "alcoholic beverage," Talmage considers the prostitute:

> *Suppose one of these wanderers should knock at your door, would you admit her? Suppose you knew where she came from, would you ask her to sit down at your dining-table? Would you ask her to become the governess of your children? . . . You would not — not one of a thousand of you has come so near the heart of the Lord Jesus Christ as to dare to help one of these fallen souls.*[16]

Are there, Talmage asks, any ways out for such girls? One way is "the sewing-girl's garret, dingy, cold, hunger-blasted":

[14] Talmage, *Sports That Kill* (London: James Blackwood, n.d.), 56. Despite the zoological vocabulary, Talmage had no sympathy for what he called the "evolutionists": "Prefer, if you will, Darwin's 'Origin of Species' to the book of Genesis, but know that you are an infidel. As for myself, since Herbert Spencer was not present at the creation and the Lord Almighty was present, I prefer to take the divine account as to what really occurred." (*Life and Teachings*, 68)

[15] An anecdote of a fourteen-year-old street girl in Brace (pp. 119-121) is repeated in Talmage's *Sports That Kill* (p. 172).

[16] *Night Sides*: reprinted in England as *The Night Side of New York Life* (Wakefield: William Nicholson, n.d.), 42.

Another way is the street that leads to East river, at midnight, the end of the city dock, the moon shining down on the water making it look so smooth she wonders if it is deep enough. It is. No boatman near enough to hear the plunge.[17]

This will be recognized as the situation illustrated in Brace's book.

However, Talmage indicates that there is yet another way: the way of repentance. The poor shivering prostitute of his imaginary tale, touched by a sermon (and by the words in it, "wounded for our transgressions and bruised for our iniquities"), drags herself away from the city , back to her old home in the country, where a forgiving mother greets the dying girl with the cry of "*Oh, Maggie!*"[18]

The coincidence of name is interesting. So is the similarity between Talmage's observations on the respectable disdain of his congregation and this episode in Crane, when Maggie has been rejected by Pete and is homeless:

Suddenly she came upon a stout gentleman in a silk hat and a chaste black coat, whose decorous row of buttons reached from his chin to his knees. The girl had heard of the grace of God and she decided to approach this man. . . . But as the girl timidly accosted him he made a convulsive movement and saved his respectability by a vigorous side-step. He did not risk it to save a soul. For how was he to know that there was a soul before him that needed saving?

Or compare another set of quotations. In his sermon, "The Massacre by Needle and Sewing-Machine" (reprinted in *Abominations of Modern Society*), Talmage says, "To thousands of young women of New York today there is only this alternative: starvation or dishonour." Maggie's brother presents the alternative to her: "Mag, I'll tell yeh dis! See? Yeh've eeder got t'go on d'toif er go t'work."

Like Talmage's young women, Maggie starts by choosing work and the near-starvation it entails. As Talmage puts it:

There are thirty-five thousand sewing girls in New York and Brooklyn. Across the darkness of this night I hear their death-groan. It is not such a cry as comes from those who are suddenly hurled out of life, but a slow,

---

[17] *Night Side of New York Life*, 43.

[18] Ibid, 47.

grinding, horrible wasting away. Gather them before you and look into their faces, pinched, ghastly, hunger-struck! . . . See that premature stoop in the shoulders! Hear that dry, hacking, merciless cough!

Maggie's work is equally incongenial:

The air in the collar-and-cuff establishment strangled her. She knew she was gradually and surely shrivelling in the hot, stuffy room. . . . She became lost in thought as she looked at some of the grizzled women in the room, mere mechanical contrivances sewing seams.

According to Talmage,

Some of the worst villains of the city are the employers of these women. They beat them down to the last penny, and try to cheat them out of that.

Maggie's companions complain of "unpaid wages." They all loathe "the fat foreigner who owned the establishment" and whose "pocket-book deprived them of the power of retort": "What do you sink I pie fife dolla a week for? Play? No, py tamn!"

We can now gather together the strands of this argument. The main contention is that Crane could easily have drawn material for *Maggie* from popular American writing of the day. We are not bound to substitute the name of DeWitt Talmage for that of Emile Zola as a certain or even probable influence upon Crane. We have no proof that Crane read either author, though it would be hard for him or anyone who looked at the New York newspapers to *avoid* having heard of the publicity-conscious Mr. Talmage. Talmage was a minister and a moralist, many of whose tirades (e.g., against "The Temptations of Summer Watering Places") would no doubt have struck Crane as ludicrous. Crane was anticlerical in tone, as several references in *Maggie* and in his correspondence make clear. Maggie's brother, for a joke, goes into

a mission church where a man composed his sermons of "you's." Once a philosopher asked this man why he did not say "we" instead of "you." The man replied, "What?"

And in a letter of 1896, discussing *Maggie*, Crane admits that "I am not very friendly to Christianity as seen around town."[19]

Still, friendly or not, a reader of Talmage or not, Crane is affected by the American religious heritage. Despite himself, he belongs to this heritage as Talmage does. Against the logic of his novel, Crane, as we have seen, makes Maggie commit suicide. It could be said that this is a naturalistic convention. Possibly; but is it not, even more, a moralist's convention? The wages of sin is death, for Brace, for Talmage (whether the prostitute dies by drowning or repentant in her mother's arms), and for Crane. This kind of death is a stock finale in the moralistic writings of the era. Talmage used it at least once before in his sermon, "Winter Nights" (from *The Abominations of Modern Society*):

> *And so the woman stands on the abutment of the bridge, on the moonlit night, wondering if, down under the water, there is not some quiet place for her broken heart. She takes one wild leap, — and all is over.*

A search among contemporary tracts would disclose plenty of other examples.[20]

Another assumption of Talmage and his kind, standard in reformist literature, is that the city is the abode of temptation and sin; purity is the prerogative of rural areas. The country boy is therefore the chief victim of city snares. So, after his hasty tour of New York brothels, Talmage asserts that these establishments were full of young men "with the ruddy colour of country health on their cheeks, evidently just come to town for business. . . . They had helped gather the summer grain."[21] Crane too, it will be recalled, speaks of Maggie as confining her lures to "those of rural or untaught pattern." (One doubts whether this notion was borne out by Crane's subsequent experiences.)

In other ways Crane's early work shows the effect of the American moral-religious climate. When he refers, in *Maggie*, to "smooth-cheeked boys, some of them with faces of stone and mouths of sin," the phrase could have come from a sermon. Or take this poem, from *Black Riders*:

---

[19] Quoted in Stallman, 655.

[20] See, for example, this description of the East Side waterfront: "Women are there, too, — some singing, or laughing a laugh with no merriment in it; but for the most part they . . . are silent. Now and then one who has walked with bent head and despairing eyes makes a sudden resolve; there is a swift, flying rush toward the dark water beyond, and the river closes over one more victim." Mrs. Helen Campbell, *Darkness and Daylight: or, Lights and Shadows of New York Life* (Hartford, Conn., 1892), 214.

[21] *Night Side of New York Life*, p. 15, "God pity the country lad," he continues (p. 16), "unsuspecting and easily betrayed."

I stood upon a high place,
And saw, below, many devils
Running, leaping,
And carousing in sin.
One looked up, grinning,
And said, "Comrade! Brother!"

This is a variation upon the theme of "you" and "we." Though it is ironical in aim, the religiosity it mocks is something with which Crane is closely involved.

In other words, he is anti-clerical though belonging to a clerical heritage. In his early work, I do not think he knows where he stands — whether it is religion or religiosity he disapproves of, whether he is adapting or burlesquing. He reacts against the familiar elements of his world where these seem to him hypocritical, but they shape his thought.[22] Nor is this surprising. His own father, Jonathan Townley Crane (1819-80), was a clergyman, who held various pastorates in New Jersey and New York:

a strict Methodist of the old stamp, filled with the sense of God's redeeming love, deeply concerned about such sins as dancing, breaking the Sabbath, reading trashy novels, playing cards, billiards, and chess, and enjoying tobacco and wine, and too innocent of the world to do more than suspect the existence of greater viciousness.[23]

Crane's mother, too, was an ardent Methodist, who came from a clerical family. Crane, praising her memory, said that "Mother was always more of a Christian than a Methodist."[24] He might have said the same of his father, whose main fault seems to have been his monumental innocence. What Crane was reacting against, therefore, was nothing very rigid or terrible; hence, his adolescent reversal of what he had been taught consisted in condemning *false* religion; in showing that there was "greater viciousness" than Jonathan Townley Crane ever

---

[22] When Copeland & Day, his prospective publishers, objected to some of the poems "which refer to God" in the manuscript of *Black Riders*, Crane replied: "It seems to me that you cut all the ethical sense out of the book. All the anarchy, perhaps. It is the anarchy which I particularly insist upon." (Letter of September 9, 1894, reproduced in Stallman, 602). Ethics and anarchy! For Crane, the two are inseparable. On the subject of Crane's religious instincts, it is interesting to note that Stallman finds *The Red Badge of Courage* "loaded with Biblical allusions and religious symbolism" (Stallman, 217).

[23] Article by E. F. Humphrey, *D. A. B.*, 4: 506.

[24] Berryman, 9.

suspected; in smoking and drinking; and in not only reading "trashy novels" but actually writing some.

Stephen Crane strives to be free of not merely a family but a national atmosphere. Its restrictions are irksome just because they are, on the whole, kindly. The American emphasis is didactic and redemptive. But not bleakly so: Crane's father's dogmatism is of the serenest order. So are the sensible, "enlightened" teachings of Talmage, Henry Ward Beecher, Lyman Abbott and other prominent clergy of the day. There is, in America no cleavage between religion and rationalism comparable to that in France (where Zola for one was, as an agnostic, thrown into violent controversies). So when young Crane writes with would-be savage candor of the slums, the preachers have been there before him. He cannot help borrowing some of their material. In later writing he pushes further and further away from subjects that can be encompassed by well-meaning pastors. He does so because he wants to write fiction; and fiction in America, is still too close to didacticism — to the religious tract and the philanthropic survey.[25] "Preaching," Crane observes, "is fatal to art in literature."[26] Like other Americans after him, Crane aims at direct experience, simply rendered; the comment, if any, often takes the form of irony (as if to say, *this is the way the preachers would put it — and it's just possible they may be right*).

This essay appeared in *American Quarterly* 7, 1 (Spring 1955): 31-44.

[25] As many commentators have said, this is true even today: *vide* the innumerable novels about alcoholism, race relations, etc. No other country has such a quantity of them in its literature.

[26] From a letter of 1897 (?), quoted in Stallman, 673.

15

What Was the Matter with Henry Adams?

This was done as a review for *Commentary*, to which I used to contribute in the 1960s, of Ernest Samuels's three-volume biography of Adams. A one-volume condensation of the Samuels biography has subsequently appeared. A few afterthoughts and details on more recent material on the Adamses are provided in the postscript to this piece.

Like a half-buried former civilization — famous, extensive, and perplexing — the Adams family is being uncovered for us. The evolution from generation to generation is made clearer, and the factors that link each. John begat John Quincy who begat Charles Francis who begat Henry. The papers of the first three are coming out in handsome amplitude. "Think of your forefathers! Think of your posterity!" was John Quincy Adams's injunction. They force us to do so — to involve ourselves in their central yet idiosyncratic chronicle. They meet us halfway, for all Adamses had an eye to posterity.

Henry of the fourth generation has especially engrossed us, because he is the most interesting and tantalizing of the lot. There have been half a dozen books about him in the last decade or so, including the very good ones by William H. Jordy and J. C. Levenson. Max Baym has discussed his French interests, Henry Wasser his scientific notions. Edward N. Saveth has examined yet other aspects. But the most complete record is the trilogy by Ernest Samuels, a solid and admirable achievement which tells us as much about Henry Adams's inner and outer life as we are ever likely to learn.[1] Samuels is sensible, pertinacious, sympathetic but not idolatrous, and modestly speculative. The picture differs a good deal, though perhaps not fundamentally, from the one disclosed in *The Education of Henry Adams* — that curious work that is both less and more than an autobiography. Here is the complete story of an incomplete man. Or is that a fair comment? Which of us is not incomplete? Whatever the answer, Henry remains a figure to tease the imagination. As Lionel Trilling has said, we cannot react consistently to Adams. "Sometimes he is irresistible. . . . Sometimes he is hateful. . . . It often occurs to us to believe that his is the finest American intelligence we can possibly know, while again it sometimes seems that his mind is so special, and so refined in specialness, as to be beside any possible point."

The hateful or at least unlikable sides of Henry Adams are not concealed by Professor Samuels. We are reminded that the English diplomatist Cecil Spring-Rice, who was later to become his devoted friend, found him "cynical" and "vindictive." Another English acquaintance, Lord Morley, irked by the tone of *The Education*, said, "If Adams had ever looked at himself naked in a glass, he would have rated other men a little more gently." Adams irritated a generation of American Presidents, from Rutherford B. Hayes to his erstwhile friend Theodore Roosevelt. Other public men were rubbed raw by his combination of arrogance and humility. A typical reaction was that of Justice Oliver Wendell Holmes, in the course of a conversation with the novelist Owen Wister:

Holmes: *"If the country had put him on a pedestal, I think Henry Adams with his gifts could have rendered distinguished service."*
Wister: *"What was the matter with Henry Adams?"*
Holmes: *"He wanted it handed to him on a silver platter".*

Not only Henry but the whole family tended to leave this impression. From John Adams onward they were regarded as stiff, perverse, moody, sharp-tongued. They showed the same disposition toward one another. Spring Rice noted that "They are all clever, but they all make a sort of profession of eccentricity. . . . Two of them were arguing. One said, 'It seems to me that I am the only one of the family who inherits anything of our grandfather's manners.' 'But you dissipated your inheritance young.' answered the other." They were all well aware of and almost boasted of their unlikableness, as if they thought it an

---

[1] *The Young Henry Adams* (1948); *Henry Adams: The Middle Years* (1958); *Henry Adams: The Major Phase* (1964), by Ernest Samuels, Harvard University Press.

essential corollary of being honest. Thus Henry's elder brother, Charles Francis Adams, Jr., served in the Civil War with the 1st Massachusetts Cavalry. In January 1864 his company, under his influence, was the only one in the regiment to reenlist at the expiration of the first agreement. Charles wrote to his father:

> *To be egotistical, I think I see the old family traits cropping out in myself. These men don't care for me personally. They think me cold, reserved and formal. They feel no affection for me, but . . . they have faith in my power of accomplishing results and in my integrity.*

The consequences within the family were sometimes bizarre. Its members had moments of intimacy, especially when they rallied together to defend the Adams reputation against strangers. Otherwise they made few concessions. Charles Francis Adams, Jr., in a stratagem concealed from his brother, wrote a long unsigned review of Henry's biography of Albert Gallatin for the *Nation*. He called the book "clumsy" and "little short of . . . an outrage" for anyone who sought a true insight into Gallatin. Henry never discovered who had attacked him. His brother's motives were no doubt high-minded, at any rate on the surface. But obscure jealousies were at work. Who was to carry on the family's great tradition? Neither Charles nor the other elder brother, John, exactly sought the office. Nor did Henry or his younger brother, Brooks Adams. But none was quite content to let the others have the limelight. "My father and brothers," Henry had acknowledged, "block my path fatally, for all three stand before me in order of promotion." The erratic Brooks, to his understandable chagrin, was once defeated by two votes in an attempt to secure election to the Massachusetts legislature. They were the votes of two of his uncles. Integrity, one might think, could be overdone. Charles, Henry, and Brooks all wrote history and on occasion were of considerable help to one another. Yet they got on one another's nerves. Henry deliberately absented himself from Brooks's wedding. True, his own wife had committed suicide in 1885, and thereafter he could not endure reminders of matrimony. But a hostile observer could wonder at the circumstances of Henry's childless marriage and could point out that Henry's impatience with Brooks was more widely based. Perhaps the impatience was justified. Like Henry, but with an extra quality of vehemence, Brooks wanted to provoke people as much as he wanted to instruct them. In his writings he preached calamity with increasing shrillness. Even at the stage in his life when he believed in reform, Brooks's sympathies were confined to his own class. In later life he became rabid — detecting conspiracies, dreaming of government by the strong. "Brooks is too brutal, too blatant, too emphatic . . . to please any large number of people," said Henry.

He himself was of a more timid disposition. Yet the brothers had a good deal in common. Each was at heart conservative and in a sense class-ridden. Henry had gone to Harvard, studied in Europe, served as his father's secretary in London from 1861 to 1868 while C. F. Adams, Sr., was minister to Britain. He then lived in Washington, taught history for some years at Harvard, and came back to Washington to lead the life of a gentleman-scholar. Never in this stretch of time or subsequently did he have close contact with commonplace people. Though he fretted now and then at his London situation, he never came back to enlist in the Union army —an experience that certainly left its mark on Charles Francis, Jr. The spectacle of poverty seems not to have moved him. The only physical suffering that appears to have made a deep impression was, typically enough, confined to the family: the death of his sister from lockjaw. H. S. Commager has drawn the contrast between Henry and Jane Addams. She devoted herself to the wretched multitudes in the Chicago slums. Henry nursed his investments and took long trips abroad. Her autobiography, *Twenty Years at Hull-House*, is a personal yet selfless document. *The Education of Henry Adams*, though impersonal and generalized, is astoundingly self-centered.

Like Brooks, Henry passed through a phase of reformism, though he finally retired from the contest and began to express a withering contempt for the reform mentality with its faith in panaceas. Even in the Adamses' Washington hey-day, during the late 1870s and early 1880s, we discover from Samuels that Henry and his wife shrank from the political hurly-burly. They lived close by the White House, they knew political leaders, and they relished political gossip. But their operations were confined to a select circle, based on an almost censoriously prim standard of selection. They condescended to President and Mrs. Hayes and shuddered at senators like Blaine and Conkling. They snubbed visiting stage-performers — Sarah Bernhardt, Adelina Patti, Lily Langtry — whose morals they suspected. Their friend Henry James found the Adams socio-political code not altogether to his taste, if we may judge from the notes for his short story "Pandora." The character in this story presumably modeled on Adams is named "Bonnycastle." James makes Bonnycastle say, in discussing a dinner-party: "Hang it, there's only a month left; let us be vulgar and have some fun — let us invite the President." Bonnycastle, he acutely remarks, "was not in politics, though politics were much in him."

Henry Adams at one stage certainly hankered after some sort of public career. But in the maneuvers between — so to speak — regulars and the volunteers, Henry and his amateur friends are easy targets for ridicule. Few were willing to soil their hands; few seemed to grasp what had happened to the old America for which they felt so proprietary an emotion. Disdainful of both major parties, the Adamses and their political intimates switched allegiances and developed temporary enthusiasms for temporary third-party movements. They wrote articles denouncing corruption and stupidity, and they ostracized political leaders at social gatherings and were then piqued to be ignored in turn, or insulted, as Henry thought himself, by the offer of a diplomatic post not in a European capital but — of all places — in Guatemala City. They recommended civil-service reform and a few other nostrums which were of only peripheral importance. They appealed to a "people" in whom they had no great confidence and to men of cultivated minds — by which they meant themselves.

They vented their discouragement on their confused expectations in political novels like Henry Adams's (anonymous) *Democracy* (1880) and Francis Marion Crawford's *An American Politician* (1884). Their inadequacy is made abundantly, if unwittingly, clear in Crawford's book. His hero is a Massachusetts gentleman-reformer: a figure much like Henry's elder brother, John, who ran unsuccessfully for the Massachusetts governorship. Like John, Crawford's hero is a Democrat. But his chief argument is that party politics are the ruination of the United States. Where then does salvation lie? Crawford resorts to wishful fantasy. America's destinies are safeguarded by a mysterious triumvirate, referred to only as "X," "Y" and "Z," "members of a small community of men which had existed from the earliest days of American independence. . . . It had frequently occurred that all three members of the council simultaneously held seats in the senate. . . . More than one President since Washington had sat at one time or another in the triumvirate; secretaries of state, orators, lawyers, financiers and philanthropists had given the best years of their lives to the duties of the council."

Crawford assures us that these men had more than once "turned the scale of the country's future." But his is a thin dream to set beside the commanding reality of control as wielded by, say, the George Washington Plunkitt of Tammany Hall who "seen his opportunities and he took 'em."

Adams's own novel is less naive. Yet it is no more useful as a guide to action. As Irving Howe has pointed out (*Politics and the Novel*), Adams affects to despise the behaviour of Senator Ratcliffe, the character in *Democracy* who embodies corrupt ambition. But Ratcliffe is a far stronger figure than his disparagers. His sentiments are debated but not refuted; there is no genuine collision of ideas, and the author's response to politics seems, in Howe's words, "that of an esthete rather than a moralist." Indeed, in *Democracy* and in his second novel, *Esther* (1884), as well as in the subsequent worship of femininity that led him to write

Mont St. Michel and Chartres (1904, privately printed), one almost feels that Adams has chosen to be a woman. Women symbolize his own, secondary role. His heroines are ambitious in a fashion. Mrs. Lee in *Democracy*, comes to Washington "to measure . . . the capacity of the motive power." There was, we are told, "a very general impression . . . that Mrs. Lee would like nothing better than to be in the White House." Again: "What she wanted was Power." The same word is used of the heroine of *Esther*, with an equally significant qualification. Esther Dudley has "an instinct for power," though "not the love of responsibility."

In his fiction Henry Adams chose to examine the world through women's eyes because they, like him, existed in a kind of graceful purdah. They may be brilliant, they may yearn for power, but they are compelled to proceed by indirection. Though they may be privy to great events, women participate merely as spectators, critics, hint-droppers — never as creators, instigators, prime movers. In crisis the sole gesture open to them is flight. Mrs. Lee runs off to Europe, Esther to Canada; Henry, too, was an incessant traveler. The only means of achieving power for such women is to be wooed by it, married by it. The only free decision left to them is whether to accept or not. Both of Adams's heroines decline the proposal. We recall Justice Holmes's caustic version of the plight of Henry Adams: *He wanted it handed to him on a silver platter* — as if "it" were an invitation to a waltz.

Within their limited realm women are permitted to be social arbiters. The dislike of Jews, so marked in Henry's later years, might be interpreted in these terms. Good society, American or European, had no properly defined place for the Jew. If Jews were more a symptom than a chief cause of the world's decline, as Henry probably conceded, he was nevertheless ready to agree with Brooks Adams that the Jew was a sinister, conspiratorial figure. The wicked bankers plotted together with an effectiveness that the gentlemanly Francis Marion Crawford would have liked to attribute to his virtuous but alas imaginary triumvirate. What was a Jew like Dreyfus doing as a French army officer? How could his purpose *not* be nefarious? Henry Adams was convinced that Dreyfus was guilty of espionage. He resisted the proof of Dreyfus's innocence, and maintained that the military were correct in closing their ranks against the clamorous Dreyfusards. Honor was at stake — the honor of the fatherland; and for a man descended from two Presidents, the word "fatherland" had an almost literal application.

The intellectual systems of Henry Adams are equally open to question. The charge against him is vigorously put in Yvor Winters's *Anatomy of Nonsense*. According to Winters, Adams was the unlucky inheritor of a debased New

England Calvinism. The Calvinist mind was an "allegorical machine." Even the most minor incident embodied some portentous significance. By the early 19th century, this attitude had broadened and weakened into the blank, generalizing tone of Unitarianism or — in the absence of easy religious belief — taken the form of "a kind of willed confusion and religious horror, best represented in literature" (says Winters) "by Melville's *Pierre* and *The Confidence Man* and by the later work of Henry Adams."

Even as a young man, Henry strove to find a pattern in the universe, yet told himself there probably was none. He was driven "to read every event with . . . allegorical precision; and since every event was isolated and impenetrable he read in each new event the meaning that the universe was meaningless." He became a seeker convinced he would find nothing, a connoisseur of bafflement and frustration. As his early ambitions for personal success dwindled, so for him mankind as a whole dwindled to pygmy scale and then to infinitesimal consequence in the scheme of things. He plunged into geology, into physics and mathematics, but less for enlightenment than in order to find fresh examples to illustrate his thesis that the universe was a weary chaos.

Formulas, dates, numbers fascinated him. He deployed them with a joking dogmatism, half frivolous, half anguished, to reinforce his contention that the only operative laws were laws of degradation or of nightmare acceleration. He fashioned numerological metaphors of the abyss: the squares that escape by giant leaps toward infinity; their opposites, the inverse squares that shrink within themselves, in pursuit of nothingness; the asymptotes that skirt the edge of non-existence. These formulas of failure can be seen as signs of an inordinate egotism. It was perhaps egotism of a solipsistic variety, in somehow equating the fate of one Adams with that of the cosmos. Louis XVI thought that disaster would overtake mankind when he was dead (*"Après moi le déluge"*): to judge from the calculations of the aging Henry Adams, the world would come to an end at about the same moment that he did. Henry knew how crushing was the sense of failure in his ancestors. John Quincy Adams, rejected by the electorate in 1828 after one unhappy term as President, remembered a song from Grétry's opera *Richard Coeur-de-Lion* which he had heard sung thirty years before and felt its bitter meaning for himself: *"O Richard, o mon roi, l'univers t'abandonne."* His grandson Henry knew the anecdote and seemed bent on turning the tables. If the universe had abandoned his grandfather, he himself could decide to abandon the universe.

In short, Henry Adams might be viewed as an extreme example of the late nineteenth-century American patriciate, endowed with the characteristic minor virtues of such a class (refinement, wit, cosmopolitanism, personal honesty) and the characteristic minor vices (snobbery, malice, diffidence, self-pity). But then, to come back to Lionel Trilling's response, a different and much more attractive interpretation may be put on the man and his writings.

It is not easy to put the two views together so that the more favorable carries due weight. An instance is the essay by Yvor Winters, already cited, in which a devastating critique of Adams's intellectual equipment is suddenly followed by lavish praise of the nine-volume *History*. Winters describes this as possibly "the greatest historical work in English, with the probable exception of *The Decline and Fall of the Roman Empire*." His analysis of the *History* is plausible, but in context we see that Winters has had to wrestle with his equivocal response to Henry Adams.

The easiest way out is to echo Winters's praise, to total up the sum of Adams's other writings, and to conclude that he is after all a major American author. The mere bulk is impressive; so is the range, from medieval to modern times, from poetry and fiction to rigorous scholarship. Major authors can be forgiven almost anything. What then if Henry Adams *was* a querulous snob? But this will not quite do. Some aspects of Adams's authorship remain perplexing. And perhaps we ought to ask whether Adams and other members of the American patriciate did not in their era have a *right* to feel sorry for themselves.

Let us consider his writings. The problem is why, if Adams is now deemed so excellent an historian, his qualities were not fully appreciated by contemporaries. Samuels offers some answers, and others suggest themselves. The volumes of the *History* were published at intervals; reviewers, dealing with isolated portions, failed to perceive the grand design — the symmetry of the work, the large generalizations on national character and on the evolution of democracies. Again, Adams did nothing to commend himself to reviewers. The cluster of friends who read preliminary proofs were disqualified from reviewing the finished product. He refrained from sweetening potential critics by distributing complimentary copies or praising *their* works. Possibly a few of them resented Adams for being who he was. The academics could well have been irritated by a man who refused the offer of honorary degrees (from Harvard and Yale) and who avoided the meetings of the American Historical Association, including the one at which he was supposed to deliver the presidential address. Nor was this office of president as flattering a recognition as might appear. In that day it went to a miscellany of professors, popularizers, and public men.

Adams was right in thinking that there was no large market for serious historical scholarship. Perhaps he hoped for too much, and attempted to satisfy incompatible desires within his own nature. Gibbon and Macaulay were much on his mind: he wanted to compose *literary* masterpieces. He was also determined to be scientific in the narrow sense of being punctilious. Hence the burrowing in sources, the long direct quotations which he (urged on by his brother Charles) took to be the hallmark of true history. And he dreamed of being scientific in some far larger way. The quest was lifelong. At the age of twenty-five, in a letter to Charles, Henry sketched his current philosophical interests. He went on to speculate that "in every progression, somehow or other, the nations move by the same process *which has never been explained* but is evident in the ocean and the air."[2] Thirty years later, in the essay on "The Tendency of History," Adams shows how much the search for this explanation has occupied him. He speaks of the tantalizing awareness among historians of standing

> *on the brink of a great generalization that would reduce all history under a law as clear as the laws which govern the material world. . . . No teacher with a spark of imagination or with an idea of scientific method can have helped dreaming of the immortality that would be achieved by the man who should successfully apply Darwin's method to the facts of human history.*

The endeavor was heroic and a factor to be reckoned with in the final assessment of Henry Adams. However he might camouflage or deride his ambitions, this was a considerable one. But the results are disappointing. Of course he was a gifted historian. Still, he did not altogether find the formulas, literary or methodological, he was looking for. The style of the *History*, and of the previous biographies of Gallatin and Randolph, is as interesting as Winters says. It is, though, too lapidary in places (too close to Gibbon?) and verges on melodrama in others (an overdose of Macaulay?). The scientific theorizing sounds more tentative than Adams probably meant it to be. The rival claims of narrative and exposition, of the exceptional individual and the average mass, are not firmly resolved. We know how perfect a style — supple, wry, allusive, entirely personal — Adams evolved in his correspondence. Perhaps we read his histories with this in mind. Reviewers at the time had no such advantage. They may have been repelled by the alternations of assertion and questioning, of national pride and headshaking pessimism; by the Gibbonian, distanced irony; and by the sheer tedium of complicated diplomatic exchanges, no matter how lucidly rendered. Adams was far more intelligent than his successor in the presidency of the American Historical Association, Senator Hoar of Massachusetts. Hoar's

[2] Italics mine.

presidential address was a humorless protest at the denigration of American history by unspecified cynics. Presumably Henry Adams was one of the offenders at whom Hoar aimed his rather clumsy darts. But one can see what Hoar was getting at. There was something unspoken, pontifical, rebarbative, caustic in the public style of Adams's middle years.

Nevertheless he does deserve to be taken seriously, as scholar and as stylist. He did aim very high. If he could not be a universal man, he did nevertheless deal in universals. Historians before his time often spoke of "universal" history. What it might amount to none could precisely explain. Even so, the idea persisted as a grand if indistinct challenge. Adams attempted to combine this earlier search for the philosopher's stone with the newer passion for "scientific" history, so as to arrive at universal scientific history. The product would have to be on the scale of Marx or Comte, Darwin or Spencer, but still more intellectually exact than these. Adams could not have labored so long and hard if he had not in his inmost being clung to the vision of winning immortality as one of the great system-builders of his time. It was odd that he went about the task in such a way as to be regarded as temperamentally frivolous and negative. Though he traveled comfortably and often and could be accused of trying to run away from himself, he never journeyed out of mere boredom. His travels had a purpose, whether he was in Tahiti or Japan, the American West or the cathedral towns of Normandy. The truest picture of Henry Adams is not of a holiday-maker in a panama hat or of a spoiled old salon-wit, but of a man alone at a table stacked with books and transcripts, absorbed in thought, and writing firmly and fluently.

Another way to see him is as a craftsman of letters. His concern with good writing far transcended dandyism. He could not bear slovenly or superfluous phrases. When he was editor of the *North American Review*, he showed no mercy to contributors' manuscripts, however eminent the author. He took enormous trouble over the style and content of some of Brooks's work. Henry was equally severe on his own writing. He wrote better in 1880 than in 1870, better in 1890 than in 1880, and so on to the end of his days. The perverse reluctance to let certain works appear at all was in part the hesitation of a perfectionist. When early essays were reprinted, he revised them with the utmost care. Another part of his hesitation came from uncertainty as to who constituted his audience and how they should therefore be addressed. The compromise of his later days, when he devised *Mont St. Michel* and the *Education* as private entertainments, was in literary terms brilliantly right. Here, as in his private correspondence, he hit upon just the appropriate form in which to disport the *persona* of one whom friends dubbed the Angelic Porcupine. By his standards it was a minuscule achievement; yet it has been the principal guarantor of immortality for Henry Adams.

There remains the final question of the quality of the American patriciate. Fastidiousness, petulance, estrangement, snobbishness, anti-Semitism: these are evident in Henry and his friends and are hard to defend without falling into the same restricted mode of thought. At least Henry suffered more than his friends from the fact of being an Adams and did his best to escape this crippling privilege. Could he be damned for feeling that the United States was *his* country and that it had gone on the wrong track? He came to despair of democracy, yet never believed that other nations were better. They were even worse, and for Adams to assert this was a demonstration of patriotism. As a young man and into middle age, he continued to think he was a citizen of a great country. His optimism gradually evaporated; so did that of scores of his contemporaries, not all of them old-stock American gentry. His misanthropy was no greater, for example, than that of Mark Twain and more firmly based on knowledge and insight. The America of the Gilded Age was a worrying spectacle for an honest and sensitive person. We may laugh at the feeble expedients of gentlemen-reformers; but what else could they have done? The choice lay between ineffective protest and capitulation to the political and commercial interests. Neither was satisfactory. Those who took the other road than Henry's lost as much as they gained. Power entailed not only responsibility, but complicity in dubious enterprises. Henry Adams, to reiterate, did his best. His best was not good enough. Nor was anyone else's, in the rarefied atmosphere of the Adams dynasty. We may say of him, as John Dos Passos has said of Thorstein Veblen, that he never could get his tongue around the essential yes. For this, in the last analysis, is Henry Adams not to be honored instead of scolded?

This essay appeared in *Commentary*, 39, (June 1965): pp. 66-71.

Henry Adams has continued to fascinate scholars — at any rate, those not hostile to his canonical-WASP standing. His two novels, also *Mont St Michel* and *Education* (1983), and his big *History* (2 vols., 1986), have been reprinted in the Library of America. *The Letters of Henry Adams*, 6 vols. (Cambridge: Harvard University Press, 1982-88), have been edited by J. C. Levenson, Ernest Samuels, Charles Vandersee and Viola Hopkins Winner in a splendidly ample expanded version. Among valuable new studies are William Dusinberre, *Henry Adams: The Myth of Failure* (Charlottesville: University of Virginia Press, 1980); Earl N. Harbert, *The Force So Much Closer to Home: Henry Adams and the Adams Family* (New York: New York University Press, 1977); John Carlos Rowe, *Henry Adams and Henry James: The Emergence of a*

Modern Consciousness (Ithaca, N.Y.: Cornell University Press, 1976); and William Merrill Decker, *The Literary Vocation of Henry Adams* (Chapel Hill, N.C.: University of North Carolina Press, 1990).

Two interpretations have occurred to me in the years since writing this review of Samuels's biography:

1. (Sketched in the 1986 revised edition of my Penguin *Literature of the United States*, 273-74) that Adams, consciously or not, presents a parallel between his own life and that of Peter Abelard, the wayward, gifted mediaeval philosopher who was castrated by the guardian of his student Eloise, never saw her again after this assault, and later wrote a *Historia Calamitatum*, a nice title for Henry's final speculations on the sad shapelessness of human evolution. My Penguin: "in *Walden*, suggesting a kind of village Sorbonne for Concord, Thoreau said: 'Can we not hire some Abélard to lecture to us?' Henry Adams, proudly unhireable, is nevertheless conceivably a sort of Abelard."

2. Adams' thirst for anonymity is still probably best understood as a personal trait. But he was not alone. Anonymity and pseudonymity remain a neglected aspect of nineteenth century authorship. Of his two novels, *Democracy* (1880) was brought out in closely guarded anonymity, while *Esther* (1884) was published under a female pseudonym, "Frances Snow Compton." Writers had mixed motives for disguising their identity. Walter Scott, turning to fiction after the success of long poems (*Marmion, The Lady of the Lake*) issued under his own name, published *Waverley* and other early novels anonymously, out of a feeling that fiction was not quite respectable. After a while, however, Scott perceived the commercial advantages of novels ascribed merely to a tantalizing "author of *Waverley*." Henry Adams probably wanted both the shelter and the paradoxical publicity of leaving the authorship of *Democracy* a mystery. Publishers of the era realized that sales might in fact be increased in this way. Roberts Brothers of Boston, a reputable company, launched a "No Name Series" of novels whose title pages bore the epigraph from George Eliot's *Daniel Deronda*: "IS THE GENTLEMAN ANONYMOUS? IS HE A GREAT UNKNOWN?" One of Roberts Brothers' anonymous books was *Mercy Philbrick's Choice* (1876), by the well-established gentlewoman writer Helen Hunt Jackson. Henry Adams, living in the nation's capital, must have been familiar with such forms of advantageous secrecy. The copy of *Mercy Philbrick's Choice* in the Gelman Library of George Washington University has a bound-in printed roster of members of the Washington, D.C. "No-Name Reading Club" — a subscription device that may have been promoted by Roberts Brothers. A pencilled note on p. 70 of the Gelman copy says: "Oh I'd like to know who wrote this story!"

16

Willa Cather and
Frederick Jackson Turner

In 1973 the University of Nebraska staged a conference in Lincoln on Willa Cather. Eudora Welty spoke of Cather as seen by another writer of fiction. Leon Edel commented as a biographer. I was asked to discuss Cather from a historian's viewpoint. These and other conference papers were published as *The Art of Willa Cather*. Unsure as to whether there actually was "a historian's" angle as such on Cather, I ventured some introductory remarks — here slightly abridged — on historians' somewhat clumsy use of imaginative writing in their classes. Then I took up a particular question. How far were Willa Cather and the frontier-historian Frederick Jackson Turner aware of one another's work? So far as I know, the issue has not been followed up, though Hermione Lee touches briefly on the apparent Cather-Turner parallels in her incisive *Willa Cather: Double Lives* (New York: Pantheon, 1990). Sharon O'Brien's recent interpretations take into account lesbian aspects, which while prominent in Cather's life are not necessarily the key to her writing. On Turner, Ray Allen Billington's remains the indispensable biography. As elsewhere, I have taken the opportunity to purge the essay of some stylistic faults, but the argument has not been tampered with.

In 1923 Frederick Jackson Turner, the historian of the frontier, remarked that "American history and American literature cannot be understood apart from each other." Yet, so far as I can determine, Willa Cather did not read Turner's essays, though they set the pattern for an entire generation of American historians from about 1900 to 1930; and Turner for his part, though in 1924 he told a correspondent that "a valuable study might be made of the pioneer woman and her place in history,"[1] seems never to have read Willa Cather.

Some imaginative writers lend themselves more readily than others to classroom citation. The historian appears to feel most at home with novelists who discuss public issues in their work or who take stands on issues in their capacity as citizens. In covering the years from 1880 to 1930 or thereabouts, the historian of the United States fastens upon such authors as Edward Bellamy, William Dean Howells, Mark Twain, Frank Norris, Winston Churchill, Sinclair Lewis, and Scott Fitzgerald. He instances Bellamy's *Looking Backward* (1888) as a novel directly concerned with social abuses and social reform. He is fascinated by the development of a social conscience in Howells's novels. He is interested in the more oblique social satire of Twain's *Connecticut Yankee* (1889), in which Twain's illustrator Dan Beard supplied caricatures for a rogues' gallery of contemporary Europeans and Americans. The historian refers students to Norris's *The Octopus* (1901) for a view of the struggle between farmers and capitalists in California and to *The Pit* (1903) for an account of the frenzied operations of the stock market in Chicago. Churchill's novels supply material for an understanding of political corruption in the so-called Progressive Era. Sinclair Lewis and Scott Fitzgerald are treated as chroniclers of the America of the 1920s. Or the historian brings in those writers who associated themselves with the causes and controversies of their day: Howells for his courageous stand on behalf of Chicago's Haymarket anarchists in 1886, Twain as an anti-imperialist in the wake of the Spanish-American War, Upton Sinclair and Jack London as socialists, and so on.

Willa Cather, being less easy to handle, has been comparatively neglected by historians. True, she is less preoccupied with purely local affairs than Sarah Orne Jewett or with abstractions of behavior than Henry James — two fellow writers whom she much admired and whose work has likewise not supplied much leverage for historians. Willa Cather is a precise observer. With James we usually have only the vaguest explanation of what his characters do for a living or how much money they make. In Cather's case the material circumstances are often stipulated. The dollars and cents are set forth. Financial disasters and successes are fairly prominent in her plots. Some of her characters, we learn, are much affected by the dramas of the time. We are told, for example, that Rodney Blake in *The Professor's House* (1925) feels strongly about the Chicago anarchists

---

[1] Ray Allen Billington, *Frederick Jackson Turner: Historian, Scholar, Teacher* (New York: Oxford University Press, 1973), 491-92.

and about the Dreyfus trial in France. But such allusions remain peripheral; they are never at the center of the story.

As for her personal response to public issues, this too seems unemphatic, when set beside those of other contemporary writers. In *The Landscape and the Looking Glass* (1960), John H. Randall suggests that Willa Cather was considerably influenced by the Populist ferment of Nebraska in the 1890s. This may well be true. But, taking her work as a whole, I do not feel that the Populist outlook was crucial and enduring for her. The aesthetic modes of the decade, which Mr. Randall also stresses, strike me as having fixed her attitudes in profounder ways. None of Willa Cather's redoubtable pioneer women emulates the Populist leader Mary Leese, who urged farmers to "raise less corn and more hell." In the next decade, after 1900, the nation became highly sensitive to political reform, temperance, women's rights, housing and working conditions, pacifism, conservation; these activities aroused a multitude of energetic and articulate Americans — women as well as men. One example is Jane Addams, the founder of the Chicago slum settlement known as Hull House, who flung herself into a variety of causes, including that of Theodore Roosevelt's "Bull Moose" Progressivism in 1912. There was abundant opportunity for the writer, through the spread of what Roosevelt called muckraking journalism. Willa Cather, with her editorial job on *McClure's Magazine*, the most enterprising of all the muckraking periodicals, was set in the midst of Progressivism. Yet for whatever temperamental reasons, she stood apart from the surface indignations and aspirations of the Progressive Era. Nor did she attune herself closely to the *Zeitgeist* in later years. Her war novel *One of Ours* (1922) is a somewhat better book than most critics have been prepared to acknowledge. But it does not reveal a comprehensive grasp of the moods of wartime America or of the immediate postwar atmosphere. Her subsequent treatment of the American scene, for instance in *The Professor's House*, is intelligent but diffuse, as if the author is unsure whether valediction or malediction is the fitter response.

Historians in their classes might have been able to draw upon Cather's writings to illustrate theories of art and literature. Here too she has failed to oblige them. Her ideas on writing are well stated and perfectly sound. But she seems to have declined to jump through the right hoops at the right moment. She did not in the 1890s become identified with the new advocates of naturalism in literature, though self professedly "Western" writers such as Frank Norris and Hamlin Garland asserted that truth in literature was something that the authors of their region were peculiarly qualified to produce. Willa Cather did not stake out a claim for herself as a woman writer. Though some of her principal characters are women, they display an almost mannish shrewdness and vigor; and in some of her novels the viewpoint is in more ways than one that of a man. Not for Cather, then, the combination of feminine perception and technical experiment evident in the stream-of-consciousness fiction of her English contemporaries Dorothy Richardson and Virginia Woolf. She may in *One of Ours* have expressed an innocent idealism that actually existed. But the historian prefers to conclude that the American experience in World War I was best rendered in the youthful avant-garde prose of John Dos Passos's *Three Soldiers* (1921) and E. E. Cummings's *The Enormous Room* (1922). Her much-quoted observation that the world broke in two in the year 1922 could be taken as her own recognition that she could not imaginatively make the transition from the old universe to the new, in part because she had never sought to keep abreast of literary fashion. So, according to this interpretation, she was able to enjoy talking with D. H. Lawrence when she met him in New York and then through Mabel Dodge Luhan in New Mexico,[2] but would never have been able to stomach most of Lawrence's fiction — any more than she could appreciate James Joyce's *Ulysses* or the plays of Eugene O'Neill. I suppose historians ought not to be blamed too much for their indifference to Willa Cather seen as spokesman for her time, when some literary critics have also displayed a good deal of uneasiness and have tended to categorize her as a "traditional" novelist. That may amount to a confession that they are unable to devise any suitable definition or "placing" for Willa Cather.

My main argument, however, is of a different order. It is that each of us is, after all, a prisoner of the *Zeitgeist*; that Willa Cather does, for the historian and possibly for the student of literature, help to shed light on her own age; and that by approaching her from this external position one may gain an additional appreciation of her individual quality. In particular, I wish to examine her as both a product and an exponent of a whole set of tensions between West and East. To some extent these are universal tensions, affecting all "advanced" civilizations at the end of the nineteenth century and all societies aware of a difference between the provincial life and that of the metropolis.

Within the American framework, it is clear that some Easterners treated the West with a casualness amounting on occasion to contempt. At various times the New Englander Henry Adams observed that the whole country west of the Alleghenies might as well be scrapped. "I do not like the western type of man," was the similar verdict of the New York journalist E. L. Godkin, editor of the *Nation*. The young literary scholar George Edward Woodberry, bemoaning the fate that had exiled him as a teacher at the University of Nebraska, told a Boston

---

[2] Lewis, *Willa Cather Living*, 138-39, 143.

friend that the Nebraska faculty was split between Eastern and Western members. Nebraska society was "characterized by blank Philistinism intellectually and barren selfishness morally." The undergraduates were unkempt and wore "shirt fronts of outrageous uncleanness." "This life," he lamented, "requires a hardihood of the senses and susceptibilities of which you have little conception, I fear. . . . I doubt very much whether the hardihood I gain will not be a deterioration into barbarism, not sinew for civilization." In about 1890 the Johns Hopkins historian Herbert Baxter Adams, reared in New England and trained in Germany, was offered a tempting well-paid professorship at the University of Chicago, which for him was in the West. Pondering the advantages and disadvantages of his present post as against the new future one, Adams drew up a balance sheet. He headed one column "Chicago," the other "Baltimore":

CHICAGO	BALTIMORE
Rush	Quiet
Broken	Continuity
Experiment	Experience
New People	Society
Boom	Conservatism
Advantage	Duty
All new	Assured position
Moving	Settled
Lost	Identification

It is not difficult to guess from this choice of vocabulary that Adams decided to stay put.[3] For a convinced Easterner, the West was raw, rude, and remote. It was worse than the provinces, in a European scheme, in being not just relatively but almost absolutely uncultivated.

However, as in the case of the European metropolis-provinces polarity, the disdain of the Easterner was often matched by the self-abasement of the sensitive Westerner. A special feature of the American Westerner was that he was often not a native provincial but someone who had come out to the West from the East and felt he was regressing into barbarism. This was, for instance, the initial reaction of the young California writer Bret Harte, who had grown up in New York City. In his contributions to San Francisco magazines during the middle

---

[3] Examples cited in Richard Hofstadter, *The Progressive Historians: Turner, Beard, Parrington* (New York: Vintage Books, 1970), 54-55, 67.

1860s, Harte sighed at the ugliness of such American placenames as Poker Flat, Red Dog, and One Horse Flat. In another piece he wrote: "The less said about the motives of some of our pioneers the better; very many were more concerned in getting away from where they were, than in going to any particular place." A few years later, as editor of the *Overland Monthly*, Harte poured scorn on the Society of California Pioneers and claimed that what the West needed instead was a Society for the Suppression of Local Pride.[4]

It was not necessary to be a settler from the East to denigrate the West. Edgar W. Howe, a thirty-year-old newspaper editor in Kansas, poured out his accumulated bitterness in a novel entitled *The Story of a Country Town* (1883). One of the characters in the novel says:

> *Haven't you noticed that when a Western man gets a considerable sum of money together, he goes East to live? Well, what does it mean except that the good sense which enabled him to make money teaches him that the society there is preferable to ours? ... Men who are prosperous ... do not come West, but it is the unfortunate, the poor, the indigent, the sick ... who came here to grow up with the country, having failed to grow up with the country where they came from.*

Nor was it necessary for a Westerner to apologize for coming East. The classic Dick Whittington-ish story of the ambitious and talented person in all eras and countries is that he demonstrates his ability by leaving the country for the city, the provinces for the metropolis. Ambition itself dictates the move; and the consolation for the provinces is that such-and-such a famous individual is "from" their area. They gain or hope to gain a minor glory from what is in fact an abandonment. There is a pathos in this recurrent drama. Sometimes the native sophisticate almost entirely loses his original feeling for the home place, as seems to have happened with William Dean Howells in relation to his Ohio childhood. Sometimes the escaper makes his living out of his store of recollections, as in large part Bret Harte did with California. Sometimes, as with Mark Twain, his best writing deals with the scenes of his early life. Usually, however, he does not go back again except on visits. Missouri-born Twain, comfortably installed in Connecticut, wrote to an old friend in 1876 about Southern politics:

[4] George R. Stewart, *Bret Harte: Argonaut and Exile* (1935; reprint, Port Washington, N.Y.: Kennikat Press, 1964), 150-51, 175.

I think I comprehend their position there — perfect freedom to vote just as you choose provided you choose to vote as other people think, social ostracism otherwise. . . . Fortunately a good deal of experience of men enabled me to choose my residence wisely. I live in the freest part of the country.

But the provinces-metropolis analogy is inexact as applied to the American polarity of West and East, and this not merely because the American "West" was an area whose geographical boundaries and whose other characteristics were continually shifting. In the American myth, as delineated by Henry Nash Smith and others, the West was never simply the back-of-beyond. It was also and to a growing degree the land of America's destiny, the locus of the westering impulse evoked in Walt Whitman's "Passage to India" (a poem that Bret Harte, incidentally, rejected when it was submitted to his *Overland Monthly*). After his death in 1865, Abraham Lincoln began to be deified as a great Western symbolic hero — the "first American" in the words of J.R. Lowell's Harvard Commemoration Ode. *The American Commonwealth* (1888), a widely read assessment by the Scottish observer James Bryce, insisted that the West was the most American part of the United States. In the traditional legend, the provinces are fatally and irretrievably backward, vis-à-vis the metropolis. In part of the American formulation, the West is not backward but forward: the place of the future.[5] According to this reversal, in important respects the "latest" is not to be found in the East but in the West; and even the "latest" in the limited sense of the latest fashions in books and clothes was swiftly becoming available in Western metropolises — including the Chicago that Herbert Baxter Adams had so summarily dismissed. This other mood was expressed in Carl Sandburg's *Chicago Poems* (1914):

> *I speak of new cities and new people.*
> *I tell you the past is a bucket of ashes. . . .*
> *I tell you there is nothing in the world*
>   *only an ocean of to-morrows,*
>   *a sky of to-morrows.*

---

[5] Turner too voiced this sentiment. He wrote in 1887: "I am placed in a *new society*, which is just beginning to realize that it has made a place for itself by mastering the wilderness and peopling the prairie, and is now ready to take its great course in universal history. It is something of a compensation to be among the advance guard of new social ideas and among a people whose destiny is all unknown. *The west looks to the future, the east toward the past.*" Quoted in Hofstadter, *The Progressive Historians*, 63.

As the nineteenth century drew to a close, Westerners were inclined to argue the strengths of their region as measured by both kinds of up-to-dateness. The historian Charles A. Beard, who had grown up in Indiana, later remembered his annoyance in the 1890s at the prevailing Eastern assumption "that all of us beyond the Alleghenies, if not the Hudson, were almost, if not quite, uncouth savages."[6] Frederick Jackson Turner, then a young teacher at the University of Wisconsin, was exasperated by an 1891 article in the *Century Magazine* by that proper Bostonian, Henry Cabot Lodge. Lodge analyzed over fourteen thousand entries in *Appleton's Encyclopedia of American Biography* to prove to his own satisfaction that practically all the talent in the United States had derived from New England, New York, and adjacent states. A generation later, in 1926, Turner offered a rebuttal on behalf of the West in the shape of an article (*Yale Review*, July 1926) entitled "Children of the Pioneers." Turner had been working on it for years. His biographer Ray Billington tells us: "It was crammed with the names of westerners who had succeeded in business, government, the arts . . . ; his westerners, he believed, gained Lincolnesque stature by their dedication to the interests of the ordinary people, inventing or writing or worshipping or painting to glorify and instruct the common man."[7]

When therefore Turner delivered his paper "The Significance of the Frontier in American History" at a conference in Chicago in 1893, the moment was exactly right. Instead of bowing to the Lodgeish assurance that the West was, so to speak, on probation and perhaps unlikely to pass the test, Turner declared that everything vitally democratic in American life had developed from the frontier experience. Within a few years every historian of note was beginning to incorporate the Turner frontier thesis in his interpretation of the national past. In Turner's lifetime, to his gratified amusement, references to the frontier spirit even became common in the utterances of politicians. There was the additional

---

[6] Hofstadter, *The Progressive Historians*, 54.

[7] Billington, *Frederick Jackson Turner*, 399-400. The article, "Children of the Pioneers," was reprinted in Turner's *The Significance of Sections in American History* (New York: Henry Holt, 1932), 193-206. In a letter of 23 December 1925 to his friend Mrs. Alice Hooper, Turner says that in the article "I examine whether the prediction of 'barbarism' made for them when their parents were going west — middle nineteenth century — proved true. It's really wonderful what places the children have filled, not only in the world of constructive business where vision was demanded, but also in the realms of art and literature, science, religion etc. etc." Ray Allen Billington, ed., *"Dear Lady:" The Letters of Frederick Jackson Turner and Alice Forbes Perkins Hooper, 1910-1932* (San Marino, Calif.: Huntington Library, 1970), 373. The article admittedly lists scores of names, with no chance to linger on any of them. Even so, the single reference to Cather (*Yale Review* 15, July 1926, p. 662) is perfunctorily second-hand: "Percy Boynton, in his recent book, 'Some Contemporary Americans,' gives especial attention to ten authors, of whom four are children of the North Central pioneers, and the fifth is Willa Cather, whose youth was spent in Nebraska."

gratification that the children of the pioneers were moving into more and more prominence in their own areas and among the strongholds of the East. He himself exemplified the process by accepting a chair at Harvard with effect from 1910; Harvard had already given him an honorary degree in the previous year.

One reason for the rapid spread of a new congratulatory attitude to the West already touched upon was that certain Easterners were now eager to claim kinship with the West out of a troubled sense that the East was no longer the repository of clear-cut, wholesome American values. "Their" America was altering rapidly and for the worse as they saw it, under the impact of urbanization, industrialization, and immigration. In the West, patrician, Harvard-educated young men like Theodore Roosevelt and his classmate Owen Wister found adventure, simplicity, manliness — indeed gentlemanliness, for they discerned chivalric qualities in the inhabitants of the great outdoors, especially those of the cattle and mountain territories. Their West, in the words of what is said to have been Roosevelt's favorite song, was the place "Where seldom is heard a discouraging word, / And the skies are not cloudy all day." Their celebration of the natural gentleman, the pioneer, the rugged individualist, is nicely analyzed by G. Edward White in *The Eastern Establishment and the Frontier Experience* (1968). Roosevelt, Wister, and the artist-writer Frederic Remington, extended the romanticizing of the West that was beginning to be essayed in works such as Mark Twain's *Roughing It* (1872) and the stories of Bret Harte. Roosevelt, who had praised the printed version of Turner's 1893 lecture, saw eye to eye with him too as to the future importance of the West. "I think it will be a good thing for this country," he told Turner in an 1896 letter, "when the West, as it used to be called, the Centre, as it really is, grows so big that it can no more be jealous of the East."[8]

Yet there was doubleness in these hymns to the West, whoever sang them. If a Westerner came East or an Easterner went out West, what did they represent and to whom? If the West evolved into the Center, in what ways could it remain distinctive? George Santayana, speaking of Whitman, has said that there is a sad contradiction in the very activity of pioneering. Once the pioneer arrives wherever his is going, he begins to "improve" — that is, spoil — the wilderness environment that temporarily ennobled him. The uncertainties are indicated in the device chosen by Bret Harte for the title page of the *Overland Monthly* (which started publication in 1868), as well as in the actual name of the magazine. The founders of the magazine had decided upon a picture of a grizzly bear: an

---

[8] G. Edward White, *The Eastern Establishment and the Western Experience: The West of Frederic Remington, Theodore Roosevelt, and Owen Wister* (New Haven, Conn.: Yale University Press, 1968), 191-92.

appropriate emblem since California was the Bear Flag state. But the bear on his own did not seem sufficient. Harte's solution was to add a railroad track beneath the bear's paws. Before the change, said Mark Twain, the bear "simply stood there snarling over his shoulder at nothing." With the change, "behold he was a magnificent success! — the ancient symbol of California savagery snarling at the approaching type of high and progressive Civilization, the first Overland locomotive!" The transcontinental railroad was then within a year of completion. But what was being symbolized? In a contest with a locomotive, the bear would clearly lose. The completion of the railroad would inevitably link California with the East and diminish whatever spirit of wilderness the bear typified.[9] In fact the railroad soon took Harte off to the East, all the way to Boston and an agreement to produce Western tales and poems for the *Atlantic Monthly*. And in any case, it had been the Eastern appetite for stories of the Wild West that had made the dandified Bret Harte realize that he had stumbled upon a literary bonanza. Was the West then truly America's future in any but the materialistic sense of a region awaiting exploitation? As a spiritual heritage, was it not disappearing almost overnight?

This ambiguity is fully apparent in the career of Frederick Jackson Turner. Did the value of the West for America lie in the formative, bygone stages of pioneering, as his frontier thesis appeared to say? He took as starting point in his 1893 paper the United States 1890 census announcement that the frontier as a continuous line of open country had ceased to exist. Yet he was offended when a critic charged him with having said that the frontier was ended and labored to prove that, through the "children of the pioneers," the West was culturally and materially displaying a favorable balance of trade in relation to the country as a whole. Having moved to the East from his native Wisconsin, Turner continued to think of himself as a Westerner. He retained a lifelong affection, indeed a personal need, for regular reimmersion in wild landscape. But he was never able to admit to himself imaginatively that his old West might have had serious shortcomings in narrowness and crudeness of spirit or that the new West might soon become indistinguishable from the East. In *Historians Against History* (1965), David Noble portrays Turner as one of several American historians who have woven scholarly legends of some splendid past era but who have been psychologically unable to come to grips with American evolution up to recent times.

---

[9] Stewart, *Bret Harte*, 159.

One curious aspect of Turner's view of the frontier West, which he shared with various Easterners, was that he liked to think of the pioneers as being pre-eminently of old, that is "Anglo-Saxon," stock. He knew with one part of his mind that this was historically not so. As a boy in Portage, Wisconsin, he had grown up in a polyglot community.[10] As a scholar he compiled material on immigrant settlement and recommended graduate students to turn their attention to immigration history. Marcus Hansen, the author of important studies on American immigration, was a Turner student. But in some other part of his mind Turner revealed a distaste not only for the city immigrants but also for those on the frontier. This is clearly brought out in the few references to Willa Cather in Turner's printed correspondence. They occur in exchanges with Mrs. Alice Forbes Perkins Hooper, an exuberant and affluent lady who had spent her childhood in Burlington, Iowa, where her father was president of the Burlington railroad. He had extended the Burlington track through Nebraska. Mrs. Hooper had already met Willa Cather by 1913, when she wrote to her friend Turner to say in passing that she had just read *O Pioneers!* and thought it "disappointing." Apparently she expected Willa Cather to "help us sometime" — presumably in lauding the pioneering enterprise of President Perkins. She implied that Willa Cather had failed to capture the atmosphere of Nebraska because she had come to Red Cloud late in the day and really knew little about it. Turner replied facetiously, also picking up a notion of Mrs. Perkins that it would be pleasant to make a return pilgrimage to Nebraska in a private railroad car:

> *But is a young thing who doesn't know her own birthplace [?] qualified to write historical fiction anyway? I haven't read O Pioneers! and I'll not until I can make that historical pilgrimage with a real pioneer, possessed of the memory, the maps and the imagination which belong only to oldest inhabitants. . . . As for me, give me Red Cloud wie es eigentlich gewesen, or give me nothing!*[11]

A decade afterward, in *A Lost Lady*, Cather did speak glowingly of the aristocratic boldness and integrity of the railroad builders, as personified by Captain Forrester. But Mrs. Hooper, as she informed Turner, resented the book:

[10] Wilbur R. Jacobs, ed., *The Historical World of Frederick Jackson Turner* (New Haven, Conn.: Yale University Press, 1968), 55-62.

[11] Billington, ed., *"Dear Lady,"* 147-49. The full citation is in note 7, above.

[Cather] drew upon her imagination and our family in Burlington and gave an absolutely false and arrogant impression of my mother and of me tho' she would probably say she had never heard of us. I didn't care for her a bit when I met her. . . , tho' I must admit some of her stories are excellent.[12]

I leave it to Cather scholars to determine whether there is any foundation for this supposed source of *A Lost Lady*. More relevant to my own account is the agreement of Turner and Mrs. Hooper, as he told her in a letter of March 1925, that Willa Cather and some other novelists had overstressed the non-British side of frontier settlement. He added: "The constructive work of the men of means, bankers, railway builders, etc. will also be recognized again after the present criticism of all things American has died down."[13] Turner's outlook is clarified in a letter he sent in the same year to his fellow historian Arthur M. Schlesinger (another Middle Westerner):

I imagine that some of the attempts to minimize the frontier theme, in the broad sense in which I used it, are part of the pessimistic reaction against the old America that have followed the World War — the reaction against pioneer ideals, against distinctively American things historically . . . to write in terms of European experience, and of the class struggle incident to industrialism. But we cannot altogether get away from the facts of American history, however far we go in the way of adopting the Old World![14]

It is time to bring back the discussion to Willa Cather. In setting her beside Frederick Jackson Turner, the first point to stress is the oddity that two writers so distinguished in their respective ways as interpreters of the American Western experience should have had so little to say to one another, directly or indirectly.

The second point is that this mutual neglect reveals more of a deficiency in Turner than in Willa Cather. As an imaginative writer she was entitled to be idiosyncratic — to read whatever suited her own needs and to ignore whatever did not speak to her. Turner, as his colleagues and students have testified, was a compulsively inquisitive and accumulative scholar. He had a feeling for the

---

[12] Ibid., 448.

[13] Ibid., 365.

[14] Jacobs, ed., *Historical World of Turner*, 164.

poetry of his subject. He sought eloquence as well as clarity in his own writing. "I always wanted to be an artist," he told a former student, "tho' a truthful one." He cherished Emerson's phrase "the nervous, rocky West"; and these lines from Tennyson's "Ulysses":

> *for my purpose holds*
> *To sail beyond the sunset, and the baths*
> *Of all the western stars, until I die.*

He was moved by Rudyard Kipling's "Explorer" poem, and also Kipling's "The Foreloper":

> *He shall desire loneliness, and his desire shall bring*
> *Hard on his heels a thousand wheels, a people and a king. . . .*
> *For he must blaze a nation's way, with hatchet and with brand,*
> *Till on his last-won wilderness an empire's bulwarks stand.*

Turner often, too, recited lines from Robinson Jeffers's "Californians" in his history lectures. But this appears to me a limited and rather commonplace record.[15] Turner's biographer does not indicate that he ever read Whitman, from whom Willa Cather borrowed her title *O Pioneers!*. He showed some knowledge of Vachel Lindsay's poetry in a letter of 1914, but only a cautious enthusiasm: "I can't say I think he is the authentic voice of the Middle West, as his friends assert." Turner appears to have remained unaware of or unaffected by Lindsay's lovely poem "Bryan, Bryan, Bryan, Bryan" from which Willa Cather took the epigraph — "Bidding the Eagles of the West fly on" — and the title of the final section of *One of Ours*.

A third point is that comparison with Turner strengthens her reputation at the expense of his. In other words, both have been accused of various deficiencies; there is a kind of parallelism in these supposed deficiencies; and Turner's seem to betray a greater deficiency of imaginative scope. Thus, it has been said that Willa Cather's mindset was formed quite early and restricted her. But by this test Turner, too, a dozen years her senior, had a restricted range. After the 1890s he wrote little and tended to repeat the essential themes he had hit upon by the time he was thirty-five. On the specific matter of immigrant frontier settlement, he was surprisingly reluctant to admit its significance. The probable reason is that

---

[15] Billington, *Frederick Jackson Turner*, 426-27. The Emerson allusion is from Emerson's 1844 lecture, "The Young American"; see Hofstadter, *The Progressive Historians*, 56-57.

like Theodore Roosevelt, Woodrow Wilson, and other historical writers of the day, he had formed an emotional image of the frontier West as the embodiment of "pure" Americanism, by which he and they meant old-stock Americanism. Willa Cather, for whatever personal reasons, showed a more original appreciation of the valuable un-Americanness of some aspects of the immigrant contribution.

In both cases, something of the quality that made them so fresh to readers of their day has evaporated or is now so much a part of our imaginative heritage that we take it for granted. Nevertheless, I would like to pursue a fourth point, also expressible negatively — though it leads toward a more positive conclusion. This point, illustrated not only by Turner but by a number of "Western" authors, is that the West in fact offers an extraordinarily elusive and frustrating theme — splendid for manifestoes and brief bursts of oratory but difficult to handle with subtlety and compassion. Hamlin Garland, Frank Norris, Jack London, and Owen Wister show a tendency to substitute geography for humanity, to be programmatic and declamatory, and to slide into either rancor and self-pity or grandiose sentimentality. Garland shifted in his literary career from bitter little pictures to roseate reminiscence. Norris in his short life could not decide whether the bigness of the West was monstrous or glorious. Stridency and unevenness marred the abundantly gifted Jack London — and can for that matter be detected in the British explorer of other far-off frontiers, Rudyard Kipling. Owen Wister, in company with Roosevelt and Remington, tended to stage heroic but stereotyped melodrama against a spectacular backdrop — making the scenery somehow more interesting than the performers.

The explanation may lie in the nature of their subject rather than in their own lack of literary ability. No doubt it was a *big* subject, but what precisely *was* it? The West was an embodiment of tender and powerful yearnings in mankind, of the kind hinted at in Wordsworth's phrase "something evermore about to be," or in Emerson's haunting juxtaposition of "the grey past, the white future," or in Kipling's "Foreloper," or in James Elroy Flecker's *Hassan*: "We are the pilgrims, master, and we shall go / Always a little further." The West was the land of possibility, "a fairer land than prose" as Emily Dickinson put it. Vachel Lindsay caught this quality of make-believe in his evocation of what the Nebraska politician William Jennings Bryan stood for in his campaign of 1896:

> *And these children and their sons*
> *At last rode through the cactus,*
> *A cliff of mighty cowboys*
> *On the lope,*
> *With gun and rope.*

> *And all the way to frightened Maine the old East*
>   *heard them call,*
> *And saw our Bryan by a mile lead the wall*
> *Of men and whirling flowers and beasts,*
> *The bard and the prophet of them all.*
> *Prairie avenger, mountain lion,*
> *Bryan, Bryan, Bryan, Bryan. . . .*[16]

That was the poetic essence of the West, a dream toward which to travel, an area of *becoming* rather than *being*. It has proved an enduring poetic myth, as a host of novels, films, and TV episodes testify. Understandably they concentrate upon the sharpest and most poignant part of the story — the first ranches, the first breaking of the sod, and even more compulsively the journey into the West, the movement of the wagons, the encampments, the Indian raids, and so on. But such sagas are fixated upon a transitory moment and upon two-dimensional displays of masculinity, of lone-wolf heroism on the part of men who, like Peter Pan in J. M. Barrie's Never Never Land, resist involvement in the subsequent chapters of the tale.

These subsequent chapters constitute the prose rather than the poetry of the Western story. Historians and novelists have the obligation to put things in sequence, to tell us what happens next. But if what happens next is in some ways a letdown, an anticlimax, as with the later career of William Jennings Bryan, they run into serious difficulties. They can try to confine themselves to chapter one, but that may seen an evasion. They can pretend there was no spiritual deterioration, as I think Turner preferred to do; but that is another evasion, not far removed from the superficialities of mere boosterism. They can turn sour, as Edgar Howe did in his novel of Kansas small-town claustrophobia, or insist that if "Go West, young man" was a stirring injunction, then "Go East, young man (or woman)" was an equally imperative need for talented Westerners. But to portray the West as a psychic wasteland is to miss the poetry, both of exhilaration and of the elegiac, that infuses the prosaic aspects of the theme.

When all these difficulties are considered, it is no wonder that the literature of the West has been so dominated by John-Wayneish, Marlboro-Country clichés of rugged maleness. What is a wonder is that Willa Cather, a woman reared in what might look like the tired fag-end of Late Victorian parlor-culture, was able

---

[16] Vachel Lindsay, *Collected Poems* (New York: Macmillan, 1925), 99. He notes having written this poem at the Guanella Ranch, Empire, Colorado, in August 1919.

to turn so much of her situation to advantage. Perhaps she was not able entirely to transcend her difficulties. Now and then I feel she is perilously near to cliché, that she is asserting a truth somewhat editorially, instead of conveying it, and even occasionally against the grain of the narrative; and that she is in such instances rescued in part by the sheer excellence of her prose — a kind of perfection of plainsong.

Nevertheless the achievement is remarkable; and my argument, to reiterate, is not that Willa Cather merely stands out in a field of second-raters, but that she made fine fiction out of alluring yet intransigent material. Thus, in her handling of Nebraska she covers all the basic stages of settlement as enumerated by Frederick Jackson Turner and other historians. There is the unmitigatedly bare landscape as young Jim Burden sees it at the beginning of *My Ántonia*: "I had the feeling that the world was left behind, that we had got over the edge of it, and were outside man's jurisdiction" (p. 7). There are the daunting early struggles of the newly-arrived farmers recounted, for example, in *My Ántonia* and in *O Pioneers!* There is the satisfaction that comes to good farmers from seeing their patch of prairie gradually turn into something fruitful, handsome, and orderly: a prosperity worked for and fitting. There is the accretion of memories, of vast significance to particular individuals though not related to public events. "Whatever we had missed," as Jim concludes of his lifelong friendship with Ántonia, "we possessed together the precious, the incommunicable past" (p. 372).

Nor does Willa Cather avoid the grubbier sides of Western life. She stresses the drabness and narrowness of the little towns and the glum resentfulness of some of the farmers. Like William Faulkner, she contrasts the generosity of the older order with the mean rapacity of would-be local tycoons such as Wick Cutter in *My Ántonia* and Ivy Peters in *A Lost Lady*. She reaches up to the present day — her present day — in *The Professor's House*. The gallery of characters is less linked and extensive than with Faulkner's Yoknapatawpha County, but it is surprisingly comprehensive. Moreover, she appreciates the magic of "Eastern" culture, whether represented by college education or by music and the theatre, and freely concedes that those who have the opportunity and wish to take it are likely to head away from the home place and may become estranged from it. Certain settlers are, so to speak, likely to become unsettled. Kipling says of the pioneer: "He shall desire loneliness, and loneliness shall bring / Hard on his heels a thousand wheels, a people and a king." There is a tinge of ironic regret in that précis of the pioneer experience. Willa Cather makes room for it with more honesty than any writer familiar to me.

The reason, I believe, is that with an instinctive wisdom she declined to identify herself as either a professional Westerner or as one of that band of esthetes in

Greenwich Village or the Left Bank who, especially in the 1920s, announced that they were escapees from the prison of the central states of America. With the dispassionate egotism of the genuine artist, Willa Cather abstracted and universalized her own situation. This idea is well put by Dorothy Van Ghent, who calls Cather's creative spirit "primitive" and "psychologically archaic" and observes that "out of homely American detail" — for instance in *My Ántonia* — "are composed certain friezelike entablatures that have the character of ancient ritual and sculpture."[17] Instead of dwelling upon the uniqueness of the American frontier, as Turner did, she sensed the recurrence of immemorial predicaments and hopes. *Tempora mutantur, nos et mutamur in illis*: both the sadness of frontier failure and the subtler regrets that came from frontier success had for her a larger dimension, stretching back to the poetry of Virgil and Horace.

She was not of a completely equable temperament. In younger life she was a rebel, in middle age increasingly dismayed by what she took to be the vulgarization of the world. Nevertheless there was an assurance in what she wrote. Her likes and dislikes and convictions were established early. In some respects they appear conventional. But they gave her a frame and a tone and suggested a literary method. The result is a curiously measured, wise style — that of a tribal elder who can explain the underlying order in even the most disorderly events.

Thus for Willa Cather there was no fundamental opposition between West and East, between "frontier" and "civilization." She knew there were differences of circumstance, which might be considerable. But she was not committed, as Turner and some of her contemporaries were, to the attractive yet oversimplified East-West polarity. She knew the strengths and weaknesses of each theoretical mode. Within the sophisticated world, refinement could become precocity and art artifice. On the frontier, hardihood could degenerate into callousness, boldness into brutality. She realized that the two extremes existed; she had after all firsthand acquaintance with both.

Yet to her, frontier and civilization were not so much opposites as coordinates. The true human being in Willa Cather's realm is innately civilized, though books and travel may heighten sensibility. The true human being is at home in all environments and is a respecter both of persons and of places. The false human being, to be found in all environments, is a hater and a spoiler, both of persons and of places. Those are Willa Cather's opposites. They are not complicated. But they work better for literary purposes than the artificial *versuses*, the false

---

[17] Van Ghent, *Willa Cather*, 5, 22-23.

male-female, tough-effete antitheses of a good deal of popular frontier fiction —
in which, for example, the reader or viewer is triggered to identify the villain as
the man who arrives wearing gloves and a fancy hat, unless this man almost
immediately gets into a victorious fight with some local tough and so proves he
is not really a corrupt dude, despite appearances. In Cather's fiction the pioneer
may well be cultivated and — in the best sense of the word — worldly, as with
one or two of the priests in *Death Comes for the Archbishop*, or Captain Forrester
and some of his visitors in *A Lost Lady*. Nor is he necessarily an innovator, at
least not in any reckless fashion. "'Change is not always progress,'" according to
Euclide Auclair in *Shadows on the Rock* (p. 119). As in *Shadows on the Rock*,
Willa Cather is fond of comparing good pioneers with bad pioneers. Auclair's
patron, Bishop Laval, has respected the needs of the Quebec citizens. His system
is overturned by a seemingly more sophisticated cleric in the name of progress.
Tom Outland in *The Professor's House* likewise respects the remnants of the
Indian mesa culture he has discovered, whereas his companion Blake — though
he may believe in justice for the Haymarket anarchists and for Captain Dreyfus
— is unable to keep faith with Tom or with the mesa Indians. In other words,
Willa Cather refuses to be saddled with the orthodox polarities of supposed East-
West behavior. Her proper pioneer is not the spoiler Santayana described, but
a conserver and a bringer of beauty. Unlike Theodore Roosevelt, he does not
worship the wilderness by killing its animals. In his supreme form, he is as
attuned to the ecology as an Indian.

Willa Cather's other main coordinates are time and space. One problem in
writing about the West, especially in her time, is that the space-dimension is large
and the time-dimension is small. Some writers, as we have seen, shrink the time-
dimension to an almost infinitesimally brief period — a sort of imaginary moment
suspended between past and future. This could be said, not too unfairly, of the
essential idea in Turner's frontier thesis, which is that the initial contact between
settler and wilderness brings about a psychic rebirth. In Cather's case, awareness
of the time-dimension is among the essential attributes of a true human being.
She and some of her principal characters extend their consciousness of time-
past through exposure to the culture of Europe. Her novel *One of Ours* makes
an interesting attempt to convey the impact of such an exposure upon an open-
minded young man from Nebraska when he goes to France with the American
army. In *One of Ours* the theme becomes entangled with other aims. But in her
most successful explorations of the time-dimension — Tom Outland's story in *The
Professor's House*, *Death Comes For the Archbishop*, and rather less powerfully in
Shadows on the Rock — she establishes with economy and authority various
previous layers of North American pioneering. If this was her way of reacting

against the disagreeable realities of postwar America, she managed to universalize her private concerns and to transform them into extraordinarily distanced and consoling images. She probably could not have accomplished this had she not been in search of American pasts appropriate to her. Other Americans were involved in similar quests; so for that matter was D. H. Lawrence. Henry Adams, her senior by a generation, had more or less concluded that medieval France was his spiritual home and that ever since the thirteenth century the world had been going downhill. Van Wyck Brooks, her junior by thirteen years, argued in his first batch of books that while America badly needed a "usable past," it did not truly possess one. The heritage, he thought, was warped and stunted.

It would be too much to claim that Willa Cather singlehandedly supplied the usable past for her country. She did however furnish authentic and valuable fragments. They could be no more than fragments or vestiges, like the Coronado sword in *My Ántonia*, because the record itself within the United States was fragmentary and discontinuous. Imaginatively, though, she brought them into a continuum. Figuratively, she was the discoverer of the cliff dwellings at Mesa Verde and the pueblo on the plateau at Acoma. She restored them to the American historical consciousness, and thereby enriched it. I myself, as a wandering student of American history, went to see them decades ago, having read about them in Willa Cather and know that they enlarged the meaning of that history for me.

We come back finally to the question: Why is Willa Cather not given her due in the average history class? No doubt some courses on the history of the frontier do include her. But during her lifetime she did not conspicuously say the right things at the obvious moments. Like other genuine artists she was essentially a private person, not a platform performer. Yet looking back, we can see that she did after all mirror her own time, in her own ways, and speak for it. She helped her country to understand itself and its momentous, momentary heritage, and she brought dignity instead of rhetoric to such understanding. Perhaps she is too good for the historians, in their everyday teaching. For in spite of what Turner said about the mutuality of history and literature, many historians are ill at ease with first-rate imaginative material. They can get more out of literature that lies nearer the surface, unmistakably signalling its intentions and its provenance.

Her "Americanness" is not in question. But perhaps she is best compared with two other novelist-contemporaries who were not American: Thomas Hardy and Joseph Conrad. None of them lived snugly. All three were deeply aware of the pain, the dislocation, the loss, and the element of heroism in ordinary lives. All three ranged widely through time and space. They were secret, sympathetic sharers in the hurts and hopes of people who are not full belongers. Hardy, not born into assured status, sensed the anguish of semi-outcasts like Tess and Jude. Conrad, the Polish-born sea-captain, knew that the surfaces of life were merely surfaces. Willa Cather was finely sensitive to the problems of women who refused to accept their conventional sexual-domestic roles, and by extension to the problems of "ethnic" immigrants stranded on the American prairie. Each recognized that, on both a geographical and a psychological plane, the profoundest possibilities of self-knowledge for people of spirit are raised not in the well-defined centers of established society but on the equivocal peripheries. What each perceived, we may conclude, was that every worthwhile pioneer is in part an exile — and that such doubleness of insight is both mournful and miraculous.

This essay appeared as 'The Two or More Worlds of Willa Cather," in *The Art of Willa Cather*, ed. Bernice Slote and Virginia Faulkner (Lincoln: University of Nebraska Press, 1974), 21-42; 259-60.

OLD WORLD, NEW WORLD

The pieces in this section generalize more broadly than the essays in other parts of the book. "America" figures as a large homogenous unit and as an *idea* held by inhabitants of the United States and by people in Europe and other countries. These final essays — final in the sense of coming at the end of the volume, though written over a quarter of a century — also betray a persistent interest in comparative themes. In one of Don DeLillo's richly speculative novels, *The Names* (1982), a character who happens to be an American archaeologist throws off a remark he does not attempt to explain, to the effect that he has sometimes thought of Europe as a hardcover publication, America as the paperback version. For me similar queries have kept presenting themselves. I have been puzzled to decide how far the United States grows out of a European heritage, how it differs, how and when such difference began, and to what extent the influence has spread outward from the United States as well as inward from elsewhere.

Thus, of the five essays in this Part IV, three examine European ideas about America and to a lesser extent what the United States has made of Europe. The theme of anti-Americanism, directly discussed in the final essay, treats the phenomenon more lightly than some of its predecessors. That reflects a growing belief on my part that anti-Americanism should not be treated by Americans merely or even mainly as the product of misinformation and spleen. I suggest that it may reflect the irritation of foreigners in the face of American xenophobia; also that anti-Americanism, so called, is a conspicuous feature of many comments by Americans themselves. Their anger and disappointment at what they sense as a loss of national integrity is to some degree a privileged, internal quarrel — sometimes verging on hysteria, sometimes justified, but nearly always ultimately a credit to a society in which criticism can not only be accepted but in some circumstances actually demanded. If certain outsiders seek to bolster their own criticisms with corroborative comment from American analysts, that is hardly to be wondered at.

Some of the older essays in this collection follow approaches that have gone out of fashion in recent years. Where generalizations about the American national character were once readily accepted, scholars of 1990 are uneasy with what they regard as loose rhetoric about "an" American "character" or "mind" in the singular or even in the plural. Assertions about allegedly unified national behavior tend, it is said, to rest upon evidence drawn from educated white males in gentrified enclaves. Such a sample, the contention goes, minimizes or ignores the several and often contrary views of women, people of color, the foreign-born, indigenous native Americans, radicals — groups which in total considerably outnumber the purportedly authoritative WASP spokesmen. "Exceptionalism," referring to the concept of the United States as fundamentally different from other societies, has come into much commoner usage than, say, a decade ago. The intended meaning, however, appears usually to be that, if people in the past ever believed that this nation was unique or exceptionally meritorious that was a superstition rather than a tenable belief.

There have been some fresh or reactivated generalizations. The most conspicuous of these is what we may call small-r "republicanism." A quarter-century ago the word was hardly to be found in writings about American history; the favored term then was "democracy." It has now been replaced by *republicanism*, to explain the ideological foundations of the American Revolution (as in Bernard Bailyn, J.G.A. Pocock, Gordon Wood and others), the new nation's attachment to popular sovereignty and civic spirit, the contrary tendencies of private enterprise, artisanal and working class impulses from New York "workies" of the 1820s to the Populists of the 1890s, and so on.

In the book I hope to complete a few months hence, nationalism, national character and republicanism will all figure as elements in a synthesis of American history from the eighteenth to the late twentieth century. But they will be put in more of a comparative context than is usual. I shall seek to show that, while belief in American "incomparability" (C. Vann Woodward's word) has been a recurrent and important factor, it has never been universal, and at times is much challenged. Like those of western Europe, American nationality has been a somewhat artificial construct, involving myths and evasions of reality. The evasions in the American record have, even more than elsewhere, involved denials of division by race and class.

Provided that perceptions of nationality are recognized as embodying various shades (most obviously in the case of the free and slave states) and as subject to change and inconsistency, I believe that it is still valuable to interpret America as a nation state enjoying, most of the time, a fairly high degree of popular if hegemonically directed support. Aspects of American national behavior, and so of "character," can usefully be posited. *Republicanism* is one such theme of marked significance, at least for the first few decades of American independence, and in particular as a feature held to differentiate the United States from the monarchies of other nations. Attachment to private property is another prominent feature of Europe as well as America. But the vehemence of American support for what I describe as "propertarianism" and of hostility to systems regarded as "socialist" has genuinely exceptionalist elements (as the Marxist origins of the word "exceptionalism" remind us).

All of these historical factors, finally, establish a frame of reference for understanding the current debates over the relative power and economic vitality of the United States between "declinists" and "triumphalists." The circumstances of the 1990s are of course new. But, whether or not they are aware of it, the debaters on both sides have predecessors as far back as the eighteenth century.

17

European Images
of America

This essay, written for a volume of pieces on American intellectual and cultural history, was also printed in *Encounter*, in tandem with an essay by Melvin J. Lasky on American images of Europe. I have shortened it in minor ways, in part to avoid excessive overlap with other essays in this book. But it remains in main shape an example of my sense of transatlantic relations as I conceived of them in the early 1960s.

IMAGE: *Artificial imitation of the external form of an object, statue (esp. of saint etc. as object of veneration); optical counterpart produced by rays of light reflected from mirror, refracted through lens, etc.; form, semblance; . . . simile, metaphor, idea, conception . . .*

IMAGINARY: *Existing only in imagination; (Math.) having no real existence, but assumed to exist for a special purpose (e.g. square root of negative quantity)*

IMAGINARY AMERICA

For most Europeans, it may be contended, America has never existed. Instead of being a "real" place it has served as an image: a symbol, a Never-Never Land. How characteristic that the whimsical Scottish dramatist J. M. Barrie should stock the Never-Never Land of his *Peter Pan* with figures of fantasy from the New World: Caribbean pirates and prowling Indians. The children who read Barrie in British nurseries took to bed another product of American folklore, the teddy bear, which derived from the near-mythical exploits of Theodore Roosevelt. What head of state in a European country has made a comparable contribution to the dreams of early childhood? The founder of the Boy Scout movement, Baden-Powell, drew their name and some of their rituals from what he had heard of Red Indian life. When the French writer of fantasies, Jules Verne, visited the United with his brother just after the Civil War, they should make a special pilgrimage to the Fenimore Cooper region and addressed one another while there as "Hawkeye" and "Chingachgook."[1] James Russell Lowell remarked in 1869, "for some reason or other, the European has rarely been able to see America except in caricature."[2]

A second proposition, which these mild instances conceal, is that European images of America have rarely been dispassionate. Samuel Gompers, the American trade-union leader, said after visiting Europe in 1909 that its peoples saw his country through one of two mirrors, either convex or concave.[3] "Has the discovery of America been useful or hurtful to mankind?" — this was the title of an article published in 1784, typical of many of the period.[4] The question has been raised again and again ever since, in essentially the same form. It was still being asked in 1960 when the Oxford University Union debated the motion, "That this house holds America responsible for spreading vulgarity in Western society." America, which by degrees has come to signify the United States, not the whole hemisphere, has been one thing *or* the other: compliment *or* recrimination, adoration *or* detestation, boosting *or* knocking, the last best hope *or* an awful warning and a cautionary tale. Convex or concave, the image has been of a hypothetical place, so enveloped in didacticisms that the French traveler George Duhamel protested:

I can't see the Americans for America. . . . Between the American citizen and me there rises I know not what monstrous phantom, a collection of laws, institutions, prejudices, and even myths. . . . I see a system rather than a people. Men, about whom I always feel an eager curiosity, in this country

---

[1] Kenneth Allott, *Jules Verne* (London, 1940), 111.

[2] From "On a Certain Condescension in Foreigners," quoted in Henry Pelling, *America and the British Left: From Bright to Bevan* (London, 1956), 161.

[3] Pelling, 161.

[4] J. Belknap, *Boston Magazine*, 1 (1784), cited in Michael Kraus, *The Atlantic Civilization: Eighteenth-Century Origins* (Ithaca, 1949), 5n. Other examples are given in R. R. Palmer, *The Age of the Democratic Revolution: The Challenge* (Princeton, 1959), 258.

*seem to me like pure ideograms, like the signs of an abstract, algebraic, and
yet already fabulous civilization.*[5]

The square root of a negative quantity. . . . Duhamel did not allow his confession
of bewilderment to inhibit him. Nor have other commentators, for whom
America has provided whatever generalization they happen to seek.
Tocqueville's admission, "J'avoue que dans l'Amérique, j'ai vu plus que
l'Amérique," could be applied to a hundred European theorizers on America.
Sometimes they are hardly talking about America at all. Franz Kafka's friends
in Prague were startled to learn from him in 1913 that he was at work on a novel
entitled *Amerika*, though he understood very little English and had probably
never met an American.[6] And despite its title, a French book, Lucien Lehman's
"Ces Cochons d'Américains!!" (1954), turns out to be a vigorous essay on the
defects of the author's own nation, with a few incidental references to the
phenomenon of anti-Americanism.

One thing *or* the other. The point may be illustrated by listing examples of a
heroic image of America and then by presenting some of the contrasting,
villainous images.

THE HEROIC IMAGE

The Earthly Paradise

The proposition that America never existed as a real place for Europeans can
be extended: the New World was invented before it was discovered. Mythology
preceded exploration; and discovery fitted previous invention. In classical and in
medieval legend there are persistent references to Atlantis; to the Hesperides;
to Avalon; to the Blessed Isles: to some lost and perfect kingdom beyond the
western seas. And we have the Garden of Eden, the earthly paradise from which
sorrowful Adam was expelled. Columbus's Caribbean landfall in 1492 gave them
all a possible, actual habitation. He himself was convinced, he wrote, that he had
found "the terrestrial paradise." In Michael Drayton's poem *To the Virginian
Voyage*, Virginia is described as "Earth's only paradise," still governed by the
natural laws of the Golden Age. True, the early panegyrists of the New World,
like the late ones, speak from mixed motives. They are often interested parties,

---

[5] George Duhamel, *America the Menace* (Boston, 1931), 42.

[6] Franz Kafka, *Amerika* (New York, 1946), preface by Klaus Mann, vi-vii. See also Richard E.
Ruland, "A View from Back Home: Kafka's *Amerika*," *American Quarterly* 13 (1961): 33-42.

promoters, advertisers. Yet they are not cynical liars: they are unable to separate fact from fancy when the two are so strangely conjoined.[7]

The Noble Savage

The natives of the new-found hemisphere (and of other, subsequently discovered territories, including the South Sea islands) likewise ministered to a European necessity. Columbus reported them to be virtuous and handsome. In the next century the picture was enlarged. "They seem to live," said Peter Martyr, "in that golden world of which old writers speak so much: wherein men lived simply and innocently without enforcement of laws, without quarreling Judges and libels, content only to satisfy nature, without further vexation for knowledge of things to come."[8] The American aborigines were thus converted into Noble Savages, free from the sins of sophistication that troubled European moralists in the seventeenth and eighteenth centuries. Full of natural dignity, integrity, and wisdom, the Noble Savage furnished an admirable contrast to the corrupt courtier or man of fashion in Paris and London.

By the eve of the American Revolution, sympathetic Europeans could assure themselves that the white settler in North America had absorbed some of the attributes of the aborigines. In the 1771 edition of *L'élève de la nature* (a Utopian novel first published in 1763 and avowedly inspired by Rousseau's *Émile*) the author, Gaspard de Beaurien, added a dedication to the "Inhabitants of Virginia":

> *In that land which you inhabit and which you cultivate, there are to be found neither cities nor luxury nor crimes nor infirmities. Every day of your lives is serene, for the purity of your souls is communicated to the skies above you. You are free, you labor, and bring forth all about you, besides your abundant crops, a harvest of all the virtues. You are as Nature would wish us all to be. I therefore dedicate to you this portrait of a man whom I have conceived as formed by nature alone.*[9]

Benjamin Franklin, "le bon Quaker," delighted Parisian society not merely on

---

[7] The evolution of one aspect of this complex fantasy is traced in Loren Baritz, "The Idea of the West," *American Historical Review* 66 (1961): 618-640.

[8] Quoted in Samuel Eliot Morison, *Admiral of the Ocean Sea: A Life of Christopher Columbus* (Boston, 1942), 232, from Richard Eden's 1555 translation. I have modernized the spelling.

[9] Quoted in Durand Echeverria, *Mirage in the West: A History of the French Images of American Society to 1815* (Princeton, 1957), 32-33.

account of his sagacity and wit but also because he contrived to appear as a backwoods philosopher, a man whose wisdom was as intuitive, as much the result of an unspoiled environment, as that of an Indian chief. He fostered the view that he was by no means unique in his self-culture. "The famous Franklin has told us," said one French journalist, "that there is no working man in Philadelphia who does not read the newspapers at lunch time and a few good works of philosophy or politics for an hour after dinner."[10]

At this juncture Crèvecoeur published his *Letters from an American Farmer* (1782) and declared — with such an uncanny appropriateness that the passage almost reads like a fake concocted by some later propagandist — that a new type of man, the American, was in the making: a glorious amalgam, actuated by new principles and behaving in new ways. In the expanded French edition, published a year after, Crèvecoeur took the idea still further. His sentiments indicate the tendency of Europeans to express their vision of America in oracular and theoretical terms. If this is not exactly what the American *is* like (and it was not for Crèvecoeur, a man well aware of frontier squalor, and so disturbed by the Revolution that he remained a loyalist), it is what the American *ought* to be like, *must* become.

The Land of Liberty

The story developed with such an air of rightness that prophecy and destiny seemed to be identical. Success was deserved and therefore attained. The rebellious colonies secured their independence. The State of Nature became the United States, the Land of Liberty. "The genuine Liberty on which America is founded," declared the English writer Thomas Pownall in 1783, "is totally and entirely a New system of Things and Men."[11] Madame de Staël, one of Europe's dominant intellectual figures, toyed with the idea of transferring her *salon* to America. In England, Coleridge and his friends spoke of establishing their ideal "pantisocracy" in the New World. While becoming the Land of Liberty, the United States produced two heroes for the world to wonder at. One was Franklin (whose autobiography, incidentally, was among Kafka's favorite books).[12] The other was the exemplary George Washington. Even the defeated British paid tribute to Washington's coolness and tenacity. The whole of Europe marveled at his subsequent patriotism and modesty in retiring from military

---

[10] Echeverria, 29.

[11] Kraus, *Atlantic Civilization: Eighteenth-Century Origins*, 239.

[12] Kafka, *Amerika*, afterword by Max Brod, 276.

command, then in returning with obvious reluctance to lead the new nation as first President under its new constitution, and finally in retiring unbidden into private life once more. "Virtue," according to Montesquieu, was a feature of republics, whereas monarchical societies valued "honor." He seemed to be correct. Washington's career revealed a republican morality of a standard rarely achieved even in the splendid days of classical antiquity.[13]

Franklin and Washington were praised as virtuous statesmen; they were also celebrated as revolutionaries. The Land of Liberty haunted the imagination of European radicals. The American experiment was held to demonstrate that armed rebellion against authority was possible: citizen soldiers led by amateurs could beat professional armies. It was thought to prove that a federal republican democracy was a feasible form of government, though to conservative eyes this was the least workable and most objectionable of all blends of government. The United States stood for the right of revolution, for the likelihood of victory in revolution, and as the living exemplar of egalitarianism. So when the Russian radical Bakunin paid a visit to America in 1861, having escaped from Siberia, he carried back across the Atlantic a copy of the autograph of that great fellow-revolutionary, George Washington.[14] For liberals and radicals in Western Europe the United States was a perennial bench mark. In England, an exasperated Conservative member of Parliament said that the radical M. P. John Bright never contributed to a Commons debate without dragging in the United States.[15] The United States of the mid-nineteenth century occupied a place in the emotions of men such as Bright similar to that occupied seventy years later, in the emotions of their spiritual heirs, by the Soviet Union. It was, they insisted, a country founded on utterly novel and pure doctrine. Humanity had been given a fresh start and was no longer subject to the frailties of the Old World. In America everything was either perfect or perfectible. Hence, no criticism was applicable. For Bright and his associates it was truly the Land of Liberty when it guaranteed

[13] Here is a typical reaction by an English clergyman who visited the United States in the 1840s: "The Americans next-to-adore, with reason, the founder and father of his country. So pure, so disinterested, so exalted a patriot never adorned the annals of time. How different a character is Washington to such charlatans as Bonaparte, and men of his class! and how equally different the issue of their work!" James Dixon, *Methodism in America* (London, 1849), 46-47.

[14] David Hecht, *Russian Radicals Look to America, 1825-1894* (Cambridge, Mass., 1947), 57. In 1858 a Neapolitan history professor was put in jail by Ferdinand II for telling his students that George Washington was a great man and a possible example for them to emulate. See Merle Curti, "The Reputation of America Overseas, 1776-1860," in *Probing Our Past* (New York, 1955), 195.

[15] Pelling, 17-18.

(in his words) " a free church, a free school, free land, a free vote, and a free career for the child of the humblest born in the land."[16]

It was this shining image that lured the potential emigrant. In leaving his own country he asserted his belief in the superiority of the United States. Even if he failed to find all that he dreamed of, his letters home tended to suppress the disappointment. How could he admit that he had duped himself? If like hundreds of thousands of others he eventually returned to the Old Country, the emigrant retained and transmitted his vision of an ideal place. In describing a village in southern Italy as it was during the 1930s, Carlo Levi speaks also for poor men in Greece and other parts of Europe:

> *Their other world is America. . . . America, to the peasants, has a dual nature. It is a land where a man goes to work, where he toils and sweats for his daily bread, . . . where he can die and no one will remember him. At the same time, and with no contradiction in terms, it is an earthly paradise and the promised land.*[17]

Europe's Future: Democracy

Even before the American Revolution, the contrast between the "New" and "Old" worlds was explained as a contrast between future and past. "Westward the course of empire takes its way," according to Bishop Berkeley in 1726, in what must be one of the most quoted lines in literature. The English traveler Andrew Burnaby, who came to the colonies a generation later, remarked that

> *An idea, strange as it is visionary, has entered into the minds of the generality of mankind, that empire is traveling westward: and everyone is looking forward with eager an impatient expectation to that destined moment when America is to give the law to the rest of the world.*[18]

In 1776 the Abbé Galiani wrote from Naples to a friend in Paris:

> *The epoch has become one of the total fall of Europe, and of transmigration into America. All here turns into rottenness, — religion,*

---

[16] Pelling, 18.

[17] Carlo Levi, *Christ Stopped at Eboli*, quoted in Michael Kraus, *The North Atlantic Civilization* (Princeton, 1957), 162.

[18] Charles Sumner, *Prophetic Voices Concerning America* (Boston, 1874), 26.

*laws, arts, sciences, — and all hastens to renew itself in America. This is
not a jest; nor is it an idea drawn from the English quarrels; I have said it
. . . for more than twenty years, and I have constantly seen my prophecies
come to pass. Therefore, do not buy your house in the Chaussée d'Antin;
you must buy it in Philadelphia.*[19]

The idea became more specific during the nineteenth century. The United
States was in the van of progress; Europe's only hope lay in trying to follow in the
same direction. In *De la démocratie en Amérique* (1835, 1840), the most reflective
European meditation on the New World, Alexis de Tocqueville viewed the
United States as a laboratory of egalitarianism, as Europe's probable destiny. It
was a generous analysis. Yet he doubted whether the Union could long survive
the centrifugal strains that threatened it. Sure enough, the Union did begin to
break apart in 1860. But for Americanophiles such as John Bright, the triumph
of the North during the Civil War proved once more the invincible power of the
democratic ideal. Destiny could be defined as the inevitable victory of good
causes. Who could now doubt the stability of the United States, the missionary
force of its spirit, when it was able to overthrow so vast and militant a conspiracy?
And when it also put an end to slavery — hitherto the dark passage in an
otherwise unblemished record? Fifty years after Tocqueville, in an equally
generous but less conjectural testimony, *The American Commonwealth* (1888),
James Bryce is also ready to interpret America as Europe's future:

*America has in some respects anticipated European nations. She is
walking before them along a path which they may probably follow. She
carries behind her . . . a lamp whose light helps those who come after her
more than it always does herself.*[20]

Bryce had to reckon with the sordid aspects of the Gilded Era. But he can
explain these away as the mistakes of the pioneer grappling with the unfamiliar.
They are temporary and incidental, not fundamental defects. On the whole, Lord
Bryce has seen the future in the United States and is quite sure that it works. To
idealism have been added experience and stability. Unlike some other countries,
America

*is made all of a piece, its institutions are the product of its economic and
social conditions and the expression of its character. The . . . vehicle has*

---

[19] Sumner, 106.

[20] James Bryce, *The American Commonwealth* (London, 2nd ed. 1889) 2: 475.

been built with a lightness, strength, and elasticity which fit it for the roads
it has to traverse.[21]

Heroes

In waging the Civil War, not only America but the world acquired a third hero
in the person of Abraham Lincoln. Franklin, Washington, Lincoln: what
European nation even in a history ten times as extensive as that of the young
United States could claim a trio which held comparable resonance for mankind?

This strong, confident land was to offer two more possible candidates for world
veneration during the twentieth century. One was Woodrow Wilson, the
"Meester Veelson" who brought the prospect of a just and lasting peace to
Europe, even if the hope was in vain. *Wilson, apôtre et martyr* — apostle and
martyr — was the title of a biography written by a Frenchman in 1933. The
second man was Franklin D. Roosevelt, a leader who in the judgment of many
Europeans (if with not so much unanimity among his own countrymen) could do
no wrong. In the homes of the peasants of Lucania where Carlo Levi was
summoned as doctor, "what never failed to strike me . . . were the eyes of the two
inseparable guardian angels that looked from the wall over the bed." These were
the local Madonna and F.D.R.:

> *I never saw other pictures or images than these: not the King not the Duce,*
> *nor even Garibaldi; no famous Italian of any kind, nor any one of the*
> *appropriate saints; only Roosevelt and the Madonna of Viggiano never*
> *failed to be present. To see them there . . . in cheap prints, they seemed the*
> *two faces of the power that had divided the universe between them. . . .*
> *Sometimes a third image formed, along with these two, a trinity: a dollar*
> *bill, the last of those brought back from across the sea, or one that had*
> *come in a letter of a husband or relative, was tacked up, . . . like the Holy*
> *Ghost or an ambassador from heaven to the world of the dead.*[22]

---

[21] Bryce, 2: 473.

[22] Kraus, *North Atlantic Civilization*, 161-162. In Fascist Italy, the study of American literature
became an oblique form of political protest among intellectuals. The first edition of an anthology,
Americana (1941), was confiscated by the authorities. See Agostino Lombardo, *Sewanee Review* 68
(Summer, 1960): 367-68, a special issue devoted to Italian views on American literature. 367-368.

THE VILLAINOUS IMAGE

The discovery of America was an affront as well as a miracle: an affront to scholarship and morality. For each heroic image there has existed a hostile antithesis. Again, these hostile images often have little to do with a "real" America. They are projections of European problems. Against the dream of an Earthly Paradise may be set the coarse invention called Cockaigne. The Noble Savage? — there is a contrary version of what we might call the Ignoble Savage. The Land of Liberty has been depicted as something that could be labeled the Land of Libertinism. In place of the notion that America anticipates Europe's democratic future is the alarmed conviction that the United States foreshadows Europe's fate — the fate pejoratively styled "Americanization." In contrast to the list of American world-heroes there is a list of American world-villains and a list of world-martyrs, Americans whose sad experiences are cited as evidence of the cruelty and hypocrisy of the vaunted Land of Liberty.

Cockaigne

The French *fabliau* of the thirteenth century, *Cocaigne*, may have been written to deride the fable of Avalon, the mythical island of the blest. To medieval Europe "Cocaigne" or "Cockaigne" represented an imaginary country situated somewhere in the West, where no one need work or worry. The very landscape was made of food; birds dropped from the air already prepared for eating (The Big Rock-Candy Mountain is a modern equivalent.) Cockaigne, also known as Lubberland, was a poor men's paradise and the fable has a certain charm.[23] But it is also a self-indulgent dream, of glut and gluttony, of life lived through the belly instead of the mind. I do not know whether America has often been explicitly identified with Cockaigne (though William Byrd of Virginia did refer to the back country of the early eighteenth century as Lubberland). But the notion clearly underlies European conceptions of American abundance, waste, and vulgarity. So the United States figures in nineteenth-century German and Norwegian novels as "a sort of dreary and vulgar fable-land, emancipated from the laws of probability."[24] Cockaigne is the medieval prototype of the Affluent

---

[23] See A. L. Morton, *The English Utopia* (London, 1952), 12, 28.

[24] "America in European Literature," from Hjalmar H. Boyesen, *Literary and Social Silhouettes* (New York, 1894), 119. Boyesen, a shrewd observer, remarks (p. 118): "If I had told my grandmother in Norway that two and two made five in America, I do not believe it would have surprised her. She had seen what was to her a much more startling phenomenon. A slovenly, barefooted milkmaid named Guro, who had been in her employ, had returned from the United States, after an absence

Society or at least of sillier and nastier aspects such as the TV "give-away" show. The stupefied Flemish peasants whom Brueghel painted in his scenes of Cockaigne (*Schlaraffenland*) are the ancestors of the greedy, idiotic creatures caricatured in *Mad* magazine.

The Ignoble Savage

To the European conservative preoccupied with achieving and maintaining order in society or to the European scholar conscious of the gradual, laborious stages by which knowledge is accumulated: to such people the Noble Savage is a dangerous and preposterous myth. Can men be wise without study, without due reverence for the past? Can they grow intellect as a plant produces flowers, merely by being? "Don't cant in defense of savages," Dr. Johnson said irritably in 1784 to the more sanguine Boswell, when Boswell tried to tell him of the innate, untutored sensibility of men raised in a state of nature.[25] What *could* come out of a raw country like the United States? The answer of the Irish poet Thomas Moore, who toured there in 1803-04, was sharp:

> *Take Christians, Mohawks, Democrats and all*
> *From the rude wigwam to the congress hall,*
> *From man the savage, whether slaved or free,*
> *To man the civilized, less tame than he, —*
> *'Tis one dull chaos, one infertile strife*
> *Between half polished and half barbarous life.*[26]

So much for Crèvecoeur and the eighteenth-century portrait of a land of simple, virtuous citizens destined to grow until the American example governed the universe.

The attack was mounted with more apparent erudition in the work of Jean-Louis Buffon and Corneille de Pauw. What lessons did America hold for the naturalist? How could its species be classified? What of its aborigines? Buffon's *Histoire naturelle* (1761) and some other treatises argued that America's "newness," scientifically speaking, connoted immaturity. Animals and humans

---

of five years, with all the airs of a lady, and arrayed in silks and jewelry which in Norway represented a small fortune. My grandmother was convinced that Guro . . . had crossed the ocean for the sole purpose of dazzling her, triumphing over her, and enjoyed her discomfiture. For she had prophesied Guro a bad end, and she bore a lasting grudge against the country which had brought her prophecy to naught."

[25] Hoxie N. Fairchild, *The Noble Savage* (New York, 1928), 338.

[26] Fairchild, 270-71.

alike were inferior to those of the "Old" World, for climatic and other reasons. Moreover this handicap was not lessening but increasing. It could be traced in the degeneration of animal species, including breeds of cattle that had been introduced from Europe. It was evident in the life-cycle of the Indians, who decayed rapidly in physique and intellect after a seemingly vigorous childhood and adolescence. The deterioration, it was argued, affected the white settler in his turn. Peter Kalm, a Swedish scientist who traveled through North America in the mid-eighteenth century, believed that the colonists matured earlier and died earlier than did Europeans. De Pauw, following Kalm and Buffon in a series of essays — including a magisterial contribution on the condition of America for the 1776 edition of Diderot's *Encyclopédie* — was sure that the colonists were less energetic and intelligent than their European contemporaries. "It has not been observed," he said, "that the professors of the University of Cambridge in New England have educated any young Americans to the point of being able to display them in the Old World."[27] The Abbé Raynal, in the first edition (1770) of his *Histoire philosophique et politique*, reproduced De Pauw's views, though he was later to modify them. Emphasizing the decadence of the English settlers, he asserted that

> *their minds have been enervated like their bodies. Quick and penetrating at first, they grasp ideas easily; but they cannot concentrate nor accustom themselves to prolonged reflection. It is amazing that America has not yet produced a good poet, a capable mathematician, or a man of genius in a single art or a single science. Almost all have some facility in everything, but none has a marked talent for anything. Precocious and mature before us, they are far behind when we have reached our full mental development.*[28]

So, in that most crucial year 1776, a European like De Pauw could maintain that mankind in America was suffering a fatal decline, through the insidious effects of heat and humidity. Though they have offered different explanations for the phenomenon, Europeans have kept on detecting it ever since. Precocity and superficiality! — Raynal's observations have been repeated over and over, though without awareness of their parentage.

"The fever is in Europe, the remedy is in America," according to Voltaire. But some would turn the statement round. Consider the old argument over the origins of syphilis. A Hessian soldier, stationed in South Carolina during the

[27] Echeverria, 11.

[28] Echeverria, 14.

American Revolution, noted that the New World had conferred upon Germany the blessing of cheap food in the shape of the potato plant; "Columbus brought in exchange for this very useful food venereal diseases, a deplorable bargain for the Americans!"[29] We recognize here a classic confrontation: corrupt Europe, innocent and benevolent America. But others believe the opposite — that syphilis, unknown in Europe until the 1490s, was unwittingly brought back by Columbus's sailors through intercourse with Caribbean women.[30] (It has also been argued that though Europe owes the potato to *South* America, the vegetable was introduced in *North* America from Europe.) Here is the opposite confrontation. Unlucky Europe, tainted America — the place of contagion of every sort, physical, moral, ideological. From *this* virulent America of the European imagination spread not only the poisons of revolution and democratic misrule but the social disorders of the frontier West, the plantation South, and the urban North. In fact the image dates from colonial days. America is the haunt of pirates in a far-from-cosy J. M. Barrie-ish sense. It is the dumping-ground for Britain's criminals and paupers and continues to be the domain of Europe's out-laws, bad-hats, remittance-men, misfits. The Abbé Prévost's novel *Manon Lescaut* (1731) opens with a wagon-load of prostitutes who are about to be shipped to America (French Canada) in order to purify France. In George Eliot's *Middlemarch* (1871-72) the unspeakable Mr. Raffles is sent off to America with "an adequate sum" in the hope and expectation that he will "remain there for life." In this context "life" is an ambiguous word. "Life in the New World" has the ring of a prison sentence. (To the dismay of his patron, Raffles returns to England, explaining that "Things went confoundedly with me in New York; those Yankees are cool hands, and a man of gentlemanly feelings has no chance with them.") Raffles is dispatched to the America of Andrew Jackson, *circa* 1830. Half a century afterward the Scandinavian Hans Mattson writes:

> *It cannot be denied that many among the higher classes in Sweden feel very unfriendly toward the United States, and it was even not long ago a common saying among them, "America is the paradise of all rogues and rascals."*[31]

---

[29] Kraus, *Atlantic Civilization: Eighteenth-Century Origins*, 18n.

[30] There is a full discussion of this problem in the two-volume edition of Morison, *Admiral of the Ocean Sea* (Boston, 1942), 2: 193-218.

[31] Hans Mattson, *The Story of an Emigrant* (St. Paul, Minn., 1892), 298. The same opinion was apparently held by the upper classes in nineteenth century Austria, for whom America was "a grand bedlam, a rendezvous of scamps and vagabonds." See Curti, *Probing Our Past*, 195. An English three-decker novel of 1856 named *Perversion: or, the Causes and Consequences of Infidelity*, by William J. Conybeare (London, 3: 120-21) mentions an English reprobate named Archer who, after

In this image, the United States was given over to libertinism. Sir Lepel Henry Griffin, a British observer who lacked the amiability of James Bryce, printed on the title page of his *The Great Republic* (1884) two harsh quotations that epitomize the tone of the book:

— "The Commonwealth of Athens is become the forest of beasts."

Timon of Athens

— "O Liberté! que de crimes on commet en ton nom."

Jeanne-Marie Roland

In the America that Griffin saw and that others have scrutinized, whites gouged, stabbed, lynched, and dueled with one another. They committed still more brutal outrages upon the Negro. They hunted down the Indian. In their cities votes were bought and sold with shameless cynicism. Only in the remote, backward corners of Europe such as Sicily was there a comparable record of brigandage; Murder, Incorporated, in the twentieth century might be affiliated with the Sicilian *Mafia* but had nothing to learn from it. From England the French language borrowed such peaceable nouns as *le weekend*, from the United States the altogether more stringent vocabulary of *le gangster*.

One scholar, Durand Echeverria, suggests that in France — and his theory would apply in part to other European countries — this vision of America has not changed except in detail from the eighteenth century to the present day. In George Duhamel's *Scènes de la vie future* (published in English as *America the Menace*, 1931) or Simone de Beauvoir's *L'Amérique au jour le jour* (*America Day by Day*, 1953) there is undoubtedly a predilection for the uglier sides, including crime, miscegenation (or rather, its consequences), rape, drunkenness, and murder. Liberty or Libertinism? "I have in my pocket," says Duhamel, speaking of the American five-cent piece, "several of your small coins on which is stamped the word 'liberty.' And what do you see immediately under the word? The figure

---

serving a prison sentence for bigamy and other offenses, takes himself off to New York:

> He professes his intention of devoting himself to political life in his adopted country; and with his talents, energy, and unscrupulousness, there can be little doubt that he will soon become a distinguished member of Congress. He has joined the ultra-democratic party, and gives out that he was a victim of aristocratic persecution in the old country. It is highly probable that he will return to this side of the Atlantic in a diplomatic capacity, like citizen Soulé, and other European exiles of kindred character. Nor is it impossible that we may one day see him representing the United States of America at the court of St. James's.

The comparison is with Pierre Soulé (1801-1870), a French-born firebrand Democrat, who was a "Manifest-Destiny" U.S. minister to Spain, 1853-1854. The perversion and infidelity of Conybeare's title, however, refer to religious and not sexual backsliding.

of a buffalo or an Indian. Oh, irony! They represent two free and spirited races that you have destroyed in less than three centuries."[32]

Europe's Fate: Americanization

Uncle Sham, Uncle Shylock: where it is not a question of American violence, the image is of a hypocritical, timid, joyless people, absorbed not in the pursuit of happiness — itself a vain quest, according to European critics — but in the pursuit of wealth. Charles Dickens popularized the expression "the Almighty Dollar" in his *American Notes* (1842). But the idea had long been in circulation. The Frenchman Louis-Félix de Beaujour, for example, offered an almost standard comment on the United States that he saw during the first decade of the nineteenth century:

Virtue has been regarded as the guiding principle or principal strength of republics. That of the American Republic appears to be a frantic love of money. It is the result of the political equality which reigns there and which, leaving people with no other distinction except wealth, invites them to acquire it by every possible means.[33]

The protracted squabble over war debts after 1918 did a great deal to intensify the European image of America as Uncle Shylock.

By the 1850s, when the word "Americanization" came generally into European usage, it was not enough merely to deplore what was thought to go on across the Atlantic. This contagion too was spreading. Far from America taking over the tasks of civilization and pointing a better way for poor old Europe, it was now

---

[32] Echeverria, 281; Duhamel, 48. The villain-view of America as it obtained during the Civil War is expressed in an editorial of September 1862 from the Spanish newspaper *Pensiamento Espanol*: "The history of the model republic can be summed up in a few words. It came into being by rebellion. It was founded on atheism. It was populated by the dregs of all the nations in the world. It has lived without law of God or man. Within a hundred years, greed has ruined it. Now it is fighting like a cannibal, and it will die in a flood of blood and mire. Such is the real history of the one and only state in the world which has succeeded in constituting itself according to the flaming theories of democracy. The example is too horrible to stir any desire for imitation in Europe." Quoted in H. D. Jordan and E. J. Pratt, *European Opinion on the American Civil War* (London, 1931), 250-51.

[33] "On a fait de la vertu le principe ou le principal ressort des républiques. Celui de la république américaine paraît être un amour effréné pour l'argent; c'est l'effet de l'égalité politique qui y règne, et qui ne laissant aux citoyens d'autre distinction que les richesses, les invite à en acquérir par toute sorte de moyens." Quoted in Richmond L. Hawkins, *Madame de Staël and the United States* (Cambridge, Mass., 1940), 69-70. Hawkins points out that Mme. de Staël never did visit the United States: she merely invested money there.

argued that Europe was the repository of a precious civilization being assailed by transatlantic barbarism. The image grew in the twentieth century of a decadent, avaricious United States in which everything including love was standardized, homogenized, and dehumanized. Cash was the measure of worth; quantity had become a value. America was afflicted with consumption, in fact, galloping consumption — not a medical but an economic and moral disease. Food was Fletcherized; production lines were Taylorized. Indeed, with the advent of the automat and the assembly line, the image became more precise. It was of a gadget and machine civilization, without savor or individuality. So in the inverted Utopia of Aldous Huxley's *Brave New World*, prayers were addressed not to Our Lord but to Our Ford. And in the years after the Second World War both radicals and conservatives in Europe, who might disagree on most other issues, could rally round the accusation that the United States was, consciously or unconsciously, tending to "coca-colonize" the rest of mankind. In *L'Américanisme et nous* (1958), Cyrille Arnavon contends that the attempt is deliberate and insidious — whether one examines the operations of NATO or of the United States Information Service or even whether one takes into account the publication of a French edition of *Reader's Digest* (a perusal of which apparently stimulated M. Arnavon to write his book).

Such views drew additional ammunition from the fact that in the twentieth century, radicals no longer looked to the United States for a lead. That role had been usurped, at least for a spell, by the Soviet Union. To the extent that the United States still symbolized the future, then, it seemed to stand for an anti-Utopia, rich and yet bankrupt. Apart from the dubious boon of "Americanization," the United States could be defined as a backward nation. That, at any rate, was the assumption in Harold Laski's *The American Democracy* (1948): lacking a left-wing political party, the United States was at a primitive stage of evolution, bound to recapitulate the experience of wiser if sadder European nations. Russian successes in outer space, in 1957, reinforced the image of America as a nation that is no longer a dream and not even a *technologically* supreme nightmare.

Villains - or Martyrs

Five heroes — Franklin, Washington, Lincoln, Wilson, Roosevelt. But not quite everyone accepted these. The poet John Keats, writing in 1818 to his brother who had just emigrated to the United States, said:

Dilke, whom you know to be a Godwin perfectibil[it]y Man, pleases himself with the idea that America will be the country to take up the

human intellect where england leaves off — I differ there with him greatly
— A country like the united states whose greatest men are Franklins and
Washingtons will never do that — They are great Men doubtless but how
are they to be compared to those of our countrymen like Milton and the
two Sidneys — The one is a philosophical Quaker full of mean and thrifty
maxims the other sold the very charger who had taken him through all his
Battles. Those Americans are great but they are not sublime Man — the
humanity of the United States can never reach the sublime.[34]

If there was some dispute as to the stature of America's heroes, there was widespread agreement that America had produced villains for the whole world to shudder at, though of course not as horrendous as Hitler. Perhaps it would be better to say groups of villains: the Robber Barons (Rockefeller, etc.), the Gangsters (Al Capone and the rest), the Demagogues (Joseph McCarthy especially), the Imperialists (headed, I suppose, by John Foster Dulles). There were, too, America's martyrs, the victims of national villainy, whose stories echo far beyond the borders of the United States: the Haymarket anarchists; perhaps Eugene Debs; certainly Sacco and Vanzetti, and the Rosenbergs, and Caryl Chessman.

From the faces in these galleries there builds up a total villainous image of the United States which owes much to Marxist coloration and the recent stresses of the cold war but which had its first shadowy adumbration several centuries ago. It is of a gross, rapacious Uncle Sam, leering, fanged, squatting on money-bags, clutching the Bomb. We may set against it the Uncle Sam in a *New Yorker* cartoon of 1958. This one is a scrawny figure, in traditional stars-and-stripes regalia that hang loose upon him, stretched out upon an analyst's couch and declaring plaintively, "Everybody hates me."

CURRENT FASHIONS IN IMAGERY

It seems that the heroic image of America has tended to yield to the villainous image, and it might seem that the tendency will continue. Human beings, always dissatisfied in some degree with their own society, devise nostalgic or radical images of superior places. The nostalgic images relate to bygone times and far-off places where life is simpler and purer than they conceive their own existence to be. The radical images relate to the future, or to some other contemporary

---

[34] Maurice B. Forman, ed., *The Letters of John Keats* (London, 4th ed., 1952), 234. Charles Wentworth Dilke was a warm friend of Keats'. D. H. Lawrence makes a similar charge against Franklin in his *Studies in Classic American Literature* (1923).

society which has a special stake in the future where the form of life already appears better than one's own and is likely to become immeasurably better. Both of these kinds of image used to apply to the United States. The nostalgic one has now, we might think, almost vanished, while the radical one has lost most of its excitement. Large-scale immigration is at an end; we perceive the accidental relevance of Kafka's description of the Statue of Liberty, which — no doubt through sheer ignorance — he equips with a sword instead of a torch. In *The Irony of American History* (1952) Reinhold Niebuhr concludes that much of America's radical thunder has been stolen by Russia. Today the majority of even friendly assessments of the United States dwell upon its loss of nerve: *Americans Are Alone in the World* (1953), by Luigi Barzini, Jr., is a case in point. There is even something a little inert about *Image of America* (1959) by R. L. Bruckberger, a well-informed French Dominican priest who sings the praises of American economic democracy in a way akin to the survey of the "permanent revolution" conducted by the editors of *Fortune*.

In the absence of either a nostalgic or a radical vision of America, we may wonder whether *any* compelling image exists other than that of bigness — of military and industrial mass, of the United States as the ponderous captain of Our Side in the dreary exchanges of the cold war. One perhaps, but not an edifying one: in an essay on "The Erotic Myth of America,"[35] the English anthropologist Geoffrey Gorer comments on the French appetite for sleazy novels like Boris Vian's *J'irai cracher sur vos tombes*, a work allegedly "traduit de l'Américain" but actually written by M. Vian. In such a genre, which also includes *No Orchids for Miss Blandish* (by René Raymond, under the American-sounding pseudonym "James Hadley Chase"), America is still a fantasy-land but of the most debased and vicious sort — "pays de cocagne," says Vian in his introduction, "la terre d'élection des puritains, des alcooliques, et de l'enfoncez-vous-bien-ça dans la tête."[36] A hundred years ago Frenchmen enjoyed Fenimore Cooper's lone wolf, Natty Bumppo. Now, it seems, they pass off as American their own morbid lone-wolf obsessions of killing and rape.

ANTI-AMERICANISM?

Articles that deal with external views of America are apt to slide into discussions of anti-Americanism. Why, the American reader asks, *why* such a lineage of error and hostility? He may concede that all human groups have fanciful images

---

[35] Gorer, *Partisan Review* 17 (1950): 589-94.

[36] Vian, *J'irai cracher sur vos tombes* (Paris, 1946), 9.

of one another that are usually out-of-date and almost invariably unfavorable. She may see that America should expect to suffer from the *Schadenfreude* of a declining Europe. But he may still insist unhappily that the images of his country differ in kind, not merely in degree, from the images that European countries entertain of one another. To be "Anglicized" or "Hellenized" was, for example, never as dreadful in general estimation as to be "Americanized." Why must America serve as a scapegoat for Europe's own weaknesses? Why must Europeans blame America for imposing upon them a mass culture which they eagerly accept and even "improve" upon?

Malice and envy do play a part, as well as Communist propaganda. But it is useful to remind Americans of their own venerable tradition of xenophobia. "Twisting the lion's tail" was once a reliable vote-raising technique for American politicians. What of the lion's discomfort? In a balance sheet of denigration, American Anglophobia would more than offset instances of British anti-Americanism. It is not surprising that Europeans should retaliate and pounce upon every discrepancy between American promise and American performance, especially when the promise is proclaimed with such grandiosity. American self-righteousness is reminiscent of that of the British, which did not endear them to Continental Europeans and which generated similar charges of hypocrisy.

This leads to the qualification that America has never been a "real," finite place to Americans themselves. There has always been a close correspondence between European *projected* images of America and American *self*-images. The United States has been a fantasy to itself: something in process, something mysterious and abstract, a democratic vista, a "willingness of the heart." What ambitious American assessment of the country does not explore its fabled quality, its mission and meaning — in short the American Dream, which Americans refer to more often than do Europeans?[37]

Similarly, the American Nightmare is a prime domestic topic. If the heroic image is cherished, the villainous image has not been neglected. There is no anti-Americanism as eloquent as that of the native American. From the strictures of Federalist authors like Joseph Dennie, through the anger of abolitionists and of their Southern opponents, down to the decades of H.L. Mencken and his "booboisie," the Dos Passos of *U.S.A.*, the Henry Miller of *The Air-Conditioned Nightmare*, or the Allen Ginsberg of *Howl*, the villainous image has to a considerable extent been a home-produced product. Like European critics they have been irritated by the disparity between *ought* and *is*. American life does have repellent features, and Americans have said so with a fine ferocity.

---

[37] For example: "There are those, I know, who will reply that the liberation of humanity, the freedom of man and mind, is nothing but a dream. They are right. It is. It is the American Dream." Archibald MacLeish, on "The National Purpose," *New York Times* (May 30, 1960): 14.

Europeans entitled to do the same? Sinclair Lewis wrote *Babbitt*: why should not C.E.M. Joad write *The Babbitt Warren* (an inferior book, alas)? Why should not Jean-Paul Sartre write a play about lynching in the South (*La putain respectueuse*) when William Faulkner has published a novel about France (*A Fable*)? Is Faulkner's France — or his South, for that matter — more "real" than Sartre's America? If an *Ugly American* by William J. Lederer and Eugene Burdick, why not a *Quiet American* by Graham Greene? Are the sadisms of Boris Vian different in any crucial respect from those of Mickey Spillane: do not the European and American publics derive the same satisfactions from such literature?

REAL AMERICA

We have suggested that

1. America has not been "real" for Europeans
2. European images of America have usually been *either* highly favorable *or* markedly pejorative
3. Pejorative images have prevailed lately over favorable ones
4. America has not been "real" for Americans either: they too have expressed extremes of admiration and anger (consider the literary career of Mark Twain, moving in one direction — glorification to disgust; and of Dos Passos, moving in the opposite direction — disgust to glorification)

Two other comments: The first has to do with the peculiar *efficacy* of the images enumerated. Most are manifestly unhistorical. Some bear palpable marks of prejudice: thus, Corneille de Pauw was in the hire of Frederick the Great, a monarch anxious to discourage emigration. Most versions of America, including that of Tocqueville, rest upon *a priori* reasoning. But no one has shown keener insight than this French theorist, on the basis of his single visit to the United States. He had the right instinct to see in America more than America. There is a poetic truth in the sequences of heroic and villainous images and in their dramatic contrast. Even the views of De Pauw and Raynal on American precocity — unscientific, Europe-oriented — have their relevance. We still catch the refrain, for instance, in the much-quoted remark by Scott Fitzgerald that there are no second acts in American lives. These are "true" sets of images of a continent and a nation which has held in suspension the extreme hopes and fears for the future of mankind under democracy and which continues to enact them for itself and for much of Europe and the rest of the world, despite the apparent drastic qualifications of the later twentieth century. Only America has had this function for Western society. The deities and devils of American democracy still fascinate Europeans. Its high gloss may have gone, but its concerns are of more immediate interest than ever.

In other words, the images of America are now of *half*-gods and *half*-devils. The United States is less loved but more liked, more criticized but less hated. It has become more "real," and our initial proposition is far less *apropos* than formerly. The relationship of America and Europe has greatly changed. The story is no longer largely of American repudiation and European condescension. The contest is no longer between America and Europe, nor even perhaps of America-plus-allies versus the Communist bloc. There are several blocs in today's world. North America and Western Europe are only two of them whose similarities are greater than their differences. Both are highly industrialized and mobile societies. We can still find absurd accounts of what America is presumed to be. But there is a growing number of expert European studies of the United States — its politics, industry, history, literature, music, art, architecture. Europe's foremost authority on the modern United States, Denis Brogan, is justly compared with Tocqueville and Bryce. But his tone is different. He *knows* infinitely more than Tocqueville did about the American scene, and considerably more than the esteemed Bryce. He is as capable as the next man of generalizing, but his approach is microscopic rather than macroscopic.

The great mythological and metaphorical European interpretations of America have ceased. D. H. Lawrence's *Studies in Classic American Literature* (1923) may have been the last of them. Europeans have not ceased to talk about the United States in broad terms. But when they do so their authorities, their large labels, are American. Current [1962] European magazines are crammed with observations on the Lonely Crowd, the Power Elite, the Organization Man, the Status-Seekers, the Affluent Society. Each is the coinage of an American author: David Riesman, C. Wright Mills, William H. Whyte, Jr., Vance Packard, J. K. Galbraith. For American literature, the grand theory is provided not by Europeans but by Americans: Perry Miller, Harry Levin, Philip Rahv, Richard Chase, Leslie Fiedler, Henry Nash Smith.

European images of America, always closer than is commonly admitted, have now almost coincided with American self-images; and the Americans are the principal image-makers. The United States will continue to be a semi-mythical place for Europeans, but mainly to the extent that the myth is rich, alive, and honest, so will be the European view. To the extent that it is commercial, vapid, and meretricious, so will it seem to Europeans. The United States will still be blamed when something goes wrong. That is America's punishment and privilege for being an imaginary as well as a real country.

BIBLIOGRAPHICAL ESSAY

In addition to the material already cited, Antonello Gerbi, *La disputa del Nuovo Mondo: storia di una polemica, 1750-1900* (Milan, 1955) covers the whole hemisphere and is a work of considerable scope. Gilbert Chinard has published several studies of Franco-American relations. Among these, *Les Refugiés Hugenots en Amérique* (Paris, 1925) has a valuable prefatory discussion of the idea of America as a "mirage" for Europe. Franz M. Joseph, ed., *As Others See Us: The United States through Foreign Eyes* (Princeton, 1959) contains intelligent essays by Denis Brogan, Raymond Aron, and other contemporary observers, as well as an appendix on the concept of the national "image." Other collections of and guides to European opinions include Henry T. Tuckerman, *America and Her Commentators* (New York, 1864); John G. Brooks, *As Others See Us* (New York, 1908); Allan Nevins, ed., *America through British Eyes* (New York, 1948); and Oscar Handlin, ed., *This Was America* (Cambridge, Mass., 1949). Frank Monaghan, *French Travelers in the United States, 1765-1932* (New York, 1933) is a bibliographical guide. Michael Kraus's *North Atlantic Civilization* (Princeton, 1957), an Anvil paperback, has a handy selection of readings, for example from William T. Stead's *The Americanization of the World* (New York, 1901). Lucien Febvre and others, *Le Nouveau Monde et l'Europe* (Brussels, 1954), the transcript of a conference on the topic held in Geneva, has some good comments interspersed among the banalities.

Alex de Tocqueville's extraordinary *Democracy in America* is available in a two-volume paperback edition (New York, 1954) with a long critical essay by Phillips Bradley. The circumstances of Tocqueville's visit and the character of his book are described in George W. Pierson's *Tocqueville and Beaumont in America* (New York, 1938; also in an abridged paperback edition, New York, 1959). *Marie*, a novel dealing with slavery in America, written by Tocqueville's companion Gustave de Beaumont (1835) and full of other generalizations, has been translated (Stanford, 1958).

Among the evidence on the reactions of particular countries, see: William Clark, *Less than Kin: A Study of Anglo-American Relations* (London, 1957); G. D. Lillibridge, *Beacon of Freedom: The Impact of American Democracy upon Great Britain, 1830-1870* (Philadelphia, 1954); Frank Thistlethwaite, *The Anglo-American Connection in the Early Nineteenth Century* (Philadelphia, 1959); R. H. Heindel, *The American Impact on Great Britain, 1898-1914* (Philadelphia, 1940); Leon D. Epstein, *Britain — Uneasy Ally* (Chicago, 1954), useful for its assessment of British opinion after World War II; Gilbert Chinard, *Volney et l'Amérique* (Baltimore, 1923); Seymour Drescher, "America and French Romanticism during the July Monarchy," *American Quarterly* 11 (1959): 3-20, on the hostile views of such men of letters as Balzac and Stendhal; Joseph E. Baker, "How the French See America," *Yale Review* 47 (1957): 239-53; Otto zu Stolberg-Wernigerode, *Germany and the United States of America During the Era of Bismarck* (Philadelphia, 1937); P. C. Weber, *America in Imaginative German Literature in the First Half of the 19th Century* (New York, 1926), interesting on Goethe and others; and Andrew J. Torrielli, *Italian Opinion on America as Revealed by Italian Travelers, 1850-1900* (Cambridge, Mass., 1941).

This essay appeared in *Paths of American Thought*, eds. Arthur M. Schlesinger, Jr. and Morton White. (Boston, Houghton Mifflin Co., 1963): 492-514, 586-589.

18

New World, Old World:
The Historical Antithesis

Richard Rose, an American political scientist at Strathclyde University in Scotland, organized a conference in 1973 to consider the relevance of American experience in various fields for European circumstances. Professor Rose took as epigraph some lines from Philip James Bailey's *Festus*:

> America, thou half-brother of the world;
> With something good and bad of every land.

Mine was one of the conference papers. It has been slightly shortened and amended for this reprinting.

PROBLEMS

What Is American History?

The history of the United States obviously can not be discussed from exactly the same position as that of the history of Western Europe. America has undergone experiences actually and figuratively remote from the preoccupations of Europe. If the American time-dimension has been smaller, the space-dimension has been larger. American attitudes to their national past sometimes appear "un-European" in a paradoxical way. The New World, that is, is apt to fall back upon historical precedent in a search for solutions to controversies of the moment — mingling past and present with a readiness that can puzzle observers from the Old World. Long before the United States became an independent nation,

"America" was a fable. Something of this large, abstract quality was incorporated into the thought-patterns of the new nation. "Our fate," according to the American historian Richard Hofstadter, "is not to have an ideology but to be one."

Novelties of circumstance, reinforced by a long-continuing self-conscious effort to put this American essence into words, have led American scholars as well as imaginative writers to make "Americanness" or "Americanity" a central theme. The process reached its height in the 1940s and 1950s. By then the greatest power in the world, the United States was also a leader among the nations in science, literature and the arts. There was an understandable desire to present and to analyze this achievement, in such books as F. O. Matthiessen's *The American Renaissance* (1941) and Henry Nash Smith's *Virgin Land: The American West as Symbol and Myth* (1950). Several brilliant and illuminating studies emerged.

In the universities this development was associated with the new "area studies" approach: the idea that every society or nation has its own special character, a unique configuration of traditions, values and styles of behavior. Anthropologists like Ruth Benedict and Clyde Kluckhohn, who had already applied these notions to "primitive" communities, now enlarged the inquiry to cover modern nations. Scholars were variously stimulated to hunt for an American tradition in the novel, in poetry, in humor, in folklore, in politics, in music, in the evolution of American nationalism. One historian, Merle Curti, explored *The Roots of American Loyalty* (1946). In *The Uprooted* (1951), Oscar Handlin saw immigration as a principal key to the understanding of national character. *People of Plenty* (1954) by a third historian, David M. Potter, was subtitled "Economic Abundance and the American Character."

None of these was a naive investigation. Curti treated patriotism dispassionately and was critical of the American version of what Germans call *Hurrapatriotismus*. Handlin implied that immigration was a disturbing and even traumatic business for the 35 million Europeans who crossed the North Atlantic: the settlers were *un*settled first of all. Potter began his book with a survey of the inadequacies of the usual treatment of national character at the hands of his fellow-academics.

Nevertheless, the assumption that the Americans were set apart from other peoples was almost axiomatic. And despite Potter's attempt to clarify, the controlling generalizations about American character or that of other nations, remained vague. One able contribution was that of the "psycho-historian" Erik Erikson. But take this passage from his *Childhood and Society* (1950):

It is a commonplace to state that whatever one may come to consider a truly American trait can be shown to have its equally characteristic opposite. This, one suspects, is true of all "national characters", or (as I would prefer to call them) national identities — so true, in fact, that one may begin rather than end with the proposition that a nation's identity is derived from the ways in which history has, as it were, counterpointed certain opposite potentialities; the ways in which it lifts this counterpoint to a unique style of civilization, or lets it disintegrate into mere contradiction.

Here difficulties arise. If every nation defines itself by means of polar opposites (law-abiding/lawless, sociable/ individualistic, etc.) can any nation be said to embody a clear, congruent identity? Or does each contain large exceptions, contradictions, dissents — such as those of the South in relation to the rest of the United States? If so, national character/ identity is a loose conception, apt to turn into self-congratulation or anecdote. Even in Erikson, there is the supposition that national identity is a state of equilibrium — leading to a "unique style of civilization" which is clearly deemed preferable to "mere contradictions".

One may still believe there are undoubted if unquantifiable differences between nation A and nation B. An Englishman and a Japanese, for instance, can sense deep differences of "character" in each other. But their two societies, and the admired or deplored forms of conduct they have generated, reflect conspicuous differences of heritage and environment. It is much harder to be sure about Euro-American or Anglo-American differences. For after all, the American colonies were once English. Neither the indigenous Indian nor the Negro slave population had much voice in colonial life; their influence was indirect and negative. When the colonies became independent, the United States continued to be closely linked with the Old World. How then can we pronounce with confidence on presumed aspects of American national uniqueness? Thus, enumerations of American characteristics almost always include "pragmatism" — the habit of thinking practically rather than theoretically. But this has also often been said about the English. An Englishwoman tells me that one of her schoolteachers used to begin each lesson with the catechistic query "What are we English?" to which the class was trained to chorus in reply: "Empiricists!" How should we set about assessing and accounting for the pragmatic or empirical element in American life? Did it come from Britain in the first place, then evolve in special American ways? If so, how and when?

Historians are interested in movement and change through time. The concept of national character, as employed in a good deal of writing about the American past, tends to be static. It assumes that, once formed, the national character acquired permanent lineaments. A prevalent idea is that Americanness was a sort of igneous formation: a coalescence produced by the intense heat of the crisis of the American Revolution, perhaps with further tempering in the war of 1812 and the Civil War. True, constant and rapid change has been recognized as a feature of American history. One could hardly ignore such a point in a country whose population, around 4 million in 1790, is now well over 250 million (1990). But this has been dealt with by including an appetite for innovation within the list of national characteristics. American historians have not much concerned themselves with the problem of whether "permanent revolution" may not be a contradiction in terms.

In part this is because they have also tended to contrast dynamic America and static Europe. In discussions of national behavior Europe has served as an unchanging backcloth against which to pose the pageant of an America on the move. This is apparent in Oscar Handlin's *The Uprooted*, which takes for granted that there was an entity called "Europe" whose component nation-states have had essentially the same set of attitudes, changing little in the past three or four hundred years. But Europe has never been such an entity. How could it be thought a static continent when, for good or ill, it has played so prominent a part in world history — colonizing, annexing, warring, industrializing?

In short, the concept of national character may seem not to have helped much in explaining the historic relationships between Old World and New. It has built upon a traditional stock of assertions: America is "new", America is "different", America is "American". In recent years, as nationalism has lost favor among intellectuals in Western societies, so national character has come to appear a somewhat dubious proposition. For some, separatism, or at any rate allegiance to a unit not familiar in the geography of orthodox nationalism, has a livelier appeal. In the United States, black spokesmen have insisted that Afro-Americans are more Afro than American; and militant women have resisted the idea that they share the same set of values as the American male.

There is, though, still a wide measure of agreement on broad propositions, such as that America grew out of and then away from Europe, under the pressure of new circumstances. Most historians, implicitly or explicitly, still believe there is such a thing as national character, even if we cannot define it with precision. Ideas about the special qualities of particular societies depend upon opinion rather than upon observable fact. In logic, every person, every town, every country is unique. Uniqueness is absolute. One cannot logically say that something is "very unique" or that A is more unique than B. In ordinary discourse, however, such things are said; and belief in the exceptional nature of one's own society (cf. Milton on England quoting Psalm 147:20 from the Bible: "God hath not dealt so with any other nation") has been an important historical factor.

Comparison: How and with What?

Another truism is that one ought to try to verify a proposition that something is unique by examining other things within the same realm. The statement that a particular society has a unique quality should involve looking at other societies to be sure they really are different. Assertions about the nature of America have always carried the corollary that we are comparing it with some other area. A difference must be a difference *from* something else.

But as historians have begun to move away from their previous concentration upon *national* history and culture — some towards a recommendation that we should be studying *world* history — comparison has enjoyed a new vogue. C. Vann Woodward has edited a group of essays entitled *The Comparative Approach to American History* (1968). There are antecedent developments in other disciplines. Courses in comparative religion or in comparative government and politics are well established. Political scientists have devoted a good deal of effort to the concept of comparison. In literature, too, there are journals and yearbooks of comparative studies and scholars accustomed to regarding themselves as "comparatists".

Harry Levin of Harvard University, one of the most eminent literary comparatists, has conceded the difficulties of comparison in a number of candid essays. Levin tells the story of a colleague who

> *enjoyed the precarious privilege of being introduced to Dylan Thomas, during one of that gifted poet's tours of American campuses. As soon as Thomas learned that my informant was a professor of comparative literature he asked: "What do you compare it with?" And in his . . . uninhibited manner, he went on to offer a monosyllabic suggestion which we could not permit ourselves to entertain.*

What do you compare, and how? It is simplest to compare only two things at a time. We can say that A resembles B or does not resemble B or reveals more or less of certain features than does B. According to this criterion, most books on comparative religion or politics are not truly comparative. They simply furnish information about a number of different systems. They may provide ingenious taxonomies; but the scale of generalization is usually too large to satisfy anyone in search of a method that can be applied to close contexts. Comparative literature often suffers from the opposite defect. It may involve, for example, looking at a couple of novels written in different languages and noting internal similarities. Taxonomies or classifications that may be illuminating, as sometimes in comparative politics, are usually too static to be of much help to historians, who operate in the time-dimension. They need to consider how ideas and institutions evolve. For American history, we have to explain how, from a European base, America generated "unique" institutions and how New and Old Worlds continued to interact upon one another.

There are broad notions that try to accommodate such needs. There is, for instance, the "convergence" theory, according to which all advanced societies, whatever their *political* form, are bound to go through the same stages of *economic* development. This experience, it is held, may lead to a more general convergence, since economic necessities and power obligations present similar problems of decision making. But the attempt by S. P. Huntington and Z. Brzezinski to apply this theory some years ago to a comparative study of the United States and Soviet Russia, while intriguing, was unsuccessful. The theory was too large to fit the detailed case-studies offered in their book; and the idea that the two super-powers were actually converging or coming to resemble one another was going out of fashion by the time the book was finished. Equally disappointing were attempts to devise a history of the whole American hemisphere, based on the premise that North and South America had been shaped by unique common experiences (immigration, slavery, encounters with aborigines, frontier settlement). The large similarities could be conceded. But the other differences seemed too considerable and too complex to be brought under one rubric; and their ties with northern and with Hispanic Europe respectively seemed to indicate that heritage might count quite as much as environment in forming a society.

The concept of comparison, like that of national character, does not in itself solve anything. We are still left with the questions of what is being compared, how it is done, and for what purpose. Clearly, comparative studies involve an inquiry into aspects of two, possibly more, cultures. These must allow comparison: there must be a reasonable symmetry, even if of apparent opposites, or the task is hopeless. As to the aim of comparison, at least where the United States is concerned, historians have quite often made up their minds before they start; they find what they are looking for.

Comparability may imply similarity. This is the sense in which students in examinations are asked to "compare and contrast" historical material: in other words, draw up a balance sheet of resemblances and differences. The notion of comparison-as-similarity may embrace a notion of *continuity in time*: an emphasis on the stubbornness of *inheritance*. That assumption underlies the "germ" theory of institutions expounded in the second half of the nineteenth century by such Americans as Herbert Baxter Adams of Johns Hopkins University and by several European historians. In their view, for example, the important thing about an institution like the New England town meeting was its ancestry, which they traced back to tribal gatherings in early German history. Some of the intellectual historians among Adams's contemporaries likewise had no doubt that, in the history of ideas, America and Europe were more or less one undifferentiated civilization, molded by a common heritage. And some of the essays in C. Vann Woodward's symposium, *The Comparative Approach to American History*, take similarity as their starting point.

But some scholars emphasize *dissimilarity: discontinuity in time*, the effect of environment. According to the French historian Marc Bloch (1928), the main value of the comparative method is not in "hunting out resemblances" but in the "observation of the differences" between societies. This was the intent of the American historian Frederick Jackson Turner, who was trained at Johns Hopkins but rejected the germ theory. Turner's "frontier thesis" (1893) maintained that the American character had been formed not by European origins but by the effects of the American wilderness upon successive waves of settlers. (In asserting the fundamental dissimilarity of America and Europe, Turner avoids the problem of how Europe, itself once a frontier society, ceased to be one; and he seems to hint at a fundamental similarity between the United States and other frontier societies, though his concern was with American uniqueness.) Comparison for the sake of contrast is a basic principle in the writing of such American historians as Daniel J. Boorstin. The assumption of dissimilarity is evident too in a number of the essays in Woodward, including that of Richard Hofstadter on political parties.

Here are two extreme positions. One enjoins us to look for resemblances. The other, generally more popular, says that the comparative approach heightens our awareness of the unique qualities of a particular society. The inheritance position presumes that people and institutions do not change greatly once the original model has been established. The environmentalist position suggests that people and institutions are plastic. There are intermediate interpretations. None is finally provable, since history is an inextricable tangle of fact and opinion. My own bias is that of a European who senses an occasional American bias towards the proposition that the United States is "incomparable": not only different from elsewhere, but incomparably better than (or worse than) elsewhere. I intend to look at historical comparisons of the United States with Europe and especially Britain with a bias towards similarity. The reasons for this approach are

— America grew from Britain, and more generally Europe; other external influences were relatively minor, until the twentieth century.

— Historically, Europe was the area Americans nearly always had in mind once they claimed to be different: they saw themselves as different *from Europe*.

— Dissimilarity has been over-emphasized, in American patriotic discourse and in the writing of American history.

THEORIES

The Belief in American Difference

Europeans as well as Americans have often taken the two continents to be not only different but diametrically opposed, as two contrasting principles. Old World, New World: the very terms indicate the supposed polarity. For the past two centuries the United States has been regarded as the embodiment of everything "American". This usurpation has annoyed Latin Americans and Canadians. But it is a matter of historical record, so we need not hesitate in using "America" and "the United States" interchangeably.

The polarity has not necessarily been in America's favor. Many Europeans, as well as self-critical Americans, have treated "America" and "Americanization" as dirty words, dire warnings of a fate likely to overtake Europe if it does not watch out. They have followed much the same lines ever since Buffon and other eighteenth-century European *philosophes* stated that America was an inferior continent, where animals and humans alike were deficient in size and sexuality, and steadily deteriorating. This approach obeys the same principle of polarity as the more frequent claim that America differed in being superior to Europe. In the standard antithesis, America has been associated with growth, space, futurity, democracy, virtue, innocence — and with the less admirable sides of these traits, such as boastfulness and naivety. Europe has been characterized as moribund, limited, antique, class-ridden, depraved, worldly — and, of course, with more admirable traits such as delicacy and intellect.

Each side of the Atlantic has historically served the other as a negative reference group: a means of defining what one is by defining what one is not. Here is a small sample:

EUROPEANS

Corneille de Pauw (1770): "We have depicted Americans as being a race of men who have all the faults of children, as a degenerate species, cowardly, impotent, without physical strength, without vitality, without elevation of mind."

Charles Dickens (1842): "I cannot change my secret opinion of this country — its follies, vices, grievous disappointments . . . I believe the heaviest blow ever dealt at Liberty's head will be dealt by this nation in the ultimate failure of its example to the Earth."

Knut Hamsun (c. 1890): "By undermining all individual yearning for freedom in its citizens, America has finally managed to create that horde of fanatic freedom automatons which make up American democracy."

Sigmund Freud (c. 1925): "America is a bad experiment conducted by Providence. At least, I think it must have been Providence. I . . . should hate to be held responsible for it."

AMERICANS

Thomas Jefferson (on European court-life, 1788): "Their manners, could you ape them, would not make you beloved in your own country, nor would they improve it could you introduce them there to the exclusion of that honest simplicity now prevailing in America, and worthy of being cherished."

George Francis Train (1860): "American character is not an imitation, but a creation — not a copy, but an original. Her power is not in armies or armadas, but in railroads and schoolmasters."

Nathaniel Hawthorne (1863): "We, in our dry atmosphere, are getting too nervous, haggard, dyspeptic, unsubstantial, theoretic, and need to be made grosser. John Bull, on the other hand, has grown bulbous . . . heavy-witted,

material, and, in a word, too intensely English. In a few more centuries he will
be the earthliest creature that ever the earth saw."

William James (1899): "We must thank God for America; and hold fast to every
advantage of our position. Talk about our corruption! It is a mere fly-speck of
superficiality compared with the rooted and permanent forces of corruption that
exist in the European states."

Not all the criticism of America has come from Europe, nor all the criticism
of Europe from America. Other examples, highly appreciative, could be given.
But the greater part of this transatlantic dialogue has drawn sharp contrasts. It
has tended to treat America as an ideal, even if an ideal lost or perverted. It
has entailed an American repudiation of the Old World — Europe as the place
to escape from. The claim to American innocence, especially where couched in
"Adamic" and primitivist metaphors, might appear hard to reconcile with
predictions that the United States would beat Europe at its own game by
surpassing it in technology and the arts. Yet the two types of claim are not really
incompatible. American visions of an unpeopled wilderness were, at any rate in
the nineteenth century, nearly always accompanied by visions of transforming the
wilderness into civilization. William Cullen Bryant begins his poem "The
Prairies":

> *These are the gardens of the Desert, these*
> *The unshorn fields, boundless and beautiful,*
> *For which the speech of England has no name.*

But by the end of the poem he imagines he can hear

> *The sound of that advancing multitude*
> *Which soon shall fill these deserts.*

America's rapid and successful industrialization, which enabled it to outmatch
British productivity by about 1890, was explained as a consequence of having a
highly mobile and resourceful labor force and a predisposition to produce for a
mass market: in short, of having a democratic society. American historians have
warmed to the writings of the sculptor Horatio Greenough (1805-52), finding in
his doctrine "Beauty is the promise of Function" an epitome of no-nonsense,
democratic pragmatism:

> *The men who have reduced locomotion to its simplest elements, in the*
> *trotting wagon and the yacht America, are nearer to Athens at this moment*
> *than they who would bend the Greek temple to every use.*

Since Europe and America have been states of mind as well as actual places, they have been expected to behave in appropriate ways. Americans in Europe have insisted on discovering Old World charm, with some assistance in recent years from tourist boards. Where they have come across a European who acted like an American, they have enrolled him as an honorary New Worlder and on occasion deported people deemed to be un-American, all this to keep the contrast tidy. An endearing example is Whitman's tribute to the works of Hegel:

> *There is that about them which only the vastness and multiplicity and the*
> *vitality of America would seem able to comprehend. . . . It is strange to me*
> *that they were born in Germany, or in the old world at all. While a Carlyle,*
> *I should say, is quite the legitimate European product to be expected.*

In reverse, Europeans have insisted that Americans should be different and inhabit a recognizably different continent.

An earlier instance is the response of the English novelist Mrs. Gaskell, when an American friend, Charles Eliot Norton, sent her some photographs of native scenery. She "thought America would have been odder and more original; the underwood and tangle is just like England." She had got a more satisfactory idea from a painting done by another Englishwoman, Barbara Leigh Smith, "in some wild luxuriant terrific part of Virginia? [actually Louisiana] in a gorge full of rich rank tropical vegetation, — her husband keeping watch over her with loaded pistols because of the alligators infesting the stream. — Well! that picture did look like my idea of America." Or there is the ironic explanation offered by the American writer John Jay Chapman for the interest conventional English critics showed in the "barbaric" poetry of Whitman. He conveyed "the un-pleasant and rampant wildness" of America as the English imagined it: "Mormonism and car factories, steamboat explosions, strikes, repudiation, and whiskey." So "the discovery of Whitman as a poet caused many a hard-thinking Oxford man to sleep quietly at night. America was solved."

Advantages of the Contrast Principle

It is our habit to think in dualisms: male and female, *yin* and *yang*, body and soul. They seem indispensable as ways of organizing our thought, even when — as with the U and non-U game of Nancy Mitford, or C. P. Snow's "two cultures" — they may be exasperatingly over-simplified. For much of their appeal lies in simplicity.

The America-Europe dualism has a stylized clarity that helps to account for its enduring appeal. It has been essential to Americans as a means of defining identity ever since the United States became an independent nation; and before 1776 the polarity was already established through legends of the earthly paradise, Puritan theories of God's New World providences, European dreams of the noble savage and the virtuous husbandman, and so on. As an ex-colonial nation the United States needed to repudiate the mother country; as a fragment or offshoot of Europe it felt obliged to deny that it was merely derivative. History and geography appeared to confirm the providential theme. "Manifest destiny" presented the United States with an immense western domain; immigration bore out the idea of a universal "nation of nations". The nineteenth-century wars fought by the United States against England (1812-15), Mexico (1846-48) and Spain (1898) brought astounding triumphs as if God were emphatically on the side of Andrew Jackson, Winfield Scott and Commodore Dewey at New Orleans, Cerro Gordo, and Manila Bay respectively. The Civil War (1861-65) was a terrible setback, but the Northerner was able to see it in retrospect as yet another predestined triumph for the American Union, which in ending slavery removed the one remaining anomaly of the land of freedom.

For some observers the American Dream has been the American Nightmare. In either case it has supplied an extraordinary drama (or melodrama) peopled with scouts and trappers, Yankees and Cavaliers, cowboys and Indians, sheriffs and badmen, Huck Finns and Nigger Jims, Abe Lincolns and Huey Longs, preachers and robber barons, do-gooders and con-men, Al Capones and J. Edgar Hoovers, hoboes and work-bosses, loners and Babbitts. No other nation has produced so rich a cast of symbolic characters for modern times. There are South American epics in prose and poetry celebrating the heroic gaucho. For all I know they are as fine as anything written about the United States. But they have not made a mark on the world's imagination. Perhaps Canadian history is full of wonderful stories waiting to be told. But I suspect they would require too many footnotes to get much beyond the walls of academe. Territorially, Canada and Brazil are as big as the United States; but their historical folklore has seemed far smaller.

The contrast principle supplies leverage for many purposes. Scores of interpretative works have made use of it. It has pervaded the writing of American historians from George Bancroft down to Daniel Boorstin and Louis Hartz in our generation. It is central to a number of interpretations of American art, architecture and literature. Again and again in their titles the word *American* refers to much more than actual latitude and longitude: it is meant to have a mythic resonance. Here are a few examples of books on literature: *The American Adam, Love and Death in the American Novel, Symbolism and American Literature, The American Novel and its Tradition, The Continuity of American Poetry, A World Elsewhere: The Place of Style in American Literature*. These assume an essential Americanness and seek to define it as contrary to European literary tradition. The same contrast is expressed by Europeans writing on American literature: for example, D. H. Lawrence's *Studies in Classic American Literature* and Tony Tanner's *The Reign of Wonder: Naivety and Reality in American Literature*. It is invoked in other European books, such as Cyrille Arnavon's *L'Américanisme et Nous* and Jean-Jacques Servan-Schreiber's *Le Défi Américain*. How could we manage without it?

Disadvantages of the Similarity Principle

Arguments that America and Europe are closely related have often appeared lame or prissy or propagandist. Geoffrey Barraclough has attacked the notion of an "Atlantic Community" as being only a extended version of the tendency to Europe-centered historical scholarship. He sees it as primarily a political or strategic idea projected backwards from the Atlantic Charter of 1941 and then embodied in the formation of NATO. There was, he concedes, a historical Atlantic *economy*; but according to him these economic ties began to loosen a century and a half ago.

An alternative notion is that of what the French call *le monde anglo-saxon*: a close historical link between Britain and America. This can be objected to as a Gaullist formula, expressing both anglophobia and anti-Americanism. Or in its historical context the notion can be regarded as an instance of French parochialism, for French scholars are notoriously casual in their allusions to non-Frenchmen. (A reputable French volume on world history describes the eminently Scottish surgeon Joseph Lister as an American.) In the United States it has unpleasant "WASP" connotations, snobbish and racist. In Britain too it is associated with late nineteenth-century visions of an imperial union, a "Greater

Britain" of English-speaking peoples who would run the world between them —
with perhaps Anglo-Saxon Germany thrown in, as with Cecil Rhodes's plan for
Oxford scholarships.   It has a ceremonial, post-prandial, Sulgrave-and-
Runnymede quality.

The similarity principle appears to overstress inheritance, to limit influences on
America to those emanating from Western Europe (what of black Americans?
Chinese? Japanese? Puerto Ricans?) and to fly in the face of a mass of beliefs
and facts about the sheer Americanness of the United States. Instead of a crisp
formulation, the similarity principle seems to substitute blurred qualifications.
The frontier thesis may be unsound; at least it gives something to hang on to
when you begin to study American history. What is there to put in its place that
wraps things up so comprehensively?

"F A C T S"

Similarity Assertions and Evidence

I believe we should nevertheless persist in questioning the validity of the contrast
principle for three chief reasons:

1. Writing about America has often claimed as uniquely American phenomena
that are manifestly not so or has made assertions without supplying confirming
evidence.

2. Writing about the American past, especially in the twentieth century, is often
misleadingly selective. It focuses upon instances of or declarations of uniqueness
but leaves out contrary material relating to similarity.

3.   Earlier commentary does not in fact always insist upon American
"incomparability" or treats the theme ambiguously, conceding the importance of
heritage or the continuing parallels with British or "Anglo-Saxon" attitudes.

On the first point, Tocqueville's *Democracy in America* is in more ways than one
a classic piece of theorizing about the New World. But often it supplies a
diagram of contrasting *theoretical* distinctions between "democracy" and
"aristocracy," instead of an actual analysis of conditions in America and Europe.
Tocqueville's Europe is Continental Europe; he finds Britain difficult to bring
into the scheme, as we see from his habit of referring to the Americans as "Anglo-

Saxons".[1] His America is the model of what a "democratic" society ought to be like. Thus, what he says about the role of the military and of warfare in abstractly contrasting societies is brilliant. But it is not an accurate picture of the situation of the United States of his day nor of the situation in Britain — whose feelings about standing armies, conscription and the like strongly influenced the Americans.[2] If Britain is not, for Tocqueville's purposes, part of Europe, how should it be schematically presented: as the mother-country, molding the United States, or as a quasi-democracy obeying some of the inevitable rules that govern such a society?

Another illustration relates to Leslie Fiedler's *Love and Death in the American Novel* (1960). He offers fascinating speculations about the evolution of a peculiarly American psyche, given to morbid fantasies. Overt sexuality is missing, Fiedler claims, from nineteenth-century American literature. Instead, in some of the tales of Edgar Allan Poe, in Harriet Beecher Stowe's *Uncle Tom's Cabin*, or in Herman Melville's novel *Pierre*, are bizarre sentimentalities, hints of incest, tears shed at the deathbed of young girls. But this atmosphere is not confined to American literature. Think of the sentimental-prurient tone of English novelists like Dickens, enormously popular in the United States, or of the French excitement over L'Inconnue de la Seine — the beautiful, unidentified, drowned girl lying on a slab in the Paris morgue, whose death-mask was once a popular item in souvenir shops.[3]

As for misleading selectivity, Crèvecoeur's *Letters from an American Farmer* (1782), the first to depict America as a wondrous melting-pot, was out of print and almost forgotten for most of the nineteenth century. Crèvecoeur was revived early in the twentieth century to furnish quotations for the controversy over whether immigration should be restricted. The American frontier West held a rather more prominent place in the nineteenth-century national imagination. But until the later part of the century, as Frederick Jackson Turner the Middle Westerner well knew, many Americans tended to think of it as an open-air slum. Turner himself as an ambitious young scholar decided he must devote his life to

---

[1] See Seymour Drescher, *Tocqueville and England* (1964). Tocqueville's mistress, subsequently his wife, was an Englishwoman. He visited her country in 1833, immediately before beginning to write *Democracy in America*, to examine what heritage "John Bull, father of Jonathan" had transmitted to his son. While at work on his book in Paris, he saw "English Mary" every evening. See the expert account by André Jardin, *Tocqueville: A Biography* (New York, English translation 1988), 197.

[2] The point is developed in Marcus Cunliffe, *Soldiers and Civilians: The Martial Spirit in America, 1775-1865* (1968, 1973).

[3] The morbidity of the European imagination is abundantly documented in Mario Praz, *The Romantic Agony*, 2d ed. (1951).

some great theme of modern history. He concluded that the most significant were the growth of cities and the settlement of virgin lands. He fastened upon the latter because it was unique to America or rather not a feature of Europe, though he was perfectly aware that urbanization was of enormous importance to the United States.

There were American "originals" whose words catch our attention today. Horatio Greenough was one of these, with his plea for functionalism and his dislike of "embellishment". But in his own day Greenough's doctrines won no following in the United States; American taste in architecture and the fine arts closely paralleled that of London and Paris. Whitman was another original. John Jay Chapman pokes fun at English critics praising Whitman but on the curious grounds that Whitman, while a great poet, was completely out of the mainstream of American culture. Much more representative of this "respectable mediocrity" were poets like Whittier and Longfellow — "read by mill-hands and clerks and school-teachers, by lawyers and doctors and divines, . . . whose ideals they truly spoke for, whose yearnings and spiritual life they truly expressed."

In short, twentieth-century scholarship conceals the extent to which the United States was "Victorian" in outlook. Victorianism coexisted with an American rhetoric of emulation and superior virtue. Yet even this rhetoric was Victorian in flavor, in calling for work, thrift, perseverance and piety. "The longer I lived in the States", the Englishman Edward Dicey said of a journey made in 1862, "the more I became convinced that America was . . . the complement of England. The national failings, as well as the national virtues of the New World, are very much those of the mother country, developed on a different and a broader scale." An American contributor to the *Atlantic Monthly*, just a few months earlier, insisted that "the features of society in Great Britain and in all our Northern regions are almost identically the same, or run in parallelisms, by which we might match every . . . incident, prejudice, and folly, every good and every bad trait . . . in the one place with something exactly like it in the other." George Francis Train, flamboyant American patriot and entrepreneur, declared that his country was *sui generis*. But he was also fond of announcing that Americans were of English stock and that the two nations were travelling the same road, well in advance of the rest of mankind.

Origins and Continuity

So we come back to the argument that the United States has a great deal in common with Europe and especially Britain. If that proposition formerly had a whiff of Pilgrims' banquets or of NATO about it, it has come to life again in new guises. Third World spokesmen like Frantz Fanon automatically align the United States with the other "have" nations of the northern hemisphere, plus such "European" zones as South Africa and Australia in the southern hemisphere. It has been given another twist by Louis Hartz and others in *The Founding of New Societies* (1965). Hartz sees the United States as a fragment-nation, broken off from Europe. His argument is that each fragment (Latin America, French Canada, South Africa, etc.) has become quite separate from Europe but is characterized by the dominant fragment of ideology taken from Europe at the formative period. Ideology in Europe has continued to be rich and to evolve through the clash of rival systems. The United States is therefore *ideologically* still caught in the late eighteenth century, although *materially* there has been great change.

There are flaws in the Hartz thesis. It does, however, hint that we are not obliged to opt for *either* the contrast *or* the similarity principle: various combinations are possible. Thus, perhaps there were several British heritages; the young United States embodied one of these — the non-aristocratic, Nonconformist, tradesman's and skilled artisan's Britain, largely North Country and Scottish — and then extended it in a favorable environment with the aid of successive waves of like-minded immigrants. Another observation is that national societies embrace a number of institutions — political and governmental, educational, religious, legal, economic, military, cultural — and that each of these has a certain autonomy within an institutional/international realm — imitating one another or otherwise evolving transnationally. Each may move at its own pace, within limits. Indeed, one would expect this to happen in an ex-colonial nation. So indigenous political forms could emerge much more easily than with literature and the arts, which were to remain derivative until the twentieth century.

Comparisons ought to specify which Europe (or which Britain) is being compared. They should not automatically assume that what holds good for one type of institution holds good for others, nor that similarity necessarily means amity, nor that mutual hostility is a sign of dissimilarity. Also, it does not follow that people who have inherited features of another culture remain conscious of the inheritance. Often they annex these to what they perceive to be their own culture. The leaders of the Taiping rebellion in mid-nineteenth-century China absorbed a certain amount of Christian doctrine. The Northern King of the Taipings, giving audience to an English official, began to discuss religion with him.

> [The King] *stated that as children and worshippers of one God we were all brethren; and after receiving my assurance that such had long been our view also, inquired if I knew the "Heavenly Rules". I replied that I was most likely acquainted with them, though unable to recognize them under that name; and, after a moment's thought, asked if they were ten in number. He answered eagerly in the affirmative. I then began repeating the substance of the first of the Ten Commandments, but had not proceeded far before he laid his hand on my shoulder . . . and exclaimed, "The same as ourselves! The same as ourselves!"*

Many Americans, like the Northern King, have no doubt professed European notions in the secure conviction that they were expounding native American articles of faith. Conversely, many Europeans have forgotten or never known that some everyday idiom or artefact, utterly habitual to them, originated in the United States. It is a nice question to decide at what moment an inheritance becomes indigenous.

During the nineteenth century, the United States developed a fairly distinct *political* culture. How distinct is a matter for debate. Robert Kelley's *The Transatlantic Persuasion* (1969) contends that Gladstonian liberalism was common to Britain and North America. Others might maintain that a stable two-party system, resting on minimal ideological disagreement, was among the outcomes of a British political heritage. Except for the Mormons (many of whose recruits were immigrants converted in northern Europe) and for Christian Science (which soon got a foothold in Europe), the American *religious* culture remained "European", though more varied and more composite than in any one European country. A possible conclusion is that *American uniqueness largely consisted in being eclectically European*: in the borrowed mix rather than in American innovation, though the resultant mix was peculiarly American. As for *arts and letters*, these were still in 1900 heavily European in feel. For the first twenty years of this century the role of the American man of letters (Ezra Pound or T. S. Eliot) was to orchestrate European culture by means of detached cosmopolitanism. He was a continentalist where many European literati were nationalists. He was still a "European" though very few Europeans were like him: he was more European than they.

Two-Way Influences

One objection to Hartz's fragment theory is that he supposes Europe and its offshoots to have had no significant effect upon one another after the separation. For Europe and America the facts are otherwise. Immigration brought many millions of Europeans across the Atlantic; indeed the flow, though at its height on the eve of the 1914-18 war, has never ceased. The United States has not managed to remain neutral in any of the big European wars. Technological, scientific and cultural exchanges have been close and continuous. Even before the steamship, Americans in droves visited Europe. European curiosity about the United States was less conspicuous; nevertheless a varied and considerable company made the trip. There was an easy and incessant two-way traffic in fads, fears, music, fiction, poetry, inventions, reforms, theories. Because of language the Anglo-American links were especially close.

Early American assertions of independence took for granted that Europe was already superseded. But these reports of Europe's demise proved premature. Britain was still in its own eyes the world's leading industrial-exporting-imperial power in 1914; and if America was contesting the leadership, so was another European power — Germany. The propaganda of nineteenth-century American nationalism understated the innovative vitality of Europe. The Europe many historians have tended to depict is the Europe of dynastic strife, of aristocracy and of class conflict, less that of city, factory and laboratory. The America they often emphasize (see, e.g., Daniel Boorstin's *The Americans: The National Experience*) is less the settled "European" East than the symbolic burgeoning West. In architecture we hear about such American contributions as the balloon-frame to house-building, almost nothing about the novelty in England of Paxton's 1851 Crystal Palace. American art historians used to take pride in the untutored originality of "primitive" drawings and paintings — until it was discovered that some were copied from magazine engravings. In other words, the facts often contradict the theory of nineteenth-century American uniqueness. Europeans did, as Americans complained, tend to be critical of the United States, sometimes ignorantly and superciliously. But a fair amount of apparent anti-Americanism may have been an understandable reaction to American distortions of what was happening in Europe.

In the nineteenth century the United States evolved many special, un-European features. Political organization is one example. In these ways it did, as James Bryce explained in *The American Commonwealth* (1888), stand as a separate society. Except among the intellectual and among the more socially pretentious classes, it did not feel like or behave like a European colony. On the other hand, as Turner's nostalgic appeal to the already fading frontier experience reveals, there was a kind of "convergence" during the latter years of the century. The United States then came up against the urban and industrial problems that Europe had been obliged to face earlier. So, at the moment when the United States was beginning to display its own characteristic, un-European combination of folkways, it was also brought closer to the common Euro-American perplexities engendered by so-called modern civilization. Some of the attempted American solutions, such as the Sherman Antitrust Act (1890), were peculiarly American. In other respects, many of America's reform expedients were borrowed from Europe: participatory devices like the initiative, referendum and recall from Switzerland, social welfare and town-planning schemes from Britain and Germany — not to mention the secret ballot from Australia.

Over the past century, whenever America has been in crisis it has tended to look abroad, especially to Europe, for curative ideas. And whenever Europe has been in crisis, this has tended to reinforce the old American conviction that Europe was iniquitous. So, in the American troubles of the Populist and Progressive era from about 1890 to 1914, the perceived parallels were close. But then in 1914, as America had long predicted, Europe appeared finished, mired in its own suicidal folly, a horrid example of what not to do. The anticipated death of Europe, however, did not quite take place; and America's own social and economic predicaments in the 1930s made her look abroad once more for possible positive answers whether from Marxism or from Keynesianism. In 1939 Europe seemed to have taken the ultimate step towards the destruction of its civilization and its empires. Once again the apparent contrast served to revive the Europe-America polarity, just when its outlines appeared blurred beyond use. For several years after 1945 theorists drew upon the old polarity, to the extent of assuming that Europe no longer counted in the world. This dismissal too has been falsified by events. Since the 1970s Europe has displayed perhaps more of a genuine and vital unity than was ever true when transatlantic commentators formerly spoke of it as such.

Has the New World-Old World antithesis outlived its purpose? In some ways Russia, Japan and China are of more concern to America than Europe is. An increasing number of Europeans regard the United States as not *the other* place, the repository of their hopes or fears, but simply as *another* place, among several regions of the world. Yet the old antithesis has not entirely lost its power. Even if they may be somewhat fallacious, or no longer relevant, historical assumptions take a long time to pass away.

CONCLUSIONS

Factors in Comparisons

We can never "prove" the question of American uniqueness one way or the other. On the largest scale, say that of a Martian arriving on Planet Earth, all homunculi are much alike. The bigger our scale of interpretation, the more similar America and Europe are: mainly Christian, mainly white, mainly affluent, mainly urban. The other extreme of scale, millimetric instead of kilometric, indicates how unlike things are. On the detailed scale, for example, Glasgow and Edinburgh not only pretend to be worlds apart but actually are so.

Neither continent has remained static. Change (for instance, the growth of political democracy in Europe), whether internally or externally caused, has been a marked feature in both. It is possible that, ideologically, Europe has changed more than America. Nor have the transatlantic societies ever been mutually isolated. The two continents have evolved in part through interaction, each modifying the other. Certain comparable decisions have faced all European and American societies, such as the degree of popular representation in government, or the priority to be given to technological development. How these actually develop is affected by many considerations, not all of them rational. But the problems themselves have an inner logic and limited options, once a society is confronted by them. America and Europe have travelled along these same routes, whether or not they wish to. There may be something in the idea that America is the same as Europe only more so.

Recapitulation

— America grew mainly out of Europe and Britain in particular.

— American claims of uniqueness have usually taken Europe as the measure.

— The belief in American uniqueness is ancient, persistent, and common to both Europe and America.

— The America-Europe contrast has an attractive symbolic boldness: it corresponds to a deep polarity in our thinking and supplies leverage for any amount of generalization.

— Assertions of Euro-American (or more particularly Anglo-American) similarity have tended to lack clarity and appeal and to be used for unlikable reasons.

— Nevertheless, many facts contradict the uniqueness claim: the two continents have continued to have a great deal in common, including mutual jealousy.

— In the arts, at any rate, some Americans have been more cosmopolitan Europeans than the Europeans.

— In the second half of the nineteenth century the United States became simultaneously more sure of its distinct identity yet in socioeconomic and cultural circumstances more like Europe.

— The two world wars of the twentieth century, apart from their many other effects, have helped to keep alive the uniqueness idea in America when one might have expected it to fade.

The question then is one of utility rather than truth. For certain purposes detailed comparison serves us best, for others broad comparison. Perhaps the conclusion can best be stated thus: *narrow comparison brings out dissimilarities and broad comparison brings out similarities*.

———————————

This essay appeared in Richard Rose, ed., *Lessons from America: An Exploration* (London, Macmillan, 1974), 19-45.

In the 1970s and the 1980s there may have been as many broad essays on comparative history as on specific studies. Among the former, see Daniel Bell, "The End of American Exceptionalism," *The Public Interest* 41 (Fall 1975): 193-224; Laurence Veysey, "The Autonomy of American History Reconsidered," *American Quarterly* 31 (Fall 1979): 455-77; George M. Fredrickson, "Comparative History," in Michael Kammen, ed., *The Past Before Us: Contemporary Historical Writing in the U.S.* (Ithaca, N.Y.: Cornell University Press, 1980), 457-73; and Carl N. Degler, "In Pursuit of an American History," *American Historical Review* 92 (February 1987): 1-12. American literary exceptionalism is queried in William C. Spengemann, *A Mirror for Americanists: Reflections on the Idea of American Literature* (Hanover, N.H.: University Press of New England, 1989). Daniel Snowman's *Britain and America: An Interpretation of Their Culture, 1945-1975* (New York: New York University Press, 1977) is a brave and readable full-length study. Other detailed exercises in comparison include Morton Keller, "Anglo-American Politics, 1900-1930, in Anglo-American Perspective," *Comparative Studies in Society and History* 22 (July 1980): 458-77; Melvyn Stokes, "American Progressives and the European Left," *Journal of American Studies* 17 (April 1983): 5-28. At a time when the dwindling "Anglo" component in the U.S. population has been accompanied by campaigning for a much greater emphasis on non-WASP and even non-European material in school curricula, an astonishing contrary direction is taken by David Hackett Fisher. His *Albion's Seed: Four British Folkways in America* (New York: Oxford University Press, 1989) is declared to be the first in a five-volume series dealing with change in American cultural history. The initial volume provides detailed material to support the argument that colonial America was essentially shaped by mother-country folkways and that these persisted after the Revolution.

19

American Watersheds

This essay has been a little abbreviated. Otherwise it stands as a reflection poised, perhaps a bit unsatisfactorily between whimsicality and seriousness, upon the frequent recourse in American historical writing to the "watershed" metaphor. Apart from the universal human reliance upon handy figures of speech often verging on cliché, I do still think there has been an American national tendency to dramatize the finality of particular episodes.

In all countries we impose divisions upon the historical continuum, as a matter of practical necessity. The bulk of material and the demands of specialized scholarship compel us to define and delimit our own "fields" or "periods." We turn naturally enough to some particular area — say the fourteenth century, or the eighteenth — and in these instances do not need to ask ourselves whether the arbitrary division into centuries has more than a provisional validity. Reigns and presidencies, wars and revolutions usually prescribe our boundaries. If they match other, chronological divisions, so much the neater. How convenient that Queen Victoria should have died at almost the exact end of the nineteenth century: though it might have suited the students of Victorianism even better if her death could have coincided with the outbreak of World War I.

Underlying the practice of chopping the continuum into manageable chunks is a notion that certain dates or episodes are more crucial than others. We assume that this element of decisiveness is not simply a useful fiction, though our terminology to describe such historical moments is inexact. We speak, for example, of "turning points," as though history could be conceived of almost as a force, possessing direction and capable of being deflected from its previous direction by the influence of some major event. In a familiar aphorism G. M. Trevelyan has referred to 1848, the year of revolutions in Europe, as "the turning point at which European history failed to turn." And in his book *Chance or Destiny*,[1] Oscar Handlin analyzes eight "turning points" in American history with reference to the blend in each of accident and predestination. A different concept, a kind of optical metaphor, is offered by Karl Jaspers. In his *Origin and Aim of History* he postulates an *Axenzeit*, or focal point in time, at which the rays of historical situation converge and from which they then spread out again.

More commonly we adopt a geographical metaphor and talk of historical "watersheds." The word in English probably derives from the German *Wasserscheide*, or water-parting. In its original German and English usages it signified "the line separating the waters flowing into different rivers or river basins; a narrow elevated tract of ground between two drainage areas." The "shed" or "parting" came to be known also as the "divide": hence the Continental Divide in North American geography. As a historical metaphor the word represented a dramatic division between two areas of time. Unfortunately, by extension, "watersheds" have also been taken to describe "the whole gathering ground of a river system" — its basin or catchment area or whatever else we like to call it. It is hard therefore to be quite sure what historians have in mind when they allude to a "watershed." Do they envisage a crest separating one age from another? Or are they thinking of some large area which receives and eventually canalizes everything that falls within it? But for the moment, we may assume that most historians use it to denote a dramatic and decisive historical dividing line, metaphorically akin to the geographical Great Divide of North America. If the term is vague, it lies ready for use, and certainly historians in Europe employ it fairly often.

My concern, however, is with "watersheds" in the American past. Here are a few instances of the word in historical writings of the 1950s. The first, in a random sample relates to 1789, which is cited as a "watershed year" by Eugene H. Roseboom in his *History of Presidential Elections*[2] Moving on one year, Richard B. Morris believes that Alexander Hamilton's "notable state paper, his Report on Public Credit (1790), constitutes a watershed in American history." It marked, he says, "the end of an era of bankruptcy and repudiation. At the same time it exposed a deepening cleavage between the Hamiltonian nationalists on

[1] Oscar Handlin, *Chance or Destiny: Turning Points in American History* (Boston: Little, Brown, 1955).

[2] Eugene H. Roseboom, *A History of Presidential Elections* (New York: Macmillan, 1957), 1.

the one hand and the proponents of states' rights, now championed by Madison."[3]
I find that I myself, in a recent little book in the *Chicago History of American Civilization* series, rather tentatively proposed the decade of the 1830s as "some sort of watershed in American history."[4] In another book published during 1959, Avery O. Craven argues (with a mixture of metaphor) that

> *The years from 1844 to 1850, which ultimately produced the Wilmot Proviso and the Compromise of 1850, form something of a watershed in the history of the democratic process in the United States. Before that period, there had been considerable creaking and jolting, but the undercurrent was strongly national and few seriously entertained the thought of disruption.*[5]

After 1850, Mr. Craven contends, the American atmosphere was quite otherwise.
   Not surprisingly, the same thing has been said about the Civil War. Thus, to Bruce Catton,

> *The Civil War was the continental divide of American history, the summit line beyond which everything was to be different. . . . For the Civil War set this nation on the course it has followed ever since. The time before the war is part of the distant past; the time since it is, somehow, the beginning of the present. This was where the great change took place.*[6]

Then, among the closing years of the century, the sociologist David Riesman sees the presidential election of 1896 as "an historical watershed: the high point of oligarchic rule."[7]
   Henry Steele Commager, in his *The American Mind*, treats the whole decade of the 1890s as "the watershed of American history":

[3] Richard B. Morris, ed., *The Basic Ideas of Alexander Hamilton* (New York: Pocket Books, 1957), 232.

[4] Marcus Cunliffe, *The Nation Takes Shape, 1789-1837* (Chicago: University of Chicago Press, 1959), 183.

[5] Avery O. Craven, *Civil War in the Making, 1815-1860* (Baton Rouge: Louisiana State University Press, 1959), 69-70.

[6] Bruce Catton, "Where the Great Change Took Place," *New York Times Magazine*, reprinted in *The American Review*, 1 (Summer 1961): 5.

[7] David Riesman et al., *The Lonely Crowd* (New Haven, Conn.: Yale University Press, 1950), 236.

> *On one side lies an America predominantly agricultural; concerned with*
> *domestic problems; conforming, intellectually at least, to the political,*
> *economic, and moral principles inherited from the seventeenth and*
> *eighteenth centuries. . . . On the other side lies the modern America,*
> *predominantly urban and industrial; inextricably involved in world*
> *economy and politics; troubled with the problems that had long been*
> *thought peculiar to the Old World; experiencing profound changes in*
> *population, social institutions, and technology; and trying to accommodate*
> *its traditional institutions and habits of thought to conditions new and in*
> *part alien.*[8]

Writing of subsequent eras, other historians have had recourse to the same metaphor. Frank Freidel says of the New Deal of the 1930s that it "achieved major shifts in the relationship between government and society which have permanently altered the American way of life. From the perspective of a quarter century and more, it seems one of the great watersheds of American history."[9] Arthur Schlesinger Jr. agrees with Freidel: "The age of Franklin Roosevelt is a watershed in the history of the United States, the great dividing line in the nation's life between innocence and responsibility."[10] And the same notion is present in various interpretations which do not actually allude to a "watershed." Henry F. May, in *The End of American Innocence*, says, "Everybody knows that at some point in the twentieth century America went through a cultural revolution. One has only to glance at the family album, or to pick up a book or magazine, dated, say, 1907, to find oneself in a completely vanished world." He

---

[8] Henry Steele Commager, *The American Mind: An Interpretation of American Thought and Character Since the 1880s* (New Haven, Conn.: Yale University Press, 1950), 41. The same thought is to be found in the editors' introduction (by Henry Steele Commager and Richard B. Morris) to George E. Mowry, *The Era of Theodore Roosevelt, 1900-1912* (New York: Harper & Bros., 1958), xii: "the real watershed of our history can be located in the decade of the nineties." Consider also these observations from Richard Hofstadter, "Manifest Destiny and the Philippines," in Daniel Aaron, ed., *America in Crisis* (New York: Alfred A. Knopf, 1952), 173-74: "The taking of the Philippine Islands from Spain in 1899 marked a major historical departure for the American people. It was a breach in their traditions and a shock to their established values. . . . The acquisition of the islands, therefore, was understood by contemporaries . . . , as it is readily understood today, to be a turning-point in our history. . . . It is often said that the 1890s . . . form some kind of a 'watershed' in American history."

[9] Frank Freidel, "The New Deal," in Richard W. Leopold and Arthur S. Link, eds., *Problems in American History* (Englewood Cliffs, N. J.: Prentice-Hall, 2d ed., 1957), 626.

[10] Arthur M. Schlesinger, Jr., *The Age of Roosevelt*, vol. 1: *The Crisis of the Old Order, 1919-1933* (Boston: Houghton Mifflin, 1957), ix. See also vol. 3, *The Politics of Upheaval* (1960), 385: "The year 1935 marked a watershed. In this year the strategy and tactics of the New Deal experienced a subtle but pervasive change."

goes on to speak of a "historical boundary," a "barrier," a "line," and maintains that: "At some point, if not an instantaneous upheaval, there must have been a notable quickening of the pace of change, a period when things began to move so fast that the past, from then on, looked static."[11] For Mr. May the crucial years of this boundary, barrier or line are from 1912 to 1917. Finally Richard Hofstadter, though he does not use the actual metaphor, discusses great changes in his *The Age of Reform*, and appears to believe that these trends in American experience came to a climax with the beginning of World War II.[12]

What general observations are we to draw from this brief list? We might amuse ourselves by compiling a schedule of, say, the ten chief watersheds in American history. . . . Or we might inquire more closely into the problem of these allegedly critical episodes in history, following the example set by Oscar Handlin's *Chance or Destiny*. In so doing, we might look more critically at a professional tendency, not confined to Americanists, to employ them as the terminal rather than as the central features of our books. If they are so vital, instead of relegating them to rhetorical endpapers, ought we not to place them right in the middle of the text, so as to examine their causes and consequences? There has been a welcome development here in American works which do not call an abrupt halt at 1865 and Appomattox, but go on at least as far as 1877 in order to see what happened when the battlesmoke was replaced by the cigar-smoke of lobbies and conference rooms.[13]

Or we might ask whether "watershed" is not a very bad historical metaphor, which, unlike the term "turning point", posits a too fundamental discontinuity between a remoter and a more recent past. Does it not conjure up a picture of events flowing away in radically opposite directions or of some crisis-hump isolating the historical cismontane from the historical transmontane?

Clearly that is not the author's intent in some of the instances quoted. Nor is it the intent of most European historians when they find themselves reaching out

---

[11] Henry F. May, *The End of American Innocence: A Study of the First Years of Our Own Time, 1912-1917* (New York: Knopf, 1959), ix, 303. A similar date, though from a quite different viewpoint, is proposed by Maxwell Geismar, *American Moderns* (New York: Hill & Wang, 1958), 68: "Although literary history doesn't watch the calendar, the year 1919 was a breaking point in American life. It marked the end of an epoch of social reform which had sprung from the populist and progressive movement at the turn of the century. It opened a decade of social anarchy under the mask of 'normalcy' - of pleasure seeking and private gain, of material success and trivial moral values."

[12] Richard Hofstadter, *The Age of Reform: From Bryan to F.D.R.* (New York: Knopf, 1955), 326.

[13] For example, the two-volume text by T. Harry Williams, Richard N. Current, and Frank Freidel, *A History of the United States* (New York: Knopf, 1959).

for this handy cliché, although their own national histories have not been lacking in dramatic and even catastrophic changes of direction. But it *is* the intention of some Americans. When they speak of a watershed or great divide this is what they mean to mean. The assertion is not true, I would suppose, of Mr. Morris' reference to Hamilton's report of 1790. I think he merely wishes to indicate that the report was a remarkable document which had important consequences. I know that when I spoke of the 1830s as a "watershed" I was only trying to indicate a transitional period in American history (and, incidentally, to discover a satisfactory way of concluding my book: the rhetorical endpaper fashion once again).

In the example from Avery Craven the matter is in doubt. He says only that the 1840s were "something of a watershed." Yet in his book he argues that a profound change took place during those years. The "Modern Era" was born and America was never the same again. Bruce Catton is certain of the importance of *his* watershed; and with Henry S. Commager we are, equally, left in no doubt. For him the 1890s form not *a* watershed but "*the* watershed" of American history,[14] and he is at pains to develop the idea of a Great Divide. "On one side" lies the old America: "On the other side lies the modern America." Arthur Schlesinger, Jr. is equally firm in his conviction that the age of Franklin Roosevelt is "*the* great dividing line in the nation's life."[15] For Henry F. May, whose subtitle is *The First Years of Our Own Time*, "our time" is separated by the years 1912-17 from a "completely vanished world." Richard Hofstadter is no less positive in his comments on the later 1930s:

> *The beginning of the war meant that Americans, with terrible finality, had been at last torn from that habitual security in which their domestic life was merely interrupted by crises in the foreign world, and thrust into a situation in which their domestic life is largely determined by the demands of foreign policy and national defense. With this change came the final involvement of the nation in all the realities it had sought to avoid, for now it was not only mechanized and urbanized and bureaucratized but internationalized as well.*[16]

[14] My italics.

[15] My italics.

[16] Hofstadter, 326.

We could make something of the fact that each of these four historians, from Commager to Hofstadter, recommends a different date for the Great Divide. They cannot all be correct, though one of them might be. But I fancy that none would quarrel ferociously with the others over their preferences; and in any case, much of the material in Hofstadter's book deals with the upheavals described by the others. In other words, all of them deal with the twentieth century (if we may stretch our century back as far as 1890), and all insist that fundamental changes separate it and us from the nineteenth century. This is a widely held view, supported by much evidence, including a number of studies of changes in the American character during the past half-century.[17]

One can indeed construct a strong case for the argument that American life began to alter profoundly toward the end of the nineteenth century and that the novelty and collective weight of such change had a more startling effect in the United States than did comparable movements in European life at the same period. Oscar Handlin has suggested that the very notion of the "watershed" (though he does not call it that) dates from this period. Immigration and industrialization combined, he maintains, with a loss of belief in progress and in the American historic mission to introduce a new pessimism into American thought — especially the thought of those Americans of older stock who now felt dispossessed. So they took refuge in nostalgia, in the half-comforting, half-dismaying idea that *their* America had disappeared at some definite moment which Handlin labels the "cut-off point":

> *The depression of 1893 and 1907 had each evoked widespread fears that all American history to that point had come to an end, and that a new era was about to begin. Strikes . . . produced similar predictions. Through much of the thinking about the end of the frontier and through much of the argument about conservation ran the same frightening thoughts. Sometimes . . . these speculations located the cut-off point in the future rather than in the past or present. . . . Stories about the ruin of old civilizations or about the forthcoming end of the world appeared frequently in the popular magazines and on the shelves of the booksellers. . . . [T]heir*

---

[17] Riesman's *The Lonely Crowd* has as its subtitle *A Study of the Changing American Character.* William H. Whyte, *The Organization Man* (New York: Simon & Schuster, 1956), discusses the shift from an "individuated-entrepreneurial" to a "welfare-bureaucratic" society. This formulation is made to serve in works such as Daniel R. Miller and Guy E. Swanson, *The Changing American Parent* (New York: John Wiley, 1959).

central incident was a cataclysm, a violent terminus to the peaceful historical process.[18]

Looking backward, Handlin says, Americans of this period fastened upon a variety of "cut-off points." For some it was the Civil War. Henry Adams, for whom catastrophe was a hobby, picked out the thirteenth century or, within his own lifetime, picked out 1844 (as Avery Craven has done more recently). Writing retrospectively, in the early twentieth century, Adams asserts that in that year 1844

the old universe was thrown into the ash-heap and a new one created. He and his eighteenth century, troglodytic Boston were suddenly cut apart — separated forever — in act if not in sentiment, by the opening of the Boston and Albany Railroad; the appearance of the first Cunard steamers in the bay; and the telegraphic messages which carried from Baltimore to Washington the news that Henry Clay and James K. Polk were nominated for the Presidency. This was in May, 1844; he was six years old; his new world was ready for use, and only fragments of the old met his eyes.[19]

Adams's friend, the Bostonian Henry Cabot Lodge, indulged in similar speculations when he came to write his autobiography. Lodge was born in 1850, twelve years after Adams:

The fact was that the year 1850 stood on the edge of a new time. . . . I have often said . . . that there was a wider difference between the men who fought at Waterloo and those who fought at Gettysburg or Sedan or Mukden than there was between the followers of Leonidas and the soldiers of Napoleon. This is merely one way of stating that the application of steam and electricity to transportation and communication made a greater change in human environment than had occurred since the earliest period of recorded history. The break between the old and the new came some

---

[18] Handlin, *Chance or Destiny*, 206. The shock of mass immigration is stressed in Nathan Glazer, "The Immigrant Groups and American Culture," *Yale Review*, 48 (Spring 1959). Glazer contends (p. 392) that "while the relatively homogeneous American culture of the middle of the nineteenth century was, like all the other national cultures of that period, seriously affected by the rise of modern industry, . . . mass immigration added something additional to the destructive impact. . . . The break between the culture of the 1870s and that of the 1920s was thus greater in the United States than it was in England or France."

[19] Henry Adams, *The Education of Henry Adams* (Boston: Houghton Mifflin, 1918), 5.

time in the thirties, and 1850 was well within the new period. Yet at that date this new period was still very new, . . . and the ideas of the earlier time . . . were still felt, still dominant. The men and women of the elder time with the old feelings and habits were, of course, very numerous, and for the most part were quite unconscious that their world was slipping away from them. Hence the atmosphere of our old stone house, with its lane, its pear-trees, and its garden-nymph, indeed of Boston itself, was still an eighteenth-century atmosphere, if we accept Sir Walter Besant's statement that the eighteenth century ended in 1837.[20]

If America began to change so drastically in the 1890s, and *if* Americans like Adams and Lodge began to project their dismay both backward and forward in time, and *if* the pace of change has continued to accelerate ever since, then there is not much left to say. "Watershed" may be a bad metaphor. But then all metaphors are inexact; and since they are indispensable to historians as well as dangerous, why not choose an abrupt metaphor to signalize abrupt change?

Well, to begin with, not all present-day American historians seem willing to locate *the* watershed in or after the 1890s — and "in or after the 1890s" itself covers a stretch in American history too long to be considered as one era. Some writers, such as Avery Craven and Bruce Catton, would push the date back considerably earlier than the 1890s. Allan Nevins, for instance, reinforces Bruce Catton:

The old Pilgrim chronicler Nathaniel Morton, relating how the founders of Plymouth had taken leave of Europe, committed themselves to a fateful experiment, and by hard labor triumphed over their first trials, concluded that from their last estate they were forever parted: "If they looked behind them, there was a mighty ocean which they had passed, and was now as a main bar or gulph to separate them." When Americans in 1863 looked back a short three years, they saw that they were separated from their former world by a stormy ocean, and that an impassable chasm shut them off from their earlier history.[21]

---

[20] Henry Cabot Lodge, *Early Memories* (New York: Scribner's, 1913), 16.

[21] Allan Nevins, *The War for the Union*, vol. 2: *War Becomes Revolution, 1862-1863* (New York: Scribner's, 1960), 482.

Possibly there may have been not one but several fundamental changes in the history of the United States. But if so, this is an important concession. It suggests that we ought not to enter such ambitious claims for the "watershed" quality of any one particular period or episode. If there have been several breaks, we may wonder whether any of them imposed as dramatic a discontinuity as its historians would maintain.

Again, we may wonder whether Oscar Handlin's comments on the 1890s, illuminating though they are, explain the whole story. It is surely significant that observers like Adams and Lodge, conscious of and disturbed by the movements of their own middle years, nevertheless went back a half-century before the 1890s to find the source of the upheaval. Nor was there any novelty in this sort of puzzled backward glance. Nathaniel Morton used the ocean metaphor because it had a literal application; yet it is equivalent to a "watershed" metaphor. Before long the "jeremiads" or admonitory sermons of colonial New England, with a different emphasis, were in effect depicting some watershed or cut-off point — some cleavage, that is, between an early American innocence and a latter-day depravity.[22] There is an interesting anguish of exaggeration, which goes beyond mere political partisanship, in the indictment of Thomas Jefferson's policies by a pamphleteer of 1808:

> *Everybody will recollect, for it is but a few years since (so rapid has been our progress from infancy to decay) when this country stood on a proud eminence. Its dawn of existence was like that of Hercules, and its maturity promised to be like his. But the poisoned garment, was thrown over her at an early age, and her premature strength has been followed by a premature old age and second childhood.*[23]

This is typical of a mass of assertions, throughout American history, that a wondrous opportunity has been ruined, a golden age has been tarnished, the old ways have disappeared or offer no useful guide to a newer generation. It is not a continuous, undifferentiated cry of woe but an ambiguous affair, half-lament, half-boast, as Martin Chuzzlewit might have discerned:

---

[22] See Perry Miller, *The New England Mind from Colony to Province* (Cambridge: Harvard University Press, 1953), esp. pp. 27-39.

[23] John T. Danvers, *A Picture of a Republican Magistrate of the New School, Being a Full Length Likeness of His Excellency Thomas Jefferson, President of the United States* (New York, 1808), 56.

"You have come to visit our country, Sir, at a season of great commercial depression," said the major.

"At an alarming crisis," said the colonel.

"At a period of unprecedented stagnation," said Mr. Jefferson Brick. "I'm sorry to hear that," returned Martin. "It's not likely to last, I hope?"

Martin knew nothing about America, or he would have known perfectly well that if its individual citizens, to a man, are to be believed, it always is depressed, and always is stagnated, and always is at an alarming crisis, and never was otherwise; though as a body they are ready to make oath upon the Evangelists at any hour of the day or night, that it is the most thriving and prosperous of all countries on the habitable globe.[24]

In other words, there is an almost inherent American tendency to believe that one has been cut off decisively from the past as if by a physical barrier. The tendency has three main elements. First, it is a consequence of the undeniable *fact* of continuous and rapid social change, since the origins of settlement. This process has revealed itself in regrets and neuroses as well as in pride and exuberance. Second, the tendency is rooted in the constant American determination to repudiate Europe — Europe equated with the Past, in contrast with America as the Future — and so to lose the Past altogether. Third, the tendency is a consequence of the American sense of a society which is uniquely free to choose its own destiny. This sense of mission, of dedication and of infinite possibility, in part a fact and in part an article of faith, has led to acute if temporary despairs, to suspicions of betrayal and the like, as well as to more positive and flamboyant results.

It may be objected that the wistful vision of a golden age is not an American monopoly. Eden and Arcadia were ancient inventions. Nearly six hundred years ago in his poem *The Former Age*, Chaucer sighed for the dear dead days before mankind began to worry and scheme and amass wealth:

> *A blisful lyf, a paisible and a swete*
> *Ledden the peples in the former age.*

And in *Gulliver's Travels*, Dean Swift harks back to a vanished England of sturdy yeomen: an England which has given way to the evils of sophistication. Nostalgia — a mild emotional indigestion which comes from the attempt to eat one's cake

---

[24] Charles Dickens, *Martin Chuzzlewit* (1843-44; reprint, London: Macmillan, 1954), 259.

and have it too — was as noticeable in eighteenth- and nineteenth-century Europe as in America. Someone has remarked that Englishmen in the Railway Era became fond of novels in which the fastest form of transport is a stagecoach. And the disquiet which Oscar Handlin notes in the America of the 1890s had similar manifestations in contemporary England: a yearning for the romantic past, together with an outcrop of novels about a future war, with pessimistic titles such as *When All Men Starve*.[25] Here too, continuous and rapid social change, though less evident than in the United States, encouraged an interest in watersheds.

But the American repudiation of Europe and the American sense of mission helped to differentiate the American version of watersheds and golden ages from those of Europe. For instance, the American golden age is not distant in time or place. It is tantalizingly near at hand. The pamphleteer of 1808 could feel that he had either just been in it or that — if only the Republicans could be swept from office — it might yet be created in the immediate future. There might still be an antidote for the poisoned garment. Later generations of his countrymen could react similarly. All these elements account for an apparent paradox: that American history, though in actuality it has had a surprising degree of continuity when compared with most European nations, has nonetheless been accompanied by a surprisingly prevalent American *belief in national discontinuity*; whereas these European nations have been able to combine actual discontinuity — revolutions, new constitutions, broken regimes, renamed streets and squares — with a *belief in their own national continuity*. True, they have sometimes accomplished this through a sort of national amnesia, like the Germans in relation to their Nazi interlude. But this is a different matter from the American feeling of isolation from the past.

If these opinions are valid, then it can be argued that American historians (and sociologists) along with the rest of their countrymen exaggerate the cataclysmic nature of the crises in American history. Obviously, their motives vary. Historians try to portray their subjects as emphatically as possible. So a crisis or controversy becomes by degrees *the* crisis, *the* controversy, *the* watershed in American history. The temptation is all the greater when the protagonists of whom the historian writes are themselves convinced that they are involved in an unprecedented and tremendous drama: the drama of choices that *is* a genuine feature of American history. There is, too, the undeniable fact of fantastic

---

[25] Charles Gleig, *When All Men Starve* (London: John Lane, The Bodley Head, 1898). (See the essay in this volume on "America's Imaginary Wars.")

change in both the internal and external aspects of America. The historian may be led to contend that change *is* American history, just as the sociologist may be led to conclude that nothing has remained the same. I suspect that no other nation has produced so many books about itself with the word *New* somewhere in the title, and with good reason. But not with entire justification. Much alters: some things do remain the same or transform themselves quite slowly.[26]

It should be said that recent historians like Arthur Schlesinger, Henry May and Richard Hofstadter are not talking in simple terms of a lost golden age, of a past regrettably shut off. For them "the end of innocence" is the beginning not of *depravity* but of *responsibility*. Schlesinger speaks of Franklin Roosevelt as "the great dividing line . . . between innocence and responsibility." Hofstadter deals in *The Age of Reform* with this very fallacy of a pristine, bygone America:

> *we may well sympathize with the Populists and with those who shared their need to believe that somewhere in the American past there was a golden age whose life was far better than our own. But actually to live in that world, actually to enjoy its cherished promise and its imagined innocence, is no longer within our power.*[27]

These are sophisticated historians. Even so, they may be yielding too readily to the old American habit of asserting that yesterday is shut off from today.

But if change is not quite the whole of American history, the problem of measuring and interpreting it is a major task for historians of America. To use clumsy metaphors of watersheds and turning-points is to miss out a great deal. If we must use analogies, they should be more precise — like, for example, the axiom in the physical sciences that quantitative change produces qualitative change by degrees: the steady addition of one calorie at a time to a liquid will eventually turn it into a gas. Another way of putting this is to say that change is a constant feature of Western society generally and of American society in particular. The change generates all kinds of responses: nostalgia, alarm, pride and so on. The nostalgia and alarm are possibly greater today than ever before in American history. But they are not entirely novel. The historian can best

---

[26] See, for example, Richard C. Wade, *The Urban Frontier: The Rise of Western Cities, 1790-1830* (Cambridge: Harvard University Press, 1959), 306-13, which suggests that some of the problems of urbanization that we regard as recent were already troubling cities like Pittsburgh, Cincinnati and St. Louis more than a century ago. The sprawl of suburbs, the loss of the sense of community, the growth of summer and weekend retreats: these are apparently ancient aspects of American life.

[27] Hofstadter, 326. And see Robert Allen Skotheim, "'Innocence' and 'Beyond Innocence' in Recent American Scholarship," *American Quarterly* 13 (Spring 1961): 93-99.

know that he understands American attitudes, instead of merely typifying them, by analyzing aspects of change in the nation's evolution. Indeed, some of the best recent work in American history has been along such lines. Richard Hofstadter's idea of the "status revolution" and its effect upon respectable citizens at the end of the nineteenth century is one instance.[28] A similar thesis has been employed by David Donald to explain the motives of the generation of abolitionists that came to maturity during the 1830s:

> *Social and economic leadership was being transferred from the country to the city, from the farmer to the manufacturer, from the preacher to the corporation attorney. Too distinguished a family, too gentle an education, too nice a morality were handicaps in a bustling world of business. They were an elite without function, a displaced class in American society.*[29]

This explanation has been criticized; and indeed it does not seem to fit the 1830s as convincingly as the 1890s. There is a danger that such theses may be rashly applied, once they are in fashion. "Status revolutions" may need to be rationed as carefully as "watersheds": otherwise they may form a continuous procession in American history. Yet would that not in a way be a correct statement of American social evolution? To explore the shifting balances of American society and the stratagems of which those who feel dispossessed avail themselves is to discover a whole field of historical interpretation.

Henry Nash Smith, Marvin Meyers, John W. Ward and other scholars have, by related but somewhat different routes, provided us with valuable ways of reinterpreting American experience.[30] Older interpretations tended to be organized round large polarities: America *versus* Europe, West *versus* East, industrialism *versus* agrarianism and so on. Recent scholarship admits the existence of these polarities and may even suggest as Leo Marx does, that "the dialectical tendency of mind — the habit of seeing life as a collision of radically opposed forces and values — has been accentuated by certain special conditions

---

[28] Hofstadter, *The Age of Reform*, chapter 4: "The Status Revolution and Progressive Leaders."

[29] David Donald, "Toward a Reconsideration of Abolitionists," in David Donald, ed., *Lincoln Reconsidered* (New York: Knopf, 1956), 33-34.

[30] See, for example, Henry Nash Smith, *Virgin Land* (Cambridge, Mass.: Harvard University Press, 1950); Marvin Meyers, *The Jacksonian Persuasion* (Stanford, Calif.: Stanford University Press, 1957); John W. Ward, *Andrew Jackson: Symbol for an Age* (New York: Oxford University Press, 1955).

of experience in America."[31] But Smith, Marx and the rest do not visualize these collisions primarily between opposed groups of men, but rather as contradictory ideals and desires held simultaneously and uneasily within the mind of the single individual. Very broadly, these opposed aspirations represent the tug between past and future: between primitivism and progress, wilderness and settlement, simplicity and multiplicity, "Arcadia" and "Enterprise."[32] To assume that the polarity is, so to speak, *internalized*, a dilemma in the individual minds of men as diverse as Andrew Jackson and Henry Adams, is to see American history in a new light. It is to understand more clearly what Longfellow may have been thinking about, in this final example, which illustrates both the idea of the watershed and the American uncertainty as to which side one would prefer to inhabit. Longfellow's poem, "The Two Rivers," begins:

> *Midnight! the outpost of advancing day!*
> *The frontier town and citadel of night!*
> *The watershed of Time, from which the streams*
> *Of Yesterday and To-morrow take their way,*
> *One to the land of promise and light*
> *One to the land of darkness and of dreams!*

The final stanza declares:

> *It is the mystery of the unknown*
> *That fascinates us; we are children still,*
> *Wayward and wistful; with one hand we cling*
> *To the familiar things we call our own,*
> *And with the other, resolute of will,*
> *Grope in the dark for what the day will bring.*[33]

---

[31] Leo Marx, "Two Kingdoms of Force," *The Massachusetts Review*, 1 (October 1959): 84. Marx maintains that "the contrast between the two cardinal images of value, the machine and the native landscape," dramatizes "the great issue of our culture."

[32] The "Arcadia-Enterprise" ambivalence of some Jacksonians — for instance — is made explicit in William N. Chambers, *Old Bullion Benton* (Boston: Little, Brown, 1956); and in Charles G. Sellers, Jr., *James K. Polk, Jacksonian, 1795-1843* (Princeton: Princeton University Press, 1957). It is studied, for a later period, in David W. Noble, *The Paradox of Progressive Thought* (Minneapolis: University of Minnesota Press, 1958); and see Louis Hartz, *The Liberal Tradition in America* (New York: Harcourt Brace, 1955).

[33] Henry Wadsworth Longfellow, *Poetical Works* (Boston: Houghton Mifflin, 1886), 3: 213-15.

This essay appeared in *American Quarterly* 13 (Winter 1961): 480-493.

While the watershed metaphor may be less used than formerly, examples can still be found in 1990. The 1890s, more precisely 1893, receive another vote in William Merrill Decker, *The Literary Vocation of Henry Adams* (Chapel Hill, University of North Carolina Press, 1990), 33-34. Decker sees the World's Columbian Exposition as "a watershed in the country's historical self-consciousness." On the other hand, consider this submission from a review by Michael E. Parrish of Bruce Allen Murphy's *Fortas: The Rise and Ruin of a Supreme Court Justice* (1988) in *American Historical Review* 95 (February 1990): 291-92:

> *Few years in the history of the United States have a greater claim to the designation "watershed" than does 1968. During this twelve-month period, the tide turned decisively against the U.S. effort in Vietnam, Lyndon Johnson was driven from the presidential race, assassins murdered Martin Luther King, Jr., and Robert Kennedy, the Democratic party imploded in Chicago, and Richard Nixon captured the White House. It was also the year in which Yale University first admitted women undergraduates, Jackie Kennedy became Jackie Onassis, student rebels occupied Columbia, the North Koreans seized the U.S.S. Pueblo, and the Beatles produced* Magical Mystery Tour.

Cosmic events? The review continues: "It was, depending on one's point of view, the year the music stopped, the final act of Camelot, the death of liberalism, the twilight of empire, the triumph of conservatism." And, of course, the year when the Senate refused to confirm Abe Fortas as chief justice of the Supreme Court.

On the idea of a drastic break in the American continuum, as believed in by historians, David W. Noble has explored this in work reaching back to his *Historians Against History: The Frontier Thesis and the National Covenant Against History* (Minneapolis: University of Minnesota Press, 1965).

20

America's Imaginary Wars

This is a revised version of an essay, first printed in a Belgian collection, on a topic that has interested me for years. There are comments on counterfactual history, a related aspect, in my essay, "What If?" *American Heritage* (December 1982): 16-23; and see the bibliographic essay for further titles.

Under the head of IMAGINARY WARS, the catalogues of antiquarian booksellers used to list all kinds of publications from preposterous to plausible, complacent to grim, linked by one common element. They all dealt with fictitious or hypothetical wars, usually set in their own near future. This literature of imaginary wars is immense, as we can discover from I. F. Clarke's valuable survey, *Voices Prophesying War* (1966). His first example, dating back to 1763, is a patriotic English fantasy, *The Reign of George VI, 1900-1925*, about a twentieth-century warrior king who would emerge victorious over the rest of Europe. Clarke's closing chapter discusses Orwell's *1984* and various pieces of science fiction relating to global or even cosmic conflicts. Many more have been produced since his book came out.

However, I. F. Clarke regards the effective modern phase of the genre as starting in 1871 with *The Battle of Dorking: Reminiscences of a Volunteer*. Originally printed in *Blackwood's Magazine*, it purported to look back half a century from the England of the 1920s to the disasters brought about by a German cross-channel invasion. *The Battle of Dorking*, cheaply reprinted as a paperback pamphlet, became a best-seller; and it was imitated by scores of writers in Britain, France and other countries. *The Battle of Dorking* was the work

of a colonel of the Royal Engineers, George Tomkyns Chesney. The fictional
form proved much more vividly readable than the usual tract advocating military
reform in a dry military prose. But Chesney's service background made his tale
sound authentic in detail and in atmosphere; there was nothing sentimental in his
description of battle casualties, in which the blood and suffering are candidly
avowed.

There were additional reasons for the success of Chesney's formula. Though
his own tone was professionally unemotional, the notion of a war could be used
to appeal to nationalism's various fears and appetites. *The Siege of London*, by
"J. W. M." (1871), a breezy riposte to Chesney, ridiculed the "crass ignorance and
impertinent presumption" supposedly characteristic of the newly unified German
nation. French scenarios often envisaged a war of victorious revenge against the
forces of Imperial Germany, after the humiliating defeat suffered in the Franco-
Prussian War of 1870-71. Some among the multitude of fictionalists argued for
a better training of civilian soldiers — militia or volunteers. Some took the
contrary tack, insisting that the regulars or standing army were the essential core.
Some sought to convert the public to a concern for particular weapons or
branches of the service. Navies had their voluble advocates. There was intense
speculation on the effect of new technology: armored vessels, submarines,
smokeless ammunition, high explosives, airships. The use of railroads for rapid
mobilization and movement of troops engrossed the attention of certain theorists.
In less palpably military contexts, there were tales of worldwide racial conflict; of
mad or masterful individuals imposing neo-Napoleonic rule with the aid of sundry
ultimate weapons; and of doom threatened by anarchist and socialist subversion,
or by a weakening of the moral fibre of a population given over to luxurious
materialism. The corruption and cowardice of political leaders were popular
topics.

Among all these imaginers, none surpassed the English author H. G. Wells.
Perhaps only the Frenchman Jules Verne rivaled him in making mechanical
marvels appear not simply believable but almost inevitable. The best of Wells,
though, as revealed in *The War of the Worlds* (1898) and *The War in the Air*
(1908), was truly imaginative instead of being merely fanciful. Technologically
inventive, adept at humanizing the catastrophic and the unprecedented, and a
lively stylist, Wells was also capable of making his narrative suggest profounder
issues. There is a Wellsian irony in the dénouement of *War of the Worlds*: the
Martian invaders, apparently invincible, crush all human opposition only to
succumb to the insignificant bacteria of our planet. Wells was almost alone too
in portraying a future major conflict (*The War in the Air*) as protracted,

unstoppable and shapeless. Other tales assumed that the next great war would be determined swiftly and irrevocably by one big battle.

Hundreds of less gifted stories were turned out in the years between 1871 and the actual outbreak of the Great War in 1914. In England there were the melodramatic yarns of George Griffith, such as *Olga Romanoff* (a glamorous international villainess) and *The Outlaws of the Air* (more international terrorists), both published in 1895. There was *The Great War of 189-* (1894) by Rear-Admiral Colomb and others, an ingenious patchwork of communiqués and journalists' reports. There were novels stressing the importance of war at sea (W. Laird Clowes, *The Captain of the "Mary Rose,"* 1892; Fred Jane, *Blake of the "Rattlesnake,"* 1895). There were slick concoctions, by William Le Queux or Louis Tracy (*The Great War in England; The Final War; The Invaders*), sometimes serialized daily to boost the circulation of Britain's recently created mass newspapers. In France there was the trilogy of Emile Driant (*La Guerre de Demain*, 1889-93), son-in-law of the ambitious General Boulanger, written under the pseudonym of "Danrit". From Germany came similar publications, including several predictive fantasies by the military historian Karl Bleibtreu.

Where does the United States figure in this huge hotchpotch? The striking feature is that, at least before 1914, the scenarios were nearly all devised by Europeans and confined to the recognized Great Powers of the era, plus their satellites and their empires. The scene is dominated by Britain, France, Russia, Germany, Austria-Hungary, with minor attention paid to Spain, Italy and Turkey. The majority of plots turn upon alliances, or the lack thereof, and warfare waged between the principal nations (excluding the United States). In W. F. Butler's *The Invasion of England* (1882), as in Chesney's *Battle of Dorking*, the main struggle is between Britain and Germany. In Clowes's *Captain of the "Mary Rose"* England is at war with France. Le Queux's *Great War in England* envisages a Franco-Russian onslaught. Charles Gleig's *When All Men Starve* (1898) has Britain defeated by the triple alliance of France, Russia and Germany. Colomb's *Great War of 189-* pits France and Russia against England and Germany.

Until the 1890's the United States plays a negligible part in these international grapplings — a peripheral status quite in accord, of course, with America's actual hemispheric preoccupation and her lack of a large army or navy. In *The Battle of Dorking*, the Americans are mentioned twice in passing, as a people indifferent to Britain's troubles except to profit by annexing Canada and the West Indies after the mother country has collapsed. A somewhat different tone prevails in British novels around the end of the century. Le Queux's and Louis Tracy's potboilers take for granted a highly benevolent American neutrality.

"Throughout this war," Tracy says in *The Invaders* (1901), "the United States had given their unstinted sympathy to Great Britain, and had poured into the country illimitable supplies of food, guns, and ammunition. Congress declined to pay any heed to statutes which defined the duties of neutral states. At a single word from England, the navy and troops of the great power beyond the Atlantic would have been placed at her disposal. But British pride forbade."

Nor were American authors immediately prompted to imitate the *Battle of Dorking*. Until the late 1880s, imaginary wars were quite rare in American literature. The twenty-year timelag is an interesting reminder of the relative isolation of the United States. And when the flow of war fantasies did begin, its first products departed appreciably from the standard European formulae. Mark Twain's *A Connecticut Yankee in King Arthur's Court* (1889) does arguably embody a sort of imaginary war, "The Battle of the Sand Belt," in which a tiny force led by the protagonist Hank Morgan wipes out 25,000 knights by means of electrocution, drowning, and a "deluge of fire" from a battery of Gatling guns. But Twain is not concerned with the military rivalries of the modern world, even though its technology fascinates him; his battle takes place in a mediaeval never-never-land. Wars occur in a few contemporary American fantasies, including a couple by the Populist writer Ignatius Donnelly (*Caesar's Column*, 1890; *The Golden Bottle*, 1892), and also *Philip Dru, Administrator* (1912; the anonymous work of Colonel Edward M. House, soon to be a close associate of Woodrow Wilson), envisioning an altruistic strong man at the head of government. However, combat is not the principal theme of these tales.

Some betray considerable uneasiness as to the social strains of late-19th century America. *The Fall of the Great Republic* (1885), written under the pseudonym "Sir Henry Standish Coverdale" and presumably the work of a conservative Bostonian, purports to describe the fate of America in 1886-88 at the hands of mainly Irish revolutionaries — socialists, anarchists, communists, "dynamiters." The belligerent chaos they induce leads to a hopelessly one-sided war with England and other European powers, which culminates in a crushing American defeat (by chance, on the old battlefield of Gettysburg) and subsequent occupation by the victors. In fantasies such as these, the strife is in a sense a civil war. Perhaps that is not surprising, since the American Civil War was still a living memory.

We pass to another phase with *The Great War Syndicate* (1889), by the American humorist Frank R. Stockton. War is the central subject of his story — a war with Great Britain, in which his own country is spectacularly successful, beating the world's foremost naval power at her own game. The contest is over in a few months. Stockton's novel is amiably optimistic; no-one is killed in combat on either side. Yet it is not exactly a burlesque. Stockton conceived of a peculiarly American solution to the problems of modern warfare. The Syndicate in his story is a group of American tycoons, who combine patriotism with financial shrewdness. They persuade the federal government to let the Syndicate run the entire war. The American army and navy, weak and ill-prepared, are not to be used, save for a last-ditch emergency. The Syndicate guarantees "to effect a satisfactory peace within one year," depositing with the U.S. Treasury an "immense sum," to be forfeited if the Syndicate's contract is not fulfilled. The Syndicate, on the other hand, stands to make additional bonus profits by winning in under a year. Faced with this offer, the authorities in Washington gladly yield the floor to the genius of private enterprise. In European fictions of the era, nongovernmental figures are portrayed as mavericks, pirates, or revolutionaries. Stockton shows an almost superstitious American faith in the energy and ingenuity of the new entrepreneurial breed. *Captains* of industry? Generals, rather, or field-marshals.

His idealized businessmen, acting with extraordinary speed, develop a pair of secret weapons that are both devastating and humanitarian. The first is the "crab," a monitor-like armored vessel, equipped with a pair of giant underwater claws, designed to rip away the screws and rudders of British warships. The second weapon, mounted on ordinary merchant ships (hired for the duration, with civilian crews), is the "instantaneous motor-bomb," fired from a special cannon. This projectile, a sort of lucky guess at the atom-bomb, minus radiation, can cause total destruction over a considerable area, as well as sending up a vast "spherical cloud."

Employing the devices, the Syndicate's flotillas disable enemy fleets, and demonstrate the awesome effects of the motor-bomb on areas that have been cleared of people. After a few such experiences the British realize the Americans are invincible and make peace. The United States, magnanimously anglophile, forms an alliance, with both nations sharing the secret of the motor-bomb and thereby able to confer a *pax anglo-americana* upon mankind. The account ends on a mellow note, with just a tinge of admonition:

> *The United States had been obliged to pay an immense sum on account of the contract with the War Syndicate, but this was considered money so well spent, and so much less than an ordinary war would have cost, that only the most violent anti-Administration journals ever alluded to it.*
>
> *Reduction of military and naval forces, and gradual disarmament was now the policy of the allied nations. . . . Now there would be no more mere*

exhibitions of the powers of the instantaneous motor-bomb. Hereafter, if
battles must be fought, they would be battles of annihilation.

This is the history of the Great Syndicate War. Whether or not the
Anglo-American Syndicate was ever called upon to make war is not to be
stated here. But certain it is that after the formation of this Syndicate all
the nations of the world began to teach English in their schools, and the
Spirit of Civilization raised her head with a confident smile.

In the years following *A Connecticut Yankee* and *The Great War Syndicate*, Europeans continued their near-monopoly of major-war scenarios. Or Americans, concerned at their own military and naval weakness, accepted the European estimate of which nations counted and which were peripheral. Henry G. Donnelly, under the pen-name "Stochastic" (meaning "Conjectural"), wrote a 16-page pamphlet *The Stricken Nation* (1890), with cover-illustrations of a battle-scarred Boston and New York, describing the humiliatingly swift defeat of the United States in a war with Great Britain. Britain annexes the United States and so owns all of North America.

But as the United States began at last to construct a great-power navy, and to show increasing interest in overseas empire, a shift occurred. One sign was the publication of Alfred Thayer Mahan's war college lectures, *The Influence of Sea Power upon History* (1890). True, their initial impact was greater in Europe than in America. Kaiser Wilhelm II announced that copies of Mahan's writings had been placed aboard every ship in the Imperial German Navy; and in 1893 the Admiral received honorary degrees from Oxford and from Cambridge Universities. Nevertheless, Mahan's reputation burgeoned at home, too, keeping pace with new-found American military activism. His ideas accorded closely with those of Theodore Roosevelt and Henry Cabot Lodge. An imagined instance of the changing climate appeared in *Harper's New Monthly Magazine* (April 1894): "A Battle-Ship in Action," by S. A. Staunton, an American naval officer. Staunton's carefully documented fiction describes a single-ship action between the U.S.S. *Farragut* and a similar warship of an unnamed enemy. The story ends with the *Farragut* about to ram the disabled foe. This is the conclusion too of a British magazine-piece that Staunton may have known: "In A Conning Tower; or, How I Took H.M.S. 'Majestic' into Action," by H. O. Arnold-Foster (first published in *Murray's Magazine*, April 1891). The eighth edition (1898) of Arnold-Foster's realistic narrative referred to the lessons of the recent naval encounters between the Chinese and Japanese and to the Spanish-American War.

The naval victories of that war, indeed, resembled fiction in their astonishing one-sidedness. Expressions of belligerent patriotism were beginning to be heard in the United States pretty much as in Europe. One example, cited by the historian James C. Malin, is the bellicosity of Eugene F. Ware, "unofficial poet laureate of Kansas," who in the years 1885-98 kept telling schoolboys and others: "Sooner or later the United States will have another war. I hope we have it soon. We need it; there is an occasion . . . for a war and we ought to open it." The first "occasion" was the 1895 Venezuelan crisis with Great Britain. One of Ware's supporters, a Kansas newspaper editor, boasted that "we never failed to whip Johnny Bull. . . . Uncle Sam's latest battleship is the greatest ever launched. . . . No English vessel can touch her" — a martial ardor shared with Roosevelt and Lodge.

Indeed, an obscure little anonymous novel, *The Great Anglo-American War of 1900* (1896), published in London but probably by an American, described a conflict in which the United States is led by a suddenly emergent military genius. He undertakes in a manner reminiscent of Stockton to repel British invaders within six months. The Americans themselves invade England, occupy London, liberate Ireland, and annex Canada, "and the Bahamas and Bermuda, which were also a menace to the United States."

Despite such signs of convergence, American forecasts of future conflict remained somewhat different from those of Europe. The white nations in both continents betrayed uneasiness over the threat to their dominance offered by non-white peoples. In a few of the European fictions, the Great Powers suspended their fight and made common cause in order to suppress wholesale native risings in Africa. The mauling received by a "white" nation in the Russo-Japanese war (1904-5) was greeted with alarm in Europe and North America and a degree of euphoria elsewhere.

The American response was to produce worried, almost obsessive scenarios of danger from the "Yellow Peril." Homer Lea, a brilliant crank of a strategist, attached himself to the Chinese during a spectacular though brief military career, attaining the rank of general under Sun Yat-sen, despite the apparently hopeless handicap of a deformed spine. Lea's version of the Yellow Peril, in *The Valor of Ignorance* (1909), a war-gaming prediction complete with charts of enemy landings on the Pacific coast, was aimed at Japan. Lea also projected a Japanese invasion of the Philippines. The climax of *The Valor of Ignorance* comes with Japan holding the Western states, whose mountain ranges then form a natural fortress against attempts by the Americans at a counteroffensive. Thwarted in these futile operations, the forces of the Union hatch "rebellions, class and sectional insurrections, until this heterogeneous Republic . . . shall disintegrate."

In the year of Lea's death, 1912, he issued another pessimistic survey, *The Day of the Anglo-Saxon*. His warnings anticipated *The Great Pacific War* (1925), by the British naval analyst Hector C. Bywater, whose subtitle was *A History of the American-Japanese Campaign of 1931-33*. Bywater allowed the Americans to win, though only after a desperate struggle.

In one bizarre piece of Yellow Peril literature of the same era, the Americans also emerge on the right side, militarily, this time against China. "The Unparalleled Invasion" (1914) is a short story by Jack London, whose hectic imagination could dwell almost lovingly upon violence and disaster. London foretells a world of the 1970s in which the population of China has grown with the "certainty and terrifying slow momentum of a glacier." The surplus spills over into adjacent countries, overrunning them without actual military conquest. An American professor "employed in the laboratories of the Health Office of New York City" comes up with an idea he presents to the U.S. president. The president, convinced of the soundness of the scheme, persuades all the white nations to join forces. Their fleets and armies ring China in a silent blockade. For a while they remain motionless. Then one day in 1976 allied aircraft appear over every city and town. Instead of bombs they drop small glass tubes containing concentrated doses of deadly diseases. Within a few weeks practically everyone in China is dead. The blockading units are unaffected, having been immunized. China is cordoned off for a few years. The country is then repopulated, not in zones as Germany had proposed but "heterogeneously, according to the democratic American program. It was a vast and happy intermingling of nationalities that settled down in China in 1982 and the years that followed — a tremendous and successful experiment in cross-fertilization," London remarks with horrific insouciance.

He does, however, add an ominous postscript. By 1987, London notes, the "Great Truce" between the white nations has dissolved. There is the threat of another Franco-German war. On the brink of the new conflict the nations convene and pledge "never to use against one another the laboratory methods of warfare they employed in the invasion of China." Given London's assumption of Nordic superiority, the reader is presumably meant to believe that the pledge will be honored. Still, a "frightfully virulent" hybrid plague-germ may be evolving.

Anxieties over the future balance of power in the Pacific thus encouraged the development of one especially American type of war scenario. Characteristic of the entire genre in the years before 1914 is the blend of confidence and catastrophism; of pride in and dread of technology; of chauvinism and racism with better-world internationalism. Utopia was just around the corner: so was doom. The actual and the hypothetical were intermingled, as in the "factoid" writings of the late twentieth century. When conflict became professionalized, the new war colleges of the world built up fanciful yet circumstantial dossiers of possible wars with other powers. One scenario in the German military archives analysed how many ocean liners would be needed to mount an invasion of the United States. No doubt the military planners read Jules Verne and H.G. Wells for recreation — and yet for something more.

With the outbreak of the Great War in the summer of 1914, the combination of reality and fantasy in American thinking was suddenly intensified. The United States had to confront an actual situation in which Germany and the Central Powers were pitted against France, Russia and the British Empire. Prewar American disquiet over German militarism, hitherto mild, was vastly stimulated by the Kaiser's invasion of a would-be neutral Belgium; the efficiency of his war-machine, surging forward on two fronts; and the skill of Franco-British propaganda in depicting their enemy as barbarous "Huns" who raped nuns and skewered babies on their bayonets.

There was fierce controversy inside the United States. American individuals, including Jane Addams, had supported the world pacifist movement of the pre-1914 era symbolized by the establishment of the Nobel Peace Prize in 1901. Among ordinary American citizens there was a widespread opposition to involvement in modern war. The humorous magazine *Life* devoted a whole issue (vol. 62, 2 October 1913) to cartoons and prose passages on the futility of war in solving conflict. This spirit, building on old suspicions of Europe, was strong in 1914 and after. Was neutrality the best policy? Did it mean impartiality or aiding the Allies short of American involvement? What was the nation's stake in a European struggle that seemed more and more a world war? Those who wished the United States to act boldly — not necessarily by joining the fight — developed a fresh set of scripts: war-preparedness literature.

Not all of this was cast as fiction. Articles by Howard D. Wheeler in *Harper's Weekly*, published in book form as *Are We Ready?* (1915), presented factual reports on the inadequate numbers, training and equipment of America's armed forces. On the opposite side was an angrily ironic statement by a socialist author, Allan L. Benson. His *Inviting War to America* (1916) was advertised as "the complete Baedeker to the land of the three Ps: Patriotism, Preparedness and Profit. . . . It is convincing proof that the invitation to bloodshed and bankruptcy is not in the interest of national defence but of profits for economic parasites." Hudson Maxim, brother of the armaments inventor Hiram Maxim, was in agreement with Wheeler, not Benson — an alignment suggested by the epigraph of his *Defenseless America* (1915): "The quick-firing gun is the greatest life-saving instrument ever invented."

Nevertheless fictional theorizing figured in much of the debate. Maxim's book became the basis of a Vitagraph motion-picture, *The Battle Cry of Peace*. The English-born producer of the film, J. Stuart Blackton, claims that he mentioned the idea for it to Theodore Roosevelt, who arranged for him to meet Admiral Dewey, Elihu Root and other important people, who talked of war-preparedness. "Get every word of that in your picture," said Roosevelt. "Drive it home to the peace-at-any-price creatures!" A motion-picture sequel, originally to be called *The Battle Cry of War* and again featuring an invasion of the United States, was renamed *Womanhood, the Glory of a Nation* for its March 1917 premiere. Roosevelt and his rival President Woodrow Wilson both made screen appearances in it. Blackton became an American citizen.

Allan Benson complained that "these moving picture plays" were propagandist and fictitious "frauds". In a movie, said Benson, it was as easy to show George Washington burning an orphan asylum as to show him crossing the Delaware: "The story the war 'movie' tells is as simple as it is horrible. During the great war in Europe," America pays no attention to 'preparedness' warnings. "A little later, New York is under bombardment, the skyscrapers come tumbling down, Washington is captured and the United States is compelled to buy peace at the price of an enormous indemnity."

Sure enough, Wheeler's *Are We Ready?* inserts a couple of chapters that envisage an invasion of New England by an unnamed enemy. The invaders smash American resistance at the "Battle of Connecticut River." A War Department communiqué admits the "hopelessness of further attempting to defend New York." One of the book's illustrations — "Madison Square, New York, After an Aerial Raid" — depicts a disaster already vividly recounted in Wells's *War in the Air*.

In J. Bernard Walker's *America Fallen!* (1915) Germany is supposed to have lost the war in Europe. The Kaiser, since his fleet is intact, decides to recoup his losses across the Atlantic. The German invasion is a stunning success. New York, Boston and Washington are seized with whirlwind efficiency. Warning of the descent on the nation's capital by a corps of "5,000 picked bicycle troops" is brought by a "modern Paul Revere," an intrepid though wounded newspaperman on a motor-bike:

> The routine of work . . . at the central telephone exchange [in Washington D.C.]. . . was suddenly broken at 3.30 a.m., April 1st, when . . . a man. . . crawled into the room, dragging after him a broken leg that left a smear of blood. . . . Propping himself . . ., he shouted in a burst of staccato sentences: "The Germans are coming — landed at Annapolis — here in

half hour — warn members of Cabinet escape United States — tell garage
send taxis each house — quick, quick, for the love of our country — the
President first, then the —" And with a groan he crumpled up and lay as
though dead before the gaping night force.

And a similar tale is told in J. W. Muller's *The Invasion of America: A Fact Story Based on the Inexorable Mathematics of War* (1916) — the fate of "a brave Nation, a greatly capable Nation, made to grovel for her life because, in a world of men, she had failed to prepare for what men might do."

The invaders of course never did set foot in the United States during the real 1914-18 war: it was the Americans who crossed the Atlantic, heading for Europe. Nor did the Japanese grab California in the next great war, though they did attack Pearl Harbor and seize the Philippines — onslaughts whose improbable audacity seemed to belong to the realm of the merely imagined. The scenarios of fiction can cast an eerie spell. Their future keeps being reached by our today (*1984!*), as in a nightmare from which (in more fortunate lands) we escape by waking into reality. Or we feel reprieved from catastrophe for the time being.

Perhaps the heyday of imaginary-war writing ended in 1918. After that most of its functions were taken over by science fiction, the more brilliant examples of which prodigiously extended the scale and scope of the old genre. Philip K. Dick's *The Man in the High Castle* (1962) hypothesized a United States defeated in World War II, its West coast a Japanese occupation zone and its East under German rule. *Wolfbane* (1959), by Frederick Pohl and C. M. Kornbluth, pictured humans as the slaves of an invasion by highly sophisticated machines.

There is a good case for admitting many such tales to the category of imaginary-war fiction. After all, some of them owe much to H. G. Wells, whose *War of the Worlds* was adapted with such extraordinary effect by Orson Welles in 1938 for his Mercury Theater of the Air program, dramatizing an invasion from Mars. Colonel House's *Philip Dru, Administrator*, or for that matter Stockton's *Great War Syndicate*, could have provided inspiration for John S. Martin's fantasy *General Manpower* (1938), about a private corporation that supplies workers and soldiers on worldwide contract and could eventually fight wars for the United States on the same cost-effective mercenary terms.

Again, just as newspapers and magazines had launched many of the pre-1914 war-fantasies, so in the aftermath of World War II *Collier's Magazine* devoted two remarkable special issues to imagined conflicts: "Hiroshima, U.S.A." (1950) on the annihilation of Manhattan by an atom bomb, and "Preview of the War We

Do Not Want" (1951) on World War III between Russia and a victorious United States.

Whatever the tone and technique of these supposings, however, they differed in one essential feature from the *Battle of Dorking* approach. In the old tales the Americans were either marginal or missing altogether. Since the 1930s (for better or worse) every scenario has the United States in the thick of things.

BIBLIOGRAPHICAL ESSAY

Particularly relevant work for this essay includes: I. F. Clarke, *Voices Prophesying War* (Oxford: Oxford University Press, 1966); Richard Gerber, *Utopian Fantasy: A Study of English Utopian Fiction Since the End of the Nineteenth Century* (London: Routledge & Kegan Paul, 1955); John Patrick Finnegan, *Against the Specter of a Dragon: The Campaign for American Military Preparedness, 1914-1917* (Westport, C.T.: Greenwood Press, 1974); Kenneth M. Roemer, *The Obsolete Necessity: America in Utopian Writings, 1888-1900* (Kent, Ohio: Kent State University Press, 1976); Volker R. Berghahn, *Militarism: The History of an International Debate, 1861-1979* (New York: St. Martin's Press, 1982), esp. chapter 1; and Neil Harris, "Utopian Fiction and Its Discontents," in *Uprooted Americans: Essays to Honor Oscar Handlin*, ed. Richard L. Bushman et al. (Boston: Little, Brown, 1979), 209-44. H. Bruce Franklin and David Ketterer have made imaginative scholarly studies of future-directed fiction. Counterfactual or "uchronic" history (also referred to as "allohistory") is ingeniously hypothesized in Daniel Snowman, ed., *If I Had Been . . . Ten Historical Fantasies* (Totowa, N.J.: Rowman & Littlefield, 1979); Nelson W. Polsby, ed., *What If? Explorations in Social-Science Fiction* (Lexington, Mass. and Battleboro, Vt.: Lewis Publishing, 1982); and *Alternative Histories: Eleven Stories of the World as it Might Have Been*, ed. Charles G. Waugh and Martin H. Greenberg (New York and London: Garland, 1986), which has an admirably comprehensive bibliography, compiled by Barton C. Hacker and Gordon B. Chamberlain. American wargaming is examined in J.A.S. Grenville, "Diplomacy and War Plans in the United States, 1890-1917," in *The War Plans of the Great Powers, 1880-1914*, ed. Paul M. Kennedy (London: Allen & Unwin, 1979), 23-38; and in an essay on German-U.S. naval planning in the same volume, 39-74, by H. H. Herwig and D. F. Trask. The material on J. Stuart Blackton and *The Battle Cry of Peace* is drawn from *The*

Big V: A History of the Vitagraph Company, by Anthony Slide with Alan Gevinson (new ed., Metuchen, N.J.: Scarecrow Press, 1987), 72-81.

This essay appeared in Gilbert Debusscher, ed., *American Literature in Belgium* (Amsterdam, Rodopi, 1988), 251-260.

21

European Anti-Americanism

In a slightly different form, this was given as a lecture in an Amsterdam symposium, held under the auspices of the lively and resourceful Netherlands American Studies Association. Rob Kroes of Amsterdam's Free University has brought out a flow of annual volumes edited from conference papers. The theme of anti-Americanism crops up in previous essays of mine. Though they do not show any big shift in attitude, I think I have become more skeptical over the years about the supposed depth and wrongness of the phenomenon.

There is much talk of "anti-Americanism" in the twentieth century world. Yet, as with a number of other terms in common use, it resists precise definition. David Strauss, author of *Menace in the West* (1978), a study of French anti-Americanism focusing on the period 1917-32, says that anti-Americanism has in recent years denoted "sharp criticism of American policies, frequently resulting in violent demonstrations against the symbols of American power abroad." In older and broader usages, anti-Americanism might refer to "a philosophy, ideology, or institutional framework based on assumptions and principles which ran counter to the Americanist position": that is, to the "values, practices, and institutions which had their origin in the United States and were far more permanent than official policies."[1] For Strauss, then, anti-Americanism may

---

[1] David Strauss, *Menace in the West: The Rise of French Anti-Americanism in Modern Times* (Westport, Conn.: Greenwood Press, 1978), 6.

signify opposition to American military and governmental activities, symbolised for example by nuclear missile-bases or by the acronym CIA; or it may be an older phenomenon, expressed as a dislike of American culture and its "Coca-Colonizing" spread.

A project headed by a French scholar (Claude Fohlen) and a German (Willi Paul Adams) began to take shape in the early 1980s. This, under the auspices of the European University Institute in Florence, envisaged a volume of essays on various aspects of European anti-Americanism. At a 1984 conference organised by the Institute, with several nations represented, it was suggested that the subject fell chronologically into four periods, each with its characteristic forms of anti-American behaviour and sentiment. These were: 1893-1917, 1917-1941, 1945-1964, and 1964-1984.

One participant at the EUI conference, the French historian Raoul Girardet, discussed *cultural* anti-Americanism (the theme of David Strauss's book). For Girardet such anti-Americanism was analogous to anti-semitism in being irrational, bigoted and generally reprehensible. Anti-Americanism could thus be defined as the *anti-semitism of the European intellectual*. Girardet could have taken this formulation from the French philosopher André Glucksmann. In a February 1984 interview Glucksmann said of the comparison between the two "antis":

> *The reproaches are the same. Einstein, Freud, Rothschild. The words are just different. They're everywhere. They're behind everything [i.e., in "anti" demonology, the Jews/Americans become universal scapegoats]. . . . You can add an additional crime now. In much of the antinuclear logic, the armed citizen becomes a criminal. The poor guy who wants to defend himself is no good. The American, the Jew in Israel, he will fight. He's a dangerous man.*[2]

The Girardet-Glucksmann analogy has in fact an older history. In 1962 I took part in a BBC radio symposium on "Anti-American Attitudes," in company with the novelist Kingsley Amis, the political scientist Denis Brogan, the Labour M.P.

---

[2] John Vincur, "Europe's Intellectuals and American Power", *New York Times Magazine*, April 29, 1984, 74. A further conference of European anti-Americanism was held at the EUI in 1985. Their work resulted in the publication of some interesting papers under the auspices of the European University Institute. On recent German assessments, see Kurt Sontheimer, "How Real Is German Anti-Americanism?"; and Frank Trommler, "The Rise and Fall of Americanism in Germany," in Frank Trommler and Joseph McVeigh, eds., *America and the Germans: An Assessment of a Three-Hundred Year History*, 2 vols. (Philadelphia: University of Pennsylvania Press, 1985) vol. 2, *The Relationship in the Twentieth Century*.

Anthony Crosland, the Conservative journalist Peregrine Worsthorne, and the anthropologist Geoffrey Gorer. Our chairman was the historian Constantine Fitzgibbon. In preliminary correspondence (January 1962), Fitzgibbon conjectured that "the main conclusion of this programme" could be that " anti-Americanism is a manifestation of stupidity-cum-envy, similar to anti-Semitism, and that most of the intelligent people in [Britain] are as immune to it as they were to the other, racial rubbish."[3]

His prediction was pretty much borne out by the tone of the panelists. We were in broad agreement that anti-Americanism, at least in its cruder forms, grew out of "prejudice," "ignorance," "resentment" and the like. Anthony Crosland, for instance, regretted the "unreasonable" belief of "many people on the Left" that the United States was "the arch-capitalist country dominated by a power elite." Such people, he said, being anti-capitalist, were therefore "inevitably anti-American." Crosland dissociated himself from such attitudes:

> *Personally, I think that this picture of America is terribly exaggerated. I do not think America is run in this crude way by a capitalist power elite, and in any case this element in America is balanced by other factors that should be attractive to a person on the Left, among them . . . that America is — at any rate compared with Britain — a relatively classless, and in some ways a very much more democratic country.*

Worsthorne, at the other end of the political spectrum, offered not dissimilar opinions. Even if conventional, older members of the British upper classes disapproved of the United States, "more and more young Tories," according to Worsthorne, "feel that the plutocratic, free-for-all American system has much more to offer than the rather inhibited, frustrated system that remains in this country."[4]

Whether such observations were representative or analytically adequate is hard to say. A few journalists and ordinary citizens who wrote to the BBC tended to complain both that we had been unduly pro-American *and* unduly critical. Someone living in Oxford described the broadcast as a "diatribe." "Isn't there," he asked, "a strong bond between our scholars and those in the U.S.A. . . .? We

---

[3] Letter from Constantine FitzGibbon to Marcus Cunliffe, January 15, 1962. This radio programme was printed in *The Listener*, somewhat abridged, April 19, 1962, 667-71. Some extracts were reprinted in the *New York Times Magazine*, July 22, 1962, with a few relevant cartoons from British sources.

[4] Crosland in *The Listener*, 668-69; Worsthorne, 670.

never hear from them such adverse criticism as we heard [from the panel]."
Another letter in the same issue of *The Listener* (the BBC's magazine) denounced
the symposium for its limited and biased approach:

> *In order to redress the balance, could we in the near future have a*
> *programme . . . with contributions from a communist, a pacifist, a socialist*
> *(not another pink Labour-ite please), an anarchist, a C.N.D. [Committee*
> *for Nuclear Disarmament] speaker . . . and perhaps someone who has*
> *taken an active part in the fight against the racial segregation in the U.S.A.?*

A third correspondent, describing himself as "a British socialist," wondered why
the symposium had not recognised that

> *a lot of the criticism of the United States and its Government did not*
> *originate from America itself . . . I always turn to American sources when*
> *I wish to indict American capitalism. Professor Wright Mills, in his Power*
> *Elite, shows that the economic system, with its giant monopolies, remains*
> *basically the same as ever, Professor D.F. Fleming and J.P. Morray in their*
> *books, . . . The Cold War and From Yalta to Disarmament, . . . argue, in*
> *my opinion convincingly, that America is as much responsible for world*
> *tension as the Russian Government, if not more so.*

"Starbuck," a pseudonymous columnist in the weekly London *Spectator*,
defended the broadcast against the letter-writers. "It is clear," he said, "that there
remain many whose anti-Americanism has now the full force of a faith, and who
react to any challenge much as the [1860] British Association for the
Advancement of Science, at which Bishop Wilberforce made an *ad hominem*
attack upon T. H. Huxley for espousing Darwin's newly published theory of
natural selection." In other words, for the *Spectator* the "anti-American" letter-
writers, though ignorant "Lefties" rather than intellectuals, were in truth guilty of
prejudice akin to anti-semitism.[5]

I confess to an almost dreamlike fascination with these old clippings from 1962.
I had almost forgotten being involved in this discussion, yet its details seem
archetypally familiar. The sensation of *déjà vu*, or *déjà lu*, is heightened by other
yellowing items in the file. Thus, a North-Country columnist expressed in his

---

[5] Correspondence in *The Listener*, April 26, 1962, 735, 737; and see further letters in The *Listener*'s
next issue, May 3, 1962. "Starbuck's" column appeared in the *Spectator*, May 4, 1962.

newspaper a general dissatisfaction with the smug assumptions of the broadcast. "No attempt," he insisted, "was made to investigate or analyse American economic penetration of the United Kingdom. According to a new book by Francis Williams [*The American Invasion*, 1962], there is now well over 1,000-million pound sterling worth of American capital invested in Britain, most of it in the growth and consumer industries. Older industries . . . are ignored by Wall Street. Surely facts like this have a bearing on anti-Americanism? . . . Nor did anybody [on the program] make very much of the U.S. forces stationed here. This was odd, since chalking 'Go home, Yank' on walls used to be the great delight of the anti-American fringe."[6]

Most of us probably had read Williams's book, though without being impressed by its contention that the British economy had been seized and held in ransom like some innocent heiress abducted by evildoers. Reviewers complained that Williams's facts were wrong or misinterpreted or that his was a superficial restatement of old European apprehensions as to "Americanization." There was indeed a considerable literature bearing on these matters, from W. T. Stead's *The Americanization of the World* (1901) and Albert Houtin's *L'Américanisme* (1904) to such works as William Clark, *Less than Kin: A Study of Anglo-American Relations* (1958) and Cyrille Arnavon, *L'Américanisme et Nous* (1958). The postwar years had spawned innumerable discussions of the American role in the modern world. One example was *Le Nouveau Monde et l'Europe* (1954), the transcript of a conference conducted in Geneva by Lucien Febvre and others and published in Brussels — old and new centres of international palaver.[7]

My ancient "Anti-Americanism" file contained too a light-hearted exercise conducted by the American humorist Art Buchwald, then a columnist for the *Paris Herald-Tribune*. In August 1957 he placed the following advertisement in the London *Times* personal column:

> *Would like to hear from people who dislike Americans and their reasons why. Please write Box R 543.*

---

[6] *Oldham* (Lancashire) *Evening Chronicle*, April 17, 1962.

[7] Francis Williams was interviewed in the London *Sunday Times*, Colour Section, April 8, 1962, in a special section, "How American Are We?" His book was not warmly reviewed: see, for instance, Iain Hamilton, "Some of Our Best Friends," *Spectator*, April 13, 1962, 481-82. For a broad discussion, see Melvin J. Lasky, "America and Europe: Transatlantic Images," and Marcus Cunliffe, "European Images of America," in Arthur M. Schlesinger, Jr., and Morton White, eds., *Paths of American Thought* (Boston: Houghton Mifflin, 1963), 465-514.

The next week brought him over a hundred replies. Most came from British citizens, although one annoyed American woman wrote: "Obviously you have some grudge against Americans. . . . If you are one of these half-baked Englishmen, then your grudge most probably is that the Americans get along better with the English girls and you are left with leftovers. So much for your stupid advert, you squirming little Englishman." An English woman correspondent disliked American men "because of their loud, raucous voices and because of their adolescent, sex-conscious minds. Five minutes in an American's room — a complete stranger — and he will want you to sit on his knee."

Other letters dwelt upon American insularity, naïveté, and chauvinism of the "how-much-is-that-in-*real*-money?" variety. An Irishman declared: "It is not of very much importance who an Englishman likes or dislikes in this world today. . . . For, thank goodness, the sands are running out. If you would like to know, however, why they dislike Americans I shall be only too pleased to provide an accurate assessment of their attitude. The theme word would be JEALOUSY." Summing up this range of responses, Buchwald concluded that

> *If Americans would stop spending money, talking loudly in public places, telling the British who won the war, adopt a pro-colonial policy, back future British expeditions to Suez [a reference to the Anglo-French descent upon the Suez Canal in 1956], stop taking oil out of the Middle East, stop chewing gum, . . . move their air bases out of England, settle the desegregation problem in the South, . . . put the American woman in her proper place, and not export Rock'n'Roll, and speak correct English, the tension between the two countries might ease and the British and the Americans would like each other again.*[8]

What are we to make of such charges and counter-charges? Even confining discussion for the moment to a single European country, Britain, it would appear that anti-Americanism is frequently invoked but rarely employed as a central category in dispassionate discussions. One example, almost contemporary with the BBC symposium, is *Community and Contention: Britain and America in the Twentieth Century* (1963), by the American political scientist Bruce M. Russett, which grew out of a Yale Ph.D. dissertation directed by Karl W. Deutsch. In seeking "to develop a body of theory . . . for analysing factors in the relations

---

[8] Art Buchwald, "Why They Dislike Americans," two articles, *Paris Herald-Tribune*, August 19 and 20, 1957.

between two countries," Russett makes only three passing references to the term, noting that "one must be extremely careful to specify the content of the attitudes in question when using broad labels like 'anti-American'." He adopts instead the more clinical typology developed by Karl Deutsch and others in order to measure degrees of integration among North Atlantic nations. Britain and the United States in such a conception have achieved a "pluralistic security-community" in which disagreements are resolved without violence because of the relatively high degree of socio-economico-political assumptions held in common.[9]

Without necessarily resorting to behavioral-science language, we do need to be particular in talking about anti-Americanism. One basic point is that anti-Americanism is, like anti-semitism, a highly pejorative label. It is an accusation levelled at other people, not an attribute people claim for themselves. Those who make critical statements about the United States tend to insist (cf. "some of my best friends are Jews") that "some of my best friends are Americans." Francis Williams began his book with a characteristic disavowal: "Because this book is concerned with the extent of the American invasion, I hope no one will make the mistake of thinking it anti-American. Sir Harold Nicolson once remarked that Americans are sometimes easy to dislike but always difficult not to love. My love affair with them is of long duration." The exception to this rule can be found in certain Left-wing pronouncements. In these, as Anthony Crosland remarked, the United States tends to be synonymous with "imperialism" and "capitalism." Examples can be found in a special issue of *Arena* (1951), a minor British Communist magazine, devoted to the theme of "The U.S.A. Threat to British Culture." E. P. Thompson, writing about "imperialist Babbit-itis" [*sic*], recounted a conversation with an American professor of literature. The professor supposedly confessed that his career had taken the wrong turn. Instead of teaching Shakespeare, he ought to have gone into business selling refrigerated meat in the Middle East: "Boy, I could have set up a *chain of slaughterhouses* throughout the Holy Land! My God, I could have *cleaned up*!" Thompson continued:

> *I did not make this story up, and the Professor was not pulling my leg. The 'American Dream' really is as childish and as debased as this and its*

---

[9] Bruce M. Russett, *Community and Contention: Britain and America in the Twentieth Century* (Cambridge, Mass.: M.I.T. Press, 1963), 213n.7. On the notion of a special relationship between Great Britain and the United States, see D. Cameron Watt, *Succeeding John Bull: America in Britain's Place* (Cambridge: Cambridge University Press, 1984); and the long review, suggesting that Watt's analysis is in effect anti-American, by H. C. Allen, "A Special Relationship," *Journal of American Studies* 19 (December 1985): 403-13.

poison can be found in every field of American life. Those who have never been to the United States and who fool themselves . . . that Hollywood, the Hearst Press and the comics, represent only a lunatic fringe of the American bourgeoisie, sometimes suggest that Babbit [sic] is an out-of-date joke on the 'twenties: unfortunately it only foreshadows the horror of to-day. In the last two or three years the dream of my Professor has acquired for me a terrible significance — and has revealed itself in a more terrible actuality for the peasants of Korea and the people of a threatened world.

In the same issue of *Arena*, Montague Slater expressed his alarm at the destruction of British indigenous culture by debased and commercialised American products —"giving up music," for example "and putting in its place jazz (and then calling it a strong working class tradition). And with this goes a loss of the taste for the wine of the country, the discovery that English writing and English beer, or Scottish writing and export ale, are insipid compared with coca-cola and Dashniell Hamnett [sic]."[10]

A second obvious yet crucial point is that reactions to the United States from other nations vary considerably according to class and political alignment. In the case of Britain, as Sir Denis Brogan contended, "anti-American" sentiment has historically been much stronger among the professional and privileged classes than among workers: many of the latter had friends and relatives who emigrated to North America or themselves crossed the Atlantic to work for a while in the United States. Broadly speaking — a claim documented by the English labor historian Henry Pelling — during most of the first century of American independence, the British left regarded the United States as "the best poor man's country," while the Right (as typified by a spokesman like Sir Lepel Griffin) was often patronising if not downright hostile. With the twentieth century, however, these positions tended to be reversed — the Right admiring American political, economic and military power while the Left perceived American strength as monopolistic, oligarchic, hegemonic, etc.[11]

A third observation prompted by a glance through my old file is that, when any debate as to "anti-Americanism" is engaged, responses are conditioned and

[10] E. P. Thompson in *Arena: A Magazine of Modern Literature* 2, new series (June-July 1951): 25; Montague Slater, 37. The reference to Sinclair Lewis's novel *Babbitt* may hark back to a rather dismissive older account, *The Babbitt Warren*, by the English pundit C.E.M. Joad. In Slater's contribution, "Hamnett" should, of course, be Dashiell Hammett.

[11] Henry Pelling, *America and the British Left: Bright to Bevan* (London: Black, 1956).

perhaps even determined by estimates of who is speaking. Buchwald's *American* correspondents assumed, whether wearily or indignantly, that his advertisement must have been placed by someone British. His British respondents took for granted they were dealing with a fellow-countryman: why would an American lay himself open to what are, in this context revealingly, called "home truths"? Having made that assessment, British readers then apparently divided sharply between confessions of "dislike" (not, *n.b.*, of "anti-Americanism") and between rebukes to the unknown advertiser for inciting "anti-Americanism." Such divergences match the experiences of all of us. Thus, we are apt to resent criticism of our own society voiced by an outsider that we would deem legitimate, even possibly valid, from the mouth of an insider. In such matters most of us are more chauvinistic that we care to recognise.

A fourth consideration is that, as the comments on the old BBC symposium indicate, much of the material cited by foreigners said to be "anti-American" comes from or could come from American sources. A *Listener* letter alludes to C. Wright Mills's *The Power Elite* (1956). Other much-cited American books of the same era include David Riesman et al., *The Lonely Crowd* (1950); Sloan Wilson, *The Man in the Gray Flannel Suit* (1954); William H. Whyte, Jr., *The Organization Man* (1956); and Vance Packard, *The Hidden Persuaders* (1957), *The Status Seekers* (1959), and *The Waste Makers* (1960): variants on the theme of American conformism that had annoyed James Fenimore Cooper in the 1830s, Sinclair Lewis in the 1920s, and the expatriate Henry Miller whose return to the United States of the 1940s prompted him to call it *The Air-Conditioned Nightmare* (1945). Apart from the authors already mentioned, seemingly harsh criticisms of the United States could be culled from citizen-authors as various as Ralph Waldo Emerson, Henry David Thoreau, James Russell Lowell, Walt Whitman, Mark Twain, Edward Bellamy, Jack London, E. E. Cummings, John Dos Passos, Arthur Miller, and Tennessee Williams — and these would be cast into insignificance by some of the stories and commentaries on their native land produced by Americans during the past quarter-century. The tally is longer and angrier than comparable literature from elsewhere: leaving out of account, that is, propagandist statements about the United States from countries within the sphere of influence of the Soviet Union. The exalted disgust of, say, Alan Ginsberg's *Howl and Other Poems* (1956) far transcends the disparagement detected by touchy citizens of the United States in European assessments like Geoffrey Gorer's *The Americans: A Study in National Character* (1948), the product of seven years of first-hand observation and of close association with the American anthropologist Margaret Mead; or like Simone de Beauvoir's more impressionistic travelogue, *L'Amérique au jour le jour* (*America Day by Day*, 1953). If Oscar Wilde pictured America as "one vast expectoration" and Sigmund Freud called it "a gigantic mistake," such apparent hostility has, as Gert Raeithel notes, nothing over the view of H. L. Mencken, whose fellow-countrymen constituted "the most timorous, sniveling, poltroonish, ignominious mob of serfs and goosesteppers ever gathered under one flag in Christendom since the end of the Middle Ages." Thomas Carlyle's "fifteen million bores" are topped by Mencken's "Commonwealth of third-rate men," peopled not by "the hardy adventurers of legend, but simply by incompetents who could not get on at home."[12]

At Sussex University in the late 1960s, red paint was thrown over a press attaché from the American Embassy invited to the campus for a "teach-in" on U.S. involvement in Vietnam. A few years later, on the same British campus, the American political scientist Samuel P. Huntington, also an invited guest, was denied a hearing by students who associated him with war crimes in Vietnam. These episodes were widely reported and condemned as examples of radical hooliganism. Far less remarked was the fact that on both occasions the leaders were American graduate students — in the latter case inspired by the anti-war essays of Professor Noam Chomsky of the Massachusetts Institute of Technology. One of the principal figures in West Germany's "Green Party" of the 1980s happens to be half-American.

In such circumstances, whether their setting is at home or abroad, Americans feel an entitlement to criticise they often deny to foreigners. Or they have a compensatory sense of full understanding that they are apt to believe eludes outsiders (or long-time American expatriates). Nathaniel Hawthorne, talking with the American sculptor Hiram Powers in Florence in 1858, believed that Powers's "long absence from our country has made him think worse of us than we deserve; and it is an effect of which I myself am sensible, in my shorter exile, — the most piercing shriek, the wildest yell, and all the ugly sounds of popular turmoil, inseparable from the life of a republic, being a million times more audible than the peaceful hum of prosperity and content, which is going on all the

[12] George Steiner, a European of exceptionally cosmopolitan experience, could be regarded as a citizen of both continents or at least an expert on both. Consider his extended essay, "The Archives of Eden," in a special issue of the quarterly *Salmagundi* 50-51 (Fall 1980-Winter 1981) devoted to "Art and Intellect in America." Steiner's onslaught, if that is what it was, brought a number of ripostes in the same issue of *Salmagundi* and in the succeeding one. See especially, for an illuminating German comment, the letter by Gert Raiethel in *Salmagundi* 52-53 (Spring-Summer 1981): 241-44; and his book *Citronen für Onkel Sam: Europäer schelten Amerikaner* (Munich, 1975).

while."[13] Here Hawthorne's argument, like that of other Americans, almost implies a claim to a special exemption from negative comment. As a democratic republic and therefore equipped with a free press, the United States will necessarily (according to this viewpoint) reveal itself *unlikeably*. Yet the display *is itself to be liked* for its candor and freshness. Carried to extremes such reasoning can lead to the notion that only Americans can properly appreciate their own society or that foreigners suffer from ignorance and prejudice if they do venture to comment unfavorably on the United States — even if they cite American material in so doing.

The books on America most praised for "insight," "truthfulness" and the like are in the main admiring rather than dispassionate. No critical foreign account has ever been accorded classic status by Americans. But if certain interpretations are thought to suffer from America-*phobia*, could other assessments be perceived as marred by America-*philia*? We speak of "fellow-travellers": people with a sentimental and gullible commitment to left-wing causes. Could those foreigners who deplore "anti-Americanism," and strive to suppress any manifestations in even their own work, risk falling into the opposite error of undue "pro-Americanism" — becoming fellow-travellers or fellow-travelling-salesmen for the United States? The question is at least worth raising.

There have been ill-informed, unfriendly and even malevolent foreign criticisms of the United States. To lump all such comments under the general rubric of "anti-American" is, however, to miss the refinements in the situation. "Anti-Americanism" may be reciprocal to American xenophobia or to expressions of American "spread-eagle" patriotism that presuppose the fundamental inferiority and foreordained decline of other nations, especially those of "Old-World" Europe. Many American literary histories dwell upon the disdainful treatment of the new nation's aspiring authors during the early nineteenth century by British journals like the *Edinburgh Review* and *Quarterly Review*. They rarely point out that some of these articles were composed during or just after the War of 1812: that is, when the two nations were in armed conflict — a war precipitated by Congress. Sydney Smith has often been reproached for asking (*Edinburgh Review*, January 1820): "In the four quarters of the globe, who reads an American book?" To the extent that Smith's article was unduly critical, he may (it has been suggested) have been stimulated to derision by a famous announcement by the House of Representatives that the United States was as a

---

[13] Entry from June 4, 1858, in Nathaniel Hawthorne, *The French and Italian Notebooks*, ed. Thomas Woodson (Columbus, Ohio: Ohio State University Press, 1980), 280. Hawthorne himself had been in Europe, initially as U.S. consul to Liverpool, since 1853.

nation, "the freest and most enlightened in the world." The temptation to respond to such *braggadocio* may have been irresistible for foreign humorists of the Smith variety.[14] American journalists and politicians were almost routinely dismissive of Old World vice and folly. In the case of Britain, "twisting the lion's tail" was a standard American vote-catching device, aimed at the Irish and other anglophobe groups. We read that the London *Punch* cruelly caricatured President Lincoln during the American Civil War. Leaving aside the point that Lincoln was jeered at by many American publications of the same period, it is salutary to look at American portrayals of European monarchs and statesmen of the same era. The staid *Harper's Monthly* of the 1870s dubbed the Prince of Wales "Champagne Charlie" and urged the British to get rid not only of him but of his mother Queen Victoria. There were of course good republican grounds for speaking out in this way; but retaliatory assaults on transatlantic mores have frequently been called unfair, indeed "anti-American."

How much validity is there, then, in the comparison of anti-Americanism with anti-semitism, given the deep irrationality and dire consequences of the latter? The comparison strikes me as far-fetched, especially for the post-1945 epoch. To accept the parallel is to be coerced into believing that *any* criticism of the United States is evil and unfounded. Then what is an acceptable and workable definition of the key term "anti-Americanism"?

Confining discussion to the American and European continents, it is evident that the relation of "New World" to "Old World" is intricate and stretches back several centuries. Antonello Gerbi and Edmundo O'Gorman are among the scholars who have revealed the shock experienced by inhabitants of the Old World when the discovery of the American hemisphere destroyed their cosmology. The origins and significance of the new, fourth continent (Australasia, the fifth, remained unknown for nearly another three hundred years) were matters for prolonged debate. By degrees a New World-Old World polarity was established; and as the United States became the dominant hemispheric power, all the attributes of North *and* South America gradually became associated with that one country. In the America-Europe polarity, one version (understandably popular with Americans) allotted to the New World the desirable features (the "smiling aspects" in the phrase of the American writer William Dean Howells), such as prosperity, benevolence, innocence, providential protection, and to the

---

[14] See A. Owen Aldridge, *Early American Literature: A Comparative Approach* (Princeton: Princeton University Press, 1982), 187-88; and the discussion in Marcus Cunliffe, "'They will *All* Speak English': Some Cultural Consequences of Independence," in Ronald Hoffman and Peter J. Albert, eds., *Peace and the Peacemakers: The Treaty of 1783* (Charlottesville: University of Virginia Press, 1986), esp. pp. 140-46.

Old World all the undesirable elements such as poverty, malevolence, depravity, and ultimate doom. Or the terms could be reversed, so that America (the continent, *and* its concentrated essence, the United States) could be seen as having become rotten before it was ripe: to Sigmund Freud an "anti-Paradise" or "a mistake, a gigantic mistake." The duality has fascinated numbers of American artists and intellectuals, causing them to oscillate between proudly hopeful visions and despairing diatribes. And some Europeans have historically been "pro-American," *philiacs* eager to extol their dream country and to go and live there. Other *phobiac* foreigners have equated the United States with everything strident, superficial, mechanized, and destructive in the modern world. Both enthusers and nay-sayers (abetted, to repeat, by abundant pronouncements from American sources) resort to an exaggerated vocabulary of praise and blame. The Americans have by hemispheric inheritance come in for a good deal of eulogy. Perhaps they ought to accept some catcalls, not as "anti-American" of a calculated sort, but rather as (so to speak) the flip side of the American Destiny one hears so much about.[15]

There are other ways of perceiving the American place in the world. Several British observers, aware of the recently departed glories of their own empire, are prepared to believe that there is such a thing as "anti-Americanism": a force of unthinking, uncharitable hostility aimed at the United States by much of the rest of the world. But instead of lamenting this anger and pleading for its removal, they take it for granted. Malcolm Muggeridge regards it as the unavoidable fate of "top dog" nations (Spain, France, England, America in centennial sequences, to refer only to quite recent history). Top dog nations, wielding power on a gigantic scale, attract to themselves a comparably sizeable jealousy and disapproval: "megaloxenophobia" in Geoffrey Gorer's coinage. Not so long ago, Continental Europe made fun of the arrogant, insular British, filling up hotels and first-class compartments along every approved tourist route. The *Maximes* of the French author Chamfort relate an anecdote of an English "milord" who unwittingly killed a serving-boy at an inn by kicking him downstairs, and then brushed aside the distraught landlord with: "The boy? *Put him on the bill.*" In

[15] Antonello Gerbi, *La disputa del Nuovo Mondo: storia di un polemica, 1750-1900* (Milan, 1955); trans. Jeremy Moyle as *The Dispute of the New World* (Pittsburgh: University of Pittsburgh Press, 1973); Edmundo O'Gorman, *The Invention of America* (Bloomington: Indiana University Press, 1961). See also Cushing Strout, *The American Image of the Old World* (New York: Harper & Row, 1963); J. Martin Evans, *America: The View from Europe* (New York and London: Norton, 1979); Hugh Honour, *The New Golden Land: European Images of America from the Discoveries to the Present Time* (New York: Pantheon, 1976); William Clark, *Less Than Kin: A Study of Anglo-American Relations* (Boston: Houghton Mifflin, 1958); and W. R. Brock, "The Image of England and American Nationalism," *Journal of American Studies* 5 (December 1971): 225-45.

such fables the English are crassly sure that their currency, the pound sterling, is indeed of sterling quality. Their American supplanters, as we have noted, reputedly hold the same faith ("how much is that in *real* money?") in the "almighty dollar."

Such antagonism, often expressed in cultural terms rather than those of military or financial overlordship, has sometimes been expressed as a broadly "Latin" distaste for the uncouthness of "Anglo-Saxon" peoples. For the French, *le monde anglo-saxon* tends to include Britain as well as the United States. Although Stendhal thought the strictures on the United States in Mrs. Trollope's *Domestic Manners of the Americans* (1832) were justified, he believed that it was a case of the pot calling the kettle black: Mrs. Trollope was every whit as bigoted and vulgar as the people she castigated. Neither country understood the fine arts of civilised life. Displaced industrially and imperially by the United States, Europe as a whole has, according to the French journalist André Visson, fallen victim to the "Athenian complex" — seeing itself, that is, as the older and finer culture ousted by the crude new "Roman" one. A similar polarity has been invoked by Latin-American writers, for whom the nation to the north is a bully and a barbarian, a "Caliban" confronting a graceful Hispanic "Ariel." To the extent that these are reactions of top-dogness, then, we might agree with Malcolm Muggeridge that they are ancient and normal mechanisms — ways in which parent cultures (say, China vis-à-vis Japan) console themselves for the apparently greater success of younger offshoots and transpose into cultural language disdain for their brash, unthinking conquerors.[16]

In this wide context, European anti-Americanism comes to look much less puzzling or pernicious. We have, to recapitulate, argued that *U.S.* "anti-Americanism" may be the most eloquent and passionate variety; that unfriendly foreign reactions may represent responses to expressions of *U.S.* xenophobia; and that all powerful societies incur the dislike of less powerful associates. A further crucial point is that certain American attitudes and policies may not be in the best *interests* of Europe (viewing foreign relations as a fairly hard-headed matter, in which all nations including the United States naturally put their own interests foremost). Or, on a somewhat higher plane, such American insistence may strike Europeans as *inherently* wrong or unsound. There is a fascinatingly relevant

[16] Stendahl's remarks occurred in correspondence with his friend Victor Jacquemont, a French naturalist who had visited the United States in 1827. See Marcus Cunliffe, "Frances Trollope," in Marc Pachter, ed., *Abroad in America: Visitors to the New Nation, 1776-1914* (Washington, D.C.: National Portrait Gallery, 1976), 42. The Ariel-Caliban comparison was developed by the Uruguayan author José Enrique Rodó in his *Ariel* (1900): see *History of Latin American Civilization: Sources and Interpretations*, Lewis Hanke, ed., *The Modern Age* (Boston: Little Brown, 1967), 2: 301-69.

editorial, "America and the Ritual 'But'" in the *Guardian Weekly* (February 16, 1986). The *Weekly*, produced in conjunction with *Le Monde* and with the *Washington Post*, is international rather than parochial in scope. The editorial observes that British politicians and businessmen invariably preface remarks with "I'm not anti-American." Then increasingly, comes the "But" — "But," for instance, "America is stripping Europe of its independent manufacturing capacity" and "America is fundamentally expansionist" — in weaponry as in economic activity. The writer himself protests that Europeans are in fact not anti-American:

> *By and large, we like Americans. We imbibe their culture day by day. . . .*
> *We swoon over their passing pop stars. How can one be against so much*
> *of this, for this is the life we know and embrace? Yet the political America*
> *we see in action is stronger, less comforting. It often seems to us to have*
> *bizarre fixations. Discuss Nicaragua (or Manila, or Haiti) for 20 seconds*
> *with a man from the Pentagon to see the point. America thinks differently.*
> *It behaves differently.*

The editorial displays an uneasy balance; Europe itself is "schizophrenic" and Americans are not unanimous about their own programs ("It was interesting to see former President Jimmy Carter, passing through London the other day, openly questioning the whole basis of Ronald Reagan's concept of superpower relations and pouring scorn on the bottomless pit that is Star Wars"). To supporters of President Reagan the piece is characteristically "Leftish" and antagonistic to the American way. Yet the writer does strive to use reason instead of rhetoric. The years since 1945 are divided into three phases: "First, the years of reconstruction — and Marshall aid — after the war. Second, . . . the emergence of Europe as a powerful industrial force in its own right — a competitor for America, with all the strains . . . that brings in train. And now the feeling across so much of the continent that the single giant engine of the American economy is beginning to win the battle against a bevy of nation states, too small to compete alone, too bemused to unite properly."

Given such complexities, loose talk of "anti-Americanism" serves little purpose. Is there then *anything* in word or deed that deserves to be dubbed "anti-American" in being inveterately prejudiced? Yes, as an emanation from propaganda machines within the Soviet bloc, in which anything American tends to be caricatured as evil, plutocratic, genocidal — the type of assertion confronted by Arnold Beichman in his *Nine Lies About America* (1972). There is a *cultural* disdain for some aspects of American life, sometimes cranky and ill-informed: the "Greek complex" operating among Europeans, with perhaps particular acerbity in past years among the French. Yet American popular culture is far more widely accepted in Europe than a generation ago. And if there are critics of American conduct there are also strong defenders of the United States, including the philosopher André Glucksmann cited at the beginning of this essay.

To conclude, anti-Americanism is sometimes a perfectly normal manifestation of dislike for *otherness*. Human groups tend to be suspicious of other human groups. Secondly, so-called anti-Americanism is sometimes a justifiable if not irrefutable complaint against some element or other of Americanness. One example is the homicide rate in the United States, especially through the use of handguns, which is much higher than among European nations. Third, there may be a type of arrant prejudice that will hear no good of the United States. That *can* be dubbed "anti-American." But is it not a mirror-image of the crasser sorts of anti-Communist talk voiced by some Americans? And where anti-Americanism is sweepingly vituperative, does it not parody itself and thereby cancel out its intended message?

———————————

This essay appeared as, "The Anatomy of Anti-Americanism," in Rob Kroes and Maarten van Rossem, eds., *Anti-Americanism in Europe* (Amsterdam: Free University Press, 1986), 20-36.

Works by Marcus Cunliffe

The following list is based on the files and collections of Marcus Cunliffe. To the best of our knowledge it is complete with the exception of unsigned reviews, reviews of fewer than two hundred words, and reviews lacking sufficient publication information. Periodical entries are identified by date and, where possible from available sources, by page number as well. Within each category works are listed in alphabetical order by title.

BOOKS AND PAMPHLETS

The Age of Expansion, 1848-1917 (London: Weidenfeld & Nicolson; History of the Western World Series, gen. ed. J. M. Roberts, 1974).

The Ages of Man: From Sav-age to Sew-age (New York, American Heritage Press, 1971).

Chattel Slavery and Wage Slavery: The Anglo-American Context, 1830-1860 (Athens: University of Georgia Press, Lamar Lectures, 1979).

The Doubled Images of Lincoln and Washington (Gettysburg, Pa.: Gettysburg College, Fortenbaugh Lecture, 1988).

George Washington and the Making of a Nation (New York: American Heritage Junior Library, 1966).

George Washington: Man and Monument (revised edn., 1982; Boston: Little, Brown & Mentor, 1958).

History of the Royal Warwickshire Regiment, 1919-1955 (London: William Clowes for The Royal Warwickshire Regiment, 1956).

The Literature of the United States (London: Penguin, 1954; various revised edns.; translations in French, German, Italian, Portuguese, Chinese, Japanese, etc.; revised and enlarged 4th ed., 1986).

The Nation Takes Shape, 1789-1837 (Chicago: University of Chicago Press, 1959, History of American Civilization Series, gen. ed. Daniel J. Boorstin).

The Presidency (3rd revised edn.; originally published as *American Presidents and the Presidency* in New York by American Heritage, 1968, 1972, 1976; 3rd revised edn., Boston: Houghton Mifflin, 1987).

The Right to Property: A Theme in American History (Leicester, England: Leicester University Press, Watson Lecture, 1974).

The Royal Irish Fusiliers, 1793-1950 (London: Geoffrey Cumberlege, Oxford University Press, 1953).

A Short Story of 21 Army Group: The British and Canadian Armies in The Campaigns in North-West Europe, 1944-1945 (Aldershot, England: Gale & Polden, 1949), with Hugh Darby.

Soldiers and Civilians: The Martial Spirit in America, 1775-1865 (Boston: Little, Brown, 1968; revised edn., New York: The Free Press, 1974).

BOOKS EDITED OR CO-EDITED

The American Destiny: An Illustrated History of the United States, edited with H. S. Commager and M. A. Jones. First published in 1975 as *The American Destiny: An Illustrated Bicentennial History of the United States*, 20 v., (London: Orbis Publishing Ltd for Danbury Press of Grolier Enterprises Inc., 1975) with essays by Marcus Cunliffe in v. 1-19. Reissued 1986 with revised and enlarged v. 20, *Post-Vietnam America*. Cunliffe essay, "The National Spirit: Aspects of Americana," 68-88.

American Literature since 1900 (London: Sphere Books, Sphere History of Literature in the English Language, v. 9, 1975; revised and enlarged edn., 1987). Cunliffe essay, "Literature and Society," 369-400.

American Literature to 1900 (London: Sphere Books, Sphere History of Literature in the English Language, v. 8, 1973; revised and enlarged edn., 1986). Cunliffe essays, "The Conditions of an American Literature," 1-22; "New England: The Universal Yankee Nation," 253-272.

Burke's Presidential Families of the United States of America, ed. Hugh Montgomery-Massingberd (London: Burke's Peerage Ltd, 1975; 2nd revised edn., 1981). Co-author of presidential biographies.

The Divided Loyalist: Crèvecoeur's America (London: Folio Society, 1978), edited with introduction, 7-18.

In the Midst of Life and Other Tales, Ambrose Bierce (New York: New American Library, Signet Classic, 1961), edited with afterword.

Life of Washington, Mason L. Weems, (Cambridge, Mass.: John Harvard Library of Harvard University Press, 1962), edited with introduction.

London Times History of Our Times (London: Weidenfeld/New York: Norton, 1971), edited with introduction and epilogue.

Pastmasters: Some Essays on American Historians (New York: Harper & Row, 1969), edited with Robin Winks. Cunliffe essay, "Arthur M. Schlesinger, Jr.," 345-374.

The Prince and the Pauper and *A Connecticut Yankee in King Arthur's Court*, Mark Twain (New York: New American Library, Signet Classics, double volume, 1982), edited with introduction, v-xvi.

ARTICLES IN BOOKS

"Aaron Burr; Theodore Dreiser; Robert E. Lee; Edgar A. Poe; George Washington," *Encyclopedia of American Biography*, ed. John A. Garraty (New York: Harper & Row, 1974), 652-654; 864-866; 1155-1157.

"Afterword," *The Jungle Book*, Rudyard Kipling (New York: New American Library, 1961).

The Almanac of American History, gen. ed., Arthur M. Schlesinger, Jr., consultant contributor (New York: Bison/G. P. Putnam's, 1983).

"America's Imaginary Wars," *American Literature in Belgium*, ed. Gilbert Debusscher (Amsterdam: Rodopi, 1988), 251-260.

"American History," *New Movements in the Study and Teaching of History* (London: Temple Smith, 1970), 116-132.

"American Literature," *The Year's Work in English Studies*, ed. Beatrice White, (Oxford: Oxford University Press for the English Association) annual volumes, 1954-1957.

"The American Military Tradition," *The Americans: 1976 . . . Critical Choices for Americans*, v. 2, ed. Irving Kristol and Paul H. Weaver (Lexington, Mass.: D.C. Heath, Co., 1976), 111-130.

"The American Military Tradition," *British Essays in American History*, ed. H. C. Allen and C. P. Hill (London: Arnold, 1957), 207-224.

"American Studies in Europe," *American Studies Abroad*, ed. Robert H. Walker (Westport, Conn: Greenwood Press, 1975), 46-52.

"American Thought," *The United States: A Companion to American Studies*, ed. Dennis Welland (London: Methuen, 1974, 453-504; paperback ed., 1976; 2nd revised, enlarged edn., 1987), 518-573.

"The Anatomy of Anti-Americanism," *Anti-Americanism in Europe*, ed. Rob Kroes and Maarten van Rossem (Amsterdam: Free University Press, 1986), 20-36.

"Comment on Dwight G. Anderson, 'Quest of Immortality: A Theory of Abraham Lincoln's Political Psychology,'" *The Historian's Lincoln: Pseudohistory, Psychohistory, and History* ed. Gabor Boritt and Norman Forness (Urbana: University of Illinois Press, 1988), 279-284.

"Comment on 'Epilogue: Soviet Historians on American History,'" *America and Russia: A Century and a Half of Dramatic Encounters*, ed. Oliver Jensen (New York: Simon and Schuster, 1962), 273-277.

"Congressional Leadership in the American Revolution," *Leadership in the American Revolution* (Washington, D.C.: Library of Congress, 1974), 41-61.

"The Cultural Patrimony of the New United States," *The Treaty of Paris (1783) in a Changing States System*, ed. Prosser Gifford (Washington, D.C.: University Press of America for Woodrow Wilson International Center for Scholars, 1985), 167-181.

"Douglas Southall Freeman," *Dictionary of American Biography*, supp. 5, ed. John A. Garraty (New York: Charles Scribner's Sons, 1977), 233-235.

"The Earth Belongs to the Living: Thomas Jefferson and the Limits of Inheritance," *Forms and Functions of History in American Literature: Festschrift for Ursula Brumm*, ed. W. P. Adams et al. (Berlin: Erich Schmidt Verlag, 1981), 56-70.

"Elections of 1789 and 1792," *History of American Presidential Elections*, v. 1, ed. A. M. Schlesinger, Jr. and F. L. Israel (New York: Chelsea House/McGraw-Hill, 1971-1972, 4 vols.), 1:3-32.

"European Images of America," *Paths of American Thought*, ed. A. M. Schlesinger, Jr. and M. White (Boston: Houghton Mifflin, 1963), 492-514.

"The First Duty of a Republic: Education in the American Scheme of Things," *Liberty and Liberal Education: Papers Presented in Commemoration of the St. John's College Charter Bicentennial, 1984-1985* (Annapolis: St. John's College, 1987), 30-40.

"Foreword," *The Changing Image of George Washington* (New York: Fraunces

Tavern Museum for Sons of the Revolution, State of New York, 1989), 7.

"Foreword," *George Washington: A Figure Upon the Stage*, Margaret B. Klapthor and Howard A. Morrison (Washington, D.C.: National Museum of American History, Smithsonian Institution Press, 1982), 10-13.

"Foreword," *Gulliver's Travels*, Jonathan Swift (New York: New American Library, Signet Classic, 1960).

"Foreword," *Ordeal by Hunger*, George R. Stewart (London: Eyre and Spottiswoode, 1962).

"Formative Events from Columbus to World War I," *American Character and Foreign Policy*, ed. Michael P. Hamilton (Grand Rapids, Mich.: William B. Eerdmans Publishing Co., 1986), 3-13.

"Frances Trollope," *Abroad in America: Visitors to the New Nation 1776-1914*, ed. Marc Pachter (Reading, Mass.: Addison-Wesley Pub. Co., for National Portrait Gallery, Smithsonian Institution, Washington, D.C., 1976), 32-42.

"Francis Parkman," *Atlantic Brief Lives: A Biographical Companion to the Arts*, ed. Louis Kronenberger (Boston: Little, Brown & Co., 1971), 576-578.

"George Washington: Too Good to be True?" *Washington Salutes Washington: The President and the State* (Seattle: Washington State Capital Museum, 1989), 4-7.

"George Washington's Generalship," *George Washington's Generals*, gen. ed. George Athan Billias (New York: William Morrow and Co., 1964), 3-21.

"The House of the Seven Gables," *Hawthorne Centenary Essays*, ed. Roy Harvey Pearce (Columbus: Ohio State University Press, 1964), 79-101.

"Introduction," *George Washington*, Woodrow Wilson (New York: Shocken Press Edition, 1969), v-xviii.

"The Invention of the Presidency," *The Great Ideas Today* (Chicago: Encyclopaedia Britannica, Inc., 1987), 157-221.

"Madison (1812-1815)," *The Ultimate Decision: The President as Commander in Chief*, ed. Ernest R. May (New York: Braziller, 1960), 23-53.

"The Making of America: Opportunities and Problems of a New World," *The Nineteenth Century, The Contradictions of Progress*, ed. Asa Briggs (London: Thames & Hudson, 1970; repr. 1985), 239-266.

"New World, Old World: The Historical Antithesis," *Lessons from America: An Exploration*, ed. Richard Rose (London: Macmillan, 1974), 19-45.

"Nord e Sud, Est e Ouest: La Crescita dei Valori in America" [North and South, East and West: The Polarizing of American Values], *Regionalismo e Centralizzazione Nella Storia di Italia e Stati Uniti* ed. Luigi De Rosa and Ennio Di Nolfo (Florence, Italy: Olschki, 1986), 41-93.

"Problems and Tendencies in American Studies," *American Studies in Spain*, ed. Enrique García Díez (Universitat de València: Tirant lo Blanch Libres, 1988), 11-20.

"Property," *Encyclopedia of American Political History: Studies of the Principal Movements and Ideas*, ed. Jack P. Greene (New York: Scribner's, 1984), 3: 1018-1030.

"Reinterpreting An Elusive Past," *The United States* (New York: Time Inc., Life World Library, 1965), 29-36.

"Teaching the Nation: The Development of American Education," *American Civilization*, ed. Daniel J. Boorstin (London: Thames & Hudson, 1972), 189-198.

"'They Will *All* Speak English': Some Cultural Consequences of Independence," *Peace and the Peacemakers: The Treaty of 1783*, ed. Ronald Hoffman and Peter J. Albert (Charlottesville: U.S. Capitol Historical Society by the University Press of Virginia, 1986), 132-159.

"The Two or More Worlds of Willa Cather," *The Art of Willa Cather*, ed. B. Slote and V. Faulkner (Lincoln: University of Nebraska Press, 1974), 21-42.

"The Uses and Dangers of the Past," *An Independent Institution in a Free Society: Essays in Honor of Lloyd H. Elliott* (Washington, D.C.: The George Washington University, 1988), 67-81.

ARTICLES IN PERIODICALS

"America at the Great Exhibition of 1851," *American Quarterly* 3, 1 (Summer 1951): 115-127.

"America Today — An Assessment from Abroad," *Boston Globe* (7 Mar. 1976): A1 + A2; successive articles: "Rx for America — More Heart, Less Head," *Boston Globe* (14 Mar. 1976): A3; "Beautifully Empty Spaces, Tragically Empty Hearts," *Boston Globe* (4 Apr. 1976): A4.

"American History in Prints — Delightful Exhibition at Manchester City Art Gallery," [Manchester] *Guardian* (6 Mar. 1954): 3.

"The American Intellectuals," *Encounter* (May 1955): 23-33.

"American Primitive Paintings — Manchester Display" [Manchester] *Guardian* (4 May 1955): 5.

"American Religious History," *Journal of American Studies* 1, 1 (Apr. 1967): 105-116.

"American Religious History," *Journal of Ecclesiastical History* 24, 2 (Apr. 1973): 185-193.

"American Watersheds," *American Quarterly* 13, 4 (Winter 1961): 480-494.

"America's Impact on the Arts: Literature," *Saturday Review* (13 Dec. 1975): 83-86.

"Backward Glances," *Journal of American Studies* 14, 1 (Apr. 1980): 83-102.

"Black Culture and White America," *Encounter* (Jan. 1970): 22-35.

"Brows of All Levels," *Daily Telegraph* [United States Supplement] (22 July 1957).

"The Causes of the American Civil War," *History Today* (Nov. 1953): 753-761.

"Comforts of the Sick-Bay," *Encounter* (July 1963): 96-99.

"Crèvecoeur Revisited," *Journal of American Studies* 9, 2 (Aug. 1975): 129-144.

"Daniel Webster," *American Heritage* [Special Issue: *I Wish I'd Been There*] (1984): 6.

"The Deep North," *Encounter* (May 1963): 70-71.

"Europe and America: Transatlantic Images I," *Encounter* (Dec. 1961): 19-29.

"George Washington," *Encounter* (June 1957): 29-34.

"George Washington: Real and Symbolic Hero," *Valley Forge Journal* 2, 1 (June 1984): 5-19.

"George Washington Scandals," *Northern Virginia Heritage* (Oct. 1982); another version in [London] *Times*, (20 Feb. 1982): 9.

"George Washington's Prodigious Metamorphosis," *GW Times*, 11, 1 (Jan./Feb. 1982): 1 + 8-9.

"The Growth of American Studies in British Universities," [Manchester] *Guardian* (22 Feb. 1963): 14.

"Harvard," *Encounter* (July 1961): 3-16.

"The Herd, the Self, and the Gulf Between," *Reporter* (2 Oct. 1958): 36-38.

"How Independence Was Finally Won," *Smithsonian Magazine* 14, 6 (Sept. 1983): 56-63.

"Humor as an American Political Style: The Case of Abraham Lincoln," *Jahrbuch Für Amerikastudien*, 11 (Heidelberg: Carl Winter, 1968): 29-40.

"Life in the Industrial North, or: A Cold Egg on an Old Tip" *Encounter* (Dec. 1962): 16-22.

"Mark Twain and His English Novels," *Times Literary Supplement* (25 Dec. 1981): 1503-1504.

"Newness as Repudiation: Styles in Modern American Thought," *Times Literary Supplement* (30 May 1980): 615-616.

"Notes on the Dorsey-Stanley Correspondence (1871-73) in the John Ryland Library," *Bulletin of the John Ryland's Library* 36, 2 (Mar. 1954): 360-385.

"Parson Weems and George Washington's Cherry Tree," *Bulletin of the John Ryland's Library* 45, 1 (1962): 58-96.

"Paul Goodman," *Encounter* (Apr. 1962): 58-62.

"Periodical Culture," *Encounter* (Aug. 1965): 82-84.

"The Presidency: A Defective Institution?" *Commentary* 45 (Feb. 1968): 27-33.

"Proud to be a Redcoat," *Observer* (3 Aug. 1975): 20-21.

"Recent Writings on the American Civil War," *History* (Feb. 1965): 26-35.

"Republicanism and the Founding of America," *World & I* (Sept. 1987): 37-45.

"Source for Hemingway's Macomber?" *Journal of American Studies* 21 (Apr. 1987): 103.

"A Soviet View of Six Great Americans: Comments on the *Soviet Encyclopedia* Account of George Washington, "*American Heritage* (Oct. 1960): 65-66.

"Stephen Crane and the American Background of *Maggie*," *American Quarterly* 7, 1 (Spring 1955): 31-44.

"Symbols We Made of a Man Named George Washington," *Smithsonian Magazine* 12, 11 (Feb. 1982): 74-81.

"Teaching United States History Abroad: Great Britain," *The History Teacher* 18, 1 (Nov. 1984): 69-74.

"Theodore Roosevelt," *History Today* 5, 9 (Sept. 1955): 592-601.

"Thomas Fuller," *GW Forum* 33 (Spring 1988): 18-21.

"Thomas Jefferson and the Dangers of the Past," *Wilson Quarterly* 6, 1 (Winter 1982): 96-107.

"The Two Georges: The President and the King," *American Studies International* 24, 2 (Oct. 1986): 53-73.

"What If?" *American Heritage* (Dec. 1982): 16-23.

"What Was the Matter with Henry Adams?" *Commentary* 39 (June 1965): 66-71.

"Whatever Happened to Flying Saucers?" *Reporter* (24 Nov. 1960): 48-52.

"Where Freud-Bullitt Went Wrong," *Encounter* (July 1967): 86-90.

"The World of L'il Abner," *Observer* (19 June 1960): 17.

REVIEWS

"*Abraham Lincoln*, Benjamin P. Thomas," *Listener* (17 Sept. 1953): 471.

"*Adams Family Correspondence*, v. 3 and 4, ed. L. H. Butterfield," *English Historical Review* (Oct. 1977): 914-915.

"*The Age of Roosevelt*, v. 3, *The Politics of Upheaval*, Arthur M. Schlesinger, Jr.," *Sunday Telegraph* (21 May 1961): 7.

"*The Agony of the American Left*, Christopher Lasch," *New Society* 19 (14 May 1970): 839-840.

"*America and the Patterns of Chivalry*, John Fraser," *Journal of American History* 71 (June 1984): 144-145.

"*America in Our Time*, Godfrey Hodgson," [Manchester] *Guardian Weekly* (9 Jan. 1977): 18.

"*America Through British Eyes*, Barbara Peterson," *Journal of American History* 77 (Sept. 1990): 723.

"*The American Age: United States Foreign Policy at Home and Abroad Since 1750*, Walter LaFeber," *New York Times Book Review* (5 Mar. 1989): 30.

"*The American Cowboy*, Joe Frantz and Julian Choate; and *Buffalo Bill and the Wild West*, Victor Weybright and Henry Sell," *Encounter* (Nov. 1956): 78-80.

"*The American Federal Government*, Max Beloff; and *The American Science of Politics*, Bernard Crick," *New Statesman and Nation* (22 Aug. 1959): 227.

"The American Frontier: Reviews of *The Year of Decision, 1846*, Bernard De Voto; and *The Far Western Frontier: 1830-1860*, R. A. Billington; and *William Bollaert's Texas*, eds. W. Eugene Hollon and Ruth L. Butler; and *David Crockett: the Man and the Legend*, James A. Schackford," [Manchester] *Guardian* (1 Feb. 1957): 6.

"*The American Henry James*, Quentin Anderson," [Manchester] *Guardian* (16 Jan. 1959): 6.

"*The American Image of the Old World*, Cushing Strout," *English Historical Review* (July 1965): 636-637.

"*The American Invasion*, Francis Williams; and *The Image, or What Happened to the American Dream*, Daniel J. Boorstin," *Encounter* (July 1962): 78-83.

"*American Literature, 1919-1932: A Comparative History*, John McCormick" *Spectator* (5 June 1971): 784.

"*An American Procession*, Alfred Kazin," *New York Times Book Review* (13 May 1984): 3 + 34.

"*The American West,* John A. Hawgood," *Spectator* (16 June 1967): 710.

"*The Americans: A New History of the People of the United States*, Oscar Handlin," *New York Times Book Review* (25 Aug. 1963): 8.

"*America's Receding Future*, Ronald Segal," *New Statesman and Nation* (18 Oct. 1968): 502.

"*Ancestors and Immigrants: A Changing New England Tradition*, Barbara Solomon; and *Goodbye to Uncle Tom*, J. C. Furnas," *Encounter* (Mar. 1957): 83-86.

"*Anti-Intellectualism in America*, Richard Hofstadter," [Manchester] *Guardian* (7 Feb. 1964): 9.

"*Anti-Slavery: Crusade for Freedom in America*; and *A Bibliography of Anti-Slavery in America*, Dwight Lowell Dumond," *Spectator* (25 May 1962): 688.

"*The Apostle of Liberty: A Life of LaFayette*, Maurice de la Fye and Emile Babeau, trans. Edward Hyams," *New Statesman and Nation* (17 Mar. 1956): 250.

"*Army Life on the Western Frontier*, Col. George Croghan, ed. Francis Paul Prucha," *English Historical Review* (Oct. 1959): 743.

"*Atlantic Legacy: Essays in American-European Cultural History*, Robert O. Mead, *American Historical Review* 75 (Oct. 1970): 1692.

"*Atlas of Early American History, 1760-1790*, ed. Lester J. Cappon," *Times Literary Supplement* (24 Sept. 1976): 1200-1202.

"*Autobiography of Benjamin Franklin*, ed. Leonard H. Labaree, et al.; and *A Transaction of Free Men: The Birth and Course of the Declaration of Independence*, David Hawke," *New York Times Book Review* (5 July 1964): 1 +.

"*The Autobiography of Mark Twain*," *Encounter* (Oct. 1960): 71-74.

"*The Bicycle Rider in Beverly Hills*, William Saroyan," [Manchester] *Guardian* (8 June 1953): 2.

"*The Bodley Head Scott Fitzgerald*," *Spectator* (24 Nov. 1961): 767-768.

"*The Bodley Head Jack London*, ed. Jack Calder-Marshall," [Manchester] *Guardian* (21 June 1963): 6.

"*The Bombing of Germany*, Hans Rumpf," *Commentary* 36, 4 (Oct. 1963): 323-325.

"Book Notes," *American Studies International* (1984-1990), Washington D.C., George Washington University.

"*The Bootleggers: The Story of Chicago's Prohibition Era*, Kenneth Allsop, *Daily Herald* (13 Oct. 1961): 6.

"*Brigham Young: American Moses*, Leonard Arrington," *New Republic* (26 Aug. 1985): 40-42.

"*Broadsides and Bayonets*, Carl Berger," *English Historical Review* (Jan. 1963): 184.

"*A Carnival of Buncombe by H. L. Mencken*, ed. Malcolm Moos," *New Statesman and Nation* (1 June 1957): 712-713.

"*The Character of American History*, W. R. Brock," *English Historical Review* (July 1961): 529-530.

"*Civil War Digest*, Ralph Newman; *The Confederacy*, Albert Kirwan; *The Civil War in America*, Alan Barber; and *The Road to Harper's Ferry*, J. C. Furnas," *The New Statesman* (21 Apr. 1961): 628-630.

"*Coast to Coast*, James Morris," *New Statesman and Nation* (16 June 1956): 706-707.

"*The Confident Years, 1885-1915*, Van Wyck Brooks," [Manchester] *Guardian* (27 May 1952): 4.

"*The Conscience of the State in North America*, E. R. Norman," *English Historical Review* (Apr. 1969): 416-417.

"*Conservatism in America*, Clinton Rossiter," [Manchester] *Guardian* (16 Mar. 1956): 6.

"*Constraint and Variety in American Education*, David Riesman," *Encounter* (Oct. 1957): 82.

"*Cora Crane*, Lillian Gilkes," [Manchester] *Guardian* (2 Mar. 1962): 6.

"*Crisis of the House Divided: An Interpretation of the Issues in the Lincoln-Douglas Debates*, Harry V. Jaffa," *Reporter* (18 Feb. 1960): 46-48.

"*The Critical Period in American Literature*, Grant Knight; and *Sherwood Anderson*, Irving Howe," [Manchester] *Guardian* (19 Feb. 1952): 4.

"*The Crossroads of Liberalism: Croly, Weyl, Lippmann, and the Progressive Era, 1900-1925*, Charles Forcey," *Spectator* (28 July 1961): 147.

"*Culture on the Moving Frontier*, Louis B. Wright," *English Historical Review* (Jan. 1957): 176-177.

"*Diary of Charles Francis Adams*, v. 1 and 2, ed. Aida Donald and David Donald," *English Historical Review* (July 1966): 618-620.

"*Diary of Charles Francis Adams*, v. 3 and 4, eds. Marc Friedlaender and L. H. Butterfield," *English Historical Review* (Jan. 1970): 191-192.

"*Diary of Charles Francis Adams*, v. 5 and 6, ed. L. H. Butterfield," *English Historical Review* (Oct. 1977): 919.

"*The Day Lincoln Was Shot*, Jim Bishop," *Listener* (9 June 1955): 1034.

"*The Death and Life of Great American Cities*, Jane Jacobs," *Spectator* (24 Aug. 1962): 278-279.

"*The Death of the Artist: A Study of Hawthorne's Disintegration*, Rudolph Von

Abele," *New Statesman and Nation* (20 Aug. 1955): 223.

"*The Degradation of the Academic Dogma,* Robert Nisbet; and *University Independence: The Main Questions,* ed. John H. MacCullum Scott," *New Society* (13 July 1972): 782 + 784.

"*The Dispute of the New World: The History of a Polemic, 1750-1900,* Antonello Gerbi," *Encounter* (Dec. 1973): 38-40.

"*Documents on Inter-American Cooperation,* ed. Robert Burr and Roland Hussey," *English Historical Review* (Jan. 1957): 190-191.

"*The Dream of Arcadia: American Writers and Artists in Italy, 1760-1915,* Van Wyck Brooks," *Encounter* (July 1959): 76-77.

"*Dream West,* David Nevin," *New York Times Book Review* (29 Jan. 1984): 10.

"*Early Americans,* Carl Bridenbaugh; and *Jamestown, 1544-1699,* Carl Bridenbaugh," *Washington Post Book World* (24 May 1981): 10 + 13.

"*Eisenhower: The Inside Story,* Robert Donovan; *The Crucial Decade: America 1945-1955,* Eric Goldman; and *Days to Remember: America 1945-1955,* John Gunther and Bernard Quint," *Encounter* (Jan. 1957): 83-85.

"*The End of Kings: A History of Republics and Republicans,* William R. Everdell," *Washington Post Book World,* (22 Jan. 1984): 9.

"*Emerson on Race and History,* Philip Nicoloff," *English Historical Review* (Oct. 1963): 809.

"*The Era of Theodore Roosevelt: 1900-1912,* George E. Mowry," [Manchester] *Guardian* (24 Oct. 1958): 6.

"*Ernst Junger,* J. P. Stern," *Listener* (8 Apr. 1954): 623.

"*Europe Looks at the Civil War: An Anthology,* Belle B. Sidemann and Lillian Friedman," *Reporter* (19 Jan. 1960): 60-62.

"*The Federalist Era, 1789-1801*, John C. Miller," *The Historian* (Nov. 1961): 116-117.

"*Felix Frankfurter Reminisces: Recorded in Talks with Dr. Harlan B. Phillips*," [Manchester] *Guardian* (10 Mar. 1961): 9.

"*Fiction Fights the Civil War*, Robert Lively; *The Land They Fought For*, Clifford Dowdey; *This Hallowed Ground*, Bruce Catton; *The Militant South, 1860-1861*, John Hope Franklin; *The Soldier and the South*, Samuel Huntington; and *Arms and Men*, Walter Mills," *Encounter* (Aug. 1957): 79-82.

"*Findings and Keepings: Analects for an Autobiography*, Lewis Mumford," [Manchester] *Guardian* (19 Feb. 1976): 9.

"*The Fire Next Time*, James Baldwin," [Manchester] *Guardian* (19 July 1963): 7.

"*The First American Constitutions: Republican Ideology...*, Willi Paul Adams; *John Taylor of Caroline: Pastoral Republican*, Robert E. Shalhope," *New Republic* (10 Feb. 1982): 36 + 38-39.

"*The First New Nation: The United States in Historical and Comparative Perspective*, Seymour Lipset," *English Historical Review* (Jan. 1966): 180-181.

"*The First of Men: A Life of George Washington*, John E. Ferling," *Journal of American History* 76 (Dec 1989): 912.

"*The Flower and the Leaf: A Contemporary Record of American Writing Since 1941*, Malcolm Cowley, ed. Donald Faulkner," *Boston Globe* (3 Feb. 1985): A10 + A12.

"*The Fremantle Diary*, ed. Walter Lord." *New Statesman and Nation* (21 Apr. 1956): 427-428.

"*From Atlanta to the Sea*, William T. Sherman, ed. B. H. Liddell," *Spectator* (27 Oct. 1961): 589-590.

"*A General of the Revolution: John Sullivan of New Hampshire*," *English Historical Review* (Jan. 1964): 184.

"*George Washington*, James T. Flexner," *American Historical Review* (July 1966): 1427-1428.

"*George Washington*, James T. Flexner," *Reviews in American History* 1, 3 (Sept. 1973): 372-377.

"*George Washington*, v. 7, John A. Carroll and Mary W. Ashworth," *Reporter* (20 Feb 1958): 40-42.

"*George Washington, A Biography*, John R. Alden; and *Cincinnatus: George Washington and the Enlightenment*, Garry Wills," *New York Review of Books* 31, 15 (11 Oct. 1984): 47-50.

"*George Washington and Religion*, Paul F. Boller," *William and Mary Quarterly* (1963): 614-615.

"*George Washington: The Making of an American Symbol*, Barry Schwartz," *World & I* (Aug. 1987): 398-402.

"*Grace Had an English Heart*, Jessica Mitford," *Washington Post Book World* (12 Mar. 1989): 5 + 7.

"*Grant: A Biography*, William McFeely," *New York Times Book Review* (22 Mar. 1981): 13 + 18.

"*Grant Takes Command*, Bruce Catton," *Spectator* (16 May 1970): 651.

"*Great Britain and the United States*, H. C. Allen," *English Historical Review* (July 1955): 467-468; also reviewed in [Manchester] *Guardian Weekly* (10 Feb. 1955): 10.

"*The Great Experiment*, Frank Thistlethwaite," *English Historical Review* (Jan. 1956): 168-169.

"*Great River: The Rio Grande in North American History*, Paul Horgan," [Manchester] *Guardian* (29 July 1955): 4.

"*Guide to the Study of the United States of America*, ed. Roy Basler, et al.," *English Historical Review* (Jan. 1962): 208.

"*Hawthorne's Last Phase*, Edward Davidson," *Modern Language Review* (1950): 540.

"*Hemingway: A Biography*, Jeffrey Meyers; *Along with Youth: Hemingway, The Early Years*, Peter Griffin; and *Dateline: Toronto. The Complete Toronto Star Dispatches, 1920-1924*, Ernest Hemingway, ed. William White," *Washington Post Book World* (3 Nov. 1985): 1 + 14.

"*Hemingway and His Critics*, ed. and introduction by Carlos Baker," *Sunday Telegraph* (9 July 1961): 7.

"*Henry Adams: A Biography*, Elizabeth Stevenson," [Manchester] *Guardian* (27 Jan. 1956): 6.

"*Henry Adams: The Major Phase*, Ernest Samuels," *Spectator* (19 Mar. 1965): 366-7.

"*Henry James: A Life*, Leon Edel; *Henry James: The Writer and His Work*, Tony Tanner; and *Novels, 1881-1886: Washington Square, The Portrait of a Lady, The Bostonians*, Henry James, ed. William Stafford," *Washington Times Book Section* (16 Dec. 1985): 4M-5M.

"*The Historian's Contribution to Anglo-American Misunderstanding*, ed. R. A. Billington, et al.," *English Historical Review* (Jan. 1968): 221-222.

"*The Image, or What Happened to the American Dream*, Daniel J. Boorstin." *Spectator* (30 Mar. 1962): 415; also reviewed in *Encounter* (July 1962): 78-83.

"*In the Days of McKinley*, Margaret Leech," *Reporter* (24 Dec. 1959): 36-37.

"*The Independent Reflector: or Weekly Essays . . . by William Livingston and Others*, ed. Milton Klein," *English Historical Review* (Apr. 1965): 410-411.

"*The Intellectual Versus the City*, Morton White and Lucia White," *Encounter* (June 1966): 42-44.

"*An Introduction to American Politics*, Denis Brogan," [Manchester] *Guardian* (26 Oct. 1954): 4.

"*James Bryce and American Democracy*, Edmund Ions" *New Statesman* (7 June 1968): 768.

"*James Fenimore Cooper*, James Grossman; *Herman Melville*, Newton Arvin; and *Nook Farm: Mark Twain's Hartford Circle*, Kennett R. Andrews." *New Statesman and Nation* (28 Apr. 1951): 485-486.

"*John Adams*, v. 1 and 2, Page Smith," *New York Times Book Review* (18 Nov. 1962): 1 + 64.

"*Journal of a Years Residence in the United States of America*, William Cobbett," *Agricultural History* 40, 4 (Oct. 1966): 329.

"*The Last Hurrah*, Edwin O'Connor; *The Public Arts*, Gilbert Seldes; *Music in American Life*, Jacques Barzun; and *The American Woman*, Eric John Dingwall," *Encounter* (Oct. 1956): 78-80.

"*Less Than Kin: A Study of Anglo-American Relations*, William Clark," *Reporter* (12 June 1958): 32-34.

"*Letters of Emily Dickinson v. 1-3*, ed. Thomas H. Johnson," *The Review of English Studies* 12, 48 (Nov. 1961): 434-436.

"*The Letters of Herman Melville*, ed. Merrell Davis and William Gilman," [Manchester] *Guardian* (2 Dec. 1960): 6.

"*The Letters of Private Wheeler, 1809-1828*, ed. B. H. Liddell; and *Peninsular Cavalry General, 1811-1813*, ed. with memoir by T. H. McGuffie." *New Statesman and Nation* (19 Jan. 1952): 77.

"*The Letters of Theodore Roosevelt*, v. 1 and 2, ed. Elting E. Morison," *Listener* (27 Mar. 1952): 523.

"*The Letters of Theodore Roosevelt*, v. 3 and 4, ed. Elting E. Morison," *Listener* (6 Nov. 1952): 781.

"*The Letters of Theodore Roosevelt*, v. 5 and 6, ed. Elting E. Morison," *Listener* (11 June 1953): 966.

"*The Liberal Conspiracy: The Congress for Cultural Freedom and the Struggle for the Mind of Postwar Europe*, Peter Coleman," *Reviews in American History* 18 (Sept. 1990): 406-410.

"*Light-Horse Harry Lee and the Legacy of the American Revolution*," Charles Royster, *Washington Post Book World* (22 Mar. 1981): 6.

"*The Lincoln Image: Abraham Lincoln and the Popular Print*, Harold Holzer, Gabor S. Boritt, and Mark E. Neely," *Washington Post Book World* (12 Feb. 1984): 5.

"*Lincoln the President*, v. 3, *Midstream*, J. G. Randall." *Listener* (26 Mar. 1953): 529.

"*The Literary Situation*, Malcolm Cowley," [Manchester] *Guardian* (16 Sept. 1955): 6; also reviewed in *New Statesman and Nation* [signed Jason Falkner] (28 Jan. 1956): 106-107.

"*Love and Death in the American Novel*, Leslie Fiedler," *Encounter* (Sept. 1961): 75-79.

"*The Loyalties of Robinson Jeffers*, Radcliffe Squires," *Encounter* (May 1957): 86-88.

"*The Machine in the Garden: Technology and the Pastoral Idea in America*, Leo Marx," *Spectator* (22 Jan. 1965): 106.

"*The Making of the Constitution*, Richard B. Bernstein with Kym Rice," *New York Times Book Review* (3 May 1987): 26.

"*The March of Folly: From Troy to Vietnam*, Barbara Tuchman," *USA Today* (9 Mar. 1984): 3D.

"*Mitre and Sceptre: Transatlantic Faiths, Ideas, Personalities, and Politics, 1689-1775*, Carl Bridenbaugh," *English Historical Review* (Oct. 1964): 851-852.

"*Modern American Poetry: Focus Five*, ed. B. Rajan," *New Statesman and Nation* (29 July 1950): 132.

"*Modern Times: The World from the Twenties to the Eighties*, Paul Johnson," *Washington Post Book World* (21 Aug. 1983): 9.

"*Money, Class and Party: An Economic Study of Civil War and Reconstruction*, Robert Sharkey," *English Historical Review* (Oct. 1961): 751-752.

"*Mornings on Horseback*, David McCullough," *Washington Post Book World* (14 June 1981): 1-2.

"*More Die of Heartbreak*, Saul Bellow," *Washington Post Book World* (7 June 1987): 1 + 11.

"*The Names and Faces of Heroes*, Reynolds Price; *The Sun's Attendant*, Charles Haldeman; and *The Centaur*, John Updike," [Manchester] *Guardian* (27 Sept. 1963): 4.

"*The Negro Novel in America*, Robert A Bone." *Times Literary Supplement* (13 Mar. 1959): 146.

"*New England Literary Culture: From Revolution Through Renaissance*," Lawrence Buell," *History Today* 37 (Aug. 1987): 52.

"*The New Radicalism in America, 1889-1963: The Intellectual as a Social Type*, Christopher Lasch," *Encounter* (Sept. 1966): 74-78.

"*New Travels in the United States of America, 1788*, J. P. Brissot de Warville, trans. and ed. Durand Echeverria," *English Historical Review* (July 1966): 606-607.

"*No Further West*, Dan Jacobson; and *In America in Doubt*, Alexander Werth," [Manchester] *Guardian* (7 Aug. 1959): 4.

"*Not By Fact Alone: Essays on the Writing and Reading of History*, John Clive," *Washington Times* (10 Apr. 1989): E7 + E9.

"Notes of a Native Son; and *Nobody Knows My Name*, James Baldwin," [Manchester] *Guardian* (28 Feb. 1964): 7.

"Le Nouveau Roman Américain, Michel Mohrt," *Times Literary Supplement* [unsigned] (16 Dec. 1955): 762.

"Observations on American Education, Robert M. Hutchins," *New Statesman and Nation* (22 Dec. 1956): 824.

"The Old Devils, Kingsley Amis," *Washington Times Books* (16 Mar. 1987): M1 + M4.

"On Revolution, Hannah Arendt," *Spectator* (21 Feb. 1964): 257.

"On the Contrary, Mary McCarthy," [Manchester] *Guardian* (27 July 1962): 6.

"One Nation Indivisible, Paul Nagel," *English Historical Review* (Jan. 1966): 179-180.

"The Ordeal of Woodrow Wilson, Herbert Hoover," [Manchester] *Guardian* (28 Nov. 1958): 9.

"The Other America, Michael Harrington; and *Challenge to Affluence,* Gunnar Myrdal," [Manchester] *Guardian* (25 Oct. 1963): 7.

"Oxford Companion to American Literature, ed. James D. Hart," [Manchester] *Guardian* (6 Nov. 1956): 4.

"Oxford History of the American People, Samuel Eliot Morison," *New York Times Book Review* (25 Apr. 1965): 1 + 32-33.

"Papers of Daniel Webster: Correspondence, v. 1, 1789-1824, ed. Charles M. Wiltse," *Times Literary Supplement* (17 Sept. 1975).

"The Papers of Thomas Jefferson, v. 20, *1 April to 4 August 1791,* ed. Julian P. Boyd and Ruth W. Lesters; *The Papers of George Washington,* Colonial Series, v. 1 and 2, *1748-April 1756,* ed. W. W. Abbot, assoc. ed. Dorothy Twohig," *Journal of American Studies* 18 (Apr. 1984): 129-130, 154-155.

"*The Past Before Us: Contemporary Historical Writing in the United States*, ed. Michael Kammen," *Washington Post Book World* (13 July 1980): 3 + 7.

"*Patriotic Gore: Studies in the Literature of the American Civil War*, Edmund Wilson," *Spectator* (22 June 1962): 829-830.

"*Patriotism on Parade*, Wallace E. Davies," [Manchester] *Guardian* (22 June 1956): 6.

"*The People Called Shakers: A Search for the Perfect Society*, Edward Andrews; and *The Undeclared War, 1940-1941*, William L. Langer and S. Everett Gleason," *Listener* (8 Apr. 1954): 621.

"*People of Paradox: An Inquiry Concerning the Origins of American Civilization*, Michael Kammen," *New York Times Book Review* (1 Oct. 1972): 4.

"*Poets of San Francisco: In Defense of the Earth*, Kenneth Rexroth," *New Statesman and Nation* (14 Feb. 1959): 227-228.

"*Politics in the U.S.A.*, M.J.C. Vile," *New Society* (25 June 1970): 1113.

"*The Power Elite*, C. Wright Mills," *Encounter* (July 1956): 78-80.

"*The Power of Blackness: Hawthorne, Poe, Melville*, Harry Levin," *Reporter* (26 June 1958): 36-38.

"*Power, Politics, & People: The Collected Essays of C. Wright Mills*, ed. Irving L. Horowitz," [Manchester] *Guardian* (5 July 1963): 8.

"*Practicing History: Selected Essays*, Barbara Tuchman; *The Past and the Present*, Lawrence Stone; and *The Mind and Method of the Historian*, Emmanuel LeRoy Ladurie," *Washington Post Book World* (27 Sept. 1981): 4 +.

"*The Pragmatic Revolt in American History: Carl Becker and Charles Beard*, Cushing Strout," *English Historical Review* (Jan. 1961): 181-182.

"*Protestant - Catholic - Jew*, Will Herzberg," *Encounter* (Dec. 1956): 83-86.

"*The Reconstruction of American History*, ed. John Higham," *English Historical Review* (Apr. 1964): 415.

"*Religion and the Rise of the American City*, Carroll Rosenberg," *English Historical Review* (Oct. 1973): 924-925.

"*Reminiscences*, Douglas MacArthur," *Commentary*, 38, 6 (Dec. 1964): 66-68; also reviewed in [Manchester] *Guardian* (15 Jan 1965): 11.

"*Report of the County Chairman*, James A. Michener," [Manchester] *Guardian* (10 Nov. 1961): 7.

"*Responsibilities of the Critic: Essays and Reviews by F. O. Matthiessen*, ed. John Rackliffe," [unsigned] *Times Literary Supplement* (10 Apr. 1953): 236.

"*Revolutionary Journal of Baron Ludwig Von Closen, 1780-1783*, trans. and ed. Evelyn M. Acomb," *English Historical Review* (Jan. 1960): 172-173.

"*The Robber Barons: The Great American Capitalists 1861-1901*, Mathew Josephson," *Spectator* (5 Oct. 1962): 516-517.

"*Le Roman Américain au XXe Siècle*, Jean Simon; *The Beginnings of Naturalism in American Fiction*, Lars Åhnebrink; and *Letters Grave and Gay, and Other Prose of John Banister Tabb*, ed. Francis Litz," *Modern Language Review* (1951): 499-500

"*Roosevelt: The Lion and the Fox*, James M. Burns," [Manchester] *Guardian* (8 Apr. 1957): 6.

"*Runaway Star: An Appreciation of Henry Adams*, Robert A. Hume; and *The Art of Teaching*, Gilbert Highet," *New Statesman and Nation* (27 Oct. 1951): 474.

"*St. John de Crèvecoeur: The Life of an American Farmer*, Gay W. Allen," *The American Historical Review* 93 (Dec. 1988): 1395.

"*The Secret Diary of Harold Ickes*, v. 1 and 2, Harold Ickes," [Manchester] *Guardian* (18 Feb. 1955): 8.

"*The Secret Diary of Harold Ickes*, v. 3, Harold Ickes," [Manchester] *Guardian Weekly* (22 Dec. 1956).

"*The Shaping of America: A People's History of the Young Republic*, Page Smith," *William and Mary Quarterly* (July 1981): 514-517.

"*The Shock of Recognition*, Edmund Wilson," *Listener* (10 May 1965): 609.

"*Sinclair Lewis: An American Life*, Mark Schorer," [Manchester] *Guardian* (29 Mar. 1963): 6.

"*The Solitary Singer*, Gay Wilson Allen," *New Statesman* (9 July 1955): 50.

"*Spheres of Liberty: Changing Perceptions of Liberty in American Culture* (1986) and *A Machine That Would Go of Itself: The Constitution in American Culture* (1986), Michael Kammen," *Journal of American Studies* 22, 1 (1988): 105-106.

"*The Spirit Above the Dust: A Study of Herman Melville*, Ronald Mason Lehmann; and *Melville's Early Life and 'Redburn,'* William H. Gilman," *New Statesman and Nation* (22 Dec. 1951): 738.

"*Ten Nights in a Bar-Room*, Timothy Shay Arthur," *New Society* (2 Dec. 1965).

"*Terrible Swift Sword*, Bruce Catton," [Manchester] *Guardian* (8 Nov. 1963): 9.

"*The Theory of American Literature*, Howard Mumford Jones," *Modern Language Review* (1950): 545-546.

"*This Hallowed Ground*, Bruce Catton," [Manchester] *Guardian* (9 Aug. 1957): 4.

"*Through the Fields of Clover*, Peter De Vries," *Sunday Telegraph* (11 June 1961): 7.

"*The Twentieth Maine: A Volunteer Regiment in the Civil War*, John J. Pullen," *New Statesman and Nation* (17 Jan. 1959): 77.

"*Vicksburg: A People at War, 1860-1865*, Peter F. Walker," *English Historical Review* (July 1962): 578.

"*The Virgin of Chartres: An Intellectual and Psychological History of the Work of Henry Adams*, Joseph F. Byrnes; and *Custer and the Little Big Horn: A Psychobiographical Inquiry*, Charles Hofling," *Times Literary Supplement* (23 Oct. 1981): 1241.

"*Walt Whitman: A Life*, Justin Kaplan," *Washington Post Book World* (9 Nov. 1980): 3 + 6.

"*Walt Whitman Reconsidered*, Richard V. Chase," [Manchester] *Guardian* (25 Nov. 1955): 14.

"*The War for Independence: A Military History*, Howard Peckham," *English Historical Review* (Oct. 1959): 736.

"*Washington and the American Revolution*, Esmond Wright," [Manchester] *Guardian* (3 Jan. 1958): 4.

"*Wellington Studies*, ed. Michael Howard," *New Statesman and Nation* (27 June 1959): 903.

"*The Western Hemisphere Idea: Its Rise and Decline*, A. P. Whitaker," *English Historical Review* (Oct. 1955): 679-680.

"*Westward the Course of Empire*, Bernard DeVoto," [Manchester] *Guardian* (Aug. 1953).

"*Whitman's American Fame: The Growth of His Reputation in America After 1892*, Charles B. Willard; and *'Leaves of Grass' and Selected Prose Writings, Part I*, Edwin Harold Eby, *Modern Language Review* (1951): 95-96.

"*Wilderness and the American Mind*, Roderick Nash," *English Historical Review* (July 1969): 629-630.

"*The Worcester Account*, S. N. Behrman," [Manchester] *Guardian* (21 Jan. 1955): 6.

"*A Writer's Journal*, H. D. Thoreau, ed. Laurence Stapleton," *New Statesman* 4 (Aug. 1961): 161.

R E P R I N T S

"American Background of *Maggie*," *"Maggie": Stephen Crane's Text and Context*, ed. Maurice Bassan, (Belmont, Calif.: Wadsworth Publishing, 1966), 128-132. Reprinted from *American Quarterly*, 7 (Spring 1955): 31-44.

"Elections of 1789 and 1792," *The Coming to Power: Critical Presidential Elections in American History*, ed. Arthur M. Schlesinger, Jr. (New York: Chelsea House/McGraw-Hill, 1972). Reprinted from *History of American Presidential Elections*, v. 1, ed. A. M. Schlesinger, Jr., and F. L. Israel (4 v., New York: Chelsea House/McGraw-Hill, 1971), 3-32.

"Elmer Ellsworth," *The Military in America: From the Colonial Era to the Present*, ed. Peter Karsten, (New York: Free Press, 1980), 117-121. Reprinted from Marcus Cunliffe, *Soldiers and Civilians: The Martial Spirit in America, 1775-1865* (New York: Free Press, 1976) 241-247.

"How Independence Was Signed, Sealed and Then Delivered," *American History; Pre-Colonial through Reconstruction*, v. 1, *Revolutionary America*, 10th ed., ed. Robert James Maddox. (Guilford, Conn.: Dushkin Publishing Group, 1989), 45-52. Reprinted from *Smithsonian Magazine* 14, 6 (Sept. 1983): 56-63.

"Stephen Crane and the American Background of *Maggie*," *Studies in "Maggie" and "George's Mother,"* ed. Stanley Wertheim (Columbus, Ohio: Charles E. Merrill Pub. Co., 1970), 34-44. Reprinted from *American Quarterly*, 7 (Spring 1955): 31-44.

"Too Powerful - Or Not Powerful Enough?" *Viewpoints: The Presidency: The Power and the Glory*, ed, Mary Klein (Minneapolis: Winston Press, 1973), 24-29. Reprinted from "A Defective Institution?" *Commentary* 45, 5 (Feb. 1968): 27-33.

"What, Gracious God, Is Man?" *Portrait of America: From the Cliff Dwellers to the End of Reconstruction*, v. 1, ed. Stephen B. Oates, (Boston: Houghton Mifflin, 1973). Reprinted from *George Washington: Man and Monument* (Boston: Little, Brown & Mentor, 1958).

Index

About the Author

MARCUS CUNLIFFE (1922-1990) was a British-born historian who wrote more than a dozen books on American history and literature. A commentator on American life, he had been University Professor at George Washington University since 1980. He was a prolific writer, focusing extensively on George Washington and the early history of the United States. He authored, among others, *The Nation Takes Shape, American Presidents and the Presidency, The Ages of Man: From Sav-age to Sew-age, Soldiers and Civilians,* and *The Literature of the United States.*

A NOTE ON PRINTING

This book was prepared for the printer by Nan Thompson Ernst with a Hewlett Packard LaserJet II P printer and an IBM Personal Computer AT using software by WordPerfect 5.0 and Glyphix fonts Tymes Roman and Helvenica. Camera-ready copy was output directly on the Laser Jet II P, and later reduced at 92% in camera for final printing. Design is by Jason Cunliffe and Nan Thompson Ernst.

The fine for this
item when overdue
is 10¢ a day.